CLINICAL IMPLICATIONS OF THE PSYCHOANALYST'S LIFE EXPERIENCE

Clinical Implications of the Psychoanalyst's Life Experience explores how leaders in the fields of psychoanalysis and psychotherapy address the phenomena of the psychoanalyst's personal life and psychology. In this edited book, each author describes pivotal childhood and adult life events and crises that have contributed to personality formation, personal and professional functioning, choices of theoretical positions, and clinical technique.

By expanding psychoanalytic study beyond clinical theory and technique to include a more careful examination of the psychoanalyst's life events and other subjective phenomena, readers will have an opportunity to focus on specific ways in which these events and crises affect the tenor of the therapist's presence in the consulting room, and how these occurrences affect clinical choices. Chapters cover a broad range of topics including illness, adoption, sexual identity and experience, trauma, surviving the death of one's own analyst, working during 9/11, cross-cultural issues, growing up in a communist household, and other family dynamics.

Throughout, Steven Kuchuck shows how contemporary psychoanalysis teaches that it is only by acknowledging the therapist's life experience and resulting psychological makeup that analysts can be most effective in helping their patients. However, to date, few articles and fewer books have been entirely devoted to this topic. *Clinical Implications of the Psychoanalyst's Life Experience* forges new ground in exploring these under-researched areas. It will be essential reading for practicing psychoanalysts, psychotherapists, psychologists, social workers, those working in other mental health fields, and graduate students alike.

Steven Kuchuck is a faculty member, supervisor, and is on the Board of Directors at the National Institute for the Psychotherapies. He is a practicing psychoanalyst in Manhattan, New York. He is also co-editor of the journal *Psychoanalytic Perspectives* and Associate Editor of the Relational Perspectives Book Series published by Routledge.

RELATIONAL PERSPECTIVES BOOK SERIES
LEWIS ARON & ADRIENNE HARRIS
Series Co-Editors

STEVEN KUCHUCK & EYAL ROZMARIN
Associate Editors

The Relational Perspectives Book Series (RPBS) publishes books that grow out of or contribute to the relational tradition in contemporary psychoanalysis. The term *relational psychoanalysis* was first used by Greenberg and Mitchell (1983) to bridge the traditions of interpersonal relations, as developed within interpersonal psychoanalysis and object relations, as developed within contemporary British theory. But, under the seminal work of the late Stephen Mitchell, the term *relational psychoanalysis* grew and began to accrue to itself many other influences and developments. Various tributaries—interpersonal psychoanalysis, object relations theory, self psychology, empirical infancy research, and elements of contemporary Freudian and Kleinian thought—flow into this tradition, which understands relational configurations between self and others, both real and fantasied, as the primary subject of psychoanalytic investigation.

We refer to the relational tradition, rather than to a relational school, to highlight that we are identifying a trend, a tendency within contemporary psychoanalysis, not a more formally organized or coherent school or system of beliefs. Our use of the term *relational* signifies a dimension of theory and practice that has become salient across the wide spectrum of contemporary psychoanalysis. Now under the editorial supervision of Lewis Aron and Adrienne Harris with the assistance of Associate Editors Steven Kuchuck and Eyal Rozmarin, the Relational Perspectives Book Series originated in 1990 under the editorial eye of the late Stephen A. Mitchell. Mitchell was the most prolific and influential of the originators of the relational tradition. He was committed to dialogue among psychoanalysts and he abhorred the authoritarianism that dictated adherence to a rigid set of beliefs or technical restrictions. He championed open discussion, comparative and integrative approaches, and he promoted new voices across the generations.

Included in the Relational Perspectives Book Series are authors and works that come from within the relational tradition, extend and develop the tradition, as well as works that critique relational approaches or compare and contrast it with alternative points of view. The series includes our most distinguished senior psychoanalysts along with younger contributors who bring fresh vision.

CLINICAL IMPLICATIONS OF THE PSYCHOANALYST'S LIFE EXPERIENCE

When the Personal Becomes Professional

Edited by
Steven Kuchuck

Routledge
Taylor & Francis Group

NEW YORK AND LONDON

First published 2014
by Routledge
711 Third Avenue, New York, NY 10017

and by Routledge
27 Church Road, Hove, East Sussex BN3 2FA

Routledge is an imprint of the Taylor & Francis Group, an informa business

Library of Congress Cataloging in Publication Data
A catalog record for this book has been request

ISBN: 978–0–415–50798–1 (hbk)
ISBN: 978–0–415–50799–8 (pbk)
ISBN: 978–1–315–88217–8 (ebk)

Typeset in Times New Roman
by Swales & Willis Ltd, Exeter, Devon

FOR DAVID FLOHR

CONTENTS

CONTENTS

CONTRIBUTORS

Galit Atlas, Ph.D. is a psychoanalyst, creative arts therapist and clinical supervisor in private practice in Manhattan. She is on the faculty at NYU Postdoctoral Program in Psychotherapy and Psychoanalysis, faculty at the Four Year Adult and National Training Programs at NIP, and faculty and Board of Directors at the Institute for Expressive Analysis (IEA). She serves on the editorial board of Psychoanalytic Perspectives, and is an author of articles and book chapters that focus primarily on gender and sexuality.

Martin S. Bergmann, Ph.D. is an Instructor in the NYU Postdoctoral Program in Psychoanalysis and Psychotherapy, and the recipient of the Sigourney Award for outstanding contributions to psychoanalysis (1997). He is the author of *The Evolution of Psychoanalytic Technique* (1976); *Generations of the Holocaust* (1982); *The Anatomy of Loving* (1987); *In the Shadow of Moloch: The Sacrifice of Children and Its Impact on Western Religions* (1992); *What Silent Love Has Writ: a Psychoanalytic Exploration of Shakespeare's Sonnets* (2007, with Michael Bergmann); and *The Unconscious in Shakespeare's Plays* (forthcoming, Karnac Books).

Sally Bjorklund, M.A. is a founding faculty member of Relational Psychoanalysis and Psychotherapy Seattle. She is a psychoanalyst in private practice providing clinical supervision, and treatment for individuals and couples. She lives and works in Seattle, Washington.

Steven Botticelli, Ph.D. is on the faculty of the NYU Postdoctoral Program in Psychotherapy and Psychoanalysis. He is a contributing editor for Studies in Gender and Sexuality and The Division/Review, and practices in the West Village, New York City.

Michael Eigen, Ph.D. Author of twenty-one books, including *Contact with the Depths*, *Feeling Matters*, and *Kabbalah and Psychoanalysis*. Faculty, National Psychological Association for Psychoanalysis and NYU Postdoctoral Program in Psychotherapy and Psychoanalysis.

Kenneth A. Frank, Ph.D. is Director of Training, National Institute for the Psychotherapies; former Clinical Professor in Psychiatry, Columbia College of

Physicians and Surgeons; and Senior Consulting Editor, *Psychoanalytic Perspectives*. Author of over fifty books, chapters, and articles, he serves on the advisory boards and faculties of several psychoanalytic institutes. He practices integrative psychoanalysis in Englewood, New Jersey and Manhattan.

Noah Glassman, Ph.D. is a graduate of the NYU Postdoctoral Program in Psychotherapy and Psychoanalysis and is a member of its Psychoanalytic Society. He teaches about human motivation research at Barnard College and is in private practice in New York City.

Hillary Grill, LCSW, is a supervisor at the National Institute for the Psychotherapies, and supervisor and faculty member at the Institute for Expressive Analysis. She is submissions editor for the journal *Psychoanalytic Perspectives* and co-author of the book *Dreaming for Two: the Hidden Emotional Life of Pregnant Women.* She is a psychoanalyst practicing in New York City.

Irwin Hirsch, Ph.D. is faculty and supervisor, Manhattan Institute for Psychoanalysis; distinguished visiting faculty, William Alanson White Institute; and adjunct professor of psychology and supervisor, NYU Postdoctoral Program in Psychotherapy and Psychoanalysis. He is on the editorial boards of *Contemporary Psychoanalysis*, *Psychoanalytic Dialogues*, and *Psychoanalytic Perspectives*, and is author of the 2008 Goethe Award winning book, *Coasting in the Countertransference: Conflicts of Self-Interest between Analyst and Patient* (Routledge).

Steven Kuchuck, LCSW, is a faculty member, supervisor and on the Board of Directors at the National Institute for the Psychotherapies, co-editor of the journal *Psychoanalytic Perspectives*, and Associate Editor of the Relational Perspectives Book Series from Routledge. He publishes and presents primarily on the impact of the analyst's subjectivity on development of theory and clinical technique, and practices psychoanalysis and supervises in Manhattan.

Eric Mendelsohn, Ph.D. is on the teaching and supervisory faculties, National Institute for the Psychotherapies Training Institute and National Training Program, Westchester Center for the Study of Psychoanalysis and Psychotherapy; Postgraduate Program in Psychoanalysis and Psychotherapy, Adelphi University; and visiting faculty, Michigan Psychoanalytic Institute. He has written about the therapist's participation and the patient–therapist relationship in analytic therapy.

Susie Orbach, Ph.D. is a psychoanalyst, activist, cultural commentator and author or co-author of twelve books including *Fat is a Feminist Issue*, *The Impossibility of Sex*, *Bodies*, and *Fifty Shades of Feminism*. A co-founder of The Women's Therapy Centre in London and The Women's Therapy Centre Institute in New York and of Psychotherapists and Counsellors for Social Responsibility, she is UK convenor of www.endangeredbodies.org. She has a practice seeing individuals, couples and consulting to organizations.

Anna Ornstein, M.D, psychoanalyst (retired). Lecturer in Psychiatry, Harvard Medical School, Supervising Analyst, Boston Psychoanalytic Institute and Massachusetts Institute for Psychoanalysis.

Deborah Pines, LCSW, is the co-editor of *Psychoanalytic Perspectives*, and former co-chair of the Candidates Committee of the International Association for Relational Psychoanalysis and Psychotherapy. She is in private practice in New York City, and is a supervisor at the National Institute for the Psychotherapies

Philip Ringstrom, Ph.D., Psy.D. is a Training and Supervising Analyst at the Institute of Contemporary Psychoanalysis in Los Angeles, on the Editorial Boards of the *International Journal on Psychoanalytic Self Psychology*, *Psychoanalytic Dialogues and Psychoanalytic Perspectives*, as well as on the *International Council of Self-Psychologists* and on the Board of Directors of the *International Association of Relational Psychoanalysis and Psychotherapy.*

Eric Sherman, LCSW, is a faculty member and supervisor at the National Institute for the Psychotherapies and the Center for Psychotherapy and Psychoanalysis of New Jersey, where he is also Associate Director of Training. He is author of *Notes from the Margins: The Gay Analyst's Subjectivity in the Treatment Setting*, and is in private practice in New York and Montclair, New Jersey.

Joyce Slochower, Ph.D. is Professor Emerita of Psychology, Hunter College; faculty, NYU Postdoctoral Program, Steven Mitchell Center, National Training Program of NIP and PINC. She has published over sixty articles on various aspects of psychoanalytic theory and technique. She is the author of *Holding and Psychoanalysis: A Relational Perspective* (1996 and 2013) and *Psychoanalytic Collisions* (2006 and 2013).

Chana Ullman, Ph.D. is Training Psychoanalyst and faculty at Tel Aviv Institute of Contemporary Psychoanalysis, faculty and supervisor at the school of Psychotherapy, Sackler School of Medicine at Tel-Aviv University, supervisor at the school of psychotherapy at Bar Ilan University, and former chair of Tel-Aviv Institute of Contemporary Psychoanalysis. Dr. Ullman is a member of the board of the International Association for Relational Psychoanalysis and Psychotherapy, author of *The Transformed Self: The Psychology of Religious Conversion* and numerous publications on witnessing, political context and the psychoanalytic process. She lives and practices in Rehovot, Israel.

Bonnie Zindel, LCSW, is Faculty and Supervising Analyst at the National Institute for the Psychotherapies. She is a Founding Editor and Creative Literary Editor of *Psychoanalytic Perspectives*. A playwright and published novelist, she runs writing groups and conducts workshops on personal expression. She has published numerous articles on creativity and presented at IARPP in Athens, Madrid, San Francisco and New York. She is in private practice in New York City.

ACKNOWLEDGMENTS

In a book that focuses on subjectivity, it seems especially fitting to acknowledge those friends, colleagues, and family members who enrich my life and, in turn, my work and these pages. First and foremost, I am grateful to Galit Atlas and Hillary Grill, dear and trusted friends and colleagues who support and inspire me, and who have each contributed to this book in numerous and important ways. Thank you both for always being there to listen to concerns and challenges, read drafts, and encourage me along the way. You are each in your own way an integral part of this volume.

I am lucky to have the friendship, support, and inspiration of colleagues at the National Institute for the Psychotherapies, a creative and nurturing psychoanalytic home. Thank you and congratulations in this 40th anniversary year to all of my fellow Board Directors, but especially to founders James L. Fosshage, Kenneth A. Frank, whose friendship and partnership in *Psychoanalytic Perspectives* is also particularly meaningful to me, Henry Grayson, and Clemens Loew, a valued journal colleague as well. I appreciate the friendship and support of Margaret Black, Board President Ellen Fries, and that of Vice President Caryn Sherman-Meyer, whose presence on the Board, in my life, and help with this book nourishes in many ways. Thank you to friends and former Board colleagues at the Institute for Expressive Analysis, an important community and holding environment: Claudia Bader, Suzanne Bien Bonet, Sara Lavner, Kristin Long, Pam Rogers, Lynn Somerstein, and Janet Sullivan, and to friends and colleagues Robert Benton, Michael Clifford, Heather Ferguson, Jill Gentile, Linda Hopkins, Phil Ringstrom, Jonathan Slavin, and Mal Slavin.

Thank you to my friend, teacher, and mentor Lew Aron, and to Adrienne Harris, also an inspiration. In their roles as co-editors of the Relational Perspectives Book Series, each has encouraged and expertly guided me throughout this process, and each adds immeasurably to the vibrancy of our field. I am fortunate to have the friendship and opportunity to work and play with reading and study group-mates Steve Botticelli, Gary Bruschi, Katie Gentile, Paula Glickman, Steven Knoblauch, Pamela Raab, Mary Sonntag, Susan Sussmann, Angela Vance, and Stephanie Zola, and greatly value the friendship, intellectual stimulation and help with thinking through the book title, working on the journal, and other professional and social projects offered by Sally Bjorklund, Sharyn Leff, Psycho-analytic Perspectives co-editor Deborah Pines, and Bonnie Zindel. To journal colleagues and friends not yet mentioned David Austern, Anja Behm, Kim Bernstein, Jill Choder-Goldman, Sheldon Itzkowitz, Janet Kelly, Sharon Mariner, Allison Mazer Katz, Alan Sirote, Rachel Sopher, and our Managing Editor at Taylor and Francis Amanda Ashworth, I owe each a huge thank you for all that you do to make our publication vibrant.

Publisher Kate Hawes and Senior Editorial Assistant Kirsten Buchanan at Routledge have been wonderful and always generous with their time, patience and support of this project, and Kristopher Spring, formerly of Routledge, and Annelisa Pedersen, have also contributed to this volume in significant ways.

Thank you to dear friends Scott Bloom, Joanne Cabello, Mary Dino, Jordan Friedman, Helen Greenberg and Michael Connor, Ronit and Shimon Greenberg, Debby Kuppersmith, Lisa Lenz, Cherie Lieberman and John Ahearn, Pamela Lotenberg, Alon Orr, Jodd Readick, Herb Stern, and Gabrielle Tessler, and to family members Phyllis, Art and Danny Kuchuck, Judith Young, the Flohrs, Spinowitzes, Caffertys, and a large extended family – Feinsteins, Handels, Harrises, Hollanders, Karpfs, Reiffs, Sadkins, Sterns, and Emma, Yali, and Mia Koch, whose love and companionship mean the world to me.

For Yiri Dollekamp, Susan Rothschild, and Angelo Smaldino, your wisdom and guidance are always with me, and in memory of Gert Karpf, Danny and Ellis Feinstein, Marilyn and Milt Green, Kay Reiff-Udell, Sam and Annette Atlas, and early teachers and mentors Gladys Gonzalez-Ramos and Jeffrey Seinfeld.

Finally, thank you to my patients, supervisees, and students, all of whom enhance my life and offer opportunities for learning and growth in ways you might not imagine.

INTRODUCTION

Steven Kuchuck

In the following pages, established psychoanalytic writers and newer contributors come together to address the phenomena of the analyst's[1] personal life and psychology. Each author explores pivotal childhood and adult life events and crises that have contributed to personality formation, personal and professional functioning, choices of theoretical positions, and clinical technique. Contemporary theory teaches that no two clinicians approach psychoanalytic work in exactly the same way. It is the intersubjective fit and patient–therapist dynamics that determine the course of a treatment. Merton Gill (1983), in fact, notes that if we were to study the transcripts of multiple therapies conducted by the same clinician, we would see clear evidence of that therapist's individual personality. The therapist's subjectivity, therefore, plays a significant role in the co-construction of the clinical fit and trajectory, though it is seldom examined as carefully as other elements of the work.

By expanding psychoanalytic study beyond theory and technique to include a more careful examination of life events and other subjective phenomena, readers will have an opportunity to explore specific ways in which these events and crises affect the tenor of the analyst's presence in the consulting room, and how these occurrences affect and interact with clinical choices. It is my hope that they will be encouraged to think similarly about their own life experiences and unique ways in which these affect clinical technique, theoretical interest, transference–countertransference dynamics, impasses, and other aspects of the treatment. For some, this is already an integral part of how you work, and perhaps these essays will inspire or shed further light on those aspects of theorizing and practice. For others, this might represent a newer way of thinking about the clinical process and/or provide courage and validation for your own subjective and theoretical investigations.

As interest in enactments, intersubjectivity, and general exploration of transference–countertransference dynamics has increased, more contemporary writers have included at least some consideration of these previously understudied variables of personal life and psyche in their work. Indeed, inclusion of such material has become a hallmark of relational psychoanalytic writing. Still, few articles and even fewer books have been devoted entirely to the topic; later in this introduction, I will elaborate on why I think that is. Though by no means an exhaustive list, notable exceptions include Kenneth Frank (1977), who edited the first and (for many years) only volume of essays related to this theme that I am aware of; Margaret Little (1990), on her experience of clinical depression and breakdown while a patient of Winnicott; Robert Stolorow and George Atwood (1993), who explore the subjectivities of Freud, Jung, and others and the relation between their internal dynamics and theoretical discoveries; Richard Isay (1996), on his evolution as a gay psychiatrist and psychoanalyst in an era of mandatory hiding; Barbara Pizer (1997), on self-disclosure of her illness; Adrienne Harris (1998) on autobiography and subjectivity as theoretical constructs; Ellen G. Ruderman and Estelle Shane's *Psychoanalytic Inquiry* issue about life experiences and their impact on treatment (2002); Darlene Ehrenberg (2004), Eric Sherman (2005), Patrick Casement (2006) and Linda B. Sherby (2013), on the interplay between subjectivity and practice; Sophia Richman (2006), on trauma and revelation via autobiographical writing; Therese Ragen's (2009) autobiographical essays; Muriel Dimen (2011), on sexual violation and theoretical aftermath; and the influential volume edited by Barbara Gerson (1996), *The Therapist as a Person*.

Lew Aron (1996) makes the point that people who are drawn to becoming psychoanalysts will by definition have conflicts around intimacy and the desire to be known by another. Aron posits that narcissistic conflicts around voyeurism and exhibitionism are the rule rather than the exception in our work. Why else, he asks, would we choose a profession where we listen so intently to others while sitting silently and hidden? The fact that analysts are never really invisible – even if they try – and that patients often want desperately to know us, raises tremendous anxiety for those struggling with our own longing to be known and defensive temptation to hide. Even relational and other analysts, who can no longer theoretically justify attempting to prevent personal characteristics and other material from entering the treatment, must contend with these likely conflicts and internalized and "real" classical mentors, teachers, analysts, and ghosts, who tell us to refrain from acknowledging the extent to which our subjectivities influence the ways in which we work.

As for clinical applications of subjective awareness and direct self-disclosure in particular, I and others in this volume are certainly not advocating the latter as anything other than a valid option to be held in dialectical tension with protecting a patient's right not to know. Rather, we are urging recognition of the inevitability of inadvertent disclosure and influence that is the cornerstone of working within a two-person psychology. More to the point of this collection, I am suggesting that as a profession, we attempt to overcome or at least address the shame, vulnerability, and antiquated theoretical prohibitions that prevent more widespread explorations of the therapist's subjectivity in the literature.

When the personal becomes professional

In keeping with the theme of this book, I will share some personal context for the evolution of my relational perspective and the subject of this volume in particular.

To begin with, let me state that I have certainly struggled with the conflicts that Aron (1996) describes, and early on, as a child, I learned to hide. While some feelings were tolerated in our house, others – like anger and sadness – were not. Ironic, perhaps, since each were such a part of the fabric of our home, though, as is often the case, rarely if ever openly acknowledged. Sexuality, as a general topic and as a complex, shifting identity, was most definitely forced into hiding. Like many of us, my interest in open exploration of the impact of the analyst's subjectivity and life experience evolved as a corrective to decades of personal and later professional indoctrination to the contrary (Kuchuck, 2008).

At a fairly early age, I entered graduate school and then institute training. As it was for those who came before me, training was quite classical, with heavy undertones of American ego psychology. Readings referred to homosexuality as resulting from arrested development, with heterosexual object choice as the only healthy endpoint of adult development. Not once did I hear a teacher, supervisor, or student question this – an experience that was dispiriting and embarrassing when not dissociated. I regret that I too was not yet at a point where I could speak out. Not only my analyst, but the entire analytic community and literature confirmed that I was damaged and therefore needed to continue fighting what was increasingly feeling like an impossible battle to win: to change fundamental aspects of my core identity, all the while hiding this from the institute and larger professional community (see Aron & Starr, 2013). Having key elements of oneself labeled pathological, especially by the field you have turned to for healing, professional identity, and development, wreaks havoc with even the most securely formed psyche. Isay (1996), Drescher (1997, 2000), Shelby (2000), and others discuss similarly painful, traumatic experiences of psychoanalytic training as closeted and even openly gay candidates.

Impeding my ability to discover or reveal a true analytic self, the state of the field was such that courses and supervisors stressed the importance of complete and absolute analytic neutrality, in those days understood and translated by many of us as secrecy in service of the treatment, rather than analytic discretion. Secrecy wears you down – as does deprivation – and, again, along with hiding, confirms a sense of badness. Strict abstinence (for both sides of the couch) – wishes and needs were very rarely, if ever, to be gratified – ruled the day, as did the notion of a one-person psychology; the analyst's personality was only a consideration to the extent that it was deemed problematic and interfered with the all-important blank slate. Though I came of institute age as recently as the early 1990s, the analyst's subjectivity was not yet a concept we heard very often in those days unless used disparagingly.

There is, of course, a tremendous irony that our profession's not-too-long-ago (and, for some, still current) ego ideal was to hide the analyst's true self or certain of what we now call the analyst's self-states – often at great psychological cost for both analyst and patient – as part of the process of helping patients to come out of hiding and uncover a fuller range of these states. I had early graduate school, institute, and clinic teachers and supervisors stress the importance of making sure that emotions never registered on my face, assuring that office and personal dress were completely "neutral," and seeing to it that, for the sake of the patient, personal needs were always suppressed. As mentioned, abstinence, even to the point of self-negation, seemed to be the key in those days, and though less and less empha- sized by many, it is still an essential goal for some analysts. I know the toll all of this took on me and colleagues. I worry about the toll it took on my patients. And I worry about the toll it might continue to take on our students and their patients if we accept the fact that no matter how far we have come, most of us still operate with some residue of this archaic analytic superego.

Our challenge then becomes to maintain our psychoanalytic ideals – our ana- lytic discretion – while also making space in the room for our real selves. Indeed, many candidates at many institutes – especially in the not-so-long-ago days I am describing – suffered to some degree from the limits imposed by theories that do not allow for acknowledgment of the analyst's subjectivity or diversity, insti- tutional resistance to incorporating and teaching newer theories, and antiquated, insensitive (if not sadistic) training and evaluative methods. For those many of us already carrying our own trauma histories before entering training, this becomes a heavy load to bear, not just a rite of passage, as some might prefer to see it (Reeder, 2004).

Some of these problems were reflective of a lack of progression in the develop- ment or assimilation of new psychoanalytic theory, and some more particular to the dynamics and practices of specific institutes. Certainly in our case, my class- mates and I were fine examples of what Jurgen Reeder (2004) refers to as normal- ized analysts in training. We were told what to think and counseled out of training if we did not follow suit in a climate that reinforced but rarely, if ever, challenged the status quo. Others have also written about this atmosphere of paranoia and infantilization engendered by the Eitingon model of psychoanalytic training, an authoritarian system characteristic of Karl Abraham's and Max Eitingon's Berlin Institute, founded in 1920, but still dominant as a training model at most tradi- tional and even some nontraditional psychoanalytic institutes (Berman, 2004).

By the mid-1990s, I was beginning to hear about psychoanalytic treatment approaches in which homosexuality was not pathologized or automatically hid- den, and in which straight and gay analysts were not afraid to share – or at least refrain from hiding – select biographical or metabolized countertransference data with their patients (Greenberg & Mitchell, 1983; Isay, 1986, 1991; Mitchell, 1988). I entered into a second analysis, and, though still what I would consider boundaried and appropriately asymmetrical (Aron, 1996), it was the first in which I felt engaged in a more mutual, less hierarchical therapeutic relationship. By the end of the millennium, for me and to a certain extent even for the profession, the groundwork for significant change and growth had been laid. It would take a tragedy, however, a life-changing event, before I would be exposed to the kind of transformative learning experience that would allow me to more fully emerge from hiding and feel intact, inspired, and awed enough by the changes in our field and world to overcome significant hurdles in the formation of my identity as a psychoanalyst. Practicing in downtown Manhattan as the towers fell, my personal and professional life was about to change forever.

Shifting terrain

As was true for most of my New York colleagues, and I suspect for others as well, September 11th, 2001, was the first time that my patients and I were experiencing trauma and retraumatization at the same time. In a matter of hours – minutes even – long-held perceptions of the world changed forever. Writing about this period, Altman and Davies (2002) note that "trauma has a way of penetrating what has been inviolate" (p. 359). Forced from hiding, we found that the playing field was more level now – strange new territory to be entering into. Reflecting on her experience of seeing patients shortly after the attacks, Saakvitne (2002) writes of shared (patient–analyst) trauma, with loss as a dominant theme for both: loss of the illusion of invulnerability, innocence, and freedom from fear. When analyst and patient are exposed to the same traumatic event, the therapist is at risk for experiencing multiple levels of trauma. Direct or primary traumatization results from the effects of exposure to traumatic events, in this case experienced by some patients who were in the vicinity of the towers when they fell and, to a lesser extent for others and me, through witnessing soot-covered survivors fleeing en masse as well as seeing and smelling the smoke and viewing the images on television. I certainly experienced a degree of secondary traumatization in relation to traumatized patients and intimate others, as well as what Saakvitne identifies as vicarious traumatization, in this case the impact on and transformation of aspects of the analyst's self-states as a result of identification and empathic engagement with traumatized patients in the context of treatment. I believe that it was in large part vicarious traumatization that accounts for many of the personal and professional shifts I discuss. All three of these levels of traumatization can and did, for me and many patients (and colleagues), lead to feelings of vulnerability, danger, loneliness, and isolation as engendered by the tragedy. Also, for many of us on both sides of the couch, these feelings were a result of a fourth level of traumatic experience: retraumatization, which manifested in the resurrection of these and other, older feelings.

For that first day and the weeks and months to follow, walls and defenses crumbled as patients shared their stories and asked about me – it suddenly felt absurd and inhumane to fall back on the already at times questionable, "Why do you ask?" Hirsch (2003) and colleagues he spoke with noted similar shifts in the direction of increased symmetry and toward engagement in what interpersonalists call participant–participant dyads. It was indeed validating to have the intensity of my experience living and working downtown confirmed when patients from uptown remarked on the awful stench that permeated our air for months – I can still smell it – and the haunting, heart-wrenching missing persons posters that covered the sides of our lampposts and buildings. Although the city came together during this period, it was blessedly easy to forget – at least temporarily – what we downtown could not escape. In sessions, we flinched and sometimes even ducked when planes flew low overhead and worried about and missed absent group members.

I did not lose anyone in the disaster, although I did not know that at first. Some patients who lived in the vicinity of the World Trade Center did not show up or respond to calls for close to two weeks, and a long-time patient lost his dearest friend in the world. We were all mourning, and I could not always stop myself from crying for – and with – some patients. For some who also shed tears, the mutuality was comforting, close, while for others it was frightening, as the care-taker seemed to suddenly need care. As Jessica Benjamin (1998) and others point out, patients are not always ready and able to accept evidence of their analyst's subjectivity. For these patients, the experience was strange, if not terrifying. For probably the first time in my practice, I knew this and yet could not always regu-late the affect enough to protect them from what surely felt impinging. Grist for the mill, to be sure, but the coarsest of the coarse.

Initially, constructivist perspectives (Hoffman, 1983) quickly shifted from genetic/historical to the crisis at hand. We now had our shared, much more recent history to contend with. In those first days and weeks, there was the here and now of physical and psychic safety to deal with until the immediacy of the crisis passed and we could begin to explore the psychic residue that had been stirred. And in those first days and weeks – in some respects, months – the guide was as shaken as the guided.

I barely hesitated when a letter arrived from a then-new organization: The Inter-national Association for Relational Psychoanalysis and Psychotherapy. A com-mittee called Psychotherapists for Social Responsibility (PSR) had formed to study the psychological effects of 9/11 and the resulting political crisis. An effort would be made to apply what was known about unconscious dynamics, trauma, and attachment theory in order to understand what many of us believed to be (at least in part) a manipulation by the Administration for political purposes, as well as the social and psychological effects of these maneuvers. Secondary to applying psychoanalytic theory in an attempt to understand the new political climate, the group was to serve as a community in which therapists could process what was happening to us; this was especially important since, in addition to our own, we were holding difficult feelings for patients and others as well.

Moving objects

Internalized analytic (and other) objects were shifting. PSR was formed and ini-tially led by some of the founders of the relational and feminist psychoanalytic movements, and so I was now exposed to a new vocabulary, a new body of lit-erature, and, for me, fresh new ways of thinking about psychoanalysis (Gentile & Gutwill, 2006; Seeley, 2008). The crisis pushed and perhaps even forced me into newer ways of being with patients: greater openness to the possibility of selec-tive self-disclosures (initially, as when overcome by affect, this felt out of my conscious control); greater appreciation of mutuality, if not direct symmetry; a more acute recognition of the inevitability and value of the intersubjective nature of treatment and enactments; and other changes already mentioned. But it was my exposure to and collaboration with these new colleagues that gave me, first, the language to express what had before seemed mostly inadvertent, and second, the opportunity for further reflection, identification, integration, and learning.

Hirsch (2003) notes that despite initial changes similar to those I have described, over time, analytic life returned to what it had been for him. He recognizes that for some analysts these newer ways of being with patients may have changed permanently, and suggests that the attacks served to highlight some important themes about analysts and their relationship to patients that he and other inter-personal and relational analysts before him had been addressing since Sullivan's original contributions. Analysts who are more inclined to denial, emotional isola-tion, narcissistic self-absorption, and hyperrationality may never have shifted in the first place or sealed over more quickly than those who had suffered previous traumas, and therefore have lower thresholds for anxiety and possibly more incli-nation toward empathic identification. This latter group, with which I obviously identify, took longer to return to normal and may have been changed in more ongoing ways. I was indeed changing. Concepts of intersubjectivity, mutuality, the third, doer/done-to, and many others stayed with me (Aron, 1996; Benjamin, 2004; Mitchell, 2003) and continue to inform my practice, teaching, and writing (Atlas-Koch & Kuchuck, 2012; Kuchuck, 2008, 2009, 2012, 2013). They not only helped to provide a framework for what had been happening in the period after the terrorist attacks, but also opened up new ways of thinking about concepts of transference, countertransference, and psychoanalysis in general. Hiding, still a tendency at times, was not as absolute an option anymore. I could no longer ignore the role that life experience and other aspects of subjectivity plays in how we think about theory and practice.

This book, then, is borne of the storming in of my own and the profession's subjectivity. This was an uprising no doubt in formation for years, but in the end heralded by a crisis and an already shifting field. It is a collection that celebrates an emergence from hiding on the part of authors, analysts, and a profession. In all but one case, it assumes an embrace of relational concepts, including the notion that minds develop only in relation to other minds (Mitchell, 1988): child to par-ent, patient to analyst, perhaps writer to reader, all in circular fashion. In the pages that follow, each author bucks classical conventional wisdom and braves a level of exposure and vulnerability not often enough afforded in this field.

Part I: Early life events, crises, and influences

Although this book is divided into two sections, it is designed with the assumption that development is nonlinear, and in that context, Parts I and II may be inter-changeable categories. Still, the primary focus of Part I is on early life events and their emergence in the consulting room, while in Part II, authors reflect on later life passages and events and consider more recent occurrences, antecedents, and theoretical and clinical implications. In both sections, authors give thought to the ways in which both early beginnings and adult internal and external events lead to particular ways of theorizing and practicing.

In Chapter 1, Sally Bjorklund takes us back to the very beginning, to a time when she was named Betty, and home was a series of temporary placements prior to adoption. As Bjorklund explains, her narrative attempts a chronological linearity that has proven as impossible to achieve in this chapter as it has in life. The facts of how she came to be have been revealed to her in fits and starts, and even then, only incompletely. Confusion, secrecy, loss, and identity politics have colored the author's development and her identification as a psychoanalyst. Learning to tolerate the unknown is an integral part of this legacy and her way of being with patients.

At 5, Susie Orbach would answer the door and ask: "Are you a socialist? Are you a Jew?" These two characteristics, she tells us in Chapter 2, marked the identity of a child growing up in an emotionally volatile political household in postwar England. Politics were either whispered or screamed, but in every case, were always imbued with secrecy. As a child, she wondered about what the other secrets might be. It took an adolescence and young adulthood to figure out the paradox of a seemingly verbal, communicative family where intimate communications were out of reach. From these beginnings, Orbach traces a lifelong interest in politics, activism, women's issues – especially around body image – and psychoanalysis.

Embedded not in European culture but rather that of the Middle and Far East, we learn in Chapter 3 that Galit Atlas was witness to a different set of secrets. Like Orbach, early on, Atlas was primed to explore cultural, intrapsychic, and interpersonal meanings of female identity. In her grandmother's kitchen and later the Israeli army and United States, Atlas had to navigate issues of shame, cultural and national identity, and immigration in order to learn what it means to be a woman and a sexual being, what it means to find a home. Personal and professional explorations continue. In her writing and clinical work, she is engaged in a complex and contextually rich investigation of sexuality.

Joyce Slochower, Irwin Hirsch, and Kenneth Frank, in Chapters 4, 5, and 6 respectively, examine household dynamics and early personal and professional identifications that led to their choice of profession and inform their theoretical and clinical stances. Slochower, the daughter of two Freudian psychoanalysts, entered graduate school and later, institute training, with a perhaps obvious predisposition for classical Freudian thinking. As she explains, however, there were too many rules in childhood and then in psychoanalysis to remain comfortably enough in that theoretical space. She soon embarks on a personal and theoretical journey that changed and continues to define her relationship to herself, her patients, and her profession. Hirsch states that his most significant learning experiences are derived from failure and disappointment. He was raised by an anxious, worried mother, identified with her tendency to expect the worst, and believes that this led to a sense of readiness and control when the inevitable bad experiences occurred. Hirsch explores how this sense of negativity and a tendency to be oppositional inform his clinical work. Frank examines his ongoing personal and professional struggle between letting others know him as fully as they or he might wish, and the strong felt need to safeguard his privacy. Early history and later experiences in graduate school, analytic training, private practice, and while cofounding a psychoanalytic institute led and contributed to these conflicts and their ongoing resolution. In reading Frank's work, my favorite Winnicott quote comes to mind: "It is a joy to be hidden, but a disaster not to be found" (1965, p. 186).

Anna Ornstein was raised in a small village in Northern Hungary. She and her family suffered the consequences of severe anti-Semitism and later, life in the ghetto and Auschwitz. In Chapter 7, Ornstein explores the influence of her close-knit family, the effects of multiple losses, and concentration camp internment. In this chapter and earlier publications (1985, 1989), she challenges the assumption of pathology that is often made about Holocaust survivors. On the contrary, Ornstein credits her ambition, strength, and resilience to early influences and wartime experiences. She recognizes her resonance with self psychology, a lifelong interest in narcissistic rage, and more recently, the psychology of mass murderers as emerging from these earlier events.

As the daughter of Holocaust survivors and a lifelong citizen of Israel, Chana Ullman is very much aware of the presence of past and current violence, trauma, hope, and renewal. In Chapter 8, she shares with us the impact of these dynamics, and delves into the interplay of these themes with concepts of forgiveness and witnessing, suffering and evil as she understands them in herself and her patients. In Israel, the personal and the political are always intertwined. While politics are not overtly discussed in Eric Sherman's contribution, the politics of sex and equality are backgrounded in Chapter 9, internalized by the author and his friends, who come of age in post-Stonewall America. Politics and other cultural artifacts contribute to the pain and shame Sherman, and later his patients, must overcome in order to face an evolving sexual identity and brave a search for intimacy and love.

Part II: Later life events, crises, and developmental passages

It might be said that Michael Eigen's writing often defies categorization, and in that respect, can be read as an embodiment of similarly complex, nonlinear thinking about development, practice, and human nature in general. In Chapter 10, we meet Eigen on a spiritual and psychological quest, an effort to better understand himself and the tensions that build when he tries to write, love, be. Although his attempt to consult with R. D. Laing about these struggles is not successful, he does find himself in sessions with Winnicott, and later, Bion. He shares with us what each man taught him about these personal challenges and psychoanalysis.

Several years ago, a longtime patient entered my office and shared some news that left me shaken, threatening to challenge what I thought I knew about professional and personal boundaries. In Chapter 11, I discuss the details of this case in an effort to address the impossible task of sorting out the personal from the professional, and in doing so, trace the course of my professional evolution and related aspects of my personal journey. In Chapter 12, we journey with Phil Ringstrom as he reflects on early experiences with siblings and parents and later challenges in starting a family that allow him to more clearly distinguish trauma from expectancy systems. He explores an additional connection between these family dynamics and later life events and his interest in working from an improvisational perspective.

Although there is a slowly growing body of work on adoption (*Psychoanalytic Inquiry*, 30 (1), 2009; *Psychoanalytic Perspectives*, 10 (1), 2013), this is an area that still remains underrepresented in the literature. In Chapter 13, Steve Botticelli and his partner Noah Glassman join Sally Bjorklund (Chapter 1) in offering their take on this complex event. Issues of gender, sexual identity, childhood longings and fears, and the bridging of personal and professional identities come to the fore as they co-write and co-parent their adopted son. Like Botticelli and Glassman, Hillary Grill also explores fatherhood, primarily in the context of her own and her patient's struggles to understand difficult, imposing paternal figures. Grill's exploration of attachment and loss are the subject of Chapter 14, and lead to larger questions about self-disclosure, the therapeutic value of the patient to the analyst, and the analyst's self-interest and care.

One of the fundamental experiences of life, loss always precedes, accompanies, and or follows change and growth. As for Grill, it is a central theme in the chapters that follow. In 1996, Eric Mendelsohn wrote about the loss of his infant daughter, and in Chapter 15 of this volume, about an almost 30-year marriage. As he tells us, the still very recent separation is in equal measures public and private. The wish to talk about this event and be known during a most difficult phase of his life is held in tension with a need for privacy and respect for his patients' needs. Feelings of failure versus emancipation, sadness and distraction versus authenticity and relief hover over his sessions with patients. Explorations of the separation's impact on the transference–countertransference are ongoing. Similarly, a large part of Bonnie Zindel's work in her training analysis centered around loss. A significant theme since the death of her mother when she was an adolescent, Zindel outlines the implications of this and subsequent losses, the meaning she and her analyst are able to make of this early trauma, and the impact on her personal and professional trajectory. In Chapter 16, we witness an expanding sense of self: a woman, analyst, and writer on the cusp. Nine years into the treatment, there are additional devastating losses: one the sudden death of her analyst Emmanuel Ghent, a founder and early leader of the relational psychoanalytic community. This treatment and its shattering end changed Zindel and informs her own clinical work immeasurably.

Illness is never a welcome visitor, and usually arrives unannounced, challenging our fantasies of unlimited strength, control, and predictive abilities, causing bodily and narcissistic injuries. We learn in Chapter 17 that while on vacation, Deborah Pines suffered a stroke, and as one might imagine, life for her and her family was forever changed. As can be the case following this type of episode, it took months to determine the full extent of the damage, and now, close to five years later, recovery is dramatic but still ongoing. Pines describe the course of the illness, its initial and subsequent impact on her patients and practice, and the nature of the continuing recovery. While the struggles have been significant, so too has the personal and professional learning and opportunity for reworking old traumas.

This book opens with a birth, proceeds through the life cycle and myriad challenges of lives and practices fully lived, and closes in old age. Thus, in the final chapter, Martin Bergmann – penning his contribution at 99 and about to turn 100 as I put the finishing touches on this introduction – is still in the full-time practice and individual and group supervision of psychoanalysis, and a faculty member at the New York University Postdoctoral Program in Psychotherapy and Psychoanalysis, where he teaches a popular course on the history of psychoanalysis. Labels are of course limited in their usefulness and often obscure the more accurate complexities and subtle gray areas of overlapping identities. Having stated that, I would venture that Bergmann is probably the only author in this collection who would self-identify as a Freudian rather than a relational or interpersonal analyst or self psychologist. His psychoanalytic knowledge is staggering, his wisdom, charm, and good humor legendary, and Bergmann brings these qualities to bear as he turns his attention to writing about clinical practice in old age. Although he begins his chapter with a discussion of old age and clinical work with elderly patients in more general terms, he soon joins the rest of the authors in this volume by turning the lens on himself as well. We learn something about what Bergmann calls his personal philosophy of life and death, and what he sees as the challenges of treating patients at a more advanced age. We should all live and be well, as my grandmother used to say, blessed with enough years to learn and grow, and the curiosity, courage, and fortitude to examine the impact of our lives on our patients, theirs on us, and the intersubjective spaces in between.

Note

1 Throughout the book, unless otherwise noted, psychoanalyst and psychotherapist are used interchangeably, assuming an interest in and awareness of psychoanalytic concepts regardless of the nature of postgraduate training. For a discussion of how and why these terms have come to be separated, and the political and theoretical ramifications of this split, see Aron and Starr (2013).

References

Altman, N., & Davies, J. M. (2002). Out of the blue: Reflections on a shared trauma. *Psychoanalytic Dialogues, 12*, 359–360.
Aron, L. (1996). *A meeting of minds: Mutuality in psychoanalysis*. Hillsdale, NJ: Analytic Press.
Aron, L., & Starr, K. (2013). *A psychotherapy for the people: Toward a progressive psychoanalysis*. New York: Routledge.

Atlas-Koch, G., & Kuchuck, S. (2012). To have and to hold: Psychoanalytic dialogues on the desire to own. *Psychoanalytic Dialogues*, *22*, 93–105.

Benjamin, J. (1998). *Shadow of the other: Intersubjectivity and gender in psychoanalysis.* New York: Routledge.

Benjamin, J. (2004). Beyond doer and done to: An intersubjective view of thirdness. *Psychoanalytic Quarterly*, *73*, 5–46.

Berman, E. (2004). *Impossible training: A relational view of psychoanalytic education.* Hillsdale, NJ: Analytic Press.

Casement, P. (2006). *Learning from life: Becoming a psychoanalyst.* London: Routledge.

Dimen, M. (2011). Lapsus linguae, or a slip of the tongue?: A sexual violation in an analytic treatment and its personal and theoretical aftermath. *Contemporary Psychoanalysis*, *47*, 35–79.

Drescher, J. (1997). From preoedipal to postmodern: Changing psychoanalytic attitudes toward homosexuality. *Gender and Psychoanalysis*, *2*, 203–216.

Drescher, J. (2000). Cornucopia: Responses to Rosario, Cohler, Orange, Roughton, and Shelby's discussions of psychoanalytic therapy and the gay man. *Gender and Psychoanalysis*, *5*, 291–319.

Ehrenberg, D. B. (2004). How I became a psychoanalyst. *Psychoanalytic Inquiry*, *24*, 490–516.

Frank, K. A. (Ed.) (1977). *The human dimension in psychoanalytic practice.* New York: Grune & Stratton.

Gentile, K., & Gutwill, S. (2006). How to create social activism: Turning the passive to active without killing each other. *Psychotherapy and Politics International*, *3*(2), 122–132.

Gerson, B. (Ed.) (1996). *The therapist as a person: Life crises, life choices, life experiences, and their effects on treatment.* Hillsdale, NJ: Analytic Press.

Gill, M. M. (1983). The interpersonal paradigm and the degree of the therapist's involvement. *Contemporary Psychoanalysis*, *19*, 200–237.

Greenberg, J., & Mitchell, S. (1983). *Object relations in psychoanalytic theory.* Cambridge, MA: Harvard University Press.

Harris, A. (1998). The analyst as (auto)biographer. *American Imago*, *55*, 255–275.

Hirsch, I. (2003). Reflections on clinical issues in the context of the national trauma of September 11th. *Contemporary Psychoanalysis*, *39*, 665–681.

Hoffman, I. Z. (1983). The patient as interpreter of the analyst's experience. *Contemporary Psychoanalysis*, *19*, 389–422.

Isay, R. A. (1986). The development of sexual identity in homosexual men. *Psychoanalytic Study of the Child*, *41*, 467–489.

Isay, R. A. (1991). The homosexual analyst: Clinical considerations. *Psychoanalytic Study of the Child*, *46*, 199–216.

Isay, R. A. (1996). *Becoming gay: The journey to self-acceptance.* New York: Henry Holt.

Kuchuck, S. (2008). In the shadow of the towers: The role of retraumatization and political action in the evolution of a psychoanalyst. *Psychoanalytic Review*, *95*, 417–436.

Kuchuck, S. (2009). Do ask, do tell?: Narcissistic need as a determinant of analyst self-disclosure. *Psychoanalytic Review*, *96*, 1007–1024.

Kuchuck, S. (2012). Please (don't) want me: The therapeutic action of male sexual desire in the treatment of heterosexual men. *Contemporary Psychoanalysis*, *48*(4), 544–562.

Kuchuck, S. (2013). When two become four: Patient, analyst, lover, friend. *Psychoanalytic Perspectives, 10*(2).

Little, M. (1990). *Psychotic anxieties and containment: A personal record of an analysis with Winnicott.* Northvale, NJ: Jason Aronson.

Mitchell, S. A. (1988). *Relational concepts in psychoanalysis: An integration.* Cambridge, MA: Harvard University Press.

Mitchell, S. A. (2003). *Relationality: From attachment to intersubjectivity.* Hillsdale, NJ: The Analytic Press.

Ornstein, A. (1985). Survival and recovery. *Psychoanalytic Inquiry, 5*, 9–130.

Ornstein, A. (1989). Treatment issues with survivors and their offspring. In P. Marcus & J. Rosenberg (Eds.), *Healing their wounds: Psychotherapy with Holocaust survivors and their families* (pp. 105–116). Santa Barbara, CA: Praeger.

Pizer, B. (1997). When the analyst is ill: Dimensions of self-disclosure. *Psychoanalytic Quarterly, 66*(3), 450–469.

Ragen, T. (2009). *The consulting room and beyond: Psychoanalytic work and its reverberations in the analyst's life.* New York: Routledge.

Reeder, J. (2004). *Hate and love in psychoanalytical institutions: The dilemma of a profession.* New York: Other Press.

Richman, S. (2006). When the analyst writes a memoir: Clinical implications of biographic disclosure. *Contemporary Psychoanalysis, 42*, 367–392.

Ruderman, Ellen G., & Shane, E. (Eds.) (2002). The analyst's life experiences and their effects on treatment: Living, learning, and working through. Special issue of *Psychoanalytic Inquiry, 22*(4), Issue Editors: Ellen G. Ruderman, Ph.D. and Estelle Shane, Ph. D., Hillsdale, NJ: Analytic Press.

Saakvitne, K. W. (2002). Shared trauma: The therapist's increased vulnerability. *Psychoanalytic Dialogues, 12*, 443–449.

Seeley, K. (2008). *Therapy after terror: 9/11, psychotherapists, and mental health.* New York: Cambridge University Press.

Shelby, R. D. (2000). Narcissistic injury, humiliation, rage, and the desire for revenge: Thoughts on Drescher's *Psychoanalytic therapy and the gay man. Gender and Psychoanalysis, 5*, 275–289.

Sherby, L. B. (2013). *Love and loss in life and in treatment.* London: Routledge.

Sherman, E. (2005). *Notes from the margins: The gay analyst's subjectivity in the treatment setting.* Hillsdale, NJ: Analytic Press.

Stolorow, R. D., & Atwood, G. E. (1993). *Faces in a cloud: Intersubjectivity in personality theory.* Northvale, NJ: Jason Aronson.

Winnicott, D.W. (1965). *The maturational processes and the facilitating environment: Studies in the theory of emotional development.* Madison, CT: International Universities Press.

Part I

EARLY LIFE EVENTS, CRISES, AND INFLUENCES

1

HOW BETTY AND VINCENT BECAME SALLY AND SCOTT

Sally Bjorklund

Betty was born in Minneapolis on 5/16/51. She weighed 6 lbs., 9½ oz. and was 21" long. When she left the hospital on 5/22/51, she weighed 6 lbs., 6½ oz. She was a full-term baby, delivery had been normal, and the hospital had described her as a normal, healthy infant. When Betty left the hospital she was placed in a Children's Home Society boarding home. A few days after her placement, she developed a tendency to spit up a good deal of her food, and she cried and appeared to be uncomfortable a good deal of the time. When she was examined by the agency's pediatrician on 6/6/51, she was found to be a normal infant, but it was recommended that she be kept in a boarding home for a while longer to see if her feeding problems could be relieved. Later, she was placed on an Olac formula™. Her weight on 6/6/51 was 7 lbs., 14 oz.

July 18th, when she was again seen by our pediatrician, she was no longer spitting up her food and was adjusting very well on the Olac formula. She was also a much happier and more comfortable baby, and was beginning to exhibit many lovable characteristics. She was now smiling frequently and was responding more to any attention given her. The pediatrician checked her physical condition and her reaction, and felt that she was a normal, healthy infant. He recommended that she be continued on the Olac formula. At this time she weighed 10 lbs., 8 oz.

Due to vacation plans of the first boarding mother, it was necessary on July 18th to move her to a second boarding home. She adjusted to this change well, and if anything, did better in the second boarding home than in the first. The new boarding mother did not notice any feeding problems at all, and said that most of the time Betty had been sleeping all through the night. Betty was now able to take more formula without spitting it up and was even beginning to like her cereal better. She was getting an oatmeal cereal because pabulum was thought to disagree with her.

V.W. (social worker) 7/24/51

On August first an agreement between the Children's Home Society and Rev. and Mrs. Clifford Bjorklund was signed, stating:

> ... That in consideration of the promises made between the adoptive
> parents, the Society places in the home of the adoptive parents Betty for
> the purpose of providing the child with a free home with adoption in view
> ... The adoptive parents agree to relinquish to the Society all custody and
> right to said child whenever, prior to the adoption of the child, the Society
> shall deem it essential to the best interests of the child that the adoptive
> parents should relinquish their rights and custody. Adoptive parents shall
> have the right to return the child to the Society at any time prior to adop-
> tion, upon reasonable notice ...

By mid-August, Betty is living with her new parents "with adoption in view."
Once the adoption is finalized, a doctored birth certificate is issued declaring the
birth "legitimate," showing the names of the new parents and renaming baby Betty
"Sally Kristin." The name of the biological mother was withheld, and the name
of the biological, or as they called it then, "natural" father, was known only to the
"natural" mother, who refused to disclose the name. She was allowed to keep his
name a secret.

My mother died while I was in the midst of considering what to write for this
chapter. I guess I should say my adoptive mother. I had flown to Chicago for
the memorial service and was sorting through several piles of her few remaining
earthly belongings. Sitting at the dining-room table at my cousin's home, I opened
the strongbox she had left in my cousin's basement, fearful of it getting lost at the
nursing home where she spent her final years. Before she lost her mind to Alzheimer's, she had reminded me about the box so I could find it after her death. I sat
looking through the birth, baptism, and death certificates of my adoptive mother,
brother, and father. Maybe these papers had to be in a strongbox because of the
power of the memories it held. There were two envelopes, one marked "Scott"
and one marked "Sally." You have just read much of what was in the envelope
marked "Sally." Someone told me it was the second boarding mother who gave
Betty a name. Along with the social worker's history for baby Betty was a note of
instructions for the new adoptive parents, written by the second boarding mother.
As I read the note I was surprised by my tears, brought on by this first appearance
of tenderness in the case history. Who was this woman? She noticed what Betty
liked and didn't like. Along with instructions for amounts and kinds of food Betty
ate, she wrote, ". . . Fusses some after 6 o'clock feeding so I have usually talked
to her or rocked her and fed her again whenever she seems to want it. She coos
and smiles when you talk to her. Needs to be burped often while eating. Prefers
sleeping on her tummy." The adoption agreement papers also included the option
to bring Betty back if she didn't work out. Good thing that was time-limited or she
might have been returned as a teenager.

In the envelope marked "Scott" was a thicker pile of papers, because although
he also was found to be a "normal" infant, by three years old he was showing
evidence of developmental deficits and was eventually diagnosed with "mental
retardation." Baby Vincent had a full name, Vincent Carter Witsiepe, and his

"natural" mother's name, Renault Smith Witsiepe, was on the adoption papers. These papers state that "paternity of Vincent Carter Witsiepe has not been established . . . and that Vincent Carter Witsiepe shall to all legal intents and purposes be the child of Clifford and June Bjorklund and . . . [it] shall be the same as if he had been born to them in lawful wedlock." It further ordered and declared that the name of said child be changed to Scott Christopher Bjorklund.

So now you know the literal details of how Vincent and Betty became Scott and Sally.

Sitting with the strong box at the dining room table, I remembered having first read the papers in the "Sally" envelope years before. I knew I was adopted since before I could understand what it meant. There is a genre of books called "chosen baby stories," and I was read to from one. The book was about chickens and was supposed to help a child understand adoption. I don't remember the story, but I know I heard it many times. There also was a book about chickens to explain "the birds and bees," which came later, and made me wonder about chickens and their relation to me. The book about adopted chickens portrayed them as "special" and talked about how much they were wanted by their parents. When, as an adult, I discovered Betty Jane Lifton's books about adoption (1975, 1979, 1994), I found that she helpfully pointed out that to be wanted by your new parents you had to be unwanted by someone else. (I think I wrote "someone else" because when you're adopted you're not supposed to think about having other "parents.") Lifton makes the point that this part of adoption gets swept under the carpet in the happy story of being "special" and "wanted."

When I read the contents of the "Scott" and "Sally" envelopes, I had this strange sense of confusion about what I've read before, what someone has told me, what the "facts" are, and what I have created. I learned from talking with other adoptees that they have a similar experience of filling in bits of narrative and images around the skeleton of facts and stories told to us by others. For example, I had this image for a long time of a room full of babies, and my adoptive parents walking up and down the aisles shopping for a baby. They chose me because I smiled at them. When I was a teenager and not getting along with them, I regretted that smile and the idea that it was me who picked them. I think I cobbled together this story from something I heard about how I first smiled at them when we were introduced and how good it made them feel. Many years later I recognized, on a greeting card, a photo from Life magazine from the 1950s of a hospital nursery full of cribs with babies. On the inside it read, "You're one in a million." What caught my attention was that it looked just like the orphanage in my fantasy.

This business about being chosen instead of – what . . . made? – is a tricky one to figure out with a child's mind. I learned, from listening to other adoptees, that it's not uncommon for adoptees to be told that they chose their adoptive parents. You recall the social worker said baby Betty "left" the hospital, as if she just got up out of her crib and hiked over to the boarding home. As I read the papers in the strongbox, I felt kind of detached, like baby Betty was someone else, like I was reading a case history. Actually, it is a case history – but "normal" people don't have case histories. The social worker's tone seems to encourage this reading, that this is all very medical, about how to get Betty to eat and gain weight and to become more lovable so she can be given to the waiting parents. I laughed out loud over how many times I/Betty was declared "normal," since that is a designation that has been eroding, with some intentionality on my part, during my lifelong drift into queerness. It seems likely that Betty was spitting up because she needed a real mother to feed her. Reading that she was returned to "the Society" so that the first boarding mother could go on vacation gave me a knot in my stomach, and I felt "I don't like that mother!" I know that back then educated people believed that anyone who took care of a baby's basic physical needs was good enough and that babies don't remember anything from infancy. Of course, now we know better (Bowlby, 1980; Stern, 1985; and others). Reading how baby Betty was treated, with a contemporary understanding of psychic development (Beebe, Lachmann & Jaffe 1997; Shore, 1994; Stern; 1985; and others) is painful, and makes me wonder why on earth they didn't just let the adoptive parents figure out the feeding problems. The note from the second boarding mother felt different. There, I feel someone tuning into Betty, finding her rhythms, matching her, creating the "one in the third" that Benjamin (2004) describes. This mother needed to give the baby a name. Why "Betty," I wonder?

As an adult and as a psychoanalyst, I came to understand something about the loss and immense grief women and couples may feel because of infertility. In my work, it has felt important to help couples process their loss before they turn to adoption. I get riled up when anti-abortion groups point to adoption as the morally correct solution to unwanted and emotionally complicated pregnancies. Despite having a pro-choice point of view, I am aware that if abortion had been legal in the 1950s, I wouldn't exist. Still, it's more complicated than that. I believe that my adoptive mother never stopped grieving her infertility or for the daughter of her imagination. How you become a family matters, although how it matters is different for different families. For many, it matters to not look like any of your relatives. My cousins and their children all resemble each other. At 5' 2", with hazel eyes and fair hair, I could pass better in our adopted Scandinavian family than my 6' 7", brown-eyed, dark haired, swarthy complexioned brother. His feet were so big his shoes had to be custom-made. We were an odd pair to introduce as brother and sister. Parents who have biological children with interests or an appearance very different from their own may be surprised, but they don't wonder, did she get this from her biological parents? My adoptive mother dreamed of having a girly girl she could sew for and dress up and make doll clothes for. I was a tomboy who hated being dressed up and whose doll bed full of dolls looked like a doll museum instead of a home for beloved toys. I put baseball cards in the purse I was forced to take to church. It wasn't so easy to turn Betty into Sally.

I was invited to contribute to this book with the idea of writing about my experience as an out lesbian analyst. As I considered it, I realized that my experience of being adopted was what I felt more compelled to write about. I had no idea how I would write about such a profoundly influential aspect of my personal and professional development. I knew I would have to begin with attachment and loss. John Bowlby (1980), in his research on attachment, found a link between psychiatric disturbances in children who have lost a parent, and the surviving parent's capacity to talk openly, to visit the gravesite, and talk about how the lost parent died. When adults either can't or won't talk openly about how the dead parent died, the child is much more likely to have troubles. Adoption is an odd case of loss. It is a loss for the child of contact with biological parents and their kin, and a huge loss for the adoptive parents who are not able to "make" their own baby. In the case of Betty, she had lost three mothers by the time she was three months old and was "placed" with her adoptive parents. (Adopted babies are placed, not born.) These are losses that are seldom acknowledged or talked about because there often is shame, secrecy, and a well-intentioned use of denial to get this new "chosen" family off to a good start.

> Sorrow concealed, like an oven stopp'd,
> Doth burn the heart to cinders where it is.
> Shakespeare, Titus Andronicus

In the 472-page volume by Bowlby called Attachment and Loss (1980), I found no mention of adoption as a cause of grieving for any member of the adoption triangle. Yet, there are many passages and literary quotes like the one above that resonate for me. Bowlby describes symptoms I recognize from working with adults who were adopted as children. I have had the experience, in professional consultation groups, that I am much more likely to attribute being adopted as a significant factor for patients than my non-adopted colleagues, although "relinquishing" a child is recognized as a significant factor. The pressures, conscious and unconscious, to make adoptive families equivalent to biologically created families is powerful.

Out of the closet

As mentioned above, when I was asked to contribute to this book, I felt pulled to write about my experience of being adopted, even though I would have enjoyed writing about how baby Betty ended up being not so "normal" after all. As an openly lesbian analyst, people are surprised to hear that I was previously married to a man and had no thought of being homosexual until I was in my 30s. For me, it was a choice, not a lifelong thing I struggled with or against. It makes me more anxious to confess to bisexuality than to say I'm lesbian. Coming out as adopted also makes me anxious. Hardly anyone knows this about me. Why would I tell anyone? I'm not ashamed ("Are you sure?" I hear myself ask), but it rarely "comes up." Surely, now there can be no other closets for me to come out of. What will you, the reader, think of me? What if my patients read this? Actually, the information age has already taken away the possibility of hiding. There are various details about my childhood available in surprising ways on the internet, as well as vital statistics like that I was divorced, the name of my ex-husband, the name of my partner, and location of the property we own. Until this chapter, though, no one could find out that I was adopted, since adoption records are still sealed in most states.

As days passed and the deadline drew near, I started to worry that I would have to tell the editor that I wasn't going to be able to finish my piece on time. I had six months to complete this, and was only able to begin writing with less than six weeks to go. It occurred to me that this is a familiar problem. There is something about writing on this topic, or doing anything connected to my adoption, that creates a tremendous amount of procrastination and anxiety. I can't write because I can't think. I feel blocked. My mind goes blank, and I don't know what to say. Then, suddenly, things break loose and there's a flood of thoughts and feelings.

Searching

I thought about doing a search for my birth mother for many years. If I mentioned it, people always said, "Oh, you should do it." I can't remember how old I was when she told me, but my adoptive mother said that when they signed the final papers, my father was able to read upside-down on the form and my birth mother's name is ___.[1] I remember the image of that handwritten piece of paper she showed me, with the name on it – written down, lest it be forgotten. I think I heard that my adoptive parents looked up her name in the phone book for the small town ___ was from. It was Farmington, Minnesota. Did they drive by her house? I think I heard they did. It was a nice house, not a trailer park. Thank God. My memory feels unreliable. I don't know what I've made up about this part of the story, and what I was told or overheard. Someone said ___'s father was a banker. Wait! It feels kind of outrageous what I just did. I wrote her name down here for the whole world to see. No more secrets hidden in sealed records.

I was in the early years of my training analysis and ruminating about whether to do a "search," as it's called. I felt my analyst was encouraging me to do it. I found all kinds of reasons not to: I couldn't afford it, what if it ruined ___'s life, what if it ruined my life somehow? My partner gave me the money, so I lost that excuse; I made the call. The adoption agency, which would do the "search," sent forms and told me I had to write a letter that would be given to the birth mother when they found her. I sat down to write my "Dear ___" letter. What a daunting undertaking that was! We had a lot of catching up to do, ___ and I. I finally got everything done, and then for weeks, literally, I would forget to mail it. The envelope would turn up unmailed in the weirdest places. After being lost and found many times, I somehow got it into the mailbox. It was hard to miss my ambivalence and fears about what the next step might be.

It wasn't very hard to find her, I guess. Several months later, I was waiting to board the Tsawwassen ferry for a vacation on Vancouver Island. This was before cell phones, and I used a pay phone to check my messages at home. I can still remember the feeling, as I walked back to the car. My head was swimming. I told my partner that the social worker had left a message saying she completed the search and I should call her. What does that mean, I wonder? How was it completed? Did they find her? I walked back to the pay phone and with uncertain hands, dialed the number. The social worker told me she had talked to ___, although of course it was my secret that I knew her name, thanks to my father's skill of reading upside-down. The social worker said ___ was very alarmed by the call. Can you imagine getting that call? I had the impression the social worker tried hard to keep her on the phone to get a little information. ___ was married and had children. (I have siblings?) She never told anyone, except her father, about me. She panicked that her secret would be let out. She refused to give the social worker the name of my biological father because she was too afraid I could find her through him (I have dangerous powers). Finally, the social worker asked if she could send "the letter." She said no. (I worked so hard on it!) The end.

This is what I had prepared myself for, what I expected. Lost. Found. Lost. Still don't want you. I had read enough to know that most "reunion" stories are not happy ones, although I was envious of the Canadian adoptee who learned that the singer Joni Mitchell was her birth mother.

When I was in college in Minnesota, where I was born, but not raised, I had a minor medical problem that led to my doctor suggesting I get a better medical history. I contacted the agency that handled my adoption, and met with a social worker, who turned out to be one of the people involved with my adoption. She remembered both my birth mother and my adoptive parents. By coincidence, I discovered that she was the wife of my favorite professor from the anthropology program I was in, Dr. S. It felt like our multiple connections allowed her to give me more information than the fill-in-the-blank data I already had. I learned that ___ had been in college when she got pregnant. She was a music major. She somehow managed to keep her pregnancy a secret from everyone except her father, who helped her arrange the adoption. When she went to the hospital to give birth, she told people she was having a tumor removed. I am that tumor. I thought of naming this piece "Mommy's little tumor." It's a joke that feels almost too dark to laugh at. It seems that everything about ___'s pregnancy was about being ashamed and trying to go on as if it never happened. That's the sense I got from what Mrs. S. tried to convey to me. So I knew my return, as an adult, to ___'s world wasn't likely to be welcome.

There's something about being adopted that is a little like being lesbian. Being adopted feels like an identity category; it is who you are, not just something that happened to you. I don't know if that's true for parents who adopt, or if ___ feels like a person who gave her baby away. My adoptive mother – and I get weary having to write that every time for clarity because it feels like there's no one who is just plain "mother" – was incredibly curious about the people who "made" Betty and Vincent. She told me the adoption agency told them that ___'s father contacted the agency, after the adoption, to make sure it worked out. My aunt repeated this part of the story to me at my adoptive mother's memorial, although I can't remember why this came up. (The ghosts from the past can show up without warning.) The point seems to be to assure me that ___'s father cared enough to check. It leaves unasked the question I think it's supposed to answer: Did ___ "care"? Did she think of me every year on May 16th? My adoptive mother told me once that she thought of August 10th as my "birthday" because that's the day I came into their lives. That's right, I forgot, I was an orphan for three months. This is why Betty Jane Lifton (1975) refers to adoptees as "twice born."

Coda #1

I feel anxious again. I don't know how to end this section. It's not like any professional writing I've ever done. What's the takeaway message I want to leave you with? What is there to be learned? I also feel powerful and scared. I have named names, opened all my closets and the closets of others. Am I still trying to be "born" instead of "placed," or needing you to accept me, despite my genealogical lack? There's no proof of bloodlines or breeding, just the diplomas and certificates I've earned.

There was a turning point in my analysis where I got tired of adoption being my life "story." I was tired of listening to myself talk about it, think about it, and feel it. I mean sick and tired of it. It wasn't a momentous insight but more of a surrender. Out of the ashes of that story of tragedy comes the possibility of writing new stories. I didn't have to be Oedipus, doomed by not knowing the truth about where I came from. I could take a place at the table of humanity and become the one who chooses, not the one who was chosen.

Finding the words to say it

As with most, mine is a story with an inside and an outside. I might have chosen to narrate the story of Betty and Vincent/Sally and Scott in a more linear, digested way, but I wanted to disturb the reading of my story in a way that conveys the disorientation, the disturbance I have felt. In the inside version, time is confused. There are questions that can't be answered: Who told me that? When did I hear that? Did I imagine this? There was no one who witnessed my experience from intrauterine life to being handed over to the fourth "mother," no one who could narrate it from the outside, to help me integrate it coherently. This part of the narrative was left to drift in the ether of preverbal, unformulated experience (Stern, 1987). Anyone who has been through analytic training or treatment knows how we automatically add order to unconscious, unformulated material. When you listen to an audio tape of a session with a patient, or read process notes taken during a session, they are quite different from the notes we write up if we wait until the end of the hour. Our minds move things around, without our awareness, into a more orderly narrative. As Mitchell (1988) said, "[To] listen is to arrange" (p. 90). The free associative process reveals things in bits and pieces that don't come with a neatly ordered through-line. We experiment with fitting pieces together, like working a jigsaw puzzle. To make matters still more complicated, we understand that a life is assembled from more than one puzzle. For an adoptee, it is even more challenging to work out these puzzles because of the missing pieces. Writing this, like the process of analysis, has been about trying to follow the rhythms of internal perception, and then to transform meanings into the structure of narrative form. I am inside then outside, the one watching and the one being watched. Winnicott (1971) said about a patient, "[S]he exists in the searching rather than in finding or being found" (p. 63). Sometimes the act of searching can be an act of freedom and agency that can enliven lost or disavowed selves. However, what we find may not be what we thought we were searching for.

Behind the couch

Writing this chapter raises the question of how my experience of being adopted figures into my choice of psychoanalysis as a profession, and of a preference for a relational sensibility and postmodern perspective. There are multiple, intersecting answers to these questions, requiring a little more self-disclosure. My father was a minister, and what he loved about his "calling" was being the shepherd of his flock. His mother died when he was five, and he grew up not only motherless, but with a father who never got over losing his wife. My father's father arrived on Ellis Island at 15 without a word of English, and a note pinned to his jacket with the name of a relative in Minnesota. He worked hard to save money so he could send for his sweetheart from the old country to come and join him in his new life. Following her death, their home was shrouded in melancholic loss. The church women provided much of the "mothering" my father had as a boy. I think my father fed his hunger for emotional intimacy through his work, which brought him into the most intimate aspects of his parishioners' lives. At his funeral, many people told me about the ways he had touched their lives: counseling them before their wedding, baptizing and confirming them, and then their children, sharing their grief when a loved one died. He participated in the major rituals of their lives. Tending to others, both their spiritual and day-to-day lives, was the service to others he practiced, but he clearly also got a lot in return.

I know that my identifications with my father are significant. Finding pleasure in service to others is clearly an aspect of my professional satisfaction. I have heard analysts quip that they spend more time in a week talking intimately with their analysands than they do with their spouses. Of course, analysis creates, by design, an asymmetrical intimacy. It has also been said that people become analysts out of their own need to find love (Celenza, 2010; Kuchuck, 2012). It does seem that many people are drawn to become psychoanalysts out of the experience of struggling with their own wounds (Celenza, 2010). We have come to think of our own wounds as the basis for our capacity for empathy, with the assumption we have found some resolution about our own losses.

I wonder: Did I become an analyst looking, as my father did, for the intimate connections with others I missed out on? Is there an intergenerational transmission of trauma at work here, leading to a search for healing by helping others? The answers to these questions are maybe, or even probably. The bond with my adopted

11

family locates me in their history and gives me kinship ties that I have internalized as part of "me." I might also ask if the experience of getting close to people, in a relationship that is set up to end, might be a repetition of being separated from biological parents, and represents an effort to master that trauma by reliving it again and again with patients. There are many ways a person's beginnings may lead to a schizoid defensive system, but the losses and foreclosures in the closed adoption system set a child, and the parents, up for troubles. The reliving of attaching and letting go, inherent in analytic work, presents me with the challenge of reworking my history of loss. Grand (2009) points to how psychoanalysis may play a similar role for others as well, since it has been structured around ". . . our own attachment problems" (p. 727). She reminds us that while creating a theory that valorized independence, mastery, and strength, Freud and his followers were ". . . enmeshed, and incestuous, and needy, and wounded" (p. 728). Attachment problems are a frequent focus in psychoanalysis. We work on these problems by living through them, with the (ironic) inevitability of termination in mind.

On the couch

Clinical accounts of adoptees list problems with attachment, unstable self and other relations, low self-esteem, feelings of unworthiness, fear of rejection, and feelings of being a fraud no matter how externally successful (Verrier, 1993). When I look for these effects in myself, I wonder about my choosing an independent institute for training and the effects of being an outsider among APA and IPA affiliates. I am not eligible to supervise or analyze their candidates, although I have been invited to be a guest instructor. As a relationally oriented analyst, I have something to offer them, but there's no reciprocity in the form of candidates to analyze or supervise. The independent institute where I trained has not been able to sustain itself, so there's another "birth mother" that can't support me. I made a comparison earlier that being an adoptee is akin to being lesbian in that it's an identity category. As with being lesbian (or bisexual), I am ambivalent about my outsider status, both affirming my difference, yet wanting what insiders get. I want what insiders get from my outsider position. Could this be the adopted child speaking?

In my work with adoptees, I have found that at least in the beginning of treatment, I am likely to view their adoption as a bigger factor in their development than they do. I understand their perspective as linked with the closed adoption system I have described, with the pressure to deny the existence of birth parents, the traumatic loss of contact with the birth mother's body, shame about infertility and unwanted pregnancies, and shame about being unwanted. Opening up foreclosed areas of experience exposes adult adoptees to the melancholic losses of their lives. I have never worked with someone who began treatment wanting to work on self-identified adoption issues. As patients open up to exploring how adoption affected them, treatment often becomes marked by ambivalence about continuing, treatment interruptions, struggles with managing unmanageable feelings, and the consequences of having no confidence or trust that someone will be there to help them survive the re-membering of what they had to endure, as children, alone. As with most survivors of trauma, it takes years of effort to establish a bond of trust in which to do the hard work of re-membering and grieving. Because opening up awareness of adoption-related losses involves other people in a patient's world, such as adoptive parents, biological parents, and siblings, treatment can disturb a hornet's nest of fears of further losses and rejections. Will it hurt my adoptive parents if I talk about this, will it hurt my biological parents if I search for them, will I end up losing everyone?

Countertransference challenges

It was challenging for me when a lesbian patient I had worked with for years decided to use untraceable donor sperm to get pregnant. My countertransference – about her "selfishness" in making this choice, and lack of consideration for the effects on her potential child – was at times considerable. I worried that these feelings might endanger the important work we had done, that had led to her establishing herself in a committed relationship, and feeling ready to undertake starting a family. When she decided to leave treatment, she said she felt ready to live her life without therapy and to save financial resources for the family-to-be. I worried that I may have spoiled the good feelings between us with my gentle questioning (and not so gentle, unspoken feelings) about her choice of an anonymous donor, though she did not give this as a reason for ending. In other situations, I felt deeply affected by the grief of several patients who had multiple abortions then were unable to conceive when they were ready to have a family. I wanted them to work through their losses before turning too quickly to adoption. I also have witnessed and shared in the joy and fears of same-sex couples who have used known donors as they negotiated the uncharted territory of becoming unconventional families.

I asked a close colleague, who I have consulted with on clinical work for a long time and who knows me well, how he thought my adoption colored my work with patients. He thought of how my practice has tended to be populated by people who operate primarily from schizoid defenses, people who are hard to reach and hard to hold. Winnicott (1971) wrote about people who exist by not being found and people who have not become "someone" yet. These are people who feel they don't really exist and live lives of profound emotional isolation. Books about adoptees often speak about loss of attachment to the birth mother's body, and how that aspect of self dies when they are separated from her (Verrier, 1993). In "Mourning and Melancholia," Freud (1917) described mourning as a loss that can be eventually resolved and from which new attachments can be formed. In melancholia, however, losses are internalized and woven into the psychological matrices of the child.

For adoptees, I believe the missing parents are internalized as an emptiness, a vacancy, an absence. I, like many adoptees, grew up feeling a sense that something was missing; there was something I didn't have words for, or know how to look for. Adoptive parents are often not able to recognize the state of melancholia that adoptees suffer from, no matter how much they are loved by their new family. I wondered, for example, when I read the social worker's report about baby Betty,

wondered, for example, when I read the social worker's report about baby Betty, if when Betty kept spitting up, she was protesting getting the milk from the wrong mother. I also felt a deep sadness, wondering if what was described as her becoming happier and better adjusted wasn't actually an act of compliance and submission. If she was going to live, she had to take the milk from whomever offered it.

Andre Green (1986) describes how a child's attachment to a depressed, emotionally absent mother can lead to an identification with her emptiness. This creates a "problem of emptiness" for the child and what Green calls "psychical holes" in the unconscious. When something activates these holes, a "blank anxiety" is triggered. Green's paper is hard for me to read. I think it triggers, as he describes, my own "psychical holes" and sets off "blank anxiety." I wonder: Can a fetus be depressed? What happens, *in utero*, to a baby whose mother wishes she didn't exist? This isn't just a misunderstanding on my part, but what ___ really felt. I can't find an object relation that precedes the catastrophic event of her emotional disconnection from me. My biological father is a noticeable absence in this paper. Was there a happy moment, prior to conception, in sexual union between ___ and her lover? Do I fit anywhere in that relation? Green speaks of "reactive symmetry" between the child and the mother's bereavement, and I am reminded of how my own adolescent sexuality, before birth control pills were easily available, was inhibited by a terror of getting pregnant. ___'s bereavement was perhaps for the loss of an unencumbered sexuality and a carefree college life.

In a back page piece in the New York Times Sunday magazine titled, "Meet the Parents: A Woman Finds Her Biological Mother and Father and Wishes She Hadn't," Lisa Lutz (May 6, 2012) says

> . . . I didn't feel a strong bond with the parents who raised me, and I had anything but a happy childhood . . . I felt as if I were living with complete strangers . . . But knowing I was adopted untethered me from some of that unhappiness. I was alone but happily so. I was free to make up any story I wanted about where I came from.

I feel some disconnect with being "happily" untethered, but the freedom to imagine the past resonates. Something about being disconnected from genetic ties creates room for imagination and, as Lutz put it, allows for a "scrappy and dogged" pursuit of finding your own possibilities. Overcoming, if that's what it is, being wished dead, or never quite measuring up to the biological daughter that didn't exist, requires some "scrappy" determination. I wonder if this might actually be a strength, something I am able to use as an advantage, as a resource in being the object that survives the other's efforts at destruction, making possible the discovery of Winnicott's other who can be loved because she survives. I also know about the self that grows around the psychic holes, that sees possibilities, in spite of the scotoma that occludes the past. I have some ideas about how to play the hide and seek game that working with people who "aren't there" requires. Maybe, because of my own experience, I have more capacity than the average clinician to bear the years of patience required for a patient with schizoid defenses to form an attachment to me. I think I really do get what is terrifying about depending on another, and the impossibility of living without attachments to people.

Coda #2

The effort of this book, to explore the various ways in which the analyst's subjectivity enters the treatment room, is a question relational psychoanalysts have always asked. What's unusual is to have a whole book devoted to the subject. Writing this piece has been a fascinating challenge because it represents a significant departure from my usual writing. I, and I suspect others, prefer to write about patients' lives rather than our own. This writing involves so much self-disclosure, including the effort to analyze my own subjectivity and analytic self, and the feelings of vulnerability that arise in the process. It invites me to imagine how my adoption experience affects my work and makes me the analyst I am, even when painful feelings are stirred and it's hard to consider these questions. I believe I have embraced a relational way of working because it fits with my own experience of healing. Especially important for me has been the holding of multiple dimensions of experience: early trauma, facts and fantasies, both conscious and unconscious, and the interplay between what happened then and what is happening now. Thinking in a both/and framework (Benjamin, 2004) helps to create coherence and inclusion. Healing from my experience of adoption has required that I accept what I can't know. As challenging as a postmodern perspective can be at times, it often suits me. It means learning to recognize the limits of what can be known, and accepting that even the most important things in life are marked by uncertainty and lack of control. Perhaps ironically, accepting that even when I think I know what I'm doing, I don't really know what I'm doing, helps me feel more at peace. That acceptance helps me enjoy learning for its own pleasure, not because I can "master" something. It frees me to be curious, instead of worrying about having answers. It allows me to enjoy being surprised by what pleases me, instead of trying to control getting what I think I want. When I can accept what I can't change, it allows anxiety to be transformed into new possibilities. It moves desire in a new direction, and as Adam Phillips (2006) put it, "Desire [could] be described as all the ways we can find of replacing knowledge with hope" (p. 179).

Envoi

Many months after writing this chapter I was informed by the publisher that I would have to redact my birth mother's name. They recommended using a pseudonym. I couldn't bear to do that, but revealing her name could expose them to a suit under tort law. A tort is defined as either intentionally, or through negligence, unfairly causing someone else to suffer loss or harm. It is an interesting question to ask, in this recounting of multiple losses, who has caused whom to suffer loss or harm. Is my wish to disclose my birth mother's name an act of aggression? A wish to take control of my "story?" A love letter? A plea for healing from shame? The note from the legal department quoted my statement that revealing my birth mother's name felt (to me) like an "outrageous act" and said that "From a moral perspective, this in not her [my] secret to share." So much for "no more secrets hidden in sealed records." Perhaps this is a reminder that secrets and shame have a way of evading resolution. As an adoptee and as a psychoanalyst, I know that all too well.

Note

1 The publisher required me to redact my birth mother's name. I opted to use a space where her name was to appear. See 'Envoi' for more on this.

References

Beebe, B., Lachmann, F., & Jaffe, J. (1997). Mother-Infant structures and pre-symbolic self and object representations. *Psychoanalytic Dialogues*, *7*, 133–182.

Benjamin, J. (2004). Beyond doer and done to: An intersubjective view of thirdness. *Psychoanalytic Quarterly*, *73*, 5–46.

Bowlby, J. (1980). *Attachment and loss (Vol. III)*. New York: Basic Books.

Celenza, A. (2010). The analyst's need and desire. *Psychoanalytic Dialogues*, *20*(1), 60–69.

Freud, S. (1917). Mourning and melancholia. In J. Strachey (Ed. & Trans.), *The standard edition of the complete psychological works of Sigmund Freud* (Vol. 14, pp. 237–258). London: Hogarth Press.

Grand, S. (2009). Termination as necessary madness. *Psychoanalytic Dialogues*, *19*, 723–733.

Green, A. (1986). The dead mother. In *On private madness* (pp. 142–173). London: Hogarth Press.

Kuchuck, S. (2012). Please (don't) want me: The therapeutic action of male sexual desire in the treatment of heterosexual men. *Contemporary Psychoanalysis*, *48*, 544–562.

Lifton, B. J. (1975). *Twice born*. New York: McGraw-Hill.

Lifton, B. J. (1979). *Lost and found: The adoption experience*. New York: Perennial.

Lifton, B. J. (1994). *Journey of the adopted self: A quest for wholeness*. New York: Basic Books.

Lutz, L. (2012, May 4). I found my biological parents, and wish I hadn't. *Sunday New York Times Magazine*.

Mitchell, S. (1988). *Relational concepts in psychoanalysis: An integration*. Cambridge, MA: Harvard University Press.

Phillips, A. (2006). *Side effects*. New York: Harper Perennial.

Shore, A. (1994). *Affect regulation and the origin of the self*. Hillsdale, NJ: Lawrence Erlbaum Associates.

Stern, D. B. (1987). Unformulated experience: From familiar chaos to creative disorder. *Contemporary Psychoanalysis*, *19*, 71–99.

Stern, D. N. (1985). *The interpersonal world of the infant*. New York: Basic Books.

Verrier, N. (1993). *The primal wound*. Baltimore, MD: Gateway Press.

Winnicott, D. W. (1971). *Playing and reality*. London: Tavistock.

2

I WANTED THE STUFF OF
SECRETS TO BE IN THE LIGHT

Susie Orbach[1]

My dad hid his Everton mints in the glove compartment of his car. My mother her Terry's chocolate orange slices at the top of his cupboard. We never had desserts or biscuits, and bread, always rye, was reserved for overstuffed Hungarian salami and salad sandwiches dropped in the rubbish bin on the way to my prim and proper English school, lest the other children with their neat white bread banana ones would make fun of me.

It wasn't the oddest thing about me. Odder was that I was opinionated and intense and came from not just a Jewish family – we had a quota at my school – but a socialist one as well. And my mother was an American who worked outside the home.

We were a kind of atheist Jewish that didn't really fit in with the Jewish assembly that was held four days a week at school, and which kindly kept us out of mainstream religious education and knowledge. There's nothing odd today about being that kind of a misfit – from some perspectives it could even be seen as quite enlightened – but it set me apart in ways that were incomprehensible. Add in, too, a blacklisted screenwriter uncle and all his friends descending on the flat we lived in (a flat, please note, not a house – wrong social class, the second form teacher told me and the rest of my grade) and the endless clandestine missions my father was on to countries in the Middle East.[2] I learned that the latter were not to be discussed outside the house. Nor if you were a child inside it either. When my dad was once in a plane crash, which became front page news, I was unsure how to explain to my classmates what he had been doing on the plane.

At 5, I would answer the door and ask: Are you a socialist? Are you a Jew? These two ineffable qualities were nevertheless the identity markers of a little girl growing up in an emotionally volatile political household as the postwar period was resettling questions of class, politics, and "race." My father fought strongly in the Movement for Colonial Freedom,[3] my mother on the left of progressive Israelis. Proto-Yiddish disguised a good deal of what was being said in front of me and my brother. Politics – that's to say, the things that mattered – were either whispered or screamed, and I imbibed the romance of the secret early on.

As a child, you don't know what the other secrets are. You don't know what's normal. It took an adolescence and young adulthood to figure out the oddness of

17

a family where screeching prevailed but no one said anything real to one another. I remember being shocked and exhilarated, when visiting friends, to discover that the parents actually talked with the children and kept sweeties in the living room. One mum even relished keeping her daughter Veronica home from school to play with her. That was inconceivable. Incomprehensible that a mother could desire having pleasure with her child. I planned for a grownupness where nothing – not the content of the chat, nor the food – was off limits. It wasn't so much that I craved plenty. I wanted to know where chat and chocolate could take you. I wanted the stuff of secrets to be in the light.

Little did I know that this was a perfect training to be a psychoanalyst. Indeed, I was set on a quite different course: city planner, historian of Russian history, then switching to Women's Studies (as it was known then). But Women's Studies in the 1970s was such a wide open field that it could take into itself what it needed – social history, literature, philosophy, economics, sociology, psychology, psychoanalysis, social geography – without academic embarrassment. As Women's Studies plundered and reworked the old disciplines, so the old reactionary practice of 1950s American psychoanalysis was subverted by the new movements to understand the relationship between the personal and the interpersonal, the personal and the political, the individual and the polis, the subjective and the social.

From differing theoretical and clinical viewpoints, left wing groupings such as the Frankfurt School, the Rundbriefe, the Mental Patients Liberation Front, Issues in Radical Therapy, and Feminism[4] were recasting aspects of the psychoanalytic project and readying it for progressive purposes. Key features of the talking cure were being used not to sequester difficult thoughts and feelings off into a consulting room, where society secreted the costs of our social and economic arrangements, but to explode them. Nowhere was this more evident than in the consciousness-raising groups which set about creating a structure to enable women to talk and women to listen.

Where once private conversations between women would touch on their personal disappointments and longings, those conversations now opened up a new territory for political understanding. What we were feeling in the privacy of our own beings, relationships, and bodies was visited not simply as an individual experience. It was an expression, we began to understand, of power relationships that created the family and the relations between parents and children, women and men, girls and boys, and adults and children with regard to a set of authoritarian structures which were imbibed in the process of growing up. Capitalism and patriarchy, we were discovering, were not structures outside ourselves we could simply challenge. They were structures inside ourselves shaping our sense of self and other.

It was exhilarating at a personal level. I was touched by the experience of trying to understand my personal history with other women who were interested. The sanctioning of personal talk, and a special kind of listening that did not rush to console or identify with the speaker but left space for what was being said to be heard and reflected on by group members, was absolutely novel within a political movement or in women's conversations. We discovered the commonality of being raised as girls, and we learned about the differences in how femininity was lived in each family and by each woman. We detailed violence in the family, bitterness and longing in mother–daughter relationships, unhappy marriages, mothers' resentment of their husbands, scant introduction to menstruation, injunctions to control our bodies and sexuality, the sense that we were all too much and should be curbing appetites of all kinds. We questioned our own acceptance of the relative privileges given to brothers, who were encouraged to go after what they wanted and who experienced very different limits.

It wasn't therapy, but it was deeply therapeutic. It was shocking to realize the ways in which our lives had followed patterns we had not been aware of, and the new knowledge gave individual women a means to understand themselves while creating a platform and camaraderie to challenge the status quo. For many women, profound friendships were created within this context. We couldn't wait to talk, to challenge ourselves, to begin to redefine ourselves and live new possibilities.

Few areas were taboo. But of course some were. My psyche, exquisitely pitched towards what was hidden, disregarded, or considered shameful, was drawn to uncomfortable issues that didn't quite get talked about, clustering around our – women's – own participation in the troubled circumstances we found ourselves enacting: the deals we made in relationships both with men and with women; the sexual denial, shame, and ignorance women still experienced; the thorny issue of emotional dependency; our relationship to our bodies and the way we looked and represented ourselves physically; our complex feelings of anger, competition, hurt, betrayal, envy, and gratitude towards other women; our internalized homophobia, class and racism.

At one level, it was an unremarkable list. At another, the attempt to understand how these issues operated intrapsychically was a considerable challenge. It was a challenge led by the wish to underpin Feminism's ground of activism over issues such as reproductive rights, divorce, equal pay for equal work, the sharing of domestic labor and childcare, into the meaning of social custom in the psyche of us all. Understanding how we had accepted what we had accepted was the task. While legislation operated in some areas to constrain women's behavior, there were plenty of ways in which the girdle of internalized restraint operated more fiercely and in such a way that, in doing things that were damaging to self, we were feeling we were doing right.

There were so many examples from the mundane to the deeply significant. Equal pay, for example, operated at the level of custom and prejudice. The question for us was how we could enable women and ourselves to challenge that prejudice since we inadvertently bought into it. For we did. Until we thought about it, patriarchy was a structure we had not even known we had accepted. How might we, for example, not intervene to change the baby's diaper and wait until the father took responsibility for it for himself? What would it mean to give up the power of being the one who decided on when, what, where, and how often? What would it mean for women not to be the social grease – to not remember Aunt Jane's birthday?

What would happen if we withdrew emotional service from men we were sleeping with? We knew the story of Lysistrata, but what we needed to explore was who we were if we withdrew sexual services or emotional nurture. Would we still be women? What kind of women? And to take an equally perplexing psychological issue: How might an individual woman refrain from negating desire, even if she did not know what she might be desiring?

These were the kinds of questions which grew inside me: In what manner and by what means did we become human in these particularly gendered forms? And at a personal level, how might I visit my own mother's life and bring some empathy to her difficulties, understanding now that these – as much and perhaps, as I reflect now, more than my own – were borne of the social and emotional restrictions on a woman's life, which left her frustrated, angry, perplexed by, and under-ambitious for her children? My mother, of course, was like other mothers. A once vibrant woman who had lived through the depression of the late 20s and early 30s had been displaced from the modernity of New York to fog- and class-bound London, where her desire to train as a barrister met the prejudice and the impediments of money and social standing. She took a route that many women did, which was to use her considerable talents looking after people – in her case teaching the adults who sought refuge in the UK during and after the war English. She became involved in Unity Theatre – a left-wing, agitprop group – and was frequently out at meetings saving the world.

No wonder, then, that I took that heritage on even while believing my life had little in common with hers. Practicing in a country where psychoanalytic ideas are part of the intellectual heritage and yet, until recently, clinically rather hidden from public view, my background and political persuasions led me to try to bring psychoanalytic insights into the public sphere. When Luise Eichenbaum and I founded The Women's Therapy Centre, we were determined to make an accessible service. We believed that a gender-conscious therapy could be valuable for women of all backgrounds, and we wanted the fact of the service to be known so that people could self-refer. We provided a clinic with the aim of providing therapy on the same basis as other "medical" services: free at the point of treatment. To this end, we applied for funding, meanwhile keeping any charges very low, and we set about talking about The Women's Therapy Centre on radio, in local and national newspapers, and on television.

While such an intervention would hardly be seen as political in North America, where therapy is so much more part of the cultural and medico landscape, this was a bold act in the UK context. It raised the hackles of the staid psychoanalytic establishment until 30 years later, when they allowed cameras in to film their work. We were bringing attention to mental health and emotional issues, which in Britain were hidden behind closed doors, finding rather a home in literature or theater or sport, not through emotional life being addressed directly. The second reason was in following Ronald Laing's trajectory – who had opened up the psychoanalytic conversation to a much larger public – we were addressing the societal and structural as well as the individual reasons we understood for emotional difficulties.

My subjectivity was rooted in the politics of the left. Like every generation, I had to make those politics my own, not only to differentiate from the specifics of my parents' politics, but because the world never sits still, and the notion of the political had, excitingly, become impregnated with the personal, the individual, and the making of gender. At the same time, my politics were suffused with my parent's legacy – the need to contribute to the public good, to make change, to stand against, and to stand for. In the creation of The Women's Therapy Centre, Luise and I were saying that this Centre stood for something. It did not offer the carapace of neutrality that the Tavistock or the British Psychoanalytic Society purported to; it said we offer therapeutic services for all women and their families because women's needs deserve to be understood afresh and to be addressed.

The Centre set about providing therapeutic services to a range of women who had never encountered the possibility of being heard before. They were women from differing backgrounds, ethnicities, ages, from women coming out of institutions, to women who identified as wives and mothers, to those who were seeking to be understood in feminist terms. In "diagnostic terms," the range was enormous. In our mission, Luise Eichenbaum and I were not only enacting aspects of femininity that we had grown up with – the need to pay attention to the needs of others, to enable them to become the driving forces of their own desires, to share what we were learning – we were bringing personal histories of having grown up with secrets and with politics, and we were engaged in a work that would make secrets less exciting and toxic and political endeavors more directly related to the texture of everyday life.

It took me a long time not to be interested in the secret(s) per se, to move away from the childhood pleasures of trying to get what you weren't supposed to know. As I have been invited to share in more and more secrets – a surfeit indeed – the thirst has gone. My interest has turned to curiosity: Why and in what way is something held to be a secret? What is the difference between sharing and privacy? Between intimacy and isolation? Between alienation and giving too much of oneself away? Psychoanalysis, of course, explores such questions indirectly. In looking at what is locked away, unformulated, or overexposed, it repositions the world of the intimate, the private and the public, the sayable and the heard.

Psychoanalysis is a practice of extraordinary delicacy. It operates at a completely different level than the brushstrokes that political theory and practice must inhabit. It is about getting the feel of a particular individual, couple, or family when they are with you (and when they aren't), and finding ways to reach them that speak to the multiple layers of their experience. We therapists are interested in the actual words that people use and how they are spoken. The pauses and hesitations that mark their speech and their bodily gestures. We are interested in their passions. We are interested in their disappointments. We are interested in the minutiae of their struggles to make meaning and emotional sense for themselves so that they can live inside of their multiple conflicting and often contradictory experiences. We do so by finding just those words that speak to experience inside of protective defense structures and behind them. We do so by finding the emotions that have been sent packing and tenderly re-introducing them. We do so by feeling with and feeling separate from the dilemmas which beset the person we are working with. We do so by finding the right space between us.

My work is driven by my own wanting to know and by my desire to enable the other to fit into her or his own life. Coming from a left background, where one endeavors to understand what doesn't fit with what the culture offers, an individuals' belief structures, emotional landscape, the tributaries through which their longings traverse and stall, their acts of courage and resistance, their adherence to what hurts and harms them, endlessly engages me in the consulting room and in theory making. And the wish to share the complexities that I have learned from them in a public conversation and public policy, where a different analysis could be brought to social phenomenon, is no doubt the legacy of being raised in the particular kind of atmosphere where changing the world was the assumption, and yet children were out of the picture while being surrounded by intrigue, controversy, and pain. The pain, of course, was felt but not acknowledged. There weren't the words to frame or understand it, and in becoming a therapist, I wanted to render that pain in ways that could legitimate the individual or the groups' experience of it.

Linked to this desire to enable others to make sense of their pain was the notion that the world was on the wrong track. I imbibed this from my parents' opposition to almost everything that was talked about on the news. I can barely remember a radio broadcast without someone in the household either muttering or talking back to the radio. Long before we had the language police, my parents were always correcting the representation of a particular event. It was not possible to believe that anything but contestation and change was of value.

The more challenging questions – how and in what ways and what is it that needs to be understood in order to make change – were what fired the making of me as a therapist and commentator. These twin concerns – how to do it and how to speak to the hurt that exists that we seem so often unable to get out of – led me to want to address people's pain and confusion, and give them a way into understanding its origins as well as what they might be able to do about it. I wanted and still want to be able to say that the pain is not trivial. That it needs to be acknowledged. That comprehending its routes in early relationships (and the context in which those relationships are formed), and the ways in which we are primed to repeat both what works and what doesn't, is the source of fitting in with oneself.

At the same time, the messianic aspect of believing that one can change the world is surely one of the madder delusions of growing up left. I am sure it is much akin to evangelical endeavors in which the glory to come and the redemptive act are what makes the abject conditions tolerable.

What the psychoanalytic process allows for is the recognition of what can't be changed. The humility of accepting that there are limits, that wishing for and strategizing for and turning your internal object relations willy-nilly don't necessarily produce wanted change. It would be wrong to say that change is finite. We know that when we approach an issue it does shift shape, but the notion that change is infinite also requires contesting. As psychoanalysts, we work with the tension between the finite and the infinite. Our job requires us to enter into the emotional territories of hopelessness, mourning, and despair and not deny them. We parse the differences between rage, disappointment, fear, and excitement. In doing so, we encounter and hold onto feeling states often denied and split from the individual until they can brace them. This can be a difficult and delicate phase of a therapy, and yet without touching such states of being, the fundamental reconfiguration of self (or of family, couple, organization, or even political group) is impaired.

In the public world, we see manic flights whose routes disclose an inability to mourn, to reflect, to accept. 9/11 is an obvious case, in which the leadership of the Nation, in the name of President Bush, took the fright and shock of the assault on New York and turned it into aggression. No thinking, no space to look at issues of vulnerability and horror. Just straight insult and fury sent into an already existing strategic game plan to control the Stans[5] and Iraq.

The machinations over the Euro and the banking crisis is another (Orbach, 2012). What really are they about at a psycho-social level? Surely the xenophobia being expressed and exported first to Greece and then to Spain, Italy, and Portugal is a way of looking for a place to dump the practices of financial institutions who created imaginary monetary vehicles by which the public were duped. The Euro and banking crises serve as a carapace for sets of values by which the post-World War II social democratic settlement was dismantled and the public was persuaded to buy into consumerist neo-liberalism. Without the political recognition of what it means to have been at the sharp end of manipulative practices, the chance to get out from their consequences is squandered. If we can feel our rage, our impotence, and our disgust – and if the political classes could – then it might be possible to start from somewhere different. To accept what is. To see how we have been suckered and to see our own complicity in the politics of greed would enable us to encounter the tasks of building a different sort of resilience. Accepting that we have been had and the delusions we too have labored under, rather, is accepting a limit. It is not a defeat but a new ground to start from. It puts us in a place from which we can grow.

Psychoanalysis gives us lots of practice with retrospectively accepting what was, especially in childhood. It enables us to move out of experiencing ourselves as either the authors of our own misfortune or the hapless victims of parental mis-attunement. In doing so, it transforms our internal world so that we don't continually rescript on to the present our archaic experience of relationships. We meet relationships more fully in the now. Through the analytic process, we come to understand what sense we made of our local world and how we dealt with its disappointments. We enter into the experience of the other. We see our parents or siblings or nannies or au pairs with their *own* inadequacies and the manner in which we might have then responded. We examine at a feeling level the parental introjects, and in so doing, we come to have an experience inside of ourselves of their perspectives. Unlike political positions which can condemn those whose thoughts differ as a form of false consciousness, psychoanalysis enables us to feel the materiality of difference, the materiality of the other. We experience ourselves in relation to differing subjectivities and the way in which we are affected by and affect the other. Understanding this tension between self and other, and the need to hold more than one subjectivity in mind, is one of psychoanalysis's gifts to the world. How we disseminate these understandings, and how they can be threaded into public discourse so that they can transform the sterility of the usual debate,[6] is a task that sits inside of me given my background.

Beyond the general are the specific themes that have interested me in the clinical and theoretical context for many years. The psychological experience of the individual feeling undeserving (or its opposite expression of over-entitlement), the confusion, disdain, and disparagement around dependency needs, the crisis around the body, food, and sexuality, are all clinical themes that are shot through with understanding our present culture's creation of particular psychic structures. Very early on in my clinical experience, I was captivated by Winnicott's experience of thousands of mother–baby pairs and his commentary about the difficulties and challenges that faced the individual mother with her individual child. It was hard not to read his observations as psycho-social commentary on the conditions of maternality within patriarchy. His descriptions were fully accurate – as were, let's say, Helene Deutsch's on women – but the eviscerating of social structure and then presenting it as an is, rather than as dynamic and relating to particular power dynamics and the space in which women's psychic structure could operate, failed to give a complete interpretation of the whys and the wherefores of women's psyches. In various psychoanalytic writings, inadvertently or purposefully, women were either the failed objects of their children or they were woeful in and of themselves. Luise Eichenbaum and I set out to account for (in our books and writings) these "failed objects" as still developing subjects; we aimed to understand "masochism," the ambivalent and sometimes murderous feelings between mothers and daughters, women's "choice" of heterosexuality, women's self-hatred, women's very deep feelings of un-entitlement, and so on, not as examples of simply the abject but as ways of understanding the psychic costs and conflicts of femininity at this point in history.

We did this not by overloading our practice with interpretation about women's experience – for that would not be psychoanalysis – but by seeing the agency within the adaptation and the particular psychic trajectories that were or were not possible. We did it by seeing what lay behind the feelings of inadequacy, competition, envy, despair, doubt, bitterness, and so on. We did it by always trying to see what, why, and how a particular frame of mind, psychic arrangement, defenses, and so on were the scaffolding for that individual. This led us to differ with conventional psychoanalytic ways of understanding which had, we felt, rather overworked or simplified roots and pre-formulated interpretations which failed to meet the lived experience and conflicts of the people we were seeing. In bridging the ways in which we saw the individual in their time and gender and inner and actual relational configurations, we saw ourselves as developing what in those days we called social object relations, which of course was another naming of what came to be called Relational Psychoanalysis. Undoubtedly, this detailed work, which continues to interest me as the generations present differing versions of these dilemmas – both the young and the old as they travel through life – is a reflection of my early desire and training in wanting to understand, to get behind the secret, to know, and to transform things.

Now back to chocolates and chat, those other overarching mysteries from my childhood. I've been endlessly fascinated by what has made bodies and food and conversation so problematic, enigmatic, and exciting. I've given myself a job where I am allowed not only to explore these difficult subjects, but at an individual level, to help others and myself make very different choices than the original offerings at my childhood home. My chocolates are on open offer along with many different kinds of chat from political discourse, writing and agitating, conversations in the consulting room, dialogue with colleagues inside and outside of psychoanalysis, and always, always, talk talk talk with friends and family.

Notes

1 Copyright 2012 by Susie Orbach.
2 Some of these were between Nasser in Egypt and Sharat in Israel, where he tried to broker peace around the Suez crisis.
3 The Movement for Colonial Freedom was a political civil rights advocacy group founded in 1954 dedicated to reversing colonialism.
4 The Frankfurt School were Marxists who created critical theory (Adorno, Habermas, Marcuse, Benjamin, etc.); the Rundbriefe was the secret communication between left wing psychoanalysts who left Germany and Austria (Jacoby, 1983); the Mental Patients Liberation Front and Issues in Radical Therapy were activist groups, and Feminism was the social movement which burst on to the international stage from the late 1960s onwards.
5 All the oil and potential pipeline states – Kazakhstan, Afghanistan, etc. – which are known as the Stans.
6 See, for example, Orbach (2000) and Samuels (1993).

References

Jacoby, R. (1983). *The repression of psychoanalysis: Otto Fenichel and the Freudians.* New York: Basic Books.

Orbach, S. (2000). The clinic, the nursery and the World Bank: Psychotherapy and social institutions. *British Journal of Psychotherapy*, *16*(4), 458–466.

Orbach, S. (2012). How psychoanalytic theory can be used in social policy: Bankers, rioters and the general public. Retrieved from http://www.crimeandjustice.org.uk/opus1915/Susie_Orbach_Eve_Saville_Lecture_2011.pdf.

Samuels, A. (1993). *The political psyche*. London: Routledge.

3

SEX, LIES, AND PSYCHOANALYSIS

Galit Atlas

War

It was a week before my 18th birthday when I left my parents' home. I recall packing my clothes in a suitcase, my mother standing silently in the corner and my father locked in his room. I fled.

He was 24 years old. I thought he was a grown man and that I was running away to the safest place on earth. I didn't think he was the love of my life, but he offered me a home, and I followed him.

I was scared, and soon enough I realized I wanted to go home. It was the first – but not last – moment in which I understood that I didn't know where my home was. I sat on a bench under his apartment on King George Street in Tel Aviv. If I had known to smoke then, I probably would have, and I thought that maybe I should have sex with him after all, maybe it will change everything. I went back up and told him that if we get married, I'll have sex with him. He looked at me and said one sentence: "I don't get your sexuality." Shrugging, I said, "Neither do I."

The next day he bought me a ring and offered to marry me. I remember packing my clothes again. I had told myself that I had chosen a grown man so that he would understand everything that I didn't, so that he would offer me answers. But he had no answers, and I left him a note: "Sorry, I'm going to look for answers," and left.

Fortunately, my inner struggle found expression in the external world; in that very same month the Gulf War broke out, and missiles hit Tel Aviv. I was then a soldier in the Israeli army. On the first night, closed in a sealed room with gas masks on our faces, we heard the missiles fall, and we realized we were all going to die. On the second night an undulating siren was sounded, and we thought that maybe the warheads weren't chemical after all. There was great commotion. Home was no longer something defined; everyone slept everywhere. One did not need a home to survive, only a mask and a public shelter. My father was drafted into the army, and like most of my friends' parents, my mother took my young siblings and moved in with relatives in southern Israel. I reported to the army base every day at noon, and at night everyone slept everywhere. Fear gave way to excitement.

26

This is how my quest for answers began. Home falling apart, war, sexuality everywhere. One fear and then another, all blending with unclear excitement, and one great question: What's wrong with all of us?

Kitchen

My Iranian grandmother had more than 50 grandchildren and great-grandchildren by the time she died. On a good day she could remember all of their names. I remembered almost all of them. In her kitchen there were large pots, the kind I saw years later in the military kitchen. Pots that were intended to contain the entire regiment's food, and that in order to wash you had to climb into.

In the army there is a rotation of duties. Each one scours the large vessels in turn. It's called "kitchen duty." In my grandmother's kitchen there was no rotation. The women would wash the dishes. They were also the ones to cook, set the table, clear it, and serve the tea.

I learned the most important rule of army kitchen duty on the very first day of my service. "Right away connect with the cook," people told me. The army cook was always a man. And indeed on the very first day, Ron, the cook, got me out of dishwashing duty. But he had one condition, that I sit outside with him and tell him stories. Quite a fair deal, I must admit. We sat under a tree and I told him I had just left my boyfriend. He told me that his girlfriend had left him a few days earlier and that he was really sad. "Why did she leave you?" I inquired. We sat for a long while, and I listened while Ron shed his tears. He was heartbroken. I was curious. I thought my ex-boyfriend must be sitting with some strange girl, crying. I hoped he was. I also hoped he'd have sex with that strange girl, fall in love with her, and marry her. I knew I wouldn't have sex with Ron the cook, that I wouldn't fall in love with him, and that I would certainly not marry him, even though marrying someone sounded like an entirely reasonable solution to most of my problems.

Ron fell silent for a moment and said that it wasn't fair, since according to our agreement I was the one who was supposed to be telling him stories, and not the other way around. "Actually, why do you prefer to be sitting here with me rather than doing the dishes? Don't you like doing dishes?" he asked. "It's a long story," I replied. "It's okay, we've got time. Unless we have to run to the shelters, it'll take them a while to finish all of the regiment's dishes," he said and lit a cigarette. "Light me one, too?" I asked, adding, "Will you teach me how to smoke?"

Over a first cigarette, outside the kitchen in Camp Number 80, I told Ron the cook about my grandmother's kitchen. I told him how the women of the family would convene there, speaking Farsi. How we, the girls, would go in and out, hearing fragments, but mostly receiving orders, which I skillfully learned to ignore while escaping outside. "You're so funny, that's exactly what you just did," he told me, as though I hadn't already known.

"You don't understand, it's the smell, the smell that I hate the most," I said, remembering the smell and recalling the embarrassment that would take hold of me when the women would scrutinize my body and whisper, "Come *goonem*,[1] come learn what you should know." "Leave me alone," I would think to myself, feeling upset that none of my Tel Aviv friends had such primitive families that talked about the blood women have between their legs and about the intimate parts of their bodies. My friends' families, I believed, were normal, and only I had a strange and embarrassing family, except for my mother, who was never part of the fuss. She, too, was embarrassed. She had immigrated to Israel from Syria when she was 4 years old, and wished only to be an Israeli, not an Arab.

They packed literally nothing but their clothes and left their homes behind on a quest for the new, promised land. Like many Jews in many places in the world, they believed in establishing a secure home for the Jews. As a girl I heard my mother describe how she and her six siblings hid in "the Arab's" wagon so that no one would hear as they crossed the border and settled in Haifa, a city with a mix of Jews and Arabs. At that moment it was clear that the only identity that must remain is the Jewish, Zionist, white identity, and that the "other" identity must be erased. We mustn't be "them," we must only be "us." And "us" is Hebrew or Yiddish or English, it is certainly not Arabic or Farsi. In class when we were required to write where our parents immigrated from, I would wait for the last kid to hand in his form and only then hand mine in, so that no one would come after me and peek and see and tell everyone. And I felt my parents' embarrassment everywhere. I knew that they were seeking affirmation for having been accepted into civilized society. My parents taught us that what "they" say is very important, and that "they" are always right; the teacher, the neighbors, the other children's parents, they are to affirm that we are one of them. Whenever this affirmation failed to arrive, I sensed the intensity of their pain. Without knowing, I recognized their self-hatred and felt they were falling to pieces.

"It's a bit disgusting to do the dishes, isn't it?" I asked Ron the cook. "It depends, it depends what kind of food there was," he replied. Even back then I thought that he was terribly concrete. "There are things that are simply disgusting," I said decisively, and I guess not entirely understanding why I was beginning to get annoyed with him, he decided to agree with me. "Yeah, there are things that are simply disgusting," he said, adding, "When are you going home?"

"I have no idea," I answered. I had no clue why everything felt so overwhelming and why I had a lump in my throat. I started crying, and Ron the cook immediately promised me that he would never force me to do the dishes. I only knew that I wanted to go home, but once again did not know where home was.

Home

Bombs hit Budapest, the capital of Hungary. Tommy's mother took advantage of the commotion and shoved him out of the procession leading Jews to their deaths and into the public toilet. They hid there and heard the bombs falling. Later they realized no one from that procession remained alive. When the noise subsided, Tommy knew something was over. He understood he had no home. Nowhere was home.

This was the key moment of my life, the moment that defines me more accurately than any other – more than anything I ever did, more than any place I ever lived or visited, more than any person that I ever met. Not because I was spared – every survivor has his story of a private miracle – but because I had nowhere to go.

(Lapid, 2012, p. 58)

Years later, Tommy tells his son that it was in that place and time, though without even knowing it, that he became a Zionist. "It is the whole Zionist idea, in fact," he says. "The State of Israel is a problematic place, and we'll all always have our arguments about it, but this is the very reason it was established: so that every Jewish child will always have a place to go" (p. 58).

"You saw what they did to the Jews in Europe," my father used to say. "This is our place. We have no other." This new home was complex, and the idealization formed by those who had no other choice was treated by us, the next generation, with a great deal of cynicism once we grew up. We were proud of our country, but couldn't ignore the faults; we criticized what had previously been accepted consensually; we asked questions and demanded answers. I saw how my parents consolidated around Israeliness, while attempting to erase all traces of their past. I saw my grandmothers being left behind, lacking the language and the resources, and having children who were very much ashamed of them. The shame was in response to not only their weakness and difficulty adapting to the new culture; the shame was chiefly about their having come from "there," and not from the right "there." They spoke the "wrong" language, listened to the "wrong" music, and brought with them non-European practices that were unacceptable to the Zionist hegemony.

Israel has always been a racist country. Discrimination has prevailed from the very beginning, and racism has been directed not only towards Israeli Arabs, but also towards Sephardic Jews, and later, Ethiopian immigrants and any others who did not fit into the definitions of Israeli Ashkenazi hegemony. The meaning of the word *Mizrah* in Hebrew is "orient," and *Mizrahim* refers to men and women who migrated to Israel from the Middle East and North Africa. One of the main concepts at the center of Israeli society was that of the "melting pot," the idea that after thousands of years in the diaspora, Jews from different countries gather together, put the past behind them, and mold a new identity. But as it turned out, the common identity was not so melted. The ideal Israeli was depicted as an Ashkenazi, secular male. When the word *Mizrahim* is used nowadays, it is heavily loaded with political, economic, and cultural connotations related to the deprivation of *Mizrahim* by the Zionist establishment. Clearly, the place of *Mizrahi* people, especially women, was set to be marginal, working class, peripheral citizens (see Dahan-Kalev, 2000; Shenhav, 2007; Shiran, 2007; and others).

Those who emigrated from Arab states were not easily able to be part of the new country and to achieve key positions in Israeli society. Their socioeconomic status was inherently lower than those of European descent (Abarjel, 2007; Shenhav,

29

2007). They were considered to be ill-mannered and culturally vile, as though they were people who had yet to see the light (cf. the film *Where is S'aday?*[2]). Their climb up the socioeconomic ladder was extremely slow, as attested to by their meager representation among physicians, politicians, lawyers, and academicians. Psychology in general, and especially psychoanalysis, were predominantly "white" professions devoid of *Mizrahim*, and consequently the theory and research in these fields lack non-Ashkenazi vantage points (see Atlas, 2012a). We, the next generation, became the epitome of Israeli Sabras as was expected of us, but we carried a great deal of shame, as we held within our bodies the ghosts of East-to-West immigration.

The hornet

"Careful lest the hornet stings you," my grandmother would whisper in Farsi. "The hornet, the hornet," the women would repeat after her, chiming in laughingly. We, the girls, learned the poetic language quite quickly, and we also understood that when rhymes and obscure metaphors are used in the kitchen, they usually refer to sex.

Years later, my sister reminded me of the hornet tune and asked, giggling, "Can you believe that Grandma was actually telling her daughters, 'Be careful not to get screwed'?" We both chuckled. From our juvenile perspective there was something mysterious about it, but also vulgar and without boundaries. It was an alien tune, different from everything our culture had been teaching us to be correct and appropriate. Today I understand that the "hornet tune" was my grandmother's way of warning her married daughters not to get pregnant again by their husbands, since when the hornet stings a woman might get in "trouble." Unlike the warnings we hear or proffer these days, that warning wasn't about having casual sex, after all; for my grandmother premarital sex was one of the biggest sins imaginable, even though she had left Iran 20 years earlier and we were already in the 1970s, and then the 1980s.

In the culture my grandmothers came from, it was permissible to talk about sex, but as mentioned, prohibited to engage in it before marriage (see Atlas, 2012b). In fact, only married women were even allowed to speak about it freely. Everything said in the presence of the girls was off the record; they were allowed to listen, but prohibited from responding or participating. Those were the rules – a very confusing reality for young girls growing up in a completely different culture: Western, urban, liberal, one in which they have permission to act, to have sex, but not to own their desire.

Sexuality and desire are therefore experienced differently; permissions and inhibitions have different faces. The understanding that sexuality is in large part culturally determined isn't new – many have pointed out the connection between the two. "The manifest diversity in forms of sexual desire indicates that sexuality (like hunger) is a cultural, not a natural, product and process," writes Dimen (1999, p. 423). Today, we challenge the binary between nature and culture and know that both play a significant role in the experience of our sexuality. Every culture contributes to the complexity of pleasure, shame, and guilt in a slightly different way. What we used to call "human nature" we now know is a possibility, not a determinate, and the enigmatic message that we receive from our caregivers (Laplanche, 1987) as well as our culture, shapes our emotional and physical experiences.

Shame

One of the things I am most aware of is the effect of emigration from East to West on women's perception of sexuality. I am a witness to the traumatic aspects of immigration for first- and second-generation immigrants. The shift from certain sexual norms to new ones that are sometimes entirely different is painful and laden with shame and anxiety. These women must now learn to cope with a different conception of what is allowed and what is forbidden; of what is considered inferior and what is considered superior; a new and different conception of the body, of courting patterns, and of nonverbal communication. Part of their adaptation, as Dahan (2011, personal communication) refers to it, is the understanding that the more desire women express, the lower their position will be on the new cultural ladder. In other words, in Western society, the more they are sexually inhibited, the higher their position in the new social hierarchy.

I have met many of these women in therapy over the years and learned to recognize the embarrassment we share. In particular, I have begun to delve into and investigate the perception of sexuality in the Arab and Persian worlds. This is an exploration of many of my identities and includes attraction and repulsion, idealization and devaluation, and an investigation that has to do with immigration and its influence on all aspects of life, but especially on sexuality.

Sexuality and sex evoke many feelings. Almost everyone blushes when talking about sex. No doubt talking about sex can be as hot as having it. Some get excited, some get overexcited, some get so excited that they can only feel anxious, guilty, or out of control (Atlas & Benjamin, 2010). But I find that for immigrants from East to West (first- but also second- and even third-generation), there is an added struggle surrounding cultural norms; what they have known as forbidden (sexual act) is now permitted, and what had been permitted in a specific atmosphere (feminine autoeroticism and permission for feminine desire, for example) is now forbidden (Atlas, 2012b). The second and third generations are trapped between cultural perceptions, understanding that their parents' sexual norms might bear impact upon their social status, but at the same time internalizing their parents' inhibitions and prohibitions. In treatment, I see women's anxiety about their sexual desire, with a deep concern that they might be perceived, even to their own eyes, as promiscuous. They fear that they might be perceived that way even if they don't *do* anything other than carry their sexual heritage.

As we know, it is very shameful to talk about shame, and in different ways, in all cultures, there is much shame around sexuality. In that sense the gap between

31

cultures is a black hole, capturing much of what we don't talk about: the horror, the shame, the confusion. It is there, in that place where there is no one agreed-upon language, that we meet silences, and these silences belong to all of us, patients and analysts, Easterners and Westerners, men and women.

Can we talk about sexuality without feeling promiscuous? How can one talk about sex without over-arousing the other? Without enacting the act itself? Are there ways to listen for, and to, the unique accents of the language of sex?

Silences

I was walking on King George Street, back and forth, only 18 years old but with much weight on my shoulders. Looking for something. When my boyfriend asked me about my sexuality, he was ready to protest and press for an answer to one question only: Can we have sex? But I had many more questions, and was looking for many more answers that I couldn't find by myself. I needed someone with me. Not only so I wouldn't be alone, but so I would be able to touch the abyss, to feel my loneliness and sorrow through desire and longing, through my mind and body. I needed to touch the intensity of life and climb back holding something I could make sense of, something real. I couldn't do it alone.

In the following few years, I found three doors and started building my home. I married my first husband, who was my best friend, and felt safe enough to explore my sexual and emotional boundaries. I wasn't an orphan anymore. I realized marriage was never about the fantasy of being a bride, but about the implicit inhibitions held in my body: my grandmothers' voice that a woman is not allowed to act sexually unless she is married. I was suddenly free. And I finally had a home, at least for a little while.

The second door led to starting therapy, meeting the woman who held my questions without answering them, living my life with me, to the answers and to new questions. She was my mother and sister and lover, and her room was my shelter for many years.

And I also opened a secret door to my mind, touching life through creation. Rilke (2011) says that "the artist's experience lies so unbelievably close to the sexual, to its pain and its pleasure, that the two phenomena are really just different forms of one and the same longing and bliss." I believe that sex and art are similar partly because they are each a promise. A promise to fill for a moment the empty parts, to retrieve all of the losses, to find all the empty boxes. A promise that is fulfilled for a moment before collapsing back to square one. To re-find and re-lose, to retrieve, to be moved, excited, to cry and mourn.

All of that is tied to the fact that sex is a homeless experience, an experience without a childhood home. Physical experiences are usually lonely. They only happen inside our own bodies and there will never be anyone who can fully participate. Illnesses are certainly the loneliest experiences of all, but to varying degrees every physical experience is lonely, including birth and maturation. Sex is also such an experience, with barely any childhood memories. Although it clearly has its antecedents there, there is no acknowledgment and processing of these in any sense. Silence.

Sexuality, then, holds within its orbit a long tradition of silence and shame. Lies and disguises are most often part of the sexual appearance. Like a homeless creature it walks around the neighborhood – yes, in the psychoanalytic neighborhood as well – and people pretend they don't see it. No one is willing to admit they know it, and there is no way we disclose we actually have known it ever since childhood. When referring to infancy, we talk about attachment. Sexuality, though hovering in the background, is usually excluded from the primary dyadic connection, especially between mothers and daughters. A woman is required to deny her original love and desire which remain only implicitly linked to the mother. This is an unspoken and unsymbolized realm that reverberates through generations of mothers and daughters, one that a daughter holds in mind and body and that continues to exist in women throughout life.

Fonagy (2008), writing that emotional regulation arises out of the mirroring of affect by a primary caregiver, suggests that sexual feelings are unique in that caregivers systematically ignore them and they are therefore unmirrored. These experiences, Fonagy claims, remain to some extent a dissociated sphere within attachment bonds; therefore, sexual feelings remain fundamentally dysregulated in all of us. In the search for our mother's body we turn to our lovers for answers. Our lovers are our new home. They touch our old injuries. They touch our bodies and our longings, but also our pain and loneliness. Sometimes we ask them to do what we fantasized and never dared to ask. At other times, we keep silent.

Voices

Silences, lies, yearnings. Sex is never just sex. It intensely touches upon Otherness, loss, disharmonious pain, and stirring excitement. The great and small longings for a mother, for home, maybe for something that we may never have had.

This time, packing my things was the most painful thing in the world. I was not excited. I was not looking forward, and I didn't think anything was waiting for me, no promised and for sure no holy land. I was terrified moving to the new country, meeting the immigrant that I am. At that point unaware of holding the old pain of immigration, I looked at my mother standing silently in the corner, my father trying to look happy, and tried to pack as quickly as I could. I locked my history in a suitcase, separated from my patients, and moved with the man who would become the father of my children to New York.

I remember thinking that from now on I'm probably safe. "Here there are no wars," I'll tell my future children. But deep inside, I felt myself to be in complete danger. I felt everything was collapsing, that I was about to lose everything I had, while I am born into a new life, space, language, where I knew no one and felt unsure of what was left of me. I was not afraid – I was gone. And I was looking for words to create a narrative, to tell myself who I was.

I packed my two dogs, bought them a seat on the airplane, and gave the three of us a sleeping pill. We will wake up soon to the smell of landing, the scent of September in New York. For many years it remained the scent of immigration. And it was the first birthday I have ever celebrated alone. Sitting on the Hudson River with my laptop, writing. Gazing at the Statue of Liberty and feeling this strange sensation of liberation. "No one knows me here," I thought. "I work really hard to understand what people are talking about. Too bad I totally don't get it." I heard myself communicating with myself in two voices, sometimes three. I touch parts of myself that I didn't know existed and as the days pass I start feeling happy, brave, excited. I start getting in touch with the parts of myself that I never knew existed.

What do we truly know about ourselves? What did I know then? Now? Every patient has taught me something about myself. And I know the most painful experiences in life have been and will probably continue to be my best teachers. Touching someone you want provides the deepest experiences of our own body. In psychoanalysis we usually talk about the need to be loved or desired by another person, but in fact love and lust for another connects us to our own minds and bodies in the most intense ways. Desire awakens the hidden parts of ourselves.

Sexuality is a discrete self-state connected to material that otherwise remains in the shadow of our existence, that we somehow know exists but usually can't experience (Atlas, in press). Stein (1998a, 1998b) emphasized the distinct feeling that sexual experience offers us of stepping out of so-called "everyday mentality" and habitual modes of functioning (Stein, 1998a, p. 594) into a different state of consciousness. "The deliberate loss of self in eroticism is manifest; no one can question it," writes Bataille (1986, p. 31). It is the falling out of your everyday sense of self (Mitchell, 1997), hence the loss of the predictable self that we know and maintain in order to function in our day to day life. But at the same time, lust promotes the finding of other parts of ourselves that we are usually not in touch with, parts that are Other to ourselves. "Sex," writes Goldner (2006), "trades on the thrill of discovering, over and over again, that we are unknown to ourselves" (p. 628). Sex is how we discover otherwise unknown parts of ourselves, and can lead us to discover unknown parts of the world.

Endings

When it comes to sex, there are many things that men and women are still not allowed to talk about. Sometimes we are allowed to whisper, but never to sing the way my grandmothers used to do. As a girl, I didn't necessarily like that music, and especially not its foreign accent. I knew exactly what that accent held within. Instead, I wanted to have my own home, to create everything from scratch, to pick up answers like flowers that you aren't allowed to pick, and to hold them in a sacred place – even when they are dry and old. I had romantic ideas about sex and love. In some ways I still do. The only difference is that I'm not waiting anymore for a war to save my life. I pray for peace and as Rilke says, live my, and my patients', way to the answers.

Notes

1 "My soul" in Farsi.
2 A movie produced by the Israeli Army in 1951 that documents paternalism and racism towards Jewish immigrants from the Arab world. The Sephardic inhabitants of the tent camps, that were hastily constructed for the new immigrants and which bred filth, disease, and crime among its inhabitants, are depicted as ignorant, primitive, and backward people. Barely human, they are shown to acquire the enlightenment of the morally and intellectually superior Ashkenazim, who are presented as their saviors.

References

Abarjel, R. (2007). The mizrahi conversation in the nineties. In Y. Yonah, Y. Naaman, & D. (eds.), *Rainbow of opinions* (pp. 140–166). Tel Aviv: November Books.

Atlas, G. (2012a). East of Freud. *Division Review*, *1*(3), 25–27.

Atlas, G. (2012b). Sex and the kitchen: Thoughts on culture and forbidden desire. *Psychoanalytic Perspectives*, *9*(2), 220–232.

Atlas, G. (in press). Touch me know me.

Atlas, G., & Benjamin, J. (2010). The "Too Muchness" of Excitement and the Death of Desire. International Association of Relational Psychoanalysis and Psychotherapy conference, February, San Francisco.

Bataille, G. (1986). *Eroticism: Death and sensuality*. San Francisco, CA: City Light Books.

Dahan-Kalev, H. (2000). Feminism and ethnicity in education: An Israeli case study. *Schools and Society*, 193–210.

Dimen, M. (1999). Between lust and libido. *Psychoanalytic Dialogues*, *9*, 415–440.

Fonagy, P. (2008). A genuinely developmental theory of sexual enjoyment and its implications. *Journal of the American Psychoanalytic Association*, *56*(1), 11–36.

Goldner, V. (2006). "Let's do it again": Further reflection on Eros and attachment. *Psychoanalytic Dialogues*, *16*, 619–637.

Lapid, Y. (2012). *Memories after my death*. London: Elliott & Thompson Limited.

Laplanche, J. (1987). *New foundations for psychoanalysis* (D. Macey, Trans.). Oxford: Basil Blackwell, 1989.

Mitchell, S. A. (1997). Psychoanalysis and the degradation of Romance. *Psychoanalytic Dialogues*, *7*, 23–41.

Rilke, R. M. (2011). *Letters to a young poet*. Cambridge: Harvard University Press.

Shenhav, Y. (2007). The mizrahi conversation in the nineties. In Y. Yonah, Y. Naaman, & D. (eds.), *Rainbow of opinions* (pp. 93–106). Tel Aviv: November Books.

Shiran, V. (2007). The mizrahi conversation in the nineties. In Y. Yonah, Y. Naaman, & D. (eds.), *Rainbow of opinions* (pp. 84–93). Tel Aviv: November Books.

Stein, R. (1998a). The enigmatic dimension of sexual experience: The "otherness" of sexuality and primal seduction. *Psychoanalytic Quarterly*, *67*, 594–625.

Stein, R. (1998b). The poignant, the excessive, and the enigmatic in sexuality. *International Journal of Psychoanalysis*, *79*, 253–268.

4

THE PROFESSIONAL IDIOM AND
THE PSYCHOANALYTIC OTHER

Joyce Slochower

Developing a professional identity

Early in graduate school, I decided to train as a psychoanalyst. That choice had a long and, in some ways, natural history; both my parents were Freudian analysts. I had grown up with psychoanalytic jargon in my ears, had listened at the perimeter to the complex and intriguing conversations of my parents' analyst friends. Something special and a bit mysterious was going on behind those soundproof office doors. And so, when a high school English teacher introduced me to the fundamentals of psychoanalytic thought, I followed my father's intellectual tradition (he was also a literature scholar) by trying to apply it to Dostoyevsky. Being only 16, I didn't do it very well. But my father encouraged me, implicitly inviting me into the grownup world and symbolically letting me know I could succeed there. That invitation would become crucial to my professional identity.

In college (Clark University), I – unsurprisingly – became a psychology major. I walked past Freud's bust (marking his 1909 lectures there) daily, and was lucky enough to get exposure to psychoanalytic thinking from some of my college professors. For reasons personal rather than academic, I transferred to NYU in my junior year.

That transfer temporarily interrupted this trajectory. NYU was as behavioral as Clark was not; psychoanalytic thinking was frowned upon. I learned some behavior theory and began taking courses in social psychology. Social psych research was fun, and probably of equal importance, it was mine: in moving toward research, I established a degree of separation from my psychoanalyst parents. And so, as graduation approached, I applied to social psych Ph.D. programs. A stroke of good fortune took me to Teacher's College, Columbia University, where the social psychology program was actually headed by a psychoanalyst – Morton Deutsch, who did interesting work in conflict resolution and distributive justice. I enjoyed his open, thoughtful manner and the intellectual challenge of operationalizing ways of assessing theory.

But the theories didn't grab me. Research felt increasingly hokey, "as if"; I wanted to do something more interpersonal. By my second year, I had become fully disillusioned. I wanted to become a clinical psychologist (yes, like my parents), and

I approached Mort and told him that I wanted to make the switch. But Mort resisted, encouraging me to consider doing a joint clinical–social degree instead.

This was a different, less formal time; Mort walked me upstairs to speak to the then-Chair of the Clinical program (Rosalie Schonbar), and together they set up a special program for me. In less than an hour it was a done deal. I could take whatever clinical courses I liked, and do externships and an internship while continuing in the social psych research program, simultaneously fulfilling only those requirements the two Chairs agreed upon.

The setup turned out to be a godsend; it exempted me from the standard requirements of each program, and gave me the run of both departments and my pick of supervisors (including Walter Kass, a wonderful Menninger-trained analyst who supervised me at Bellevue). The clinical program offered good courses in psychodynamic theory. I was especially fascinated by the object relations theorists and became even more so when a psychoanalyst friend of my parents gave me what would be a prescient gift: a copy of Winnicott's (1957) BBC lectures to parents, entitled *The Child, the Family and the Outside World*. Winnicott's writing evoked a whole new psychoanalytic vision, one embedded in notions of repair more than dynamic interpretation.

Wanting more, I quickly pushed through graduate school, did a data-based dissertation on a clinical topic (obesity), and finished my coursework. I was ready to defend in my third year, and was considering where to apply for internship when a tenure track job opened up in Hunter College's Psych department. They were looking for a clinical psychologist who could do research and teach experimental social psych. Once again, I was lucky; the Chair of that department (Florence Denmark) gave a talk at T.C., where she mentioned the search to one of my professors (Harvey Hornstein), who connected us. I seemed to fit the bill, and with Harvey's encouragement, decided to postpone my internship and applied for the position. I would keep that job for 32 years, though I never did feel like a research psychologist. Despite teaching Experimental Social Psychology for three decades, my identification was first and last as a clinician.

I went into analysis in 1975. That experience, combined with several years of a part-time postdoctoral internship at Bellevue, helped me develop a tentative sense of clinical competence. The terror with which I met a prospective patient gave way. I was sometimes able to listen and think on my feet. I began to notice myself in the room in a way that allowed me to think; I didn't feel it so necessary to cling tightly to a professional role. Increasingly, I was interested in my countertransference feelings rather than being simply frightened by them. But I wanted more, and a few years later (1980), decided to apply to the NYU Postdoctoral Program. It became my true home; I began the decades-long task of building a new psychoanalytic identity.

Theory as a personal idiom

When I decided to train to be an analyst, I took a leap of faith. Will I have what it takes – emotionally, intellectually? Will I be able to absorb the vast body of theoretical and clinical literature that comprises psychoanalytic thinking? Will I help my patients, and how will I know if I am?

I brought a Freudian *Weltanschauung* to my graduate training. It had its roots in childhood, in my identification with my psychoanalyst parents' theory and also with their authoritative, knowing stance. In college and graduate school, classical theory and technique defined the clinical exchange and provided a comforting sense of certainty. There were clear rules of technique to follow, an explicit set of assumptions on which to rely. Together, they helped counter my anxious sense of incompetence.

But there had been too many rules in childhood (and now, in psychoanalysis), and their constricting effect began to outweigh their value (see Kernberg, 1986, 1996). I too often felt like I was "playing a role"; I wanted to be freer to "be" within the therapeutic setting, to use myself. I didn't want to answer *every* question with a question. Some unmet baby needs found their way into the appeal of the British Middle School; their emphasis on the impact of early (preverbal) experience and on transitional and symbolic phenomenon felt emotionally compelling. Here was a vision of patient as baby and analyst as parent; psychoanalysis could repair me, my patients, and my parents.

What we choose: relational influences

Most of us (myself included) need to belong, to please, to fit in to some degree; these needs meld with those of the larger group, teacher, supervisor, or analyst for loyalty. Both inner and external pressures color how we experience theory and respond to training (Berman, 2004; Friedman, 1978, 1988; Grossman, 1995; Slavin, 1992, 1997). The felt need to echo or support a mentor's theoretical position probably carries particular weight in clinical fields because of the dynamic meanings of the theories we choose, as well as the deeply personal relationships we form with those whom we emulate, including our own therapists or analysts. Early in my training, I experienced considerable pressure to conform to my supervisor's theory. At NYU Postdoc, competing pressures for allegiance pulled me in conflicting directions. Depending on whom I worked with, I was "supposed" to interpret and remain neutral or focus on the transference–countertransference mix. Yet, like most of us, I also struggled with the wish to go my own way.

NYU Postdoc in the 1980s had three tracks (Freudian, Interpersonal, and Independent). Most of my supervisors and teachers identified with either the Freudian or Independent track. My Freudian supervisor was lovely and warm, but she held tightly to the Freudian ideal. She expected me to be rigidly interpretive. All this came to a head when a patient requested a 2-month-long vacation from New York and analysis. My supervisor wouldn't "let" me "let" my patient take it. "Either she's in analysis or she's not. If she takes this vacation you can't continue with her." Unable to protest, I conveyed her stance to my patient, who complied. The impact of this stance reverberated on the analysis; I think we never entirely recovered though we worked together for many years. I continue to regret my refusal to this day, both because of its effect on the treatment and because in complying with my supervisor I did something that felt profoundly ego dystonic – indeed, inauthentic.

But the Freudian ideal wasn't the only one with which I struggled; an interpersonal supervisor reacted even more critically when I offered concrete parenting suggestions to a vulnerable patient whose husband was being somewhat abusive to their little girl. She accused me of mixing up social work and psychoanalysis, and pushed me to stay focused on the transference–countertransference interaction. "Why are you telling your patient how to raise her child? This is not psychoanalysis! You need to focus on what she's doing to you when she talks about her relationship to her child." There was something far too narrow about this clinical view and within it I felt unrecognized but unable to adequately protest. In this instance, I secretly ignored my supervisor and worked with my patient on how to moderate her husband's (and her) way of treating their child, but I felt guilty and subversive vis-à-vis my supervisor.

Happily, these painful experiences were counterbalanced by many others with supervisors and teachers who recognized and supported my clinical capacity and made plenty of room for me to go my own way. Increasingly, that way took me toward the object relations theorists.

A backdrop to these personal influences lay in the political arena. Analysts (like me) who came of age during the 1960s and 1970s carried an anti-authoritarian belief system into psychoanalytic training. Involved as a young adult in the anti-Vietnam movement, I grew up with a lively sense of agency and suspicion toward authority. Authority (political or psychoanalytic) should not be taken at face value; issues of compliance or submission found their way into the consulting room. First entering psychoanalytic training in my early 30s, I chose NYU largely because of its anti-authoritarian stance: candidates didn't have to choose or "pledge allegiance" to a given theory. And while, on one level, I felt compelled to comply with my supervisors' clinical demands, on the other, both personal and political identifications pulled me to push back, albeit quietly.

NYU Postdoc symbolically legitimated a vision of psychoanalytic multiplicity while serving as a backdrop support for my shaky sense of authority (Eisold, 1994; Greenberg, 1997). It introduced an outside (third) element into the patient–analyst interaction (Aron, 1998, 1999; Spezzano, 1998), representing the larger context within which I could function. On another level, my professional community was sufficiently idealized early in my training that it also evoked a sense of vulnerability (Langs, 1978); would I live up to my mentors' and teachers' expectations? That worry dissipated only very gradually.

I graduated in 1987 but remained involved with NYU Postdoc. This was a time of lively theoretical conversation. Egalitarian clinical models offered a compelling new point of entrée that clashed with the Freudian vision. Relationalists challenged the absoluteness of the analyst's knowledge, power, and certainty in a way that fit right in with the residue of the anti-war movement. I had an opportunity to enact my egalitarian, anti-establishment roots (my father was a non-card-carrying communist). I didn't recognize any of this until some years after the fact.

In 1988, the relational track came into being and in some respects I found a home. But this home was not unconflicted because the relational turn threatened to upend my object relational identity; critiquing the British Middle Group's emphasis on patient as baby and analyst as parent, they threatened core aspects of Winnicott's thinking. I felt caught between the two.

The professional other and the professional community

The professional community doesn't exist in a vacuum. As we face the fragmented and sometimes fractious psychoanalytic world, our professional identity is typically articulated, at least in part, *against* the position of the community or communities that hold opposing or divergent theoretical/clinical positions.

Often implicit in our theoretical identity is the rejection of an antithetical belief system. I call this the professional *other* – a subjectively defined "outside" force that represents a "not-me" element, the position(s) from which we seek to *disidentify*. This other may be experienced as a single oppositional voice – the underside of the psychoanalytic coin – or as a Greek Chorus of sorts, a cacophony of discordant voices, all articulating shadings of difference from our own professional community.

A psychoanalytic other remained a theoretical thread that informed my professional identity over the early years of my training and professional development. The "other," a partial caricature of an alternative, clashing theory, served an important organizing function; it helped me delineate and solidify my self-definition. The psychoanalytic other was initially defined as both Kleinian ("I would never interpret aggressively like they do") and Freudian ("I don't want to be a 'blank screen' analyst"). Gradually, interpersonal theories added another clashing strain ("I don't believe in being continuously interactive. I want to be a warm yet contained, responsive analyst. I want to repair.").

Like the synagogue or church that one *does not* attend, the psychoanalytic other creates a dialectic (or multiple dialectics). The tension between one's professional ideal and the psychoanalytic other can stimulate a sense of intellectual passion, lively internal (and real) debate, and a deepened understanding of clinical and theoretical complexity. Awareness of difference sharpens our professional identity and pushes us to more fully define our own perspective, enhancing our sense of professional community and respectful difference with other positions, rather than a reflexive rejection of those that feel "not-me" or "not-us."

But issues of theoretical identity – the need to become and remain part of one's professional community *and* separate from the psychoanalytic other – often become intensely loaded. I have heard (and occasionally participated in) the following sort of interchange innumerable times:

X is in analysis with a [Freudian, Kleinian, relational, interpersonal, self-psychologically oriented, and so on] analyst. It is dreadful. *I* would never be in treatment with someone like that. Can you believe that the analyst refuses to answer the most basic questions/interprets everything as aggression/constantly talks about his reactions to the patient/is incredibly confrontational and unempathic/does nothing but mirror and never challenges the patient?

In a self-congratulatory way, the psychoanalytic other is caricatured, rendered inadequate, bad, certainly not deserving of respect. Difference is used to affirm the rightness of one's analyst's or one's own theoretical position.

Building theoretical bridges

The more I read, the more constrained I felt both by Freudian guidelines based in a position of neutrality and the interpersonalists' insistence on a model of patient-as-adult. The object relations theorists' emphasis on intimate dyadic connectedness suggested a different therapeutic position, one based in part on a symbolic parental connection. Winnicott's work was especially inspiring and evocative; it opened a whole new way of thinking about the clinical arena.

This wasn't a purely theoretical, intellectual shift. Here was a model of treatment that felt right; I felt a personal resonance with object relational writings that I had never felt when reading Freudian and ego psychology. As my own analysis progressed, it gradually became clear that my fascination with the role of nonverbal experience also had personal sources. Winnicott inspired hope and promise – I could repair my patients' pains (and perhaps my own as well). In particular, I responded with a sense of surprised recognition to his double statements about the mother's (analyst's) vulnerability and hate. Here was a model that made room for the non-resonant, that might allow me to be both human and reparative.

I carried this professional ideal into my private practice only to confront a striking collision. Very few of my patients were prepared to enter an intense therapeutic relationship with me, and even fewer expressed unconflicted longings for parental repair. Most were quite disturbed and had trouble managing both their lives and our relationship. Some were explosive, others provocative or extraordinarily demanding, still others seemed impervious to my (not always so skillful) interventions. And my reactions didn't seem to fit the Winnicottian notion of a maternal, holding analyst. It was difficult to remain attuned or empathic; I felt, at moments, frustrated, helpless, and/or intimidated in reaction to patients' anger and reactivity. There seemed to be neither idealized baby *nor* mother in the consulting room.

To make matters worse, the Winnicottian model to which I had aspired clashed with my sense of the clinical moment. The Winnicottian analytic model felt too idealized; it seemed to demand that I feel what I did not. Even Winnicott's notion of hate in the countertransference was idealized – Winnicott said the mother (analyst) hated when it was developmentally or clinically useful (see Kraemer, 1996). Where was a discussion of the analyst's vulnerability to feeling or doing the *wrong* thing at the wrong time? And what about holding work when the patient's dominant affect was not dependence but hate, narcissism, ruthlessness, and the like? It seemed to me that at least as much holding was needed in those moments as when patients were regressed.

To complicate all this, social constructivist and feminist thinkers had been voicing strong and cogent critiques of the idealization of motherhood and the analytic function that contradicted the Winnicottian vision of a responsive, resonant analyst. They underscore the importance of owning maternal (analytic) subjectivity – of mother-as-subject.

Here, then, was a theoretical collision. On one hand, I found the relational critique compelling, but I was reluctant to abandon the idea of holding. Could the two models be reconciled?

I had the good fortune to be thinking and writing during the late 1980s and 1990s, a time of intellectual ferment and theoretical openness, a time that invited, even welcomed, collisions. There was room for multiple viewpoints. My mentors and colleagues (especially Larry Epstein, Lew Aron, and Steve Mitchell) encouraged me to voice my differences with prevailing views. The radical end of relational and feminist theory became a new and different psychoanalytic other, one that I wanted both to embrace and to distinguish myself from.

I began writing about holding but located the holding paradigm *between* analyst and patient, rather than squarely in the analyst's domain. Arguing against the assumption that mutuality is always clinically possible, I proposed a perspective that viewed intersubjective exchange as a relational goal but not always a therapeutic reality. At times, patient and analyst *together coconstruct* a holding illusion that allows the patient to set aside disturbing aspects of the analyst's separate perspective (Slochower, 1992, 1993, 1994, 1996a, 1996b, 1996c). This kind of holding process can support a gradual evolution toward collaborative, intersubjective work involving two separate subjects (Benjamin, 1995), that is, toward the relational ideal.

Further extending the Winnicottian vision of holding in regression, I used the holding metaphor to characterize a range of difficult emotional situations within and outside the treatment context (Slochower, 1991, 1993, 1996c). Analysts hold aversive emotional states like hate and ruthlessness by working toward a containing affective position and attempting to bracket but not negate disjunctive aspects of their subjectivity.

I used relational ideas to further suggest that, ultimately, the analyst can't hold alone. When patients need holding, they unconsciously exclude evidence of the analyst's otherness so that a mutual bracketing process takes shape: Potentially disruptive dimensions of the treatment relationship are temporarily sidelined in order to "smooth out" therapeutic exchange and support the illusion of analytic attunement.

Although it is certainly true that the analyst is incapable of complete emotional attunement, and further, is rarely in a position to know fully what to do, both parties bracket this piece of awareness for a time, behaving "as if" it were not the case . . . Yet it is only the deluded analyst who enters any kind of holding situation with absolute confidence about its therapeutic efficacy . . . the analyst . . . retains the capacity to acknowledge the paradoxical nature of the holding metaphor even while it is experienced as simply real.

(Slochower, 1996c, p. 32)

The theoretical position I was shaping, then, reflected an attempt to create a bridge between divergent perspectives (Winnicottian and relational). To a considerable degree, it emerged out of my theoretical interests and intellectual style, which leans toward inclusive models. Yet alongside the abstract, personal themes also informed my position: by proposing a solution to an apparent collision of ideas, I found a way to bridge difference. The wish to bridge difference had a very personal history that went beyond the realm of the theoretical.

Our professional idiom over time

Over the course of the next two decades, I continued to write about holding (as well as other themes). The power of the psychoanalytic other dimmed, and its position shifted. In fact, I recently gave a paper about how contemporary relational thinking integrated the idea of the patient as baby (Slochower, 2012); the earlier collision between these models has been more or less resolved. As my struggle to reconcile object relations and relational thinking quieted, I increasingly settled into a position that felt like my own. I became comfortably connected to my professional community, no longer anxious about finding my place within it.

And so it is with most of us. With time, our professional identification tends to solidify; we ordinarily feel more comfortably "in our own skin," less bothered or threatened by difference, by the professional community or the psychoanalytic other (though neither disappears altogether). Nevertheless, our implicit clinical theory often continues to shift across the professional lifespan as we integrate new experiences and respond to new or alternative viewpoints.

How all this happens depends in part on the degree of homogeneity within our particular professional community. Some of us are exposed to far more theoretical controversies and shifts than others. But unless we entirely envelop ourselves in a self-protective buffer – neither reading nor listening to different perspectives – we will all confront subtle and marked paradigm shifts over our professional lifetime. Some may be easily integrated; others challenge core theoretical or clinical assumptions, introducing new psychoanalytic others with which to contend.

New perspectives can be exciting; they give us alternative ways of approaching our patients and thinking about our own role in the clinical encounter, keeping the work fresh and alive. But new ideas can also disrupt deeply held beliefs about

43

the work in ways that are disturbing. After a long career, we become strongly identified with a particular way of thinking and working; it's not easy to simply abandon or drastically modify a dearly held professional idiom. Will we resist this challenge, clinging to dearly held beliefs about the treatment process in an effort to avoid becoming destabilized, or will we stretch our professional idiom?

Of course, our professional identity isn't simply a reflection of identifications and counter-identifications. Ideas have intrinsic value; we develop a psychoanalytic position by working *and* thinking about the work. Most of us can become playfully and creatively engaged in clinical/theoretical thought despite twinges of discomfort, and use that engagement to define and redefine ourselves. And perhaps most importantly, our professional idiom is profoundly influenced by clinical experience, which teaches us what "works" and what doesn't, and with whom. The more freely we can engage in the world of ideas and with our patients, the less constraint we're likely to feel as we negotiate a position within our community and in distinction to the psychoanalytic other.

But can we ever altogether remove ourselves from the arena of comparison without becoming isolated? If we are to hold a position, to negotiate our own place within the world of psychoanalytic ideas, we must engage the psychoanalytic other and address other theories without negating, exaggerating, or in other ways distorting them. This dialogue is, inevitably, ongoing, involving a cycle of recognition, destruction, and recognition (of ourselves and the other; Benjamin, 1995).

Theory's dynamic function

Psychoanalytic writers have long emphasized the analyst's personal and conflicted relationship with theory (Abend, 1979; Arlow, 1981; Crastnopol, 1999; Freud, 1937; Friedman, 1988; Grossman, 1995; Parsons, 1992; Sandler, 1983; Sharpe, 1935). We choose our theory partly for dynamic reasons and sometimes use it defensively to express needs or to ward off areas of personal conflict (Stolorow & Atwood, 1979). I certainly recognize the influence of my personal history on my preference for clinical theories that emphasize nurturance and empathy. In fact, Almond (2003) suggests that theory serves a holding function for us; it supports our sense of conviction about the work, bolsters self-esteem, and provides reassurance when ideas appear to be disconfirmed in the treatment hour. Stolorow and Atwood (1992) have underscored how theory can be used defensively to support efforts at self-regulation while sacrificing theoretical complexity. Aron (1998, 1999), addressing theory's self-organizing and self-regulatory functions, proposes that analysts select a particular theoretical focus because it's either concordant with or complementary to one's sense of self.

All good clinicians do their best to think about where a patient "is" within a given hour and use that material to inform their theoretical understanding. Yet because we work under the press of time, we only rarely fully think through an intervention before we make it. To the extent that our interventions are theoretically driven, we most often use theory implicitly and even procedurally (Friedman, 1988), discovering how (and if) our intervention fits our theory only ret-rospectively. Still, even if the discovery is retrospective, we inevitably confront moments of collision, moments when we find ourselves acting in opposition to our beliefs. Some of us are both more conscious of, and more bothered by, those moments of collision than others.

Like most of us, I more often experience the phenomenological rather than the theoretical during the analytic hour. I don't return to the abstract level until I try to make broader sense of what happened. But phenomenology is not divorced from theory; rather, it's informed by it. Even in the clinical moment, I most con-sistently focus on my patient's affect state and the dominant affective ambiance between us. I think many of my clinical moves reflect an implicit attention to my patient's tolerance for my "otherness" along with her capacity to access and work with interior experience. This focus reflects the core themes with which I identify professionally.

Yet there are plenty of times (see Hamilton, 1996; Mayer, 1996; Sandler, 1992) when my intervention doesn't reflect my theoretical position at all, and I can experi-ence a sense of collision when I recognize this. For example, I hear from more than a few patients that I don't mince words, that I'm very direct and don't let them "get away" with anything. They often, but certainly not always, say this with apprecia-tion. I recognize that this characteristic is part of my analytic self; I *am* capable of pushing (and pushing with some urgency). I try to find a way "in," to work deeply, and that focus doesn't always fit neatly with a theory that places the patient's toler-ance for the analyst's otherness at its center. Does my theory represent an attempt to balance who I am and who I want to be, in line with Aron's (1999) idea? Or does my spontaneous response sometimes override my theoretically informed analytic stance? Do I ignore areas of theoretical inconsistency (Sandler, 1992), or have I integrated a variety of theories and used them intuitively rather than consciously? I suspect that the answer to each of these questions is . . . yes.[1]

The analyst's personal response to each patient often intensifies or diminishes her tendency to think theoretically or use theory rigidly. In my own experience, when my relationship with a patient stirs up areas of personal vulnerability or conflict, I'm more likely to use theory in a (quasi-unconscious) attempt to create some emotional distance for myself so that I can think more freely. In contrast, when I work with patients whose issues overlap less with mine, I experience less conflict about how to move and am less likely to invoke theory as a support. Yet the possibility exists that this apparent "freedom" obfuscates other, more complex dynamics that operate outside my awareness. An example of each follows.

Neil approached me with chronic contempt and controlled rage at my inability to meet his need for "brilliant" interpretation. He dismissed most of my interven-tions scornfully, denigrated me, and sometimes attacked me directly for what he saw as my inadequacy. I was left feeling defensive and sometimes angry; less consciously, I felt as inadequate as his characterization. In especially difficult peri-ods, I found myself retreating from him and using theory in a way that was both self-protective and, at least at moments, clinically useful. I reminded myself that

Neil needed me to remain emotionally present and resilient but contained. I used that idea to support myself while trying to remain affectively alive and (sometimes sharply) responsive. This use of theory (especially my ideas about patients' inability to tolerate the analyst's separate subjectivity) supported the work. It also helped me to counter self-doubt, serving a self-righting force that allowed me to insulate myself from Neil's hostility and my painful feelings of helplessness. At moments, though, I suspect that my attempt to "hold" Neil may have frozen our interaction and interfered with a fuller and more affectively alive exploration of his rage and my defensive response.

In contrast, Adam's issues felt less related to my own, and I experienced less anxiety and conflict about how to move within the clinical moment. Adam is working on his sexual inhibitions and painful feelings related to his father's dismissive attitude toward him. He experiences me at different moments as a validating, loving parental figure, the object of his sexual desire, and his dismissive father. Although I have momentary strong (positive and negative) feelings toward Adam, neither his hostile or sexually intrusive transference evokes my own issues very intensely. Probably for this reason, I feel freer to use myself in the clinical moment without consciously invoking theory than I do with Neil.

On one level, I view my more emotionally present position with Adam as clinically "better." Yet it's also possible that my relative removal from theory masks, rather than clarifies, the complex dynamics of the moment.

In the intense heat of difficult clinical exchanges, it's often impossible (and probably not desirable) to find the space to think about our theory. For example, I seldom think consciously about whether or not a patient experiences me as a subject; however, that awareness infuses and ultimately shapes my understanding of our interactions and shapes my emotional stance. When my patient is highly sensitive to issues of *difference*, for example, I unconsciously adopt her language as I broach a difficult area in the hope that she will hear me. It's mainly retrospectively, though, that I identify the theoretical basis for my intervention.

Probably all of us work in far more complex and varied ways than is reflected by our theoretical allegiances. And while we may consciously work outside the theoretical arena, the implicit use of theory helps us define and sustain a personal idiom. We confront and attempt to negotiate theoretical and professional collisions that challenge that idiom across our careers. By *preserving rather than resolving* a variety of personal and clinical conflicts, we keep ourselves less complacent and more alive as we do this work.

Note

1 Mayer (1996) believes that the discontinuity between our private and public psychoanalytic theories is replete with problems and may leave us with a feeling of fraudulence with respect to our clinical work. Sandler (1992) argues that our unconscious use of these theories allows us to work effectively and does not arouse conflict precisely because it is unconscious. I suspect, however, that we continue to struggle consciously with these issues *outside* the clinical moment.

References

Abend, S. M. (1979). Unconscious fantasy and theories of cure. *Journal of the American Psychoanalytic Association, 27*, 579–596.

Almond, R. (2003). The holding function of theory. *Journal of the American Psychoanalytic Association, 51*, 131–153.

Arlow, J. (1981). Theories of pathogenesis. *Psychoanalytic Quarterly, 50*, 488–514.

Aron, L. (1998). Clinical choices and the theory of psychoanalytic technique. *Psychoanalytic Dialogues, 8*, 207–216.

Aron, L. (1999). Clinical choices and the relational matrix. *Psychoanalytic Dialogues, 9*, 1–30.

Benjamin, J. (1995). *Like subjects, love objects: Essays on recognition and sexual difference*. New Haven, CT: Yale University Press.

Berman, E. (2004). *Impossible training: A relational view of psychoanalytic education*. Hillsdale, NJ: Analytic Press.

Crastnopol, M. (1999). The analyst's professional self as a "third" influence on the dyad: When the analyst writes about the treatment. *Psychoanalytic Dialogues, 9*, 445–470.

Eisold, K. (1994). The intolerance of diversity in psychoanalytic institutes. *International Journal of Psychoanalysis, 75*, 785–800.

Freud, S. (1937). Analysis terminable and interminable. In J. Strachey (Ed. & Trans.), *The standard edition of the complete psychological works of Sigmund Freud* (Vol. 23, pp. 216–253). London: Hogarth Press, 1964.

Friedman, L. (1978). Treatment puzzles and training paradigms. *Contemporary Psychoanalysis, 14*, 456–467.

Friedman, L. (1988). *The anatomy of psychotherapy*. Hillsdale, NJ: Analytic Press.

Greenberg, J. (1997). Analytic authority and analytic restraint. Paper presented to Division of Psychoanalysis (39), American Psychological Association, Denver, CO.

Grossman, W. I. (1995). Psychological vicissitudes of theory in clinical work. *International Journal of Psychoanalysis, 76*, 885–899.

Hamilton, V. (1996). *The analyst's preconscious*. Hillsdale, NJ: Analytic Press.

Kernberg, O. F. (1986). Institutional problems of psychoanalytic education. *Journal of the American Psychoanalytic Association, 34*, 799–834.

Kernberg, O. F. (1996). Thirty methods to destroy the creativity of psychoanalytic candidates. *International Journal of Psychoanalysis, 77*, 1031–1040.

Kraemer, S. (1996). "Betwixt the dark and the daylight" of maternal subjectivity: Meditations on the threshold. *Psychoanalytic Dialogues, 6*, 765–791.

Langs, R. J. (1978). Responses to creativity in psychoanalysis. *International Journal of Psychoanalytic Psychotherapy, 7*, 189–207.

Mayer, E. L. (1996). Changes in science and changing ideas about knowledge and authority in psychoanalysis. *Psychoanalytic Quarterly, 65*, 158–200.

Parsons, M. (1992). The refinding of theory in clinical practice. *International Journal of Psychoanalysis, 73*, 103–115.

Sandler, J. (1983). Psychoanalytic concepts and psychoanalytic practice. *International Journal of Psychoanalysis, 64*, 35–46.

Sandler, J. (1992). Reflections on developments in the theory of psychoanalytic technique. *International Journal of Psychoanalysis, 73*, 189–198.

Sharpe, E. F. (1935). Similar and divergent unconscious determinants underlying the sublimations of pure art and pure science. *International Journal of Psychoanalytic Psychotherapy*, *16*, 186–202.

Slavin, J. (1992). Unintended consequences of psychoanalytic training. *International Journal of Psychoanalysis*, *28*, 616–630.

Slavin, J. (1997). Models of learning and psychoanalytic traditions. *Psychoanalytic Dialogues*, *7*, 803–817.

Slochower, J. (1991). Variations in the analytic holding environment. *International Journal of Psychoanalysis*, *72*, 709–718.

Slochower, J. (1992). A hateful borderline patient and the holding environment. *Contemporary Psychoanalysis*, *28*, 72–88.

Slochower, J. (1993). Mourning and the holding function of shiva. *Contemporary Psychoanalysis*, *2*, 352–367.

Slochower, J. (1994). The evolution of object usage and the holding environment. *Contemporary Psychoanalysis*, *30*, 135–151.

Slochower, J. (1996a). The holding environment and the fate of the analyst's subjectivity. *Psychoanalytic Dialogues*, *6*, 323–353.

Slochower, J. (1996b). Holding and the evolving maternal metaphor. *Psychoanalytic Review*, *83*, 195–218.

Slochower, J. (1996c). *Holding and psychoanalysis: A relational perspective*. Hillsdale, NJ: Analytic Press.

Slochower, J. (2012). The psychoanalytic baby in relational bathwater. Plenary address, 2012 Annual IARPP Conference, New York.

Spezzano, C. (1998). The triangle of clinical judgment. *Journal of the American Psychoanalytic Association*, *2*, 365–388.

Stolorow, R. D., & Atwood, G. E. (1979). *Faces in a cloud: Intersubjectivity in personality theory*. Norwood, NJ: Jason Aronson.

Stolorow, R. D., & Atwood, G. E. (1992). *Contexts of being: The intersubjective foundations of psychological life*. Hillsdale, NJ: Analytic Press.

Winnicott, D. W. (1957). *The child, the family, and the outside world*. London: Tavistock.

5

EMERGING FROM THE OPPOSITIONAL AND THE NEGATIVE

Irwin Hirsch

Learning from disappointment

As noted previously (Hirsch, 2008), my most significant learning in life, and in my work in particular, has come from failures. Learning from disappointment is a theme I consistently preach to students in the context of presenting analytic treatments that are not going well or have already failed by virtue of patients leaving therapy prematurely. This is an apt attitude for me, one who was raised with a legacy of maternal anxiety and worry and who identified with the tendency to expect the worst. It was adaptive for me to embrace a certain dysphoria and sense of the darkness in life. This gave me a sense of control when the inevitable large and small bad experiences emerged. To this day, personal analysis well behind me, I still believe with conviction that matters are more likely to turn out badly for me when I am optimistic.

My tastes in movies, literature, and humor tilt strongly to the dark and noirish (e.g., Hirsch, 1999, 2011; Hirsch & Hirsch, 2000). They tend to confirm my fundamental way of looking at the world, as well as my expectancies. I have grown used to adversity; indeed, all too often in life I have brought it on myself, as with all self-fulfilling prophecy. There is, however, a brighter side to this core way of looking at the world. I seem to do better in rebounding from negative experience than I do from creating rich experience from the outset. I think of sports teams or of individual professional athletes who always seem to be at their best when coming from behind. An occasional upside of my characterologic negativity has emerged clearly in my professional life. I have always been inclined to reject conventional wisdom, the forces of what is normally expected or of the majority way of thinking. I am highly skeptical, and often have been disrespectful or even mocking of expert authorities. This has caused me some serious trouble over the years, but has also helped me define points of view that I strongly believe and try to defend. Perhaps in part because I do not accept much of what is generally accepted, this reflexive negativity has led to feelings of a strong sense of identity with what I do come to embrace.

In my young years, I was the class joker, readily mocking teachers and gaining status by my classmates' laughter and awe at my rebelliousness. I was asked to leave my Hebrew school before graduation, and was paid back in public school in poor grades, until the point where there was danger that I would not be admitted into a decent college. At this point, I began to be a serious student, with my back against the wall, reaching my academic potentials for the first time. As an adult professional, I was almost fired from my initial post-doctorate hospital job, was asked to resign from my first stint as a teacher and supervisor in an analytic training program, and was essentially excommunicated for 20 years from the cherished analytic institute where I trained. I will say more about these later in the chapter, though for now I will note that despite the acute misery that these punishments caused me, ultimately each yielded a net result of my becoming far more productive than I would have been had I not brought them on. And, eventually, I learned to be less argumentative and confrontational and more measured and diplomatic. My oppositionalism, at least in person to person encounters, is now largely contained.

In the beginning

I will indulge readers with only a bit of narcissism in referring to familial autobiographical configurations that have helped shape the way I developed professionally and the way I think about matters psychoanalytic. Neither of my parents finished high school, though my father worked very long hours to provide his small family with a reasonably comfortable, what would now be called working-class or lower-middle-class life, quite commensurate with most families in our Jewish and Italian Brooklyn neighborhood. However, he was exploited both by his owner/bosses and the union he joined to help with this. In the end, he was screwed and felt like a failure. Unfortunately, I began to perceive him as both a failure and a sad figure. My parents had no particular expectancy for me to attend college, and they did not know what graduate school even meant. They provided minimal structure and, for better and for worse, gave me much leeway. I will never forget my father's primary, perhaps only piece of advice: "Find a nice boss." This is what he had hoped for and never got, and his experience and his counsel had much to do with my frequent pursuit of the opposite.

My inclination toward negation of prevailing or expected adherence began with the early rejection of what I perceived as my father's and community's belief in god and religious practice. This was followed by attendance at Baruch College of Business and Public Administration of the City University of New York, and quickly rejecting the accounting and business major that I and most others were there to study. Finding psychology, which was one of only two liberal arts options that one could take as a major, existed in tandem with my highly critical and mocking attitude toward any business related courses. While I received all A's in my psychology, history, and literature courses, my business professors took my skepticism into account in grading me for this part of the curriculum. Parenthetically, if I had any way of knowing the financial rewards eventually reaped by many of the economics and finance majors, I likely would have been more humble. Imme-

50

diately after graduation, I began the clinical psychology doctoral program at the then-mediocre University of Maryland. Because of my compromised grade point average, this was the only school that accepted me, and certainly the only one that offered me an assistantship along with waiving all tuition. My undergraduate psychology professors, men toward whom I looked with admiration and strivings toward identification, all had a psychoanalytic bent. I and they had no idea that much of academic psychology outside of New York City eschewed psychoanalysis and embraced the alien area of experimental psychology. In contrast to my undergraduate experience, in my graduate program, clinical psychology was behavior therapy, and psychoanalysis was seen, as one senior professor noted, as "the greatest hoax of the 20th century." If any of the graduate students had been known to be in personal analytic therapy, they likely would have been booted out of the program. I went undercover, learning and manifestly embracing the early behavior therapies while rejecting this privately, spending as much time as possible in a local Veterans Administration clinic where some psychologists had a psychoanalytic bent. I secretly plotted to pursue analytic training if I ever survived the University of Maryland. I had learned, at least in this setting, that my oppositional ways and my negations had to be private – I would clearly not have received my doctorate otherwise. In this setting, there was zero tolerance for oppositionalism, and in the context of great fear, I adapted. However, in most other professional venues, I continued to develop my identifications more often than not by open negation of what was prevailing. As readers will see, this often led to a combination of acute misery and eventual reward.

I will speak in more detail about each of these eras, but in prologue, oppositional thinking and/or behaving dominated my graduate school years as a young clinician at the Veterans Administration, during my internship at a well-respected hospital and mental health center, and then later, at my first hospital job in another well-regarded setting, as well as in my first psychoanalytic teaching appointment. In my subsequent analytic training, I embraced the Interpersonal psychoanalytic tradition, what was then known as both a minority and oppositional psychoanalytic perspective. Though I found a home in this rebellious community, I nonetheless conveyed open criticism to some of my weaker Interpersonal teachers and also toward others holding different theoretical viewpoints. This eventually came back to haunt me. However, having ultimately survived the often difficult positions in which I placed myself through excessive oppositionalism and negativity, I forged a way of thinking that has consistently defined the way I work and think, much of this expressed in the body of my work as an analyst, a teacher, and in my published writing.

A behavioral start

Let me start with the behaviorism of my graduate school days, a period in the early to middle 1960s when this perspective was in its burgeoning infancy. As noted, though I embraced this as a survival mechanism, I found it easy to learn and quickly felt like an expert, while I was critical of its limited range and simplicity in private. Indeed, learning behavioral therapies could not be more different than the extremely slow and gradual process of developing as a psychoanalytic practitioner. By the time I completed my dissertation, focusing on teaching mothers in groups to do reinforcement therapy with their diagnosed autistic and schizophrenic young children, I had co-authored three papers and believed that I had mastered these techniques to the point that I could establish a lucrative practice and a public name at the ground floor of a new clinical field. My dissertation results were positive, but rather than embrace the mode of treatment that produced this, I began to try to deconstruct this therapy process. I eventually concluded that the benefit these seriously disturbed children derived from their mothers' behavioral ministrations was more a function of their mothers' intense constructive/positive attention and involvement than the behavioral techniques per se. I concluded that when therapy succeeded, it was a function of the improved quality of the mutual relationship that was most responsible. I had no way of knowing at the time that this way of thinking was the precursor of my ideas about the therapeutic action of psychoanalysis, indeed, about the very essence of psychoanalytic praxis (e.g., Hirsch, 1994, 1996, 1998).

My experience with and rejection of behavior therapy in general, and my vision of what had happened with the children and parents who were my subjects, were very important to my subsequent psychoanalytic thinking in two other ways. First, I developed a distaste for technical ideas and applications, believing that these were too wooden and concrete to capture how people may change. "It's the relationship, stupid," ultimately became a sort of a mantra for me. Second, and more controversial than this, was the beginning embrace of the nurture position in the "nature vs. nurture" controversy. Because I was able to see, even to measure changes that occurred in the context of a new kind of relationship for some profoundly dysfunctional children, I concluded, and still do to this day, that emotional problems and personality formation have little to do with inherited biology or neurology and everything to do with the history of internalized relations with key others, and the unconscious repetition of these patterned configurations. Though many of my current colleagues may agree with me that this might be true for what may be called "normal" neurotic problems, most disagree that this holds for phenomena like psychoses, addiction, severe depression, extreme obsessive–compulsive behavior, and other more troublesome symptoms. My graduate school exposure to the behavior therapies led directly to an embrace of its opposite, as well as to a negation of the highly technical aspects of all therapies and to any endogenous explanation of personality formation.

Skepticism

My skepticism toward and opposition to the various prevailing wisdoms to which I was exposed was reinforced by a series of experiences with the profession of psychiatry. Given my family background, my response to the plight and the counsel of my father in particular, it was almost inevitable that I searched for the flaws of the "bosses," the medical mental health hierarchy. Starting with my experiences working with the Veterans Administration, these flaws were not hard to find. Though I have always been deeply indebted toward my psychoanalytically oriented colleagues and supervising psychologists, I found the psychiatrists in the V.A. either totally incompetent bureaucrats or professional bottom-scrapers who used tyranny to compensate for their inadequacy. This certainly has not been my experience of many psychiatrists, particularly psychoanalytic ones who I have met subsequently, but the former were easy targets for my mockery. Their efforts to apply the diagnostic and medical model to personal problems only served to reinforce my distaste and rejection of this model. Szasz's (1961) powerful and controversial exposition of the *Myth of Mental Illness* helped give my views some heft and beautifully articulated my emerging point of view. At the V.A., veterans were treated for "service connected disabilities." Their disability pensions were totally dependent on the maintenance of a diagnosed emotional disability. Most of them did not work and earned their total living from their disability pensions. To get better amounted to a 100% loss of income, and it was rare to find any of these many outpatients becoming less symptomatic. They would cycle through one psychology trainee after another, and both parties would engage in the pro forma ritual of psychotherapy. We trainees needed to practice our psychotherapy, and the patients needed to come in and do everything possible to maintain their diagnosis and their otherwise dysfunctional way of life. It paid to be crazy and to stay crazy.

This most frustrating but important experience helped me to further negate the diagnostic and medical model, and to begin to think of symptoms as largely adaptive – anything but illness or disability. At this time, the middle 1960s, not only Szasz, but Searles (1965, 1979) was scathingly skewering the medical model and notions of symptoms as expressing anything analogous to medical illness and/or simply pitiable affliction. For Searles, following Sullivan (1953), all problems in living were seen as adaptations to life circumstances, and acts of consciously or unconsciously motivated will and resilience. As miserable as any given patient might be, he or she is likely to hold on dearly to symptoms that create a familiar and a personal equilibrium. Searles turned the notion of illness on its heels, viewing the therapist as weak in his usually futile efforts to get patients to change what is all too comfortable and familiar, if not misery-making and unfulfilling as well. Nothing could have reinforced my rejection of authority and of conventional wisdom more than Searles' profound articulation of my nascent observations.

I took these views into my clinical internship, spending one year at one of the premier psychiatric settings in the Midwest at the time (middle 1960s), the Lafayette Clinic of the Wayne State School of Medicine in Detroit. Once again, the psychologists tended to be psychoanalytically oriented, while most of the psychiatrists, even those psychoanalytically trained, tended to wear white medical coats and espouse views about therapy that were diagnostically based. That is, they stressed the significance of evaluating patients' problems as either neurotically based or as structurally damaged, the former group amenable to analytic treatment and the latter clearly not so. Residents were taught what looked to me like a wooden method of distinction – enumerating behavioral signs that added up to a profile of one or another diagnosis, a method clearly in continuity with medical school training. In their defense, the notion that psychoanalytic treatment is relevant only to problems not especially debilitating had been long held, and now, 47 years later, is yet even more prevailing. As is the repetitive theme in this chapter, this experience only reinforced my oppositional embrace of the idea that personality is purely a function of lived and internalized experience, and that psychoanalytic therapy is applicable, albeit often quite difficult, with highly dysfunctional individuals.

It was during this period, with the aid of writers like Harold Searles and Thomas Szasz, two of the very few who also thought critically, that I began to interpret privately that conceptions of medical illness and diagnostic thinking serve two basic defensive functions for those in the mental health field: for one, I believe that it provides a false sense of clarity and a diminishment of uncomfortable ambiguity, considerably reducing the anxiety of uncertainty; for another, it allows practitioners to live with the illusion that they are well in contrast with their ill patients. I gradually grew to believe that this affirmation of relative wellness is often a motivating factor for many who enter the mental health field, and is a most destructive force in the practice of all forms of psychotherapy. Sullivan's (1953) assertion that we are all more simply human than otherwise, and Racker's (1968) proclamation that psychoanalysis is decidedly not a relationship between a well therapist and an ill patient, have served as guiding lights for me. To this day, they represent rare voices of diminished hierarchy between patients and those of us who treat them and/or write about them.

My early development in life that led to skeptical and rebellious thinking and behaving toward authority found fertile ground in what I had hoped and expected to find in a field that was less hierarchical than other professions. It is fitting that when I began to write in the late 1970s, my first published article focused on the authoritarian aspects of the psychoanalytic relationship (Hirsch, 1980–1981), and my second article on criticizing diagnostic thinking (Hirsch, 1986). It is worth noting that my first published article was in a rather radical journal that soon folded, and that my second paper, written in 1981, took five years and multiple rejections before finding its way to print. In spirit, my fourth published paper (Hirsch, 1984) was a critique of the conception of the ability to objectively assess analyzability. These ideas, all oppositional and based on highly skeptical attitudes toward majority thinking, as well as some direct negative personal experiences, were formed very early in my training, and to this day are continually affirmed, perhaps rigidly.

After receiving a degree from my behavioristic clinical doctoral program, I immediately escaped back to the psychoanalytic climate of New York City, and to a highly regarded two-year postdoctoral fellowship at Albert Einstein College of Medicine, at the time a beacon of both psychoanalytic thinking and innovation. Some of the psychiatrist–analysts did wear white coats; however, this institution was the most open to wide-ranging ideas and was the least hierarchical among the professions of any medical institution that I had seen and have seen to this day. I flourished here, felt little in the way of rebellion, and wished I could stay forever. And, unfortunately, I began to expect optimistically that subsequent institutions would reflect this atmosphere. I began my first real salaried staff job at Hillside Hospital on the Queens/Long Island (New York) border with this expectancy, and once again learned that expecting the worst was a safer route for me than any sort of optimism. Before describing this experience, let me circle back to one important personal negative experience referred to in the previous paragraph, for this occurred while I was on my fellowship at Einstein, and could have completely derailed me from pursuit of analytic training. Also, it is most relevant to the questions of diagnosis and analyzability and my fourth published article.

Starting treatment

During the last months of my time at the analytic mecca in the Bronx (Einstein), I had decided to pursue analytic training and to finally address some of my personal problems – to start the process of personal analysis. My financial situation required that I see someone in analytic training and who needed an additional patient to complete training. Through a trusted colleague, I was referred to a very advanced candidate, a psychiatrist at the well-regarded Columbia Psychoanalytic Institute (I now desperately wish I could recall his name). At the end of our initial consultation, I was told by this analyst that he could not see me – that I suffered from a narcissistic personality disorder and that I was not analyzable. His accuracy in assessing my narcissism notwithstanding, I was devastated. Until my next consultation with a far more senior analyst at the William Alanson White Institute (an enterprise for which I borrowed money), I believed that I would never be allowed to begin analytic training. When I was accepted into treatment by the man who was to become my one and only analyst, I almost jumped into his lap and embraced him. Readers can readily see how reinforcing this initial rejection was to my sentiments about diagnosis, though at the time I could only feel that this rejection was for good reason. Of course, rebounding from this awful negative moment led to my finding what was a much better analyst for me, and my deconstruction of this experience formed the basis of what I still believe is one of the best articles I ever published (Hirsch, 1984). This experience also went a long way in helping me begin to formulate how inherently subjective all analytic perceptions and interpretations are – to appreciate the very essence of Sullivan's (1953) conception of participant-observation, and for the relational turn that this core idea precipitated.

In the throes of my early enthusiasm about my own personal analysis, I happily chose Hillside Hospital expressly because of their specialization in working analytically with seriously disturbed, acute patients. The facility was developed by former Menninger Foundation psychiatrists and aspired to be "the Menninger of the East." I was so pleased with finally being a patient myself that I wanted to analyze everyone. The very negative part of this experience, however, related to my hopeful expectancy of a repeat of the diminished medical hierarchy that I had experienced during my postdoctoral fellowship, and to the unfortunate shift, within three and a half short years at Hillside, of a psychoanalytically oriented ethos to one that emphasized diagnosing patients empirically by how they responded to various drug treatments. During this time, the hospital directorship shifted from a renowned psychoanalyst to a leading expert on drug treatment. My angry ranting, initially against the psychiatric hierarchy and then about the increase of drug treatment, led to my nearly getting fired, and then to my leaving for full-time practice much sooner than I had planned. I had failed to find "a good boss," as my father had counseled, and at great financial risk and with enormous anxiety (I was about to become a father and was still in the middle of my analytic training at the NYU Postdoctoral Program), I became my own boss prematurely at age 33. I should add that I had wanted to become a "boss" myself at Hillside Hospital, and found it emotionally unbearable that psychiatrists less experienced and capable than me were promoted repeatedly to be my boss. Although I lived for some time with considerable anxiety[1] about being exclusively in practice, this premature move ultimately did work out well for me and for my family. Had my experience at this hospital not dissolved, I might have stayed too long and sacrificed some of the financial rewards that a full-time practice can provide.

In all fairness to Hillside Hospital, I do want to add that my experience was by no means all a negative one. I did meet my wife of now 40-plus years there, and I was part of a subset of the hospital (the Day Hospital) that did continue to work psychoanalytically in spite of the increased use of heavy-duty medications. Indeed, the experiences I had working analytically with patients who had recently made serious suicide attempts and/or were still in the throes of a psychotic break were among the most meaningful and richest of my whole career. Most of what I had come to believe through earlier experience, the support of my analytic supervisors at NYU and of my wife to be – also about to begin analytic training at the time – as well as the literature support of Harold Searles, was reinforced, though self-fulfilling prophecy cannot be discounted. Perhaps most significantly, I learned to not be especially frightened by explicit or implicit threats of suicide or of regression, and to not reflexively view very troubled patients as weak or fragile. The more anxious my colleagues and I were about what we saw initially as fragility, the more patients were likely to act this out, regress, and so on. The more we analyzed their motives for their actions and addressed the adaptive, willful, and agentic aspects of these, the more our patients became stronger. My clinical emphasis, as I originally learned in the Veterans Administration, tended toward the examination of each patient's conflicts around being a more functional person, and of the equilibrium, personal and familial, that led to extreme symptoms and regressive actions – what made them, in Searles (1979) words, "love their pathology." Working in this analytic way, I saw many instances of considerable psychological growth, often with minimal or no drug intervention, in many of those who passed through our day hospital. This was contrary to the pessimistic attitude characterized by a view of biologically or neurologically based endogenous wiring, a viewpoint which to this day dominates the thinking of the vast majority of psychotherapists and psychoanalysts.

My nurture over nature beliefs became etched in stone, as did my contempt for diagnostic categorization. Any notion of a biological or neurological etiology of psychological problems seems profoundly limiting, and ironically, in this context I am unusually optimistic about the possibility of shift in productive functioning. Indeed, if we are the usually unconscious agents of our own dysfunction, we have the power to do otherwise. Many of my interventions with patients of all types focus on pointing out how the problems that they consistently make for themselves are unconsciously motivated by the usually unconscious wish to maintain personal and familial equilibrium. This way of thinking about the origins and maintenance of the range of deficient fulfillment in love and in work absolutely guides my own work.

It is also ironic to me that with all of the evolution in psychoanalytic thinking characterized by the postmodern or relational turn in our field, conceptions of endogenously based biological and/or neurological chemistry are used to explain the genesis of even more personality qualities than during the earlier era I have just described. For example, what used to be referred to as psychologically based neurotic depression is now often described as an endogenous "bipolar" disorder, with medications viewed as the primary form of therapy. Popular diagnoses like "OCD," with its implication that obsessive and compulsive characteristics are inborn, stimulate the highly critical attitude that I otherwise have tried so hard to modify in myself. Unfortunately, I would say that most of my respected psychoanalytic colleagues would subscribe to such views, and also have embraced a more nature over nurture view than in earlier generations of analysts. My own position is in stark opposition to this – simply stated, emotional states produce changes in biology and in brain function, not normally the reverse. When we are miserable, our serotonin and testosterone (in men) levels drop – our misery is not caused by an endogenous decline. Fortunately, I am not alone in embracing this perspective, and indeed, there has even been some neurological research in particular (see Schore, 2005) that supports this reversal of what has become a majority held nature bias in understanding the development of personality.

Fragility vs. agency

My strongly critical and too often contemptuous attitude toward what I believe is a significant bias toward viewing patients as more weak, fragile, and frankly egoless and deficient (biologically, neurologically, and psychologically) than they actually are, cannot be separated from my own personal history and life experience. As noted earlier, my own mother lived her life as a highly anxious woman who conveyed that any sort of change may create a level of anxiety that was intolerable. Though never in therapy or on medication, she raised her only child in a way that was very protective, symbiotic, and confining. I was infantilized, treated as fragile and as dependent as she experienced herself. How I emerged from this was a major subject of my own analysis and far too indulgent to present in this venue. Needless to say, however, therapeutic points of view that emphasize patients' weakness and fragility are subject to my disdainful ire and to my sometimes overt criticism – they come too close to the home from which I have desperately tried to emerge.

A critique of what I viewed as overly nurturing and infantilizing modes of therapy, particularly how I understood Winnicottian and Kohutian ideas of therapeutic action to play out in the transference–countertransference matrix, was the subject of my third published psychoanalytic article (Hirsch, 1983). My embrace of a minority Interpersonal perspective while in analytic training seemed in stark opposition to what had become the prevailing non-Freudian perspective of the time, the developmental arrest model. Alongside exposure to Searles, my experience with teachers/authors like Wolstein (1959), Levenson (1972), and Singer (1977), and to the writing of their teachers (Fromm, 1941; Thompson, 1950), supported my intuitive embrace of patients as agentic, as unconscious repeaters of earlier experiences and as designers of their own lives.

I am critical of general conceptions that emphasize explanation of current problems as reflective of passive victimization, in contrast with the more likely propensity to unconsciously repeat the past in the present. I feel unabashedly opposed to a common bias that is more inclined to see the weakness in people than to see resiliency, to see passivity instead of unconscious choice, to see only injury and to never see aggression (or sexuality, for that matter). It is clear to me, of course, that the passivity of both of my parents and the infantilizing ways of my mother lead me to sometimes recoil when I read or hear clinical material with a strong Winnicottian or traditional self psychology bent. I know that these analysts help people too, though the rejection of these perspectives that have such a large following in our field has, for better or for worse, helped me to clearly define my own point of view and to actively teach and write about these comparisons as well.

The reference made earlier to having been dismissed from my first analytic teaching and supervisory experience is relevant here. This occurred in the late 1970s at the Institute for Contemporary Psychotherapy in New York. Because this institute was founded by graduates of William Alanson White and had many Interpersonally identified colleagues on its faculty, I thought I would find another place that I could call home. While teaching and supervising, however, I found that the theoretical position of the key administrators had shifted toward something closer to the developmental deficit conceptualizations alluded to above. In my immaturity and arrogance, I openly railed against this thinking with my supervisees, classroom students, and in faculty meetings to the point of intolerability to the administration. Of course, I still believe that my criticisms were most warranted, though this was the first of a number of injuries that I had to go through before learning to contain some of my feelings, and to channel them into my writing and work with my own patients. And, on the theme of turning the negative into something constructive, my having been fired was the first step of my initiating a dialogue with six of my colleagues from NYU Postdoctoral about forming a new psychoanalytic institute with a decidedly Interpersonal bent. The Manhattan Institute for Psychoanalysis was born in 1981, and I was its first co-director, and then director. This institute, alive and well today, would never have happened had I and one other of my close colleagues not first been fired in 1978.

Opposing the ruling class

It is difficult to organize this chapter entirely chronologically, for there are too many overlapping experiences and events to allow this. Also, some of my inchoate influences did not become clearly articulated for me for many years. For a moment I will dip back in time, tracing a bit the evolution of my interest in psychoanalysis and some of the origins of what grew out of opposition to what was the "ruling class" in the field. For example, the evolution of my Interpersonal psychoanalytic identity began before I even knew that there were competing psychoanalytic points of view, and were gradually shaped by my exposure to academic, clinical, and personal experiences, many already described in preceding paragraphs.

As noted, my interest in psychoanalysis originated during my undergraduate exposure to psychology professors who were analytically oriented therapists (and patients) themselves. A few were charismatic teachers and seemed extremely self-possessed and at ease with themselves and with speaking openly about sex. I wanted to be like them. I assumed that their personal analyses were largely responsible for their apparent free-spiritedness and strength of character, and hoped that one day I might arrive at a similar place. Despite all parties residing in the ecumenical city of New York, psychoanalysis as I was introduced to it referred to classical Freudian psychoanalysis only, and the undergraduate dimension of this was my exclusive exposure. The heart of the Freudian theory seemed to be all about sex, and this was very exciting to my 20-year-old self. I would enthusiastically race to the bookstore after class and skim through all of the psychoanalytic books with sex or perversion in the title, though time after time I found nothing erotic in the texts. The writing sounded very technical and scientific (e.g., "cathexis," "counter-cathexis," "negative/reverse oedipal"), though I assumed I would find something in the literature that sounded like erotic experience as I knew it – indeed, with which I was preoccupied. I never did during this period and any time after. I sensed that somewhere there must be a psychoanalytic literature that spoke to me, though I could not read Freudian literature without becoming drowsy. I have a very non-technical mind, and starting as an undergraduate, through analytic training and to this day, I find the significant majority of this literature to be both so technical and/or so overly theoretical that it fails to capture for me very much about the flesh and blood of people. Essentially, though I had no knowledge of alternate ways of thinking, I started personal analysis, quite coincidentally, with someone representing the Interpersonal tradition. Soon after this I began training at the NYU Postdoctoral Program and pursued courses and supervision with its Interpersonal faculty. Once again, the often called oppositional school's (aka Interpersonal) rejection of what was the dominant and prevailing perspective helped define my choices.

Returning to only some semblance of chronology, in part influenced by my identification with my own analyst, by the time I was ready to begin analytic training I clearly wanted to be a non-Freudian analyst. At NYU, I found an ideal home with a group of virulently anti-Freudian teachers and supervisors. Most of them had been trained in the minority tradition of the Interpersonal school, primarily at the William Alanson White Institute. At the time (early to middle 1970s), the Interpersonal perspective was considered by the vast majority of credentialed psychoanalysts as an oppositional school – that is, as having little to offer that was constructive and as relishing the position of being radical and contrary for its own sake. The terms "wild analysis" or "cultural school" or "social psychology" were often used to discredit this perspective. I loved the position of again being one among a group of some charismatic teachers who indeed relished skewering what was the psychoanalytic ruling class – the Freudian hegemonic bosses. Initially, this aspect of my analytic identity was more important than the actual substance of Interpersonal thinking. I was, however, able to enjoy and to understand at least a reasonable amount of the Interpersonal literature, and along with my supervision and personal analysis, began to appreciate this tradition for reasons beyond rejection and opposition to the majority.

What I most embraced was the decidedly non-hierarchical attitude characterized by Harry Stack Sullivan's (1953) credo of the shared flawed humanity and subjectivity of both patients and analysts. That is, we analysts are no more inherently healthy than are our patients, nor do we view matters with any more objectivity than do our patients. Of course, this emphasis on mutual subjectivity as well as mutual influence became the hallmark of the postmodern turn in psychoanalysis, though Sullivan (e.g., 1953), Erich Fromm (e.g., 1941), Clara Thompson (e.g., 1950), Benjamin Wolstein (e.g., 1959), Edgar Levenson (e.g., 1972), Erwin Singer (e.g., 1977), and their Interpersonally identified colleagues writing between the 1940s and 1970s rarely get the credit they merit for initiating this contemporary spirit. Rejection of and opposition to the overly hierarchical attitudes of Freudian analytic objectivity, and then to Winnicottian and Kohutian views of patients as inherently fragile and deficient and in need of repaired parenting, still stand as central to my thinking, working, teaching, and writing. However, since the postmodern turn, there is now much to embrace in some of the literature of all the current theoretical orientations. Aside from Interpersonal and Relational writing per se, some analysts identified as Freudian, Self-Psychological, and Object-Relational are writing in ways that converge powerfully with the less hierarchical and more intersubjective thought which has always resonated with me. I have written about this convergence (Hirsch, 1996, 1998) and I celebrate it, though I am still fueled to oppositional passion by those individuals from all traditions who embrace biological or neurological antecedents of personality, or who speak of some diagnostic categories of patients as egoless, lacking internal structure, and as otherwise deficient (inherently in contrast with the allegedly sufficient therapist).

Expelled

This chapter would be incomplete without reference to the most negative experience in my career – my essential expulsion from my comfortable home in the Interpersonal track of NYU in the dawn of the early 1980s, five to six years after graduating this program in 1975. This experience affected me so deeply and made me so miserable that I could probably write a short book about it, though a brief summary only makes sense in this context. Yet, alongside the acute unhappiness and loneliness that I felt having been kicked out of my cherished home at NYU, the net outcome of this trauma (I believe this term is warranted) has been a level of ambition and productivity that never would have materialized otherwise. This theme reflects the consistent thread throughout this chapter.

Avoiding the temptation to excavate all of the ugly details and perceived villains involved, I was nominated by the faculty selection committee of the Interpersonal track (after the minimum five years post-graduation) to become a supervisor in the program, a highly prestigious appointment at the time for such a recent graduate. When this nomination came to the governing body of the entire Postdoctoral community, some members of my own track spoke so violently against me that my nomination was withdrawn before it was even put to a vote. Three years later, the same committee, believing that an injustice had been done, re-nominated me. The initial violent objections were repeated, despite original apologies for the earlier experience and a promise by some who spoke against me that this would not happen again. My nomination was defeated by one Postdoctoral senate vote. I became disengaged from my former home for roughly 20 years, until some of those who most objected to me had either retired or had become old and ill, and a new core leadership approached me and asked if I were willing to once again go through the nomination process. Despite great fear of repetition, I did, and this time there were no objections and the process went smoothly for me.

Though I believe I was treated most unfairly, and that my punishment far exceeded my crimes, it would be most inconsistent with my thesis throughout this chapter to claim simple victimization. The Interpersonal track at NYU at the time, like most organizations, had "bosses," albeit unofficial ones. In a variety of ways that at the time I did not consider especially egregious, I both disagreed with and took actions that were contrary to some of the principle leaders. A number of these disagreements were related to the formation of the Manhattan Institute, which to our gratitude was endorsed and backed by our senior teachers and supervisors. This backing, however, became contingent on the seven founders of the Manhattan Institute paying heed to the wishes of some of our seniors, and we did not consistently do this. As first co-director and, all too arrogantly I am sure, as spokesperson for our differences, I became the lightning rod for the wrath of some of our seniors. They conveyed a sense of having been what they referred to as betrayed and disrespected. These important administrative faculty of the Interpersonal track claimed to be very hurt by me, and subsequently went against the track's recommendation of my supervisory appointment, with the argument that I was a hurtful person and would likely hurt my students. I have no doubt that my oppositional qualities and my inclination to give all too unfettered voice to my strong opinions made these charges appear plausible. Indeed, as reported, I did almost get fired from my first salaried hospital job, and did get fired from my first appointment at an analytic institute. Both of these earlier painful experiences led directly to my embrace of something ultimately very productive, and I struggled for years to do the same with this, my most negative experience of all.

Though I would never again consciously put myself and my family through what occurred at NYU, I credit this awful experience and my response to it for much of what has proven productive in my subsequent professional and even personal life. On a personal level, I believe that I finally learned to contain what had been a tendency to give aggressively tinged free voice to strong beliefs and to what I opposed. I have become far less argumentative and confrontational in personal contact with colleagues, more inclined to give voice to my strong beliefs in the more positive and constructive realms of teaching and writing, as I hope is in evidence in this chapter. I also think that I feel at least somewhat more accepting of some disparate points of view than I used to feel, though I do wonder if I just have had enough battle wounds to finally learn the virtue of diplomacy in direct contact with colleagues.

I wish to be very clear, however, that the level of ambition that has fueled my writing, public presenting, and subsequent psychoanalytic affiliations would never have developed to the degree that it has if I had remained safe and secure at NYU Postdoctoral. Shorn of the security of this home, I was terrified that I would not survive professionally and financially. This terror, with two young children to co-support, led to an enormous pressure to redeem myself, to reclaim my respectability once again, and to do everything possible to get patient and supervisory referrals in order to earn a decent living. I pushed myself to write – to write a lot – and to make a good name for myself through this vehicle. I began to get published, and used this to secure speaking engagements and teaching and supervisory appointments at other institutes. This level of ambition, with its origins in terror and desperation, has become an integral part of my professional self. I still push in order to solidify my place in my profession, and I still have some fears that I could lose this. I certainly remain cautious of any trace of unmitigated optimism in any realm of my life. Despite what some would argue, I believe – following the credo of Erich Fromm (e.g., 1941) – that anxiety is often a great motivator for me, perhaps the most powerful.

Final thoughts

In summary, both learning from and forming an identity from negation, oppositionalism, and in rebounding from frank negative experience has characterized my professional life, and though to a now far lesser degree, my personal life as well. That this still remains a strong motivating force probably speaks to a certain intransigence and rigidity. The fact that I still push myself in order to avoid being either "bossed" or viewed as fragile, and enjoy taking at least some strong positions that reflect a stance in strong opposition to the majority, reflects something about the adaptive nature of personality development, including characterological problems. In spite of injury and derailments, this way of being works for me. This is inextricably connected to so much of what I consider to be the essentials of whatever professional achievements I have enjoyed. Aside from the inherently indulgent personal background information I have provided here, I hope I have made clear some of my valued points of view that are distinct from what I believe to be the perspectives shared by the considerable majority of psychoanalysts. Indeed, I am disappointed if this is not so.

Note

1 The common anxiety about the ability to earn a sufficient income in full-time practice for oneself and/or one's family is rarely written about and is something I have tried to address in my book (Hirsch, 2008). Though my wife, also a psychoanalyst, contributed equally to our earnings, the terror of not holding down my share of income, with nothing guaranteed, stayed with me for quite some time. In part because of the power of this experience, two full chapters of my book are devoted to issues related to money. Indeed, I suggest that anxiety centered around needed income is the single biggest countertransference related problem in our field. Related to financial concerns, analysts are prone to make enormous compromises in the analytic work, much of it within ethical boundaries, though often marginally so. I believe that the most common of these compromises is the inclination to keep patients in therapy too long, often far too long. Almost all clinical examples in my book come from my own practice and my guilty self-reflection about my own work. Of course, it is possible that given my own lower-middle-class roots, economic anxiety has been more pronounced for me than for others of us. For an excellent additional discussion of the financial anxieties involved in being in full-time private practice, see also Bandini (2011).

References

Bandini, C. (2011). The good job: Financial anxiety, class envy and drudgery in beginning a private analytic practice. *Contemporary Psychoanalysis, 47*, 101–117.

Fromm, E. (1941). *Escape from freedom.* New York: Holt, Rinehart & Winston.

Hirsch, I. (1980–1981). Authoritarian aspects of the analytic relationship. *Review of Existential Psychology and Psychiatry, 17*, 105–133.

Hirsch, I. (1983). Analytic intimacy and the restoration of nurturance. *American Journal of Psychoanalysis, 43*, 325–343.

Hirsch, I. (1984). Toward a more subjective view of analyzability. *American Journal of Psychoanalysis, 44*, 169–182.

Hirsch, I. (1986). Sexual disorders: A perspective. *American Journal of Psychoanalysis, 46*, 239–248.

Hirsch, I. (1994). Countertransference love and theoretical model. *Psychoanalytic Dialogues, 4*, 171–192.

Hirsch, I. (1996). Observing-participation, mutual enactment and the new classical models. *Contemporary Psychoanalysis, 32*, 359–384.

Hirsch, I. (1998). The concept of enactment and theoretical convergence. *Psychoanalytic Quarterly, 67*, 78–101.

Hirsch, I. (1999). Contrasting classical American film with, "The Crying Game." *Journal of the American Academy of Psychoanalysis, 27*, 151–166.

Hirsch, I. (2008). *Coasting in the countertransference: Conflicts of self-interest between analyst and patient.* New York: Routledge.

Hirsch, I. (2011). Narcissism, mania and analysts' envy. *American Journal of Psychoanalysis, 71*, 363–369.

Hirsch, I., & Hirsch, C. (2000). Seinfeld's humor noir: A look at our dark side. *Journal of Popular Film and Television, 28*, 116–123.

Levenson, E. (1972). *The fallacy of understanding.* New York: Basic Books.

Racker, H. (1968). *Transference and countertransference.* New York: International Universities Press.

Schore, A. (2005). A neuropsychoanalytic point of view. *Psychoanalytic Dialogues, 15*, 829–854.

Searles, H. (1965). *Collected papers on schizophrenia and related subjects.* New York: International Universities Press.

Searles, H. (1979). *Countertransference and related subjects.* New York: International Universities Press.

Singer, E. (1977). The fiction of analytic anonymity. In K. Frank (Ed.), *The human dimension in psychoanalytic practice* (pp. 181–192). New York: Grune & Stratton.

Sullivan, H. S. (1953). *The interpersonal theory of psychiatry.* New York: Norton.

Szasz, T. (1961). *The myth of mental illness.* New York: Harper & Row.

Thompson, C. (1950). *Psychoanalysis: Evolution and development.* New York: Hermitage.

Wolstein, B. (1959). *Countertransference.* New York: Grune & Stratton.

6

OUT FROM HIDING

Kenneth A. Frank

Approaching this chapter with carte blanche to write about virtually any subjective topic I might choose, ironically, and surprisingly to me, I found myself confronting some of the very same issues that inspired me to undertake *The Human Dimension in Psychoanalytic Practice* way back in 1977. That book, a compilation of essays exploring the analyst's subjectivity, was similar in spirit to this one. In it, I criticized the paucity of self-revealing publications by analysts at the time, noting that there existed – publicly, at least – a "phobic attitude toward the inner life of the analyst" (p. 2). I saw analysts' personal openness and the dialogue associated with what I then called the "human dimension" in our work as essential – beneficial to us, to patients, and to the field in general.

As I considered how far both the field and I have and have not come since then, I saw the echoing of my past experience as commentary on the enduring power of issues of openness and concealment as they affect the analyst's professional life. Like all individuals, analysts are always balancing this tension, consciously and unconsciously, as part of self- and mutual regulation. Often, we do not realize it, don't necessarily know much or anything about *what* we are concealing, or *why*. The compelling struggle I have experienced over the trajectory of my career – between letting others know me as fully as I or they might wish and the need to safeguard my privacy, and the role that has played professionally and especially clinically – has led me to discuss that theme here. I approach "Out from hiding" hoping it will have didactic value, at the very least aiding or inspiring struggling young therapists who are coming into the field.

Introduction: writers' anxiety

A long-term patient of mine, also a therapist, apologetically and tentatively expressed interest in my personal and professional development. Her questioning piqued my reservations about my role in this project. She observed admiringly, "You always seem so calm, comfortable with yourself. Were you always like that?" In recent years, I've heard that observation made by patients time and again, and they have many reactions to that quality, while finding it basically reassuring. I chuckled and told my patient about this chapter, candidly explaining that becoming more relaxed and open had, in fact, been a long and often difficult journey. Her question also caused me to wonder: What effect might my openness have on an unprepared patient who might happen upon this intimately written memoir? For that matter, I questioned what faceless readers unknown to me, who undoubtedly would see *through* these transparent pages as well as read what I had written on them, would think of me. Feeling proud of certain milestones that resulted from and also led to and reinforced my growth and willingness to be known, could I discuss them openly without appearing boastful? Would some interpret certain admissions as weaknesses or psychopathology? Or might they identify and appreciate the feelings of self-esteem I have gained? Struggling with how to approach this chapter, which among other concerns I had to write in a voice unfamiliar to me – more literary than scholarly – raised many questions and doubts. How open could I, would I, or ought I be? I came to realize that this chapter is itself an enactment of its title and theme, embodying my personal struggle between concealment and a willingness to be known. I realized, too, that it's time for those of us who endorse openness, to "walk the walk."

The early years

I'll start with the beginning of my professional journey. During the early stages of a psychotherapist's career, hiding is inevitable, given how little the beginner actually knows about the process and the high level of therapeutic expectations (real and imagined) we and our patients often have of us. When I was 22 and in graduate school studying clinical psychology, my classmates and I were so anxious before phoning to arrange our first clinical appointments that we informally role-played those intimidating assignments. Despite our having completed our first year of training, and now entering the second year, it seemed as though the interviewing skills we had been taught in the classroom would be of little use in the consulting room. My introduction to "real life" clinical work only corroborated my fears. I can recall sitting across the room from my earliest patients feeling overwhelmed by their accounts of their difficulties. Feeling pressured to make some sense of what I was hearing, I would hurriedly shuffle through a mental catalogue of options simply for understanding, no less helping – among them, schemas for diagnosis, psychodynamics, developmental history, the interaction process between us, and more – all rudimentary and blurred by my mounting anxiety. I later learned to dignify that anxiety by naming it "countertransference." Great! It had a name. But that didn't help me understand myself and what I was feeling or do much for the suffering person seated across from me, whom I seemed to understand so poorly.[1] That person was in need of some meaningful help and was looking to *me* of all people to deliver it. During those early days, I felt ineffectual, like a poseur.

At that time, when analytic therapy was informed by a positivist epistemology, emphasizing knowledge over uncertainty and the "right way" to proceed technically that would lead to given results, my becoming able – ever – to do psychotherapy effectively, seemed impossible. Given the intense anxiety I felt at moments during those early sessions – sometimes accompanied by the impulse to flee the room – hiding seemed like one of the more reasonable options. Unlike taking flight, which was tantamount to abandoning my patient, retreating into analytic abstinence and anonymity were "legitimate" forms of hiding.

I have many memories of agonizing moments during my early years in the field. An example of one that intensified my anxiety and encouraged my penchant for hiding involved an attractive young woman, the second outpatient assignment to me during my hospital-based psychology internship, and perhaps my third or fourth case. She was a well-functioning woman in her early 30s, older and apparently worldlier than I, and during our first session she told me the story of her abusive relationship with her estranged husband. I listened attentively, feeling, well, dumbfounded as I attempted to understand her and process my experience with her. I felt paralyzed – by her story, by my own clinical ignorance, and by a host of reasons I couldn't even formulate – not knowing where to break in, how, what to ask, or why. To make matters worse, as if out of nowhere, at the end of this very uncomfortable session, I was shocked when I had a sudden impulse to kiss her goodnight!

It dawned on me much later that my discomfort during the session had been informed by my attraction to her, a new experience for me as a clinician, and one I apparently had worked unconsciously to disavow. This was a moment of awakening – when I realized as a clinician that, try as I might, I could not leave myself outside the room, that there was no place to hide. Moreover, I thought, one can never know for sure what to expect of the clinical interaction at any given moment. Becoming aware of both the inherent uncertainty and the necessity for constructive improvisation within the work at a time when I was hardly capable of handling either, did nothing to improve my comfort level. I simply hoped this woman would be able to find herself a *real* therapist. And how was I to discuss this professionally inappropriate, thoroughly unexpected "lapse" and embarrassing role confusion with my supervisor, who was, by the way, the tyrannical psychiatric director of the outpatient service and was skeptical of having psychology interns on his service? Today I might consider, among other more informed ways of understanding my reaction, her potential wish to be romantically rescued. How helpful it would have been to be able to think about it that way! But I never got close to finding that out – that patient never returned, and my shame prevented me from discussing it.

Internship was my most trying year. The hospital atmosphere was charged, tense, and competitive. Gamesmanship abounded, especially between the psychiatry residents and the clinical psychology interns, whom the residents, comfortably ensconced in their medical setting, preferred to view as second-class. I entertained many and intense self-doubts. At times, I remember struggling painfully over whether I had even chosen the "right" profession. Did I have the temperament to handle the "hot seat" the therapist's chair seemed so often to become, especially when patients turned their passions to me directly, rather than talking about feelings toward others? Was I even smart enough? Could I ever square theory with practice in a way that would truly help others? I recall one mortifying day when, seated together in our shared office, I cathartically shared some of these intimate questions with my officemate, a close friend. I opened up the full measure of exasperation and pain my struggle involved. As I glanced out through the open door, I cringed as I spotted a patient of mine hovering there. Had he been in the nearby men's room, or was he listening in the hall? Had he heard my agonized rant? I suspected he had, although I would never know with certainty – that topic was one neither of us could dare to open up, presumably because I was in such an early, fragile stage of my professional development, which I imagine he recognized. In moments of mutual hiding such as these, treatment deteriorates into inauthentic, hollow play-acting.

In *The Human Dimension* (Frank, 1977), Avrum Ben-Avi writes about his early struggles in analytic training, and his own feelings of personal unsuitability for a career as an analyst. I imagine virtually all beginning students of psychotherapy have to contend with aspects of that concern. I remember being surprised to learn during those early days how predisposed I was to projection – that is, to seeing in my patients, in a manner I initially thought perceptive, what *I* would have experienced in their shoes, rather than what they actually did. When I was off the mark, they would correct me, helping me to hone my empathic skills and my sense of humility, but also causing me to experience feelings of self-doubt. Yet I always retained a quotient of optimism about my abilities, in no small part because of the encouragement and recognition I had received earlier in my clinical psychology training, such as when I was among a handful of clinical psychology students selected to supervise underclassmen. Such developments helped engender a sense that I had "the right stuff" to do the work. That offset many doubts and provided reassurance during challenging moments that came later.

Years later, as a senior clinician, I would realize how much we all need and rely on recognition and feeling legitimized by approval from our mentors, teachers, and supervisors. They all help us "come out of hiding," toward achieving what I see as the ultimate goal of training – blending who we are as individuals with clinical skills. But at that time, I felt very much alone. My lonely struggle to establish a solid sense of competence seemed to me at the time my unique problem. In those days, there were no forums for discussing such feelings. The formal medical culture at the hospital looked unfavorably upon discussing such feelings, which were viewed judgmentally.

Initially, I used the classical belief in analytic anonymity to justify maintaining a low profile. It was, after all, *the* standard analytic stance at the time of my training, and it dovetailed beautifully with a familiar self-protective penchant for hiding in my personal life. As an early adolescent, for instance, I had been a strong basketball player, yet in important games, I would never perform as well as in lesser ones or scrimmages. Instead, I felt disabling performance anxiety and choked, missing big shots that I'd nailed in practice, or even easy layups. If the coach benched me, I felt relieved. Eventually, with practice and playing time, I overcame that problem. I can recall the pleasure and satisfaction I felt as I grew into an effective power forward on the court, capable of using what I had – my size, strength, and skill – to compete comfortably and forcefully. My basketball experience is in many ways analogous to that in the consulting room, where hard study and long practice eventually brought pleasurable feelings of mastery that overcame my chronic uncertainty and anxiety. I have found this pleasure to be inherent in growth and mastery. I count on it in my patients and explore its absence with them when it is not felt.

Another sustaining factor during those early, trying years was purely intellectual; there had never before, nor has there since been a subject that challenged and fascinated me as much as human psychology, the mind, how people become the way they are, and how they change. To this day, and remarkably – it's more than half a century since I embarked on my career in psychology and psychoanalysis – I continue to be fascinated by the field, and as much as ever, want to learn all I possibly can.

Learning to hide

I first entered therapy as a freshman in college, when bored and underachieving academically, I was about to enlist for pilot training in the Air Force. Paradoxically, the initial insight into myself holding the most explanatory power for me was my need to keep low, not allowing myself to soar or others to discover all I could (or might not!) be. I had never been willing to risk "going for it," which meant taking the risk of either excelling or coming up short. That wasn't limited to basketball, I knew, but affected me in other areas like academics and dating. I avoided leadership roles and, especially, public speaking, anything that involved posing my secret grandiose self against my hidden potentially disappointing self.

An array of childhood factors accounted for my inclination to hide, which in many ways protected and served me well during my earliest years. In a nutshell, my mother was depressive and phobic. My job as her phobic companion and pint-sized therapist probably played a role in my career choice, as I suspect such childhood enactments do for many others in the helping professions. My father, more courageous and bold, was largely absent from my childhood, and when present he was rarely supportive. He was not available as the good friend and strong identification figure he later became for me. My sister, five years older than I, was troubled, erratic, and aggressive, and my parents couldn't control her. So a central challenge in my personal growth involved putting myself out there more and becoming able to freely express myself. There's no doubt that in my case, becoming a *relational* analyst, willing to be out there in the service of connecting constructively, is intimately tied to personal growth.

Given my shaky professional start, I never would have imagined that my course as a professional would ultimately form one of my most confidence-building experiences. Over the years, I gained confidence in my clinical intuition. For instance, my psychodynamically based internship training during the 1960s was steeped in an essentialist vision. I recall the moment when, witnessing a clinical interview, I had the unexplored idea that one of the many processes that occurred in therapy, despite therapists' assiduous attempts to minimize them, related to our constructive relationality and inevitable influence. I believed that a significant part of clinical success somehow involved communicating a more adaptive vision to the patient than the one s/he brought us. That undeveloped impression, I realized much later, was a precursor of the perspectivist position I came to endorse years afterward, along with recognition of the helpful role of therapists' influence. I did not come out with those early impressions, which many of us now take for granted, so they were solitary insights. The strained atmosphere of my internship setting was not conducive to expressing such opinions. But I did share these ideas with the much more supportive clinical faculty at downtown Columbia after I completed my internship and returned to my final academic year of doctoral training. There, I found my thinking and views discussed, considered, and appreciated, which was a great relief to me.

After receiving my doctorate, I sought analytic training at the Postgraduate Center. Understandably, I wanted a relaxed, open atmosphere that would be receptive to discussing controversial ideas, one that would, I now realize, help me come out of hiding. Although for the most part I did not find that atmosphere at Postgraduate and its classes, fortunately I did with some supervisors, who were mostly validating and progressive. Unfortunately, I was being indoctrinated into ego psychology in most of my classes and, for the most part, I tiptoed quietly through the training, tolerating what I was being taught despite my strong, developing disagreement with it. I was always impressed with those few fellow students who somehow found ways to challenge ideas without becoming provocative or alienating themselves. I also saw several who crossed that line and were subsequently "asked" to leave training. Keeping my clinical disagreements and developing perspectives to myself had become familiar behavior, but partly, too, it was reinforced when early on a senior supervisor and department head warned me that I was developing a reputation as defiant. (At year's end, he indirectly apologized.) But I suspect my inability to speak up consistently led me to do so in frustration at times, and in a manner that came across as intolerant of the ideas cherished by others. An inner tension was building, and I remember one day in class when I made the point to one of our most popular and progressive teachers that the model being endorsed and I just weren't getting along. I took some class time – fairly unusual for me in those days – to stick my neck out and try to explain that drives and impulses were not meaningful to me as a way of understanding, connecting with, or helping people. After I finished speaking, the teacher went on, almost as though I had said nothing. (Isn't it nice to feel not heard?)

The training analysis is crucial for developing one's own way of thinking and being and behaving, both as a person and as a clinician. A further problem of my analytic training was that my training analyst and I did not make a good match. Far from a sense that he had affirming feelings toward me, I felt him as disapproving. Known to be authoritarian, he struck me as threatened by our differences, and countered many of my attempts to break out. It felt to me as though he wanted to be right and be on top in a way that discouraged my expansiveness. If I'm describing unresolved transference, well, wasn't it his job to help me resolve it? It's always difficult to leave one's analyst; it's especially difficult to leave your training analyst, the Clinic Director, in mid-training. What would "the Institute" think?

A turning point

During the next phase of my career, after analytic training and into the early years of private practice, I began to accumulate evidence of my skills. Competing feelings of effectiveness and uncertainty did not coexist easily or comfortably, and I reentered therapy with an analyst and former supervisor at Postgraduate Center who had struck me as gifted and wise. This fortunate decision represented a turning point for me. I remember one session in particular. I was on the couch, and it was a time when he had chosen to remain silent in response to something I said, sitting behind me and out of view. I don't remember what I was discussing, but I needed some sort of response and wasn't getting one. I paused several times, waiting, but heard nothing. It didn't take long before I assumed he had fallen asleep, like my boyhood father, sitting in his club chair, dozing. I raised my voice to stir him. Still, there was no reply. Finally, quite certain that he was sound asleep, I announced that I was now going to turn to look at him (and face the rejection), which I did – only to find him staring at me wide-eyed and apparently amused, a living contradiction of what I expected! I was far more relieved than embarrassed, and we shared a good laugh over the incident. My analyst's very obvious and fundamental confidence in me and my abilities, and encouragement of my efforts, as well as his affection – a new experience compared with both my childhood father and my formal training analyst – were extremely helpful to me, as much if not more than any particular insight achieved.

This analyst, now deceased, was enormously helpful to me, and I hold him in deep affection. There is a great deal that I appreciate about him and the way he worked with me, and at the time I often emulated him. Yet he has always remained somewhat enigmatic to me. I didn't take well to certain qualities – his self-concealment, for example – and so also learned what I didn't want for myself as a practitioner. He also was less interactive than I would have liked and have become (notwithstanding the beneficial example I gave). In any event, I felt free with him as with no one before, safe to fully express myself, feeling deeply affirmed yet occasionally challenged. I took advantage of my newly felt freedom and expansiveness, and during that analysis, I began to write scholarly papers, seizing the opportunity to formulate my own ideas. Our work occurred during an unusually fertile time for me. Having completed analytic training, I was finally free from the oppressive influence so much of my training represented, and was in the process of co-founding the National Institute for the Psychotherapies (NIP). If he ever regarded our new institute as a competing one, I never felt it. He seemed fully supportive. (It never could have been that way with my training analyst.) It was also during this period that I met the woman I would later marry, and he was very helpful with intimacy issues that arose.

I attribute a great deal of my personal and professional growth to that analysis. Looking back, I can see that my coming out of hiding had been happening in fits and starts all along the way, but until this analysis I did not find enough encouragement and support to follow through. Unlike in the beginning of my career, I became much more confident about my clinical work, and to this day feel like I am becoming the person I was "meant to be." At Columbia, the same setting in which I initially quaked with anxiety as an intern, I later became a full Clinical Professor and for a period was director of the clinical psychology internship. Visible accomplishments, positions of influence and power which early on I could never have imagined for myself, went a long way toward filling my reservoir of self-esteem.

As once I grew comfortable on the basketball court, I likewise have grown more and more comfortable in the consulting room and beyond. I have learned to remain calmer and more optimistic with the uncertainty of the future, of not knowing, and to trust myself, my judgment, and the growth process. Getting to know these people, my patients, deeply, and their getting to know me well, has bolstered my sense of trust in others. Although I have a great hunger for further learning, I have settled certain basic controversies internally. For instance, I'm satisfied with a unique balance I have worked out between intrapsychic and interpersonal concerns – patiently exploring deeply, yet considering practical reality and "real-life" accountability and knowing that we don't have forever, that analysis happens in "real time."

Some relational implications: the frame

As my views have evolved and I've become more willing to be known by my patients, so has my clinical work. I see the "frame," once prescribed and constricting, as flexible and negotiable. Recently, I accompanied a single patient in her late 30s to her first gynecological appointment since college. She had lost her mother (at age 13), maternal grandmother, and maternal aunt to breast cancer and was traumatized by witnessing her mother's multiple hospitalizations and the extreme side effects of her chemotherapy, followed by her death. Clearly, my patient was at medical risk and it was essential that she be followed, but for years she had been terrified of visiting a doctor. No amount of analysis or encouragement had succeeded. When my patient returned to join me in the doctor's waiting room after her physical examination, she was sobbing, partly with relief over her healthy report, but I suspected that on some level, also from the now-ruptured bond to her deceased mother.

I was keenly aware, too, that I was *in locus parentis*: her father had become her primary caregiver after her mother's death, and he had died of cancer while my patient and I were working together. Because she was very upset, I didn't feel I could simply leave her directly after the appointment, as I had intended; instead, we spontaneously went to the hospital cafeteria for coffee, so that she could decompress and process her experience. Among other topics, she spoke about how she had used illness and the sick role as a basis for attachment, an enactment which, we realized, she and I were in the midst of. I knew I was "breaking the frame," was conflicted about what I was doing, and had consulted with respected colleagues before engaging in this admittedly unusual behavior. Beforehand, I had wondered how I would feel as I lived through this experience with her and was pleased that throughout I felt comfortably natural, in part, perhaps, because it took place at Columbia Medical Center, familiar to me as a faculty member for many years. Later, we attempted more thoroughly to understand the meanings of the experience, which was not disruptive but growth enhancing. As I left for my August break some months later, I told her I felt sad about our being separated for a while, more than in the past. She suggested it might be the result of the deepened bond her medical experience fostered between us. When I returned, I referred back to her observation, and that opened up a crucial exploration of her reflexive need to withhold appreciation and affection.

Many analysts would see my behavior – my involvement, a willingness to openly self-disclose and become authentically known in this way in an intimate, person-to-person relationship – as extreme or inappropriate. I cannot explain exactly how I arrived at this position because it evolved gradually over many years. It's attributable to a variety of personal, clinical, and didactic considerations – the totality of a life lived. And I am fully committed to it.

I'd like to share some major themes I've come to recognize. I can see that I progressively fulfilled and owned the confidence others had in me that I had used in former years to prop me up during difficult times – the academic successes and the supervisors who believed in and nurtured me, for example. Among the admired and highly accomplished colleagues who have personally shaped and encouraged my views were Stephen Mitchell, Paul Wachtel, and Irwin Hoffman. There have been many extra-professional considerations that have fostered my personal and professional growth as well. One is my 40-year marriage to a woman who I originally thought wouldn't give me a tumble. As intimate relationships grow and deepen, like many of our analytic relationships, I might add, one comes to question old lessons that taught mistrust and the necessity to hide. Likewise, raising children I feel proud of, who have lived their young lives fully, courageously, and richly, has had an enormous impact on me. My kids confirm Bowlby's (1979) thinking that life is best organized as a series of daring ventures from a secure base. If I helped create their foundation, in many respects they have grown beyond me, providing me with a sense of confidence in my generativity.

These personal and other developments emboldened and encouraged me to challenge what I had been taught and to push the analytic envelope. They also reinforced my belief in the extent to which new behaviors and interactions in the interpersonal world can affect us deeply. They bring to mind Atwood and Stolorow's (1979) work, describing how personal and contextual factors, and not necessarily purely clinical or intellectual ones, ultimately shape our theoretical visions.

Making it home

As I briefly mentioned earlier, I co-founded NIP. I did that with four other disenchanted graduates of analytic training when we were all around 30 years old. Given our youth at the time and the Institute's subsequent success, I often joke about our being "clueless wonders." The institute has been a very important factor in my life and growth, personally and clinically. The NIP suite – the site of its administrative offices, classes, treatment center, and meeting rooms – is also the location of my New York private practice. Apart from conducting the "business" of the Institute, the arrangement has demanded that I maintain multiple relationships with the many colleagues, supervisees, students, and even the occasional training analysand of mine. In the beginning – as a recent analytic graduate with what I would see as little more than a fair quality of training and modest experience – this complexity felt very uncomfortable. I had little to teach others at that stage of my career. But as a founder and director of an institute, how was I to learn to live with that conflict?

Although I tried to distance myself from the community of candidates early on, fortunately, over time, I grew to enjoy mingling with them, serving on committees with them, for instance, and seeing them at the Institute's gatherings. I most enjoy being among and getting to know candidates who themselves dare to be known and to get to know me, pushing my limits rather than standing off deferentially in filial transference – the latter being the kind of student I was inclined to be. A few candidates have even become social friends. I would also say the individual patient with whom I learned the most about the therapy process and myself is one who wouldn't settle for facile answers and superficial relating, but pushed me hard to let her know me.[2] She helped me know myself better through an exploration of territory I never would have entered without the external impetus she provided.

At NIP, I became comfortably "at home," being able to relate naturally while shifting fluidly among the work demands of different roles. I was relieved as I became less concerned with rank, and I no longer felt a need to be, or to be seen as, anything more than I was, or to be seen as someone I wasn't. As I grew to know many of the students, I recognized that apart from where we are on the learning curve, ours are relationships of equals, founded on my respect for others and their lives before and while at NIP. Looking back, I also can see that my role was more challenging when I was 40, when libidinal tensions ran higher than now. Then I managed many attractions by suppressing and discouraging contact. In later years, I became more of a father figure, in my own mind as well as in the minds of candidates. My discomfort eased with the passing of time, as I developed a more supportive and generous role with younger professionals.

I've been asked about how I manage my relationships with training analysands around the Institute. First of all, as I explain to them initially, I remove myself as fully as possible as an "official" involved in their formal training experience. But it has always struck me as artificial, hypocritical, even rude to remain aloof, or to snub a person – anyone – at a gathering to whom, in my office, I'd open myself and respond warmly. So unless he or she made clear a discomfort with our informal meeting, which I would of course respect, I've made it a point to be accessible and responsive around the Institute. I pretty much take my cues from them by "averaging" the distance between us. Then, if it seems appropriate, we use sessions to discuss what the experience of an outside meeting was like, treating it as grist for the analytic mill, without robbing the outside encounter of its authenticity. Nothing inappropriate, no boundary transgressions ever occur – just a natural, open, and honest directness.

As my various and sometimes conflicting roles began to meld more seamlessly, I realized how much I had come out of hiding. That also applies to my clinical work. To my surprise and delight – and contrary to many of the clinical warnings I had previously learned and heeded – I also discovered that a less reserved, freer, more open relatedness with my patients made my clinical work more effective, while often bringing a playfulness, vitality, and fun to the clinical exchange. I also learned not to hold back overt expressions of concern for the well-being of my patients, further rejecting an earlier convention about neutrality that I had been taught. Within that new framework, I discovered there was still plenty of room for transference analysis.

Writing became uniquely important in the development of my professional ideas and finding my voice, empowering my clinical work, and, in general, in my coming out of hiding. Working on scholarly articles on an ongoing basis became a very important instrument for working out others' and my own ideas – of syncing theory with clinical experience. The process of writing, of formulating ideas, enables me to integrate and extend what I'm learning. Much of my writing has involved a process of deconstruction and reconstruction of what I was previously taught. That makes me more effective clinically, which emboldens me. I find writing to be an oddly relational experience. As I am working on papers, the written words and ideas take on a life of their own and become separate and important presences in my life. It is as if "we" confer, and they – the emerging, incomplete, sometimes challenging and incompatible ideas and other material that find their way onto the page – and I somehow write "together." Through my writing practice, the publication of my work, and the affirmation of others' interest in it, I have found myself coming to a more clinically secure position. Writing has become a vital aspect of my professional development and occupies much of my "free" time. I take pleasure in being the Senior Consulting Editor of *Psychoanalytic Perspectives*, the journal published by NIP and its Professional Association. Individuals at some mainstream institutes feel tacit pressure to endorse an official party line; I am grateful that I never felt that pressure at NIP, which allows for and respects differences, as the journal's subtitle (*An International Journal of Integration and Innovation*) makes clear.

Another development that strongly influences my working model is my home office. Again, I only began to appreciate this influence retrospectively. After my youngest child left for college, I moved my Englewood, New Jersey, practice from a suite in a nearby apartment complex into my home in the suburbs. My office is closed off from most of the living quarters, but I see patients in what doubles after hours as a family room, complete with sound equipment, TV, personal books and art, personal artifacts, and the like. My patients see my home and the cars I drive. Some have had occasion to see my wife and, at times, my grown children, as they come and go. Those experiences stimulate material for analysis, but also define me as an individual and contribute to what I have come to think of as the personal, or person-to-person, therapy relationship (Frank, 2005), which I see as playing a very important role in therapeutic action. Working in a home office setting, it always has seemed fatuous to me to remain closed.

My patients also get to know Tazzy, my large silver-haired standard poodle, a certified therapy dog, and my "co-therapist," as we sometimes joke. When not enjoying visiting patients in hospitals and residents in nursing homes, she spends much of her time with me and my patients. Tazzy is affectionate toward those patients who show her affection. Demonstrating human-like affect attunement, she will curl up at their feet during sessions, especially when they are experiencing distress. Tazzy definitely has her favorites, welcomes them enthusiastically, and she and I let patients know if they are members of her inner circle, which usually pleases them. She is rarely intrusive, and has a bed off to the side where, after greeting her friends, she usually naps. Only once has she backed away from a patient who tried to befriend her. He was a young man with Asperger's syndrome, and Tazzy apparently sensed something unfamiliar. It felt important to me to help them make a connection, both as a prelude to my forming a relationship with him and as a means of promoting his ability to connect. In addition to seeing my personal life all around me, I'm certain that my patients also learn about me from witnessing my interaction with Tazzy – my affection, tone, gentleness, patience, and firmness with her, and her responses to me. A few have belittled her or said they see me with a retriever or a more "masculine" sort of dog. Of course, such reactions, while admittedly stirring my own stereotypic conflict related to "real" men having poodles, raise interesting issues, which we sometimes discuss.

Patients also see that I raise plants, mainly orchids and African violets. This is not the ordinary clinical office; as mentioned, it is in my home (and I confess to a "new age" belief that the healing vibes acting in that room nurture the growth of my patients, like my plants, which thrive there). Working in a home office is inherently self-revealing, far more than in the ordinary clinical setting. In a manner that feels natural in that context, I've relaxed many of the customary boundaries dictated by the original psychoanalytic axis of analytic anonymity, neutrality, and abstinence, and I am pleased to have done so. The resulting beliefs and qualities, in turn, have carried over to my Manhattan practice as well. As you can see, these experiences have both shaped and found a compatible position in my theoretical convictions.

Final thoughts: "faces in a cloud"

As I approach the end of this chapter, I find myself hoping I have not painted too rosy a picture of the later years, making my transition from hiding sound too easy, too much of a transformational fairy tale. That is hardly the case. I've described the struggle of the early years, and my personal and professional growth have often been a struggle in later years, too, although of a different magnitude. As I mentioned earlier, I never felt very comfortable speaking in front of an audience. I lacked confidence in my ability to think on my feet and speak articulately while my autonomic nervous system attempts vigorously to co-opt my cortical functioning. It's much easier to sit behind my computer, as now, without that sense of self-consciousness that remains inherent in public performances, and to operate privately as a wordsmith, manipulating obedient words and phrases to comply with my wishes. Did I say earlier that writing helped me to come out of hiding? Ironically, it also helped me hang on to a way of hiding while still making myself known.

Although the evolution I have experienced has progressed naturally as I discovered the rewards of coming out of hiding, it has also taken a toll. The way for me to grow most substantially, I learned, is to push myself beyond my comfort zone, being willing to fail but optimistic about succeeding, mastering new challenges, and achieving the attendant growth and benefits. If certainty is an enemy of new possibility, avoidance opposes growth. For example, finally accepting and even seeking out speaking engagements, my bête noir, while causing notable anxiety, has created feelings of wholeness and new possibilities. Speaking publicly also enables me to share my ideas more effectively with others, and thereby to meet what I feel is an important professional responsibility.

Once a hidden analyst and person, I have gradually become more open and "exposed." Successive publications have marked my professional trail, each paper representing the progressive working through of emergent ideas I have had about psychotherapy. Although my writing has always developed organically, covering fairly wide-ranging topics, in retrospect I can see that, basically, it has been concerned with three themes. They include: (1) acknowledging that therapeutic action is above all else derived from engaging *openly* in a caring personal relationship and the exploration of that relationship's dimensions; (2) working with and from one's own experience in the relationship; and (3) "technique," specifically, assimilating non-analytic theories and methods into analysis.

I have recounted how these personal and clinical discoveries came together to shape the faces I see in the clouds, as Atwood and Stolorow (1979) put it. I'll end with a few quotes from the publications that have marked my trail. In them, I attempted to capture, on a theoretical level, the strengthening convictions I reached during my personal journey. First, as the French say, *plus ça change, plus c'est la même chose* – the more things change, the more they remain the same. Thus a fundamental belief has endured since relatively early in my career, before the relational revolution, when abstinence, analytic anonymity, and neutrality prevailed. In 1977, I wrote,

The techniques of the analyst are optimally effective only when imple-
mented within the context of a real, caring, human relationship . . . The
personal, subjective experience and attitudes of the analyst, especially
while conducting treatment, contribute importantly to those interpersonal
subtleties and uncharted techniques, which may, in fact, comprise the
effective core of all psychotherapy.

(pp. 1, 2)

I have elaborated many of the nuances of those beliefs over the years. In 1997, I
wrote,

To the extent that technical choices are deliberate, one ought to have
good reasons for doing or for not doing either disclosure or concealment
at any particular time. To date, analysts really have not been that open
and balanced about the possibility of articulating their participation, and
have placed the burden of proof on the disclosing analyst.

(p. 358)

And later (2004), I wrote,

Working together along a deepening, if irregular, spiral of reciprocal trust,
both [patient and analyst] come to feel safe enough with one another to
progressively relax the self-protectiveness that prevents their vulnerability to, and thus recognition of, the other . . . Transferences are worked
through [and] . . . the analyst ordinarily comes to more fully know, respect,
and thus trust the patient, and consequently to unconsciously move closer
and to become more open and vulnerable (Kantrowitz, 1997).

(pp. 353–354)

Most recently, in an article incorporating my growing interest in neuroscience and
the limits of self-awareness (2012), I concluded:

If we, as analysts, hide or even believe we can . . . we may think we are
making ourselves appropriately difficult to discover, but, in fact, we are
artificially attempting to isolate ourselves within the relational matrix
and thereby introducing our own handicap in being found and in finding
our patients . . . We do best by approaching our patients open-mindedly
as collaborators. This assertion, appreciative of the mutual nature of the
analytic process, no longer can be considered just a stylistic preference;
in the light of the present findings, it becomes a *necessity*.

(p. 319)

These days, I wrestle with the role of transference analysis – which many regard
as the centerpiece of psychoanalysis – and the extent to which it, compared with

the power of the personal relationship, influences constructive change. We tend to emphasize the new relational, or person-to-person, relationship as the *result* of transference analysis, rather than stressing its *causal* role in therapeutic change. I wonder if we have neglected the role of transference analysis as the *protector* of the personal relationship, which carries a major share in therapeutic action.

The greater one's knowledge, especially of theory and methods, the better clinician he or she will be. In the end, however, I believe our clinical effectiveness depends on our ability as individuals to join our patients at the center of the therapeutic process, working together in a relationship that is deeply personal and mutual. It is vital, therefore, that we try and remain naturally authentic, honest, and to the extent possible, open with, as well as devoted to – rather than hidden from – those who seek our help.

As I've tried to show, my writings reflect this theme of a willingness to be known. I now see myself as being "out there" more than most, fully appreciative of the value of an open, sensibly transparent clinical stance. I believe in the value of a mutually expressive relationship, asymmetrical in some respects, involving a visibility and sharing of my personal associations, even personal life experiences when it seems helpful to do so, which is often. I'm happy to explain to patients why I'm interacting with them as I am, and I try to put my explanations in plain terms and clarify them in a constructive manner that honors the mutual trust, authenticity, and honesty that binds us. I am still evolving as a clinician and feel a continuing need to grow, yet I am more comfortable than ever with where I am now.

Notes

1 I hasten to point out that I would not define countertransference in the same way today as then. At that time, countertransference was considered in a condemnatory way as a one-sided, disturbed response of the therapist. Its solution was to be found in one's own analysis. Now we understand the transference–countertransference interaction in far more sophisticated, transactional ways, recognizing the role of mutual influence.
2 I (2012) have written about "Joan."

References

Atwood, G. E., & Stolorow, R. D. (1979). *Faces in a cloud: intersubjectivity in personality theory*. Lanham, MD: Rowman and Littlefield.

Bowlby, J. (1979). *The making and breaking of affectional bonds*. London: Tavistock Publications, Limited.

Frank, K. A. (1977). *The human dimension in psychoanalytic practice*. New York: Grune & Stratton.

Frank, K. A. (1997). Reply to commentaries. *Psychoanalytic Dialogues*, 7, 347–361.

Frank, K. A. (2004). The analyst's trust and therapeutic action. *Psychoanalytic Quarterly*, 73, 335–378.

Frank, K. A. (2005). Toward conceptualizing the personal relationship in therapeutic action: Beyond the "real" relationship. *Psychoanalytic Perspectives*, 3(1) 15–56.

Frank, K. A. (2012). Strangers to ourselves: Exploring the limits and potentials of the analyst's self awareness in self- and mutual analysis. *Psychoanalytic Dialogues, 23,* 311–327.

Kantrowitz, J. L. (1997). A different perspective on the therapeutic process: The impact of the patient on the analyst. *Journal* of the *American Psychoanalytic Association, 45,* 127–153.

7

REFLECTIONS ON THE DEVELOPMENT OF MY ANALYTIC SUBJECTIVITY

Anna Ornstein

The village in which I was born and lived the first 15 years of my life in Northern Hungary was a small agricultural community of about 3500 people. Socially and culturally, the 40 Jewish families in the village were totally separated from their peasant neighbors. The Jews constituted the "middle class": the doctor, the pharmacist, the baker, and several shopkeepers. At the time I was growing up, in the 1930s and 1940s, severe anti-Semitism closed the doors to all universities for Jewish boys and girls. Not only was attending a university an unattainable dream, but so was attending a college preparatory high school (gymnasium). All schools were parochial in Hungary. There were only four Jewish college preparatory high schools in the whole country and only one, in Budapest, was for girls. My two brothers, who were three and five years my senior, attended college in a gymnasium in the city 40 kilometers away from home.

My brothers, who did not survive the forced labor lamps, had a great influence on my emotional and intellectual development. I admired both of them; both were bright but in different ways. My older brother was resourceful and practical. The younger one was a dreamer; had he lived, I believe, he would have pursued something academic, possibly philosophy. Much of my competitive spirit comes from my efforts to keep up with them physically and intellectually. They were good swimmers, so I became a good swimmer; they played a fierce ping-pong game, so I insisted they play with me and take me seriously. I often think about my brothers and wonder how they would have lived their lives had they had a chance . . . I always had the strong conviction that my life had to reflect, academically at least, what our parents had expected of them even more than what they may have expected of me.

My formal education consisted of four years in a one-room Jewish elementary school and not quite two years in a gymnasium. The rest of my education depended on my mother's patience and available time. My mother, who herself was self-educated, instructed me in the basics of mathematics, history, and the German language. This was a "hit or miss" arrangement as the time for studying had to fit in with the many physically demanding household chores that rural

81

living, without plumbing and electricity, demanded of women and girls in all families. Hungary followed many of the German anti-Jewish laws that were passed in the 1930s, and my father, like all heads of Jewish households, was frequently under house arrest on drummed-up charges. My father was a gentle, generous man not meant to live in these trying times; he was fearful and could not easily absorb the many humiliating blows that came his way. My mother was pragmatic and very competent; she took care of the store 15 kilometers away and managed our dwindling finances. As the only girl, I was expected to be responsible for our household at an early age.

Ours was a traditional, observant Jewish family but not Chassidic or ultra-Orthodox. My parents' interests were primarily in secular matters; they were strongly influenced by the intellectual currents coming not only from Budapest but also from Vienna and Prague and other German-speaking cities. My father, who served in the army of the Austro-Hungarian Empire during World War I, spoke German and wished that we, his children, learn the language as well. My parents also read and admired Russian and French literature in Hungarian translations. This was the paradox in which I grew up: technically, conditions could not have been more primitive, but intellectually this was a well-informed, enlightened family with ambitions and dreams for a better future for the children. Eventually, in the school years 1942/43 and 1943/44, I was able to attend a gymnasium in Debrecen. This high school for boys admitted a few girls who were willing to take the entrance examination and could pass four years of Latin, algebra, and French. I was ecstatic about the opportunity to attend a school with regular hours for instructions and be taught by professors who were considered experts in their respective fields. I also had classmates and friends, a wonderful experience for an eager and highly motivated 15-year-old girl.

In spite of my parents' secular interests, we observed Shabbat, the Jewish holy days; I grew up with a strong Jewish identity and with Zionist ideals. These served as major protections against the impact of daily humiliations and injustices that we were exposed to in this anti-Semitic environment. My feelings regarding my Jewish heritage are well captured in an old myth about a Jewish sage who, shrouded in his Sefer Torah (the Holy Scripture), was burned alive and bore witness from the flames: "The parchment is burning but the letters are soaring aloft." The parchment, which is the people, had been threatened with total destruction many times in Jewish history. But from the embers the letters have risen with which ideals and ethical principles have been written, keeping the survivors of the many fires alive through the long history of Jewish existence.

Values and ideals are transmitted from one generation to the next through *cultural patterns* that are embedded in the core of every relatively homogenous group. Such patterns are being transmitted through mythology, ideology,[1] religion, and child-rearing practices. Similar to the superego, ideals and ethical principles derive their *contents* from the standards and values of the family and the cultural and social environment. Kohut's (1978 [1966]) reformulation of the ego ideal gave ideals a prominent position in the psyche. Our ideals, he wrote,

82

are "*our internal leaders; we love them and are longing to reach them*" (p. 434, italics added). It is the *idealized position of ideals* in the psyche that assures the survival of cultures and societies that had repeatedly been threatened not only with physical but also with spiritual annihilation. The Holocaust was only the most recent such event in Jewish history. It is my strong conviction that it is *the transmission of ideas, ideals and ethical principles from generation to generation* that best explains how I, and other young people, have been able to persevere and live creative and productive lives after the loss of our families and communities during the terrible years of 1933–1945. For Hungarian Jews, the significance of this became most obvious during the last years of the war, in 1944 and 1945.

The deportation

In March 1944, German troops occupied Hungary. We were trapped. Jews were not allowed to use public transportation; they were arrested on the streets, in their homes, wherever they happened to be. I managed to go back to my hometown from Debrecen where I was attending the Jewish gymnasium at that time. Within weeks, we were gathered into a temporary ghetto. Early one morning in June, trucks appeared in front of the ghetto – trucks in a town that rarely saw a car on its dusty roads! It was now clear that for the Germans, the deportation and liquidation of the Jews had priority over winning the war. By the summer of 1944, the Germans had suffered severe defeats on the Eastern front which encouraged the Hungarian Jews to cling to the hope that the war would be over before they too would suffer the fate of other Jews in occupied Europe. I can still see the faces of our neighbors, people who knew us well, crossing their arms and watching impassively as our families were herded onto trucks and taken to the train station where long cattle wagons were waiting for us. Since the Jewish men between the ages of 17 and 46 (which included my brothers) were taken earlier into Forced Labor Camps, the 100 or so women, children, and elderly could easily be pressed into a single wagon.

By the first week of June 1944 – the week that American troops landed in Normandy – we were in Auschwitz. My father, grandmother, and other members of my extended family were taken to the gas chamber. My mother and I were selected for labor, and after a brief stay in Auschwitz, we were shipped to Plashow (near Krakow) where we worked in a stone quarry. Toward the end of the summer, as the Russian armies were approaching Krakow, we were taken back to Auschwitz in cattle cars similar to the ones that transported us there the first time. Not all of us understood the great danger that this trip represented. My mother, 46 years old at the time, had lost a great deal of weight and the hard work in the stone quarry had made her look old and haggard (we were carrying heavy stones from one pile to another in extraordinary heat with little food and no water). Mother understood that an entry to Auschwitz meant another selection. Her ability to recognize the situation for what it was saved her life – and my life as well. Trying to look younger and fit, she put a piece of red rag on her head that she found somewhere. Still, she was waived into the direction of the gas chambers. I remember her holding my hand firmly and daring to tell the SS officer that she was capable of more work. It is not possible to describe the sense of relief when she was permitted to join me. However, as long as we were in Auschwitz, the possibility of being taken to the gas chambers always remained a real possibility.

During the summer and fall of 1944, the gas chambers and crematoria in Auschwitz were working constantly. This was the time during which, in about 6 weeks, 480,000 Hungarian Jews were exterminated. Survival in Auschwitz was a random event – my mother and I spent one night in front of the chambers but eventually were returned to our barracks. It was no wonder then that when, a few days later, we were assembled to receive tattoos, I was convinced that this meant that our lives would be spared. I don't know whether it had anything to do with the tattoo or not, but about six weeks later, after still another selection, we were shipped to Parschnitz, a labor camp in Czechoslovakia. From Parschnitz, we were taken by train daily to Tratenau, where I worked in an ammunition factory and my mother survived the winter of 1944/45 by scraping rusty metal on the factory's courtyard. I will never stop admiring her courage and fortitude.

I am frequently asked, mainly by schoolchildren, what we had to eat and where we slept. I welcome these questions because it is easy to forget that along with the large-scale and industrialized murder there was torture and slow death by starvation, exhaustion, and exposure to freezing temperatures. In Parschnitz, for example, after we were awakened around 4:00 a.m., we would get some liquid that was made of the shafts of various grains and was called "soup" but looked and tasted more like grey water. When lucky, we would find a potato peal or some other kind of vegetable in this liquid. Those of us who were able to resist devouring the piece of bread we received the day before as we entered the camp had something to eat during the day. I was very disciplined, and mother and I had a piece of bread around noon when we got about a half-hour rest and were given some black liquid called "coffee." Placing small pieces of bread into my mouth and drinking the black liquid, I could still the terrible hunger we experienced all the time. At night, when we got back to the camp and had a thin soup again, we tried to go to sleep. This was not an easy task. It is very difficult to fall asleep when one is very hungry, and we had the additional problem of trying fight off the bedbugs. But most importantly, we worried about our bread being stolen. To keep it safe, we placed the 7 oz. piece of bread – which was our only nourishment for the next day – in the nape of our necks.

Russian troops reached Parschnitz in late afternoon on May 8, 1945. This was not how we imagined our "liberation." The single Russian soldier on a motorcycle, his face covered with dust, his voice so hoarse we could barely hear him, told us in Yiddish that he had seen hundreds of such camps that day and he had nothing to offer us. We were free and could go wherever we wanted. But where could we go? While trying to find our way back to Hungary, we also had to eat and sleep somewhere. There were about 50 women who lived in the same area in Hungary and we started our journey as a group. We walked most of the way and often did not know whether or not we were going in the right direction. We had heard that the Russian soldiers were raping women, so rather than approaching them for help, we tried to avoid them. Most of the villages we passed through were totally bombed out. Whenever we found some lived-in houses, we would approach the people and beg for food. Looking at us, they knew where we were coming from and wisely decided not to invite us to enter their homes. Instead, they would dig a hole in their yards and cook potatoes for us in large kettles. During the two to three months of wandering, we lived mainly on potatoes, water, and salt.

Inside Hungary, as we walked along rails that looked fairly intact, we heard a train approaching – indeed, a very long train filled with boisterous Serbian soldiers returning from the Eastern front pulled into a small station. Heading toward Zagreb, they had to go through Budapest. They emptied one of the wagons for us and gave us food; we were overjoyed about our good luck.

The new beginning and the mourning process

We arrived in Budapest sometime in late July or early August, 1945. There, the cruelest news of all awaited us: my mother and I were almost the only survivors of our immediate and extended families. My 21-year-old brother died in Mauthausen and my 23-year-old brother disappeared somewhere in the East; I was never able to find out where and how he died. By then, we knew that my father, who was 61 years old in 1944, had perished in the gas chamber.

Here we were, back in Hungary without our families, without a home, and without financial resources. What were we to do? My mother's sister and her husband made room for us in their small apartment. I picked up the thread of my life where it had been interrupted, and enrolled in the Jewish Gymnasium in Budapest.

And then something unexpected and wonderful happened: Paul Ornstein, whom I had known before the German occupation, was told that someone saw me after liberation, that I was alive. He appeared at my bedside, waking me from a long, restless sleep. Our reunion is one of the most unforgettable moments in my life. Paul escaped from a forced labor camp in the Ukraine and survived the last few months of the war hiding in the cellar of the Swiss Consulate Annex.

My mother was lucky to be offered a job as a directress of an orphanage for 40 Jewish children; she felt needed, and she found purpose in her life again. I often wondered how she was able to give meaning to her life after losing her husband and her two much-adored sons. When I reflected on this, she would say "life loves living," meaning that just being alive makes one want to live.[2] Paul's father, who lost four children and his wife and survived a death march from Northern Hungary to the concentration camp Mauthausen, rebuilt his life in a similar manner. After the establishment of the state, he immigrated to Israel where he sought out young families with children whose ages approximated those of his lost children. He became a "father" to them and attended all their celebratory events. This, along with feeling pride in Israel's rapid development, gave meaning to his new life. At no time was this more evident than in the boundless joy he and my mother experienced with the births of each of their grandchildren.

Freud (1917) conceptualized mourning as a process in which old attachments have to be given up for new ones to occur. To me, the sequence appears to be in reverse: new attachments offer opportunities for healing, making possible the mourning of those we lost.

Paul and I got married in March 1946, and a few weeks later, we escaped from Communist Hungary into Western Europe with the help of the Israeli underground. Paul and I grew up in almost identical social, cultural, and religious environments and had similar hopes and dreams for our lives and our future family. Our marriage provided us with a foundation that was crucial in those uncertain, turbulent postwar years.

Immigration either to Palestine or the USA took a long time, and we decided to spend this time acquiring a medical degree. It was under these circumstances that we first enrolled into medical school in Munich and later, when it was possible, in Heidelberg. I always dreamed of becoming a doctor. It was an essential aspect of my heritage; there were several physicians in my extended family. I also admired my mother's sister, the poet. These early idealizations of people I knew personally had contributed significantly to the evolution of my own ideals and provided the stimulus to pursue my goals once this had become possible. As I was growing up, however, it did not seem possible that any of these dreams could ever become a reality. It still appears like a miracle to me.

Living in postwar Germany was a mixed experience. As housing was limited, we could only rent in homes that were assigned to us by the City Hall. This turned out to be fortunate: it offered us the opportunity to get to know Germans with a variety of political orientations, which protected us from a prejudicial attitude and taught us not to generalize about the German people. The first room we rented was in the home of an SS officer, the second in the home of a National Socialist, and the third in the home of a Social Democrat. In Heidelberg, we also befriended a most remarkable man, Kreisdekan Hermann Maas, who himself was in a concentration camp because of his affiliation with an underground anti-Nazi movement. Kreisdekan Maas secured a small stipend for us, and after we left Heidelberg he looked after my mother, who had to escape Hungary because she was discovered helping to smuggle the children in her charge into Palestine.

When we tell our friends that we went to medical school in Germany, they wonder how it was possible for us to live in a country whose population had elected a National Socialist party with disastrous consequences for the Jewish people. The matter for us was simple: our goal was to get out of anti-Semitic Eastern Europe that had embraced a Stalinist Communist regime. As stateless refugees, we had to go to a place where the American Government and the American Jewish Agencies established and maintained Displaced Persons Camps, which were located mainly in West Germany.

The years in the medical school at the University of Heidelberg (1947–1951) were devoted to our studies without any contact with our German classmates. Instead, we became members of a Jewish Student Union where we could establish warm and loyal relationships with other Jewish colleagues, who, like us, survived various concentration camps and had lost either all or most members of their immediate and extended families. Sharing meals and our limited resources, we became a family and remained friends for the rest of our lives.

In 1951, when our immigration numbers came up, Paul and I left for the USA. My mother joined us two years later. She loved this country and found great joy in taking care of her grandchildren, but her life with us was short: she died in 1961, at the age of 63. I was now a medical doctor and could choose any specialty I liked. In Germany, I was not aware of a specialty called child psychiatry. Once I learned about it, I thought the specialty was created for me: This is what I wanted to do. But first, I had to have training in general psychiatry.

As graduates of a foreign medical school, we did not have free choice of where we could train and settle down. We were very fortunate that the University of Cincinnati had an excellent training program in psychiatry and that Ohio was one of the states where we were admitted to take the medical board examinations. In Cincinnati, we met and befriended many wonderful people, among them Margaret Mead and Michael Balint. We could better appreciate Balint's influence on our clinical work after we became acquainted with self psychology; "the basic fault" and other of his non-traditional ideas were good preparations for what awaited us in Chicago, where Paul and I had our analytic training.

I was now living my parents' dreams. We had a large, comfortable home and I could practice a profession I loved. In addition to our analytic practice, Paul and I embarked on an academic career in the Department of Psychiatry and began to publish jointly as well as individually. But most importantly, we became parents to three healthy children. I have been asked many times how I explain that all three children had become physicians and had chosen psychiatry as their specialty (two became psychoanalysts and one a child psychiatrist). This is a difficult question to answer because they have been exposed to a variety of influences throughout their lives. Maybe the best answer would be that the dreams of my parents and the aspirations of previous generations that had guided me in my life had continued their path into the next generation.

My analyst, Dr. Maurice Levine, was the Chairman of the Department, an arrangement not unusual in small communities with very few training analysts. Dr. Levine was a kind and well-meaning person whose psychoanalytic training did not prepare him to deal analytically with experiences of which I had to speak. From his responses I learned early on that it was preferable for me not to share my Holocaust experiences with him. Dealing with these issues had to occur in conversations with fellow survivors and by lecturing and writing. Writing, in particular, appeared to offer me a wonderful opportunity not to deny or repress the magnitude of the losses that I and others in similar circumstances had suffered. Writing, similar to an analytic dialogue, liberates affect and facilitates mourning. This is beautifully captured by David Grossman (2007):

I write. In the wake of the death of my son Uri . . . the awareness of what happened has sunk into every cell of mine. The power of memory is indeed enormous and heavy, and at times has a paralyzing quality to it. Nevertheless, the act of writing itself at this time creates for me a type of "space," a mental territory that I had never experienced before. I write and I feel how the correct and precise use of words is like a remedy to an illness.

In 2008, in a plenary address to the American Psychoanalytic Association, I was finally able to articulate my own understanding of how mourning may occur following multiple losses suffered in collectively experienced major disasters (Ornstein, 2010a).

Comments regarding the Holocaust-related literature

Psychiatrists and psychoanalysts had missed a unique opportunity to research a most remarkable phenomenon in modern history when they failed to try to answer the question: What made psychological survival in concentration camps – hiding in forests, living with false papers, and especially the loss of one's family and community – possible? Instead, the professionals restricted their inquiry to the study of the pathological consequences of this unparalleled historical event and then proceeded to theorize about the transgenerational transmission *only* of the traumatic aspects of the survivors' experiences (Auerhahn & Laub, 1984; Barocas & Barocas, 1973; Bergmann & Jucovy, 1982; Grubrich-Simitis, 1981; Kestenberg, 1972, 1977, 1982; Krystal, 1978; Levine, 1982; Niederland, 1968). Focusing only on psychopathology and then *generalizing clinical findings to all survivors* had unexpected consequences: accepting "the findings" of the original investigators without reservations, a new generation of psychotherapists have been "interpreting" any emotional problems children of survivors may have as the direct consequence of their parents' Holocaust pasts. In my view, these "second generation" patients deserve the same empathic immersion in their inner lives and the same recognition of their individuality as other patients.

Generalizations are unavoidable in scientific writings, even for psychoanalysts who pride themselves on being more interested in the uniqueness of each individual than in statistics and generalizations. In relation to Holocaust survivors, they found justification for their far-reaching generalizations by asserting that the horrendous losses and horror-filled experiences had "washed away" the survivors' childhood experiences that could have preserved the unique organization of their personalities. This meant that regardless of the age they may have been affected by these events, whether they were adults or children, in hiding, or in a camp, how long their ordeal may have lasted, and how severe the conditions may have been – *all* survivors are supposed to suffer from "profound emotional regression" from "survivor guilt." The shared view among these authors that every survivor's life had to be forever permeated by "deep and chronic depression" is particularly critical, because it meant that survivors could not live their lives with hopeful expectations, that their activities always would lack zest and initiative.

Life-long depression and lacking zest and vitality are attributes which most profoundly affect the parenting of one's children. This explains the professionals' dire predictions regarding the emotional lives of the second and third generations. Because of the magnitude of the trauma, they say, no one generation is expected to deal with these memories adequately.

One of the problems with the assessments of the professionals was that they had made them from the perspective of civilized existence. It was indeed difficult, or maybe impossible, to put themselves into the shoes of people who were in hiding with false documents or living in forests for many years, and they could not fully comprehend how life was possible in a ghetto or in a concentration camp. This created a gulf between patients and therapists that resulted in survivors being treated as experimental subjects, people totally different from themselves. Listening to extreme atrocities created hard to overcome countertransferences in these well-meaning psychoanalysts, so they were quick to offer theory-based *explanations* to their survivor-patients. If one keeps in mind that there existed a generally accepted assumption that the Holocaust trauma was "unknowable," it is striking that so many analysts claim knowledge of the most intimate psychic processes that are, by their own admission, beyond anyone's capacity to access – for example, the claim to know that on the deepest psychic level, the survivors' experiences were worse than the worse imaginable oral-cannibalistic or anal-sadistic fantasies, or that survivors were abandoned by their internal objects and forced to internalize their Nazi aggressors (Grubrich-Simitis, 1981). This kind of thinking was not surprising in the 1950s and 1960s when psychoanalysis was considered to be an explanatory psychology (Hartmann, 1958); these were the times when analysts were supposed to have had all the answers based on patients' histories or their theory of psychopathology.

But even more recently, when the co-construction of meaning in psychoanalysis is generally accepted, Holocaust survivors' emotional lives are still conceptualized in idiosyncratic, theoretical terms. The particular theory employed differs from time to time as new psychoanalytic theories gain popularity. Exploring "the psychological states and dynamics faced by survivors of genocide and their children in their struggle to sustain life in the midst of unremitting deadliness," Samuel Gerson (2009, p. 1341) uses the concepts of the "dead mother" (Green, 1986) and "the third" (Ogden, 1994) to explain what it is like to live the lives of Holocaust survivors and their children: "So imagine life when the third is dead; when the container cracks and there is no presence beyond our own subjectivity to represent continuity. It is a world constituted by absence, where meaning is ephemeral and cynicism passes for wisdom . . ." (p. 1343). The more extreme the language, the more likely it will be quoted by others: "Gaps, phantoms, voids, and negative identities are all concepts that attempt to describe the living experience of deadness, alive somewhere in the realm between presence and absence – this is the deathlife of the self" – described by Langer (2001) and quoted by Gerson (2009,

p. 1348). I consider these metapsychological speculations to be not only poor substitutes to an attempt to *understand* what the survivors have been actually experiencing, but also ideas that could have prevented a meaningful therapeutic engagement. This may explain why – after detailing the survivors' severe psycho-pathology – very few articles include reports of a treatment process.

The inmates of concentration camps did not necessarily experience what the professionals have been attributing to them. To an external observer, the behavior of camp inmates had to appear passive and helpless; to survive physically, they had to follow orders without protest and resistance. But emotional survival was not possible *in a passive state of mind.* This required a great deal of activity and resistance in all aspects of camp life: not to fall asleep when standing in line for several hours, not to sit down when totally exhausted, not to eat the piece of bread that was to last for a whole day. All these required extraordinarily high levels of alertness that was anything but passive.

To the external observer, inmates of concentration camps succumbed to sav-agery: a crowd in the shadow of death, breaking moral laws, ignoring social customs, betraying others so that they may live. From within the inmates' per-spective, the picture looked different: revisions in the hierarchy of moral values had to be made which required flexibility and creativity. The ability to reduce one's material needs (which was easier for those who grew up in the country as poor than for those who came from the city and were used to comfort) and to be responsive to the needs of others was the only way one could survive not only psychologically but physically as well: If I am not for others, who will be for me? Theft was rampant in camps; depending on what was stolen and from whom, it was either deplorable or a highly esteemed heroic act. To steal from someone weak was immoral, but to steal a head of cabbage that escaped from a German truck was worthy of praise, a feat that I myself had accomplished.

Many survivors of concentration camps preserved their capacity for empathy and the sense of morality by living double lives; they were able to preserve their internalized values and ideals because they spontaneously created small social groups which functioned like families. Prisoners arriving together made every effort to occupy neighboring bunks. The groups were created by sisters, cousins, rarely a mother, and friends from neighboring towns. These were small groups, maybe three or four women, five the most. In order to weaken morale, the Ger-mans repeatedly interfered with these life-sustaining groupings. As groups were disrupted, new groups would be formed indicating the need – and the capacity – to establish some form of social structure that made emotional survival possi-ble. The latrines served a similar function. With some foresight, a prisoner could meet and exchange a few words with a friend or a previous bunk mate. Finding out who lived, who died, or who was sent to another camp kept the social network alive.

Retrospectively, I can better appreciate these groups' great psychological sig-nificance; they provided the setting in which ordinary human affects, rivalries, hostilities, and jealousies – but also love, loyalty and caring – could be experienced and expressed. There were fights, disagreements, and reconciliations in these groups but also fierce commitment and much sacrifice, similar in intensity to ordinary family life. It was in these small social groups that they could express their innermost selves that were essential to their human, rather than purely biological, survival. The small family-like units permitted behavior that reinforced one's internal value system, which served as a bulwark against the constant attempts to undermine the victims' human qualities. There were obvious exceptions, but most survivors were neither corrupt nor saints. Adjusting to the extreme conditions without heroism or rebellion helped preserve their physical existence, and they preserved their dignity and humanness by holding on to and tenaciously maintaining the values they had brought with them into these inhuman conditions (Ornstein, 1985, 1989). Similar observations were made by Davidson (1979) and by Goffman (1961): "The practice of reserving something of oneself from the clutches of an institution is very visible in mental hospitals and prisons . . . I want to argue that this recalcitrance is not an incidental mechanism of defense but rather an essential constituent of the self" (p. 319).

In camps and in ghettos, Jews had lived under conditions not meant for human existence. They were stripped of the essential elements of civilized life. This, upon their return to civilization, helped them rediscover the simple joys in everyday life: the joy of waking up in one's own bed in clean and comfortable bedding, the joy of a hot shower and eating tasty, nourishing food. And the joy of knowing that when they become sick they will be cared for, and when their time comes they will die a human death and be buried in their own, individual graves. My children and my friends' children tell me that this particular feature of their survivor-parents is the one that had impressed them the most; they had learned from them that the everyday joys of life ought never to be taken for granted.

Comments on my analytic subjectivity

When I now focus on those factors that I believe have shaped my analytic subjectivity – specifically, my analytic listening perspective and my choice of a guiding theory – I am placing my quest within the larger historical/social and cultural contexts which I have briefly sketched on the previous pages.

There are many unconsciously interacting factors determining the choice of one's guiding theory in psychoanalysis. An obvious, certainly not unconscious factor was my having trained in psychoanalysis at the Chicago Institute for Psychoanalysis, where Heinz Kohut developed his new ideas. In 1969, in the last year of my training, Kohut began to write *The Analysis of the Self* (Kohut, 1971). I felt privileged when I was invited to join a small group of colleagues who met with him to discuss his evolving ideas. I also sought him out for supervision. I probably can never become fully aware of the extent to which supervision with Kohut and attending the small group meetings shaped my analytic subjectivity.

Retrospectively, I would say that one reason for my choice of self psychology may have been that this is a psychoanalytic *developmental* theory in which selfobject transferences are recognized as efforts to complete self-development. Responding to reactivated childhood needs for affirmation and/or merger with an idealized other in an open-ended, tentative manner are invitations for patients to correct our understanding of what they are experiencing. These "therapeutic dialogues" (Ornstein, 1991; Ornstein et al., 1977), in which meanings are arrived at jointly, create the experience of "feeling understood," which, in our experience, has a major therapeutic impact. Patients come to us with a curative fantasy, an unconscious expectation that in analysis, they will have developmentally needed experiences which, because of their repeated frustrations, have resulted in symptomatic behavior and created features in their personalities, causing suffering and an inability to live life productively and creatively (Ornstein, 1991; Ornstein et al., 1977). For too long, we have been so preoccupied with these pathological constructions in our patients' lives that we failed to recognize and to respond to the "tender tendrils" of their healthy strivings that survived the entanglements with pathological accommodations and defensive operations. Self psychology is a psychoanalytic theory which pays attention to the dreaded repetition of old, maladaptive patterns, while privileging the ways in which patients use their analysts for a "new beginning" (Ornstein, 1974, 1991; Tolpin, 2002).

One of the most obvious aspects of my subjectivity that has entered my clinical work is related to my attention to the subtle changes that indicate a "new beginning" in the course of an analysis. In my opinion, these changes have to be recognized and validated to become permanent psychological faculties (Ornstein, 2010b). The psychological processes that bring about lasting changes in the course of an analysis are closely related to the process of mourning; the two processes have a great deal in common. Mourning, writes Bowlby (1963), is not restricted to the loss of another; changes of all kinds involve the process of mourning; moving progressively forward, we are continually mourning the loss of the old. Affects involved in change in the course of an analysis (for example, the co-existence of a new sense of vitality with old fears and concerns) are usually subtle. In the process of mourning, however, the co-existence of seemingly contradictory affects may be powerfully experienced. Having experienced joy and sorrow simultaneously myself, I learned to appreciate the significance that the co-existence of contradictory emotions have for the process of mourning. Profound joy seems to invite intense sorrow mixed with rage – I experienced these mixed emotions for the first time after moving into our home in Cincinnati. Finding infinite delight in watching our three children play together, I experienced a sudden sharp, piercing pain around my heart and a desire to scream out loud to relieve the heaviness in my chest. This was the first time after 17 years that I could feel the anguish of acute grief; survivors of major disasters need a period of recovery before they can engage the demanding psychological task of mourning. More recently, I watched a young woman being lifted up in the air in celebration of her Bat Mitzvah and, at the same time, I "saw" her grandmother, a member of the Polish Resistance, carrying a gun in the sewers of Warsaw. The thought "this is victory" flashed through my mind, and I joined the dancers in celebration.

Putting these non-clinical experiences into theoretical terms, I would say that the emergence of previously dreaded affects and memories at times of great joy indicates that disavowal of these affects, which had made the survival of extreme conditions and multiple losses possible, is now being relinquished. This is a signal that one is ready to engage the life-long process of mourning. In the clinical situation, it is the feeling of being understood by an empathically responsive analyst that increases self-cohesion and allows previously feared affects to emerge without the threat of fragmentation.

My conviction of the centrality of the empathic listening perspective in psychoanalysis was reinforced by my witnessing the unfortunate impact that the absence of this mode of listening had on my fellow survivors and their children. My friends frequently shared with me the theory-based formulations they had been offered to explain whatever difficulties may have brought them to a professional. This failed to relieve their presenting problems. While the empathic listening perspective is not limited to self psychology, self psychology depends on this mode of observation: *understanding* and empathically responding to the patient's *experiences* here are privileged over theory-based *explanations.*

Embracing the empathic listening perspective raised questions among my colleagues whether or not as a self psychologist, in order to deny my own aggression, I failed to recognize aggression in others. They thought that this was particularly evident in my Holocaust-related publications, in which I wrote about survival and recovery but not about rage and a wish for revenge. Where was my hate toward the perpetrators, the need to retaliate against those who had done us the greatest harm one human being can do to another?

While self psychology has been faulted for not dealing with manifestations of aggression, it was the empathic mode of observation and the study of narcissism that lead Kohut (1978 [1972]) to the close examination of one of the most destructive human affects, that of narcissistic rage. I am quoting Kohut's definition here because of the relevance that revenge has not only in personal relationships but also in relationships between nations, ethnic, and religious groups:

> Narcissistic rage occurs in many forms; they all share, however, a specific psychological flavor which gives them a distinct position within the wide realm of human aggression. The need for revenge, for righting the wrong, for undoing a hurt by whatever means, and a deeply anchored, unrelenting compulsion in the pursuit of all these aims, which gives no rest to those who suffered a narcissistic injury – these are the characteristic features of narcissistic rage in all its forms and which sets it apart from other kinds of aggression.
>
> (pp. 637–638)

In other words, narcissistic rage, with its imperative need for revenge, is an expectable response to injustice and humiliation. Where were the signs of this need in us on the day of liberation in May 1945? On that day, a few Polish–Jewish girls caught two young female guards who were trying to flee. The former inmates cut off the women's hair, dunked their faces into an overflowing toilet bowl and let them go. Nobody was killed or was seriously injured. For most of us, taking revenge was the farthest thing from our minds. We were preoccupied with finding food and water, overcoming sores on our bodies and other not yet diagnosed illnesses, getting back our strength, and finding members of our families. It appears that one has to feel strong and able to exact revenge. Or, can one forgo the imperative need for revenge without forgiving an unforgivable crime? Thinking about this, I found the work of the philosopher Emanuel Levinas particularly remarkable. Born in 1906 in Lithuania, Levinas' life was inextricably bound to the horrors of 20th century Europe: World War I, the Russian Revolution, the Dreyfus affair, the events of the 1930s, and the Holocaust in which he lost many family members. How did this man with these life experiences come to formulate a philosophy of radical empathy and compassion? I believe that having witnessed the brutalities and the suffering that men are capable of inflicting on their fellow men, Levinas developed a philosophy *in which anything less that the adoption of a totally radical ethical attitude toward "the other"* could save mankind from the destructive powers which it is capable of unleashing. Kohut expressed similar sentiments in two of his papers (1978a [1973], 1978b [1973]).

However, compassion and radical empathy are not applicable to perpetrators of great crimes; where crimes have been committed, justice has to be served. Nor can evil be combated with revenge. The opposite is true: narcissistic rage, with its imperative demand for revenge, has been keeping nations, ethnic, and religious groups perpetually at war with each other. Not to seek revenge is a moral demand on victimized individuals as well as on victimized nations because only then can we hope to stop the cycle of violence in this troubled world.

Narcissistic rage may take circuitous routes in the human psyche. I had often wondered whether or not my interest in the symptomatic manifestations of the chronic variants of this destructive affect could, in some way, be related to my wartime experiences. In my practice, I found that patients may express repressed and/or disavowed chronic narcissistic rage either directly or indirectly. Sadistic behavior expresses the rage directly; there can be no question regarding its intent and intensity. In masochistic behavior, on the other hand, the rage is expressed indirectly and the unrelenting demand to right past wrongs may find a variety of manifestations in features of one's personality: an angry, chip-on-the-shoulder attitude, holding grudges, and collecting injustices or a feel-sorry-for-me behavior, haughty withdrawal, self-recrimination, and various degrees of depression (Ornstein, in press). I suspect that in view of the many humiliating experiences in my life, I may have become sensitized to the direct and/or indirect manifestations of narcissistic rage.

More recently, I also became interested in the psychology of mass murderers; specifically, I have been trying to articulate the drastic changes I assume to take place in one's sense of morality and capacity for empathy to make killing of unarmed women and children possible (Ornstein, 2011, 2012). I believe that my clinical interest in these subjects as well as their non-clinical, political, and social implications may well be related to the need to deal intellectually with a personal experience that can be neither forgiven nor forgotten.

Notes

1 Ideology is a system of commanding ideas held together more by totalistic logic and utopian convictions than by cognitive understanding or pragmatic experience (Erikson, 1970).
2 A keen observer, she described many details of camp life to my aunt, who shaped her narrative into a ballad. After translating it into English, the ballad was published along with our camp experiences that I fashioned into short stories (Ornstein & Goldman, 2004).

References

Auerhahn, N. C., & Laub, D. (1984). Annihilation and restoration: Post-traumatic memory as pathway and obstacle to recovery. *International Review of Psychoanalysis*, *11*, 327–344.

Barocas, H., & Barocas, C. (1973). Manifestations of concentration camps effects on the second generation. *American Journal of Psychiatry*, *130*, 820–821.

Bergmann, M., & Jucovy, M. (1982). *Generations of the Holocaust*. New York: Basic Books.

Bowlby, J. (1963). Pathological mourning and childhood mourning. *Journal of the American Psychoanalytic Association*, *11*, 500–541.

Davidson, S. (1979). Massive psychic traumatization and social support. *Journal of Psychosomatic Research*, *23*, 395–402.

Erikson, E. (1970). Reflections on the dissent of contemporary youth. *International Journal of Psychoanalysis*, *51*, 11–22.

Freud, S. (1917). Mourning and melancholia. In J. Strachey (Ed. & Trans.), *The standard edition of the complete psychological works of Sigmund Freud* (Vol. 14, pp. 243–258). London: Hogarth Press.

Gerson, S. (2009). When the third is dead: Memory, mourning, and the witnessing in the aftermath of the Holocaust. *International Journal of Psychoanalysis*, *90*, 1341–1357.

Goffman, E. (1961). *Asylums: Essays on the social situation of mental patients and other inmates*. Chicago, IL: Aldine Publishing Company.

Green, A. (1986). The dead mother. In *On private madness* (pp. 142–173). London: Hogarth Press.

Grossman, D. (2007, May 13). Writing in the dark. *New York Times*, available at www.nytimes.com.

Grubrich-Simitis, I. (1981). Extreme traumatization as cumulative trauma: Psychoanalytic investigations of the effects of concentration camp experiences on survivors and their children. *Psychoanalytic Study of the Child*, *36*, 415–450.

Hartmann, H. (1958). Comments on the scientific aspects of psychoanalysis. *Psychoanalytic Study of the Child*, *13*, 127–146.

Kestenberg, J. (1972). Psychoanalytic contributions to the problems of children of Nazi persecution. *Israel Annals of Psychiatry and Related Disciplines*, *10*, 311–325.

Kestenberg. J. (1977). *Psychological consequences of punitive institutions humanizing America*. New York: Knopf.

Kestenberg, J. (1982). Metapsychological consequences based on the analysis of a survivor's child. In M. Bergman & M. Jocuvy (Eds.), *Generations of the Holocaust*. New York: Basic Books.

Kohut, H. (1971). *The analysis of the self: A systematic approach to the psychoanalytic treatment of narcissistic personality disorders*. Chicago, IL: University of Chicago Press.

Kohut, H. (1978 [1966]). Forms and transformations of narcissism. In P. Ornstein (Ed.), *The search for the self* (Vol. 1, pp. 427–460). New York: International Universities Press.

Kohut, H. (1978 [1972]). Thoughts on narcissism and narcissistic rage. In P. Ornstein (Ed.), *The search for the self* (Vol. 2, pp. 615–658). New York: International Universities Press.

Kohut, H. (1978a [1973]). Psychoanalysis in a troubled world. In P. Ornstein (Ed.), *The search for the self* (Vol. 2). New York: International Universities Press.

Kohut, H. (1978b [1973]). The psychoanalyst in the community of scholars. In P. Ornstein (Ed.), *The search for the self* (Vol. 2, pp. 685–724). New York: International Universities Press.

Krystal, H. (1978). Trauma and affects. *Psychoanalytic Study of the Child, 33*, 81–116.

Levine, H. (1982). Toward a psychoanalytic understanding of children of survivors of the Holocaust. *Psychoanalytic Quarterly, 51*, 70–92.

Niederland, W. (1968). The problem of the survivor. In H. Krystal (Ed.), *Massive psychic trauma* (pp. 8–22). New York: International Universities Press.

Ogden, T. H. (1994). The analytic third: Working with intersubjective clinical facts. *International Journal of Psycho-Analysis, 75*, 3–19.

Ornstein, A. (1974). The dread to repeat and the new beginning: A contribution to the treatment of narcissistic personality disorders. *The Annual of Psychoanalysis, 2*, 231–248.

Ornstein, A. (1985). Survival and recovery. *Psychoanalytic Inquiry, 5*, 99–130.

Ornstein, A. (1989). Treatment issues with survivors and their offspring. In P. Marcus & J. Rosenberg (Eds.), *Healing their wounds: Psychotherapy with Holocaust survivors and their families* (pp. 105–116). Santa Barbara, CA: Praeger.

Ornstein, A. (1991). The dread to repeat: Comments on the working through process in psychoanalysis. *Journal of the American Psychoanalytic Association, 39*, 377–398.

Ornstein, A. (2010a). The missing tombstone: Reflections on mourning and creativity. *Journal of the American Psychoanalytic Association, 58*, 631–648.

Ornstein, A. (2010b). Tracing changes in psychoanalysis and psychoanalytic psychotherapy. *Selbspsychologie, 42*, 299–331.

Ornstein, A. (2011). The function of groups at times of war and terror. *Forum: Journal of the International Association of Group Psychotherapy*, 25–36.

Ornstein, A. (2012). Mass murder and the individual: Psychoanalytic reflections on perpetrators and their victims. *International Journal of Group Psychotherapy, 62*, 1–20.

Ornstein, A. (in press). Self-abuse and suicidality: Clinical manifestations of chronic narcissistic rage. In N. Kulish & D. Holzman (Eds.), *The Clinical Problems of Masochism*. New York: Jason Aronson.

Ornstein, A. & Goldman, S. (2004). *My mother's eyes: Holocaust memories of a young girl*. Cincinnati, OH: Emmis Books.

Ornstein, P., Ornstein, A., Zaleznik, A., & Schwaber, E. (1977). On the continuing evolution of psychoanalytic psychotherapy: Reflections and predictions. *The Annual of Psychoanalysis, 5*, 329–370.

Tolpin, M. (2002). Doing psychoanalysis of normal development: Forward edge transferences. In A. Goldberg (Ed.), *Progress in self psychology: Postmodern self psychology* (Vol. 18, pp. 167–190). Hillsdale, NJ: Analytic Press.

8

THE PERSONAL IS POLITICAL, THE POLITICAL IS PERSONAL

On the subjectivity of an Israeli psychoanalyst

Chana Ullman

In memory of my father.

Writing autobiographically on the development of one's subjectivity is not an easy matter. There is the awareness that as much as one is revealing, there is also, always, the simultaneous, inevitable need to conceal. There is the awareness of the limitations of our insights into our history and makeup even if "well-analyzed." There is the apprehension about how an invisible audience – including perhaps patients, students, colleagues – will read these revelations. Aron's (1996) argument about self-disclosure in analysis is no less relevant to the disclosures of the writer. Describing the conflict between a need to know and be known, and the need to protect some aspects of ourselves that need to remain private and reserved, he writes: "We are always concealing while we are revealing! If it is inevitable that we will reveal aspects of ourselves, it is equally inevitable that we will conceal aspects of ourselves" (p. 234).

I write as an analyst and as an Israeli. "Israel is not only a place but an obsession" (Margalit, 1998, p. ix). It makes a total claim on those who live there. Israeli politics is saturated with the mad intensity of victims and perpetrators, heretics and saints, survival and luxury, dreamers and schemers. It is a sociocultural, political "pressure cooker" in which the uncanny, the presence of the absence, coexists with a mostly dissociated sense of chronic threat to safety in the here and now, along with a vitality and a creative energy. It is a melting pot in which immigrants from culturally divided diasporas, from Morocco to Byelorussia, from Ethiopia to the USA, have to share a common language revived from ancient biblical times. It is a society in which claims for democracy, freedom of speech, economic miracles, and academic excellence coexist with a 45-year-old occupation of the Palestinians, with constant daily violations of human rights, and with military discourse and violent traces of military service dominating civilian life. This is where I was born, in the same year that the state of Israel gained independence, and this is where I grew up, eventually graduating from the Hebrew university and (many years later) receiving psychoanalytic training at the Tel-Aviv Institute of Contem-

98

porary Psychoanalysis. It is, therefore, no wonder that I see the intertwining of the personal and the political in the making of my professional identity. Professional identity always emerges in a context. For me, this context has been the multilayered politics (in the most general sense) of survival, of profound losses and past trauma along with the promise of a new start. This chapter focuses on aspects of my personal history that I see as inseparable from my politics, from my work, and from what I consider valuable in psychoanalysis.

I shall focus on two pieces of my biography that I believe exemplify and clarify the merger of the personal and the political, the individual and the collective or cultural, and the merger of the intrapsychic and the professional. The first is an episode that continues to inform my interest in witnessing as a therapeutic stance and curative factor; the second is a complex building block of my family history that continues to inform my interest in relational theory.

When forgiveness is not possible

My father was born in a small village in Czechoslovakia, a fourth son in a family of nine. He lost his father at the age of nine and was sent away by a loving but devastated mother who could not support the family, to study at a Yeshiva. Away from home, he was invited to eat at the homes of wealthier families, who did not always treat him generously.

The Nazi occupation started for him in 1939, when he was drafted to the Hungarian army as a forced laborer, building roads and bridges for the advancing Germans. He saw his entire family taken by trucks to a place from which no one returned, and was violently pushed away by his mother, when he tried to climb on the truck and join them.

Despite the enormous losses and traumas he endured, the internalized father of my childhood was a heroic figure. He was, for me, a fighter who came out victorious, although victory was never important for him and the glee of the victor or the drive for revenge was far from his temperament. He remained strikingly capable of seeing the point of view of the other without giving up his own. He remained, throughout his life, optimistic and grateful for the new life he had been able to create.

A few years ago, I participated in a workshop with German analysts from Heidelberg and Israeli-Jews, analysts from the Tel-Aviv Institute of Contemporary Psychoanalysis. The workshop consisted of a professional dialogue, which in this meeting occurred in the context of a powerful, poignant, personal encounter between two groups separated and yet inextricably connected by the traumatic history of the Holocaust. At the end of the second day of the workshop, having heard the personal and moving testimonials of members of the two groups, having struggled with our reservations and rage, with blame and guilt over our own (Israeli) role as perpetrators of suffering, and having told the group about the history of my parents who are both survivors of the Holocaust, I told some of the German colleagues that I was going to visit my parents later that evening. One of them said: "Will you tell them about the workshop? Tell them we ask for their forgiveness, and tell us what they said." Visiting my parents later that evening, I indeed told them about the workshop and about the German analyst's request. My parents were both visibly shaken. My father, who was the sole survivor of his large family, said: "Tell them we recognize that they want our forgiveness." I was struck by this simple but profound response. It clarified for me a question I have been struggling with, both in my work as a psychoanalyst and as an Israeli living under chronically traumatic and threatening circumstances: What do we do when there does not seem to be a possibility of forgiveness or reparation? What if the evil and suffering endured is too monstrous? Is there a possibility of reconciliation when lives are shattered and the losses cannot be mourned? My father's response offered a possible stance: there can still be recognition given for the need or desire for forgiveness and reparation. When forgiveness or reconciliation is impossible, when mutuality cannot be achieved, there can still be an acknowledgement of a desire for them.

Witnessing behind the couch and outside the office

This clarified for me my interest in the idea and nature of witnessing both in the consultation room and in society. My father's response, it seems to me, holds within it the respect for inevitable otherness, the understanding of differences that cannot be erased, as well as the offer of recognition while acknowledging the impossibility of reciprocity. As I elaborated elsewhere (Ullman, 2006), I participated for several years in the human rights group "*Machsom* watch" (Checkpoint watch), an experience that formed and transformed my awareness of the context in which I live and practice and which I call home. This experience was transformative because it brought home for me the corrosive power of and unbearable steep slide towards dehumanization. It impressed upon me the power of denial as a collective experience, the denial of an acutely proximate social reality of suffering and evil, as well as the potential for reversing it. As an eyewitness to the military checkpoints that closely control and monitor Palestinian civilian movements within the West Bank (during the years 2002–2005), I confronted a reality that was previously absent from my supposedly sophisticated, well-informed political worldview. At the checkpoints, I was suddenly faced with the concrete human meaning of life without any semblance of the autonomy that I take for granted, with the humiliating routine and the helpless submission and fear that it breeds.

Eyewitnessing shattered my blindness as I faced the suffering of the stranger and the face of the other. Felman and Laub (1992) defined massive trauma as an event without a witness. Self-knowledge of the trauma does not exist prior to being witnessed; the knowledge evolves through the process of witnessing and is inseparable from it. In this process, a crisis is inevitable. As I encountered a world in which familiar categories failed, I was forced to meet the Palestinian in her world. This generated a crisis in which my own identity was threatened. How can I, a mother of soldiers in the Israeli Defense Forces (IDF), argue with the young

Israeli soldiers at the checkpoints? Who am I at this juncture – a perpetrator? An accomplice? A victim? A well- intended but naïve participant, ignorant of the dangers threatening my own people? Bearing in mind and heart my parents' history, am I denying possible imminent threats to my security? At the checkpoints, my identity was also threatened by the gaze of the Palestinian.

During a particularly difficult and frustrating watch at a checkpoint near Jerusalem, I conversed with a Palestinian youth whose entry was refused. He told me of his family and his studies. Suddenly, he said: "You know what I feel like? I feel like throwing this huge stone straight at his [the Israeli soldier's] head." I was shocked. In sharing this impulse with me, I felt he erased my identity, treating me as an accomplice, as someone who shares his hatred. This episode (Ullman, 2006) marked for me the boundaries of merger, and underscored the impossibility of mutuality and symmetry in situations of social violence, as well as in other professional and personal encounters. It brought home a realization of the violence that is inherent in the erasure of differences, in assimilating the other to what is known, and highlighted for me the dictum (cf. Peperzak, 1993) not to turn away from otherness, not to expect similarity or reciprocity and to face asymmetry. It also points to the danger of the mingling of the political and the personal – in attempting to save the other, we may be denying his complicated face and the dangers that are inherent in the encounter. In attempting to cross the barriers to meet the other, am I giving up self-protection, natural anxieties that should guide me (cf. Govrin, 2011)? There is a crisis of subjectivity here (cf. Straker, 2006).

It is only through this process of crisis that true recognition can emerge – seeing the face of the other without the patronizing use of the other to affirm us, without what Mitchell (2000) calls "guiltiness" or what Straker (2004) describes as "white guilt." This crisis in subjectivity introduced me to a constant danger in the work with victims of trauma, as well as in political activism: we may be tempted to pseudo-reparation in which there is a fantasy of salvation while the complicated face of the other is denied. At the same time, it introduced me to the possibility and necessity of the witness in reversing the process of dehumanization.

Reflecting on my experience at the checkpoints, I am aware of the multiplicity of selves and of the complex intertwining of the personal and the political, the autobiographical memory and collective memory. My presence at the *machsom* (checkpoint) does not only attest to the trauma of the other, it is also born out of the shame and guilt of being on the powerful side. On another level, it reveals the traces of the guilt of the survivor, or the guilt of the child who cannot cure her parents.

In a way, at the checkpoints, I am the perpetrator asking for forgiveness that cannot be given. My presence at the checkpoints is stamped by the scars of my own traumas. While I belong to the side of the perpetrators, I am also on a side that has been victimized. In my political activism, I am a carrier of multiple selves. I belong to the powerful, privileged side of the aggressor, as well as to the side of the victim. However, in emphasizing my role as a witness, I resist identifying with either role. As a witness at the checkpoints, my presence delivers a complex message. It announces: I do not identify with and I feel ashamed by policies committed in my name. It also announces: I know what it means to be a victim, humiliated and helpless, but I refuse to take part in the "doer-done to" seesaw (Benjamin, 2002) and in the cycle of violence that disavowed and unwitnessed trauma may create. In retrospect, my father's message, in fact his entire life, epitomized for me the possibility of recognition – even following the trauma of genocide – while respecting the impossibility of "saving" the other or even identifying with her.

Like many others (e.g., Boulanger, 2007; Orange, 2010; Poland, 2000; Stern, 2010), I have been interested in the role of the analyst as witness (Ullman, 2006, 2010). In exploring our role as the professional other in analysis, there are important distinctions to be considered, distinctions between the role of the analyst as witness and other functions that we attempt (and fail) to perform (Benjamin, 2010; Poland, 2000). Regulating, holding, interpreting, acknowledging harm, and surviving enactments – all are crucial processes through which we participate in the complex relationship in which one can recover a dissociated or shattered self.

But our presence as witnesses to patients' traumas requires a particular stance. It requires the moral responsibility of acknowledging a reality, an external reality, of evil and suffering, and a lingering without recoil on the detailed narrative of this reality. As witnesses in the office and beyond, we have to be clear, we have to take a stance. This is not so easy for the psychoanalyst trained to look for ambiguity, complexity, dialectics.

In treating survivors of trauma, I have to feel and say clearly to my patients: what happened to you is horrible and should not happen to anyone. I have to acknowledge that there is evil in the world and in the person or people who did this to you. There is no complexity here. There are victims and perpetrators, and there was nothing you could have done to prevent the trauma.

This is easy enough for me with regard to immense catastrophes such as the Holocaust or to sexual abuse. What about lesser evils? What about ongoing oppression in one's own backyard? What about patients' participation in acts of violence that are socially sanctioned and even celebrated? Whether we intend to or not, our discourse becomes political. No witnessing can be politically free.

Even bearing witness to ongoing social trauma in our offices is a political act that involves risk. This is a risk encountered every day in Israeli clinical practice. It is in bearing witness to social violence in my own backyard that I risk the most. If I speak about a process of brutalization, of gradual dehumanization, of growing a thick skin to evils practiced in my own society, as part of a slippery slope in which we gradually become indifferent to evil and suffering, am I comparing these lesser evils to genocide or the Holocaust?

As a psychoanalyst in Israel, I live and practice under the same traumatic circumstances that my patients testify about. This complicates my role as witness. Witnessing ongoing social violence incurs risk and attracts hostility. In some places in the world, people who speak up may risk their lives. Here, I may risk being blamed by my community, at best being blamed for my simplemindedness, naiveté, or for ignoring complexities. At worst, I may risk being treated as a traitor.

I risk losing the sense of safety that group identifications give us. I risk the guilt or shame of being identified as oversimplifying or ignoring profound anxieties and pain that indeed may underlie a situation of oppression. As a psychoanalyst in Israel, I live and practice under the same traumatic circumstances that my patients testify about. This complicates my role as witness.

The intertwining of the personal, the political, and the professional becomes clearer to me as I write about witnessing behind the couch and in society and in emphasizing the curative role of the witness (cf. Ullman, 2006) and the moral imperative of witnessing (cf. Boulanger, 2012) in our role as mental health professionals in Israel (cf. Ullman, 2010), I am also, once again, the child who is a witness to her parents' silent suffering. There is reparation in the reproduction: turning the passive into active, helplessness into agency, silence into speech. It is a reparation motivated by complex dynamics informing my political and professional interests: the emphasis on an otherwise denied reality of evil and suffering which my parents endured, the focus on the role of the witness exposed to and walking the distance to the world of the other at the same time that she remains an observer of it – much like the child who feels the presence of a reality that she can barely apprehend and attempt to enter, at the same time that she remains insulated and separated from it.

"We never moved from one another"

While the first episode I shared refers to my father's retrospective acknowledgement of the impossibility of forgiveness, the second refers to my mother's story of survival. My mother, too, was born in a small village in Czechoslovakia (in an area that now belongs to the Ukraine). She was one of ten children, the youngest daughter followed by three boys. She grew up in a relatively affluent orthodox Jewish family. This is her testimony, using mostly her words: the war started for them in 1939 with Nazi confiscation of stores, with the humiliation and harassment of Jews. Theirs was the only store allowed to remain open. On Passover of 1944, the Jews of the entire area were taken to a ghetto, and the transports to Auschwitz began right away. My mother, her parents, her sisters, including a sister with a baby and a small child, and the three younger brothers (ages 7, 9, and 14) were taken in the cargo train on the trip to another planet (Kaztnick). Arriving in Auschwitz in the dark, they were separated from the men, from their parents, and from the younger children, never to see them again. Younger men, Jewish guards, shouted in Yiddish – give away the children, let go of the children if you want to live – forcefully taking the children from the younger women. The screaming reached the sky, but there was no heaven, only hell. My mother found her two sisters in the morning, shaved and stripped of their clothing; they could hardly recognize each other. They were shoved into the barracks, six in one bunk. They stuck together: "We did not move from one another, went together even to the latrines."

After two months in Auschwitz, the three sisters (then 16, 18, and 19) were taken to work at a German ammunition factory. For six and a half months, they worked inspecting bombs and grenades produced by the Germans. Occasionally, one of them worked in the kitchen, saving some bread for the others. They bought a needle, paying with bread. The older sister sewed the cloths given to them to make them fit better and saved some cloth. When one was burned by the hot machine oil, she made a bandage and sleeves they could wear to protect themselves. They washed themselves and their clothes in the snow. My mother, the youngest, was watched particularly closely by her sisters. In 1945, as the Russians approached, they were forced to walk with the fleeing Germans. In the midst of constant shelling they miraculously stayed alive, pushing carts that protected them from the freezing snow. They arrived in Mauthausen "which was even worse than Auschwitz," and then taken again to Bergen Belsen where people died like flies, and the only food was uncooked potatoes. Her older sister was sick with typhus. The others sold a diamond ring that was sewn into a dress, and managed to buy sugar and beets, placing a little bit of this everyday on her lips. My mother and her two sisters did not move from one another until the day of liberation, when British troops entered the camp.

This is an abbreviated version of my mother's testimony. There is a lacuna in these words which tell the facts, while the story remains unspeakable, neither fully remembered nor ever forgotten. There is a muteness in the midst of the words. It is a story of the living experience of deadness and the enduring presence of an absence (cf. Faimberg, 2005; Gerson, 2009). And yet there is a message that conveys the courage of living with the memory of loss, and upholding the ties that sustain life. This message remained with me throughout my childhood and to this day. I believe that my mother's mantra – "We never moved from one another to the end of the war" – has been a formative influence engraved in my character and professional identity.

Relational bubbles

In a number of important papers, Anna Ornstein (e.g., 1985, 2001, this volume), herself a Holocaust survivor, critically reviews the psychiatric and psychoanalytic literature on survivors, arguing for the variability of experiences of survivors, and suggesting the factors that enabled resilience even within the valley of death. Ornstein cites several factors accounting for adaptation in the camps. She emphasizes the difference between trauma endured alone and secretly, and trauma endured collectively, poignantly describing relational bonds as the foremost protective factor:

> Prisoners arriving together made every effort to occupy neighboring bunks. The common sleeping space functioned as a home and family and was fiercely protected from "strangers." In order to weaken morale, the Germans repeatedly interfered with this life-sustaining grouping. Still, as groups were disrupted, new groups formed, indicating the need – and the capacity – to establish some form of social structure that made survival

psychologically possible . . . Finding out who lived, who died, who was sent to another camp kept the social network alive, and feeling oneself to be the member of such a network had more than a sociopsychological significance. The capacity to actively seek out social contacts was the most significant "carryover" from the pre-Holocaust personality to camp conditions.

(1985, p. 108)

Ornstein describes small kinship groups protecting and aiding one another as much as was possible, as a major source of resilience: ". . . the differences in the degree of adaptation achieved . . . can be related back, above all, to the varying degree of initiative taken in making contact with others and to differences in the amount of comradeship displayed" (p. 108).

Reading Ornstein, I remember my amazement in discovering that what I thought was a unique and idiosyncratic biographical aspect of my mother's story – her luck in staying together with two of her sisters, the three of them keeping each other alive – also emerges in Ornstein's work as characteristic of life in the midst of the death and labor camps, where inmates formed small kinship groups with family or people they knew from their previous life, sustaining each other. It appears that what we can call insulated relational bubbles were created, perhaps increasing chances, if not of physical survival (no one in my mother's environment would have survived if the war lasted even a few days longer), then perhaps for the possibility of preserving some continuity, emotions, humanity, touch, enabling psychological survival.

Thus, the ability to hold on to the incommunicable in the presence of another, the presence of the other with whom one can live through the unspeakable shattering of all that was familiar, became a self-evident truth engrained in my biography. This seems to me to be a guiding principle that cuts across the terrains that we travel in our work. It is a theme that informs our understanding of attachment and development, of psychic survival versus deadness and "empty" zones, of life during and post-trauma, and a principle that guides our understanding of the therapeutic endeavor. This simple truth cuts across many of the illuminating contributions to relational theory. It is, therefore, no wonder that when I became acquainted with relational writings at later stages of my professional training, I felt I found a professional home. This is the kind of analyst I can and want to be, I thought, as past met present and resonated with the writings of Mitchell, Aron, Benjamin, Davies, Altman, and others who shaped the relational approach.

Risk and resilience

Ornstein's papers (1985, 2001, this volume) are critical of the automatic assumptions regarding psychopathology of survivors and of the transgenerational transmission of the trauma and losses endured. She argues that a second-generation syndrome is too readily applied in the psychiatric literature:

Patients who are second generation have come with complaints not different from their contemporaries . . . But the answers offered to the children of survivors have been formulated with far greater ease and with greater certainty than the answers for their contemporaries. Being children of Holocaust survivors was expected to explain their symptoms more than adequately, and everything from drug-abuse to schizophrenia was explained as the consequence of the parents' Holocaust experiences.

(1985, p. 100)

Ornstein's arguments for the specificity of survivors' experiences, her description of the forms resilience took within the death camps, and her criticism of the assumed psychiatric syndrome of second-generation survivors, are unusual in the clinical and psychoanalytic literature. The early literature tended to emphasize the psychopathology of survivors and their offspring (e.g., Bergmann & Jucovy, 1982; Kestenberg, 1972). The later literature focused on the inevitable transmission of wounds across the generations (Faimberg, 2005; Gample, 2010; Gerson, 2009; Laub & Lee, 2003), suggesting the pathways and manifestations of such transmission. There is also, however, support for Ornstein's premise. Her argument is consistent with research on second-generation survivors which points to the complexity of the variables involved, and the difficulty of assuming specific causal connections between the Holocaust trauma of parents and pathology in their children (e.g., Bar-On, 1996; Last, 1989; Rivnitzki, 1984). This research often fails to find differences between second-generation and control populations, and in fact points to better coping and better adjustment among second-generation than normal samples (e.g., Tytell, 1998; Zahn-Waxler & Kochanska, 1990).

These findings are also consistent with research I supervised on patterns of parenting among second-generation Holocaust survivors and their adolescent children (Yogev, 2004). Yogev (2004) did not find any differences in parental awareness, parental functioning, and communication with adolescent children among second-generation parents and a control group. There were, however, specific patterns unique to this group: a greater emphasis on continuity and a mission to transmit the memory and family history to their children, greater self-criticism regarding their own role as parents, and greater commitment to aid their aging parents. In this respect, Yogev's sample exemplified some constructive modes of serving as "memorial candles" (Vardi, 1990) to the parents' trauma.

It is impossible to do justice here to the vast and complex literature on second-generation survivors, but my aim is to elucidate what I see as relevant or influential in my professional and political identity. Is there a way to reconcile the complex, sometimes inconsistent claims of transgenerational transmission as deadening or contaminating (Gample, 2010) and the findings of no differences in pathology and even better adjustment among second-generation survivors? A recent paper by Shahar, Elad-Strenger, and Henrich (2012) argues against the clear-cut distinction between risk and resilience common in the psychosocial literature. They suggest the term "risky resilience" or "resilient risk" to convey a dialectics: any psychosocial factor, by its very nature, should be expected to include elements of both risk and resilience, any quality that increases vulnerability (risk) can also produce resilience as part of its consequences, and vice versa. With respect to the issue at hand, the propensity for guilt and oversensitivity to parental suffering, the difficulty handling aggression, a drive to compensate or undo parents' losses – all identified in the literature as producing risks in the development of second-generation survivors – can also produce circumstances that bolster adjustment (e.g., empathy, caring, drive for achievement). In particular, and in terms of my focus here on the personal and the political, I believe my own worldview and professional values are, in part, a manifestation of a guilt prone position, a drive to repair damage and a need to minimize aggression, and a depressive position which can be traced to the legacy of the second generation, which in my own life serves as a vulnerability as well as an asset.

The shadow of memory

Growing up in Israel in the 1950s and 1960s, I was very much aware of my unspoken membership in a secret subculture, the affinity with those who were second-generation Holocaust survivors. It was an ambivalent affinity, at once saturated with shame and pride, a sense of being marked at the same time that it bestowed specialness. The specialness had to do with a vague sense of mission – to uphold the memory, to serve as memorial candles (Vardi, 1990), as well as an acute sense of a precious promise to be the future. I needed to be perfect and to protect my parents from any pain or harm that I might experience. Mine was an experience that has been a variation on a theme, shared by many in my generation. When I was growing up, none of my close friends had grandparents. This was an accepted "absence," dissociated, taken for granted, and not talked about. I knew very little of my own grandparents and of the large families on both sides who perished, murdered by the Nazis. Until later in my adolescence, I knew little of the details of what my parents endured during the war. The information came in bits and pieces, sometimes in response to a question, sometimes in spontaneous revelations, sometimes in segments of conversations overheard by me. Often it was a cloud (not always a burden) of nonverbal, ritualistic traces of my parents' memories.

A patient tells me that in her grandparents' home there was a box full of shoelaces. Grandfather accumulated shoelaces and did not allow any to be thrown away. We might need them, he said, if we have to run away. Another tells me of her envy, as a child, when she discovered that she cannot have a number engraved on her arm, just like the one her grandmother has. This reverberated for me with the envy I felt, as a child, realizing the intimacy and unwavering closeness of my mother and her sisters from which I felt excluded. Familiar to me and to my second-generation friends are rituals around food ("never throw away bread"), and memories of old black and white pictures hidden in drawers that one knows not to talk about. These are dissociated traces of the absence that threatens to become transgenerationally transmitted wounds. And yet, there is a "risky resilience" (Shahar et al., 2012) at work here as well.

The personal is political in my treatment room

As I mentioned earlier, I live and practice under the same traumatic circumstances that my patients endure, which complicates my role as witness. I am caught in dilemmas of "ethical non-neutrality" (Dimen, 2009). I am primarily engaged in maintaining a haven where patients can safely express and explore the selves that are shaming to them and sometimes appalling to me. I am part of a relationship that always feels personal and specific and caring, not impartial (cf. Frosh, 2010), at the same time that I am a witness to traumas acknowledged and unacknowledged by them, and to their wrongdoings as well as suffering.

R is a male patient, in his 30s. In his civilian life, he is an architect who takes a lot of pride in his independent business. He sees himself as someone who gets along with everybody, is identified with a mother who recently died of cancer whom he describes as nurturing, caring, and docile, while he presents a conflicted relationship with a critical and intrusive father. Most of his father's family perished in Salonika, Greece, but the grandparent who survived was particularly close to R.

He came to therapy because he wants to become more assertive in his relationships with his clients and his wife. During the second year of our work together, he comes back to treatment following a stint of reserve duty in the occupied territories. R is anxious, depressed, has trouble sleeping. He tells me of an episode in which he feels he failed his soldiers. They were carrying out searches in a Palestinian village, and the soldiers were violently harassing some bystanders who were getting in their way. At this point he suddenly became confused, "like a blackout," he says, and he did not know what they were supposed to do next. He moves away. Someone else takes over, and the platoon continues their mission. When they return, he is reprimanded by his superiors, who threaten him with a court martial if this ever happens again. He is very upset. He sees this as his failure and feels worthless and ashamed for disappointing his soldiers. I feel his pain. I realize the social and professional pressures to perform as commander. I can sense the fear and the tensions of walking in "enemy" territory. I am also aware of my own reaction of anger at the harassment of civilians that he described.

As we talk about his experience preceding the blackout, I try to point out that his "blackout" may have been related to the harassment of civilians, which clashes with his usual nonbelligerent self, perhaps placing him in conflict. I am thinking of his "blackout" as a dissociative episode activated by the terror of perceived danger and by the aggression unleashed in him (cf. Boulanger, 2007). He objects vehemently. No, they deserve this; he does not feel any remorse or empathy for the Palestinians, only for his soldiers. He wants me to help him to be able to face his soldiers again, and prepare him to shoulder the burden with them, fighting the "dirty" war that he feels is imperative. I am surprised by this strong objection to my interpretation, an objection which is unusual for him. I am aware that my own "outsider" perspective, my attempt to humanize his response and the "enemy," cannot meet his own traumatic experience and is possibly construed as a weakness that he needs to disavow. I feel unable to further explore the meaning of this episode beyond focusing on his loyalty and dedication to his soldiers.

A few months later, he goes on a business trip. His last stop on this trip is Vienna. While there, on his day off, he wanders into a park and walks around in an idyllic setting. Suddenly, as he hears some people approaching him speaking German, he experiences a "blackout" again. He becomes paranoid, feeling he is being followed, experiences mounting panic, and rushes back to his hotel, where he gradually calms down. This time he experiences great relief when I relate this experience to the collective Jewish history of persecution, and his own third-generation identification with the history of his grandparents, who survived the Holocaust. Later on, we are also able to return to his "blackout" in the Palestinian village. In his recollections, he felt the same mounting panic and a need to escape as he watched the aggressive harassment of helpless civilians. It becomes possible to explore the complexities revealed by the reversal of roles, by what seems to be a split-off, disavowed identification with the victim in the first episode, which then becomes the primary experience in the second one, in which he experiences himself as being surrounded by powerful perpetrators. Together, we were able to mourn the loss of a sense of omnipotence and agentic control, previously experienced in his military service and lost in the experience of the first panic attack, as well as to recover underlying guilt and remorse about the pain he inevitably inflicted, without losing what he called the "fraternity of his friends in arms" and pride in his national identity.

Personal reverberations

R's story can be looked at through different theoretical lenses. The Oedipal drama of a child haunted by an internalized persecutory father, and struggling with an identification with a beloved but weak mother, enacted in the alternating positions of victim/victimizer, did not escape our notice in his treatment. It has been a theme in many of our sessions that focused on his relationship with his aging father and with his wife. It would have been, however, impossible for me to look at the pivotal episodes described here solely or primarily from this perspective.

It is the striking personal reverberations of the intrapsychic and biographical with the political and historical context that informed my work with R as well as other patients. I cannot escape the political in the personal and the personal in the political; he touched familiar nerves of my own biography and context. I recognized the identification with the Jew as victim embedded in the history of my own parents (and his grandparents). Simultaneously, I am responding to my inner calling to attest to a dissociated reality of suffering and evil. It is an inner calling that reflects, I believe, the way my engagement with my parents' history entered the formation of my character and thus the transference and countertransference (cf. Altman, 2011) experienced in my work. In the work with R, I recognize my proclivity to an identification with the "weaker" party, a sort of chronic depressive position, which calls for acknowledging the opposing points of view and which may be common to second-generation survivors, as suggested by the literature I briefly reviewed here. This may be the same partiality that blinded me to dangers that my patient felt were imminent and real in the first episode, therefore experiencing my interpretation as abandonment.

I believe that these vignettes from R's treatment demonstrate a power reversal that is endemic in the Jewish Israeli consciousness, and may be universal in the seesaw of guilt and terror (cf. Benjamin, 2002). In making the connection between the West Bank and Vienna, my patient's unconscious reconnected a dissociation between the personal and the collective, between the intrapsychic and the political. It is also a connection that I am not likely to miss, and which is particularly salient in my own subjectivity. With R and others, I travel a familiar intersubjective territory of multiple selves and shifting identifications, without losing the coherence of an identity.

References

Altman, N. (2011). Response to Ullman's paper, "Between denial and witnessing." *Psychoanalytic Perspectives*, *8*(2), 201–206.

Aron, L. (1996). *A meeting of minds: Mutuality in psychoanalysis*. Hillsdale, NJ: Analytic Press.

Bar-On, D. (1996). Studying the transgenerational after effects of the Holocaust. *Israel Journal of Interpersonal Loss*, *1*(3), 215–247.

Benjamin, J. (2002). Guilt and terror. *Psychoanalytic Dialogues*, *12*, 473–484.

Benjamin, J. (2010). Acknowledgment of collective trauma in light of dissociation and dehumanization. *Psychoanalytic Perspectives*, *8*(2), 207–214.

Bergmann, S. M., & Jucovy, M. E. (1982). *Generations of the Holocaust*. New York: Basic Books.

Boulanger, G. (2007). *Wounded by reality: Understanding and treating adult onset trauma*. Mahwah, NJ: Analytic Press.

Boulanger, G. (2012). Psychoanalytic witnessing: Professional obligation or moral imperative? *Psychoanalytic Psychology*, *29*(3), 318–324.

Dimen, M. (2009). A crisis in the subjectivity of the analyst. IARPP Colloquium series. No. 15, April, available at www.iarpp.net.

Faimberg, H. (2005). *The telescoping of generations: Listening to narcissistic links between generations*. London: Routledge.

Felman, S., & Laub, D. (Eds.). (1992). *Testimony: Crises of witnessing in literature, psychoanalysis and history*. New York: Routledge.

Frosh, S. (2010). *Psychoanalysis outside the clinic: Interventions in psychosocial studies*. Basingstoke, UK: Palgrave Macmillan.

Gample, Y. (2010). *The parents who live through me*. Tel-Aviv: Keter.

Gerson, S. (2009). When the third is dead: Memory, mourning, and witnessing in the aftermath of the Holocaust. *International Journal of Psychoanalysis*, *90*(6), 1341–1357.

Govrin, A. (2011). Forget the Palestinians, you are our mother: Why therapists should not be dead right with their patients. *Psychoanalytic Perspectives*, *8*(2), 215–229.

Kestenberg, J. S. (1972). Psychoanalytic contributions to the problems of children of survivors of Nazi persecution. *Israeli Journal of Psychiatry*, *10*, 311–325.

Last, U. (1989). The trans-generational impact of Holocaust trauma: Current state of evidence. *International Journal of Mental Health*, *17*(4), 72–89.

Laub, D., & Lee, S. (2003). Thanatos and massive psychic trauma: The impact of the death instinct on knowing, remembering and forgetting. *Journal of the American Psychoanalytic Association*, *51*, 433–463.

Margalit, A. (1998). *Views in review: Politics and culture in the land of the Jews.* New York: Farrar, Straus, Giroux.

Mitchell, S. A. (2000). You've got to suffer if you want to sing the blues. *Psychoanalytic Dialogues*, *10*, 713–733.

Orange, D. (2010). *The suffering stranger: Hermeneutics for everyday clinical practice.* New York: Routledge.

Ornstein, A. (1985). Survival and recovery. *Psychoanalytic Inquiry*, *5*, 99–130.

Ornstein, A. (2001). Survival and recovery: Psychoanalytic reflections. *Harvard Review of Psychiatry*, *9*(1), 13–22.

Peperzak, A. (1993). *To the other: An introduction to the philosophy of Emanuel Levinas.* West Lafayette, IN: Purdue University Press.

Poland, W. S. (2000). The analyst's witnessing and otherness. *Journal of the American Psychoanalytic Association*, *48*, 17–34.

Rivnitzki, A. (1984). Psychological characteristics of second generation to Holocaust survivors as a function of perceived similarity to parents. MA thesis, Psychology Department, Tel Aviv University.

Shahar, G., Elad-Strenger, J., & Henrich, C. (2012). Risky resilience and resilient risk: The key role of intentionality in an emerging dialectics. *Journal of Social and Clinical Psychology*, *31*, 618–640.

Stern, D. B. (2010). *Partners in thought: Working with unformulated experience, dissociation, and enactment.* New York: Routledge.

Straker, G. (2004). Race for cover: Castrated whiteness, perverse consequences. *Psychoanalytic Dialogues*, *14*, 405–422.

Straker, G. (2006). A crisis in the subjectivity of the analyst: The trauma of morality. *Psychoanalytic Dialogues*, *17*, 153–164.

Tytell, T. (1998). Trauma and its aftermath: A differentiated picture of aftereffects of trauma in daughters of Holocaust survivors. PhD thesis, New School for Social Research, New York City.

Ullman, C. (2006). Bearing witness: Across the barriers in society and in the clinic. *Psychoanalytic Dialogues*, *16*(2), 181–198.

Ullman, C. (2010). Between denial and witnessing: Psychoanalysis and clinical practice in the Israeli context. *Psychoanalytic Perspectives*, *8*(2), 179–200.

Vardi, D. (1990). *The carriers of the Seal: A dialogue with second generation of Holocaust survivors.* Jerusalem: Keter.

Yogev, R. (2004). Parental perception and awareness among second generation of Holocaust survivors towards their adolescent children. MA thesis, The Hebrew University of Jerusalem.

Zahn-Waxler, C., & Kochanska, G. (1990). The origins of guilt. In R. Thompson (Ed.), *Symposium on motivation and socioemotional development* (pp. 183–258). Lincoln, NE: University of Nebraska Press.

9

SWEET DREAMS ARE MADE OF THIS

(Or, how I came out and came into my own)

Eric Sherman

Spring, 1979. I am a high school senior in Brooklyn, New York. Not the trendy borough 20-somethings flock to today, but the birthplace of disco, bad accents, and *Saturday Night Fever*. I fit in like a ham sandwich at a Kosher deli. I am tall and awkward and have an acerbic wit that hides my insecurities like my ridiculous white-man's Afro obscures my oily face. Fortunately, I have a clique of friends who, like me, don't fit in to any larger group – not the jocks, the stoners, not even the super nerds with whom we share advanced placement classes. (Thank God, because I wouldn't want to feel *that* unacceptable.) We cling to our otherness since, at least in our group, it makes us feel the same. We even have a clever name that flaunts our tenuous rebelliousness: The Wicked Dicey Ones. Lynn Eisenberg saw it spray-painted on the side of a subway car and appropriated it for our group.

Lynn is my girlfriend. Sort of. We have been going out for months, and I don't know how much longer I can put off having sex. I try to convince myself I am doing this out of respect for Lynn – but Lynn *wants* to have sex. And I know I'm supposed to want to, also. Well, I do – just not with Lynn. Or any other girl. Oh, Lynn, you have no idea how wicked and dicey things feel inside me.

There is a boy in my math class at whom I often stare. For just a second. As soon as he looks in my direction, I panic. I turn away so quickly it's a miracle I don't get whiplash. Without realizing it, I manage to undo the powerful feelings that just gripped me. It's as if they never existed. How successfully I have quarantined these dangerous desires, like any virus that poses a threat. It will be more than a decade before I learn the word "dissociation," but already I am master craftsman. It is a coping skill with which many gay kids are familiar (Blechner, 2003).

For years now, I have both known and not known at the same time. At home, I lock the bathroom door and masturbate to images of male athletes. (I dare not even consider buying gay pornography; I wouldn't even know where to find it.) I flush the toilet and also my longings. Excitement is replaced by self-loathing.

I have another date with Lynn tonight, and I am already anxious. She will want to go to the playground near our high school to smoke pot and make out. But there is not enough marijuana in the world to calm my jangled nerves. I so much want to be straight, to fit in and feel accepted. To feel *normal*. I excel in school, yet I experience my father's disapproval constantly. This will only seal my fate. My mother will still love me, won't she? I don't know. How can anyone accept me when I cannot accept myself? I think these thoughts and not think them all at once. I think I may throw up.

I have come to a decision. I will break up with Lynn tonight. I will tell her that it doesn't make sense for us to continue going out when I will be leaving for college soon and she will be staying behind. Surely I must realize how ridiculous this logic is. I am a smart kid, but I cannot afford logic at this moment.

After the breakup, Lynn and I remain friends, and I leave for college several months later. Lynn begins to date another boy in our group, who soon comes out of the closet. He will be dead of AIDS in five years. A third Wicked Dicey male comes out in graduate school. I know now, from both life experience and years of being an analyst, that it is not unusual for closeted gay kids to somehow find each other and become friends without ever knowing they share a secret. It's not a surprise that Sullivan put so much theoretical emphasis on the idea of the chum. Who better than a closeted gay man to come up with a theory of interpersonal anxiety? (Blechner, 2005).

Summer, 1982. In a couple of months, I will return to college a senior – that much closer to graduation, to becoming an adult. Life is good, an unfamiliar experience for me. I have a decent summer job, a growing self-confidence, and hope as I look to the future.

I have already told two people about my attraction to other men. Three if you include admitting it to myself. One is a friend of a friend who has the audacity to be openly gay. The other is a college counselor – the first person I worked up the nerve to tell face-to-face. Well, in truth, I told my sneaker. I was so terrified of the counselor's rejection, I was unable to look her in the eye. But she waited patiently, gently encouraging me to speak what seemed unspeakable, somehow casting a lifeline of approval just as the shame threatened to engulf me.

There are wonderful new feelings within me – a wish to feel happy, whole. I want to act on my frightening, exciting desires. I no longer wish to banish them from awareness. I want to come out and come into myself, to be gay in all senses of the word.

I want to have sex.

I am standing on the corner of Christopher Street in Greenwich Village. I have only minutes ago emerged from a 45-minute subway ride from Brooklyn, where I am living over the summer break with my mother and sister. I am filled with both excitement and trepidation. I have never been to a gay bar, although I have walked by, furtively hoping to catch a look, even as I avert my eyes. Tonight I will set foot inside. That is what I must do, want to do, can't wait to do – am desperately avoiding. What if someone I know sees me? What will they think of me? What if my family finds out?

My head feels blurry as I start down Christopher Street. The sidewalks are crowded with people, both gay and straight. I am startled that there are so many straight people, people I fear will judge me. It would feel safer if everyone were gay – yet wouldn't *that* be even more scary?

I come to a bar and peer nervously inside. It is dark and relatively empty. The men inside stand mostly alone, huddled over drinks. I am frozen with fear. I tell myself this is not the right place for me. I tell myself to walk on, take my time. There are plenty of bars on Christopher Street. Relax. *Relax*! RELAX, DAMMIT!

I walk on past several bars, each one as foreboding as the next. I am deeper into Christopher Street, closing in on the piers. Men walk hand-in-hand and there are few (if any) straight people on the streets. The bars, with names like Rawhide and Anvil, are more crowded. The mood is more vibrant, urgent, sexual. I can feel terror swelling within me. I cannot tell whether the awful pounding in my ears is from the throbbing music in the bars or from my racing heart. I am unable to will myself into one of the establishments. By the time I reach West Street at the end of Christopher, I feel almost nauseous as I see two men in chaps leaning against a car, kissing and groping one another. I cannot bear this. This – this is not me. It *can't* be me. I turn on West Street and walk one block downtown, away from the excitement. Then I turn back toward the subway station feeling doomed and defeated.

I cannot do this. I can't. It's too much. I imagine the terrible train ride back to Brooklyn. I am approaching Sixth Avenue and the subway. My eyes are filled with tears. I admonish myself brutally. Weakling. Coward. You will always feel trapped.

As I reach the stairs to the subway station, I pause for a minute. I notice a McDonald's across the street. I take a deep breath and somehow, for a moment, am able to steady myself. Maybe if I go in to the restaurant and have a Coke, I can calm down and work up the nerve to try again.

That is what I do. For 10 or 15 minutes, I sit on a hard, swiveling chair bolted to the floor of the McDonald's. I somehow calm myself. The barrage of self-recriminations slows, and I am able to hear more soothing voices. You can do this. Just try, just one more time. If it doesn't work out, then you can go home.

With equal parts dread and determination, I head back to Christopher Street. It is no more easy this time, but halfway down the block, I somehow, *somehow* work up the nerve to walk into a bar. When my eyes adjust to the smoky darkness, I stare down my urge to run and instead approach the bartender and order a drink. I head to a dark corner, the glass shaking in my hand. The expression on my face screams to everyone, "Please talk to me! Please stay away!"

Not surprisingly, they stay away. But the rum soon works its magic. I spot an attractive man in an alligator shirt. (It *is* 1982, after all – the age of alligator shirts and feathered hair.) It takes me just a second to plan out what I will say, and five minutes to force my feet into action. But ultimately they work – one in front of the other. And, thankfully, so do my verbal skills. "I'm afraid my polo pony trumps your alligator," I say, pointing to our shirts and doing my best to flash a playful smile.

A small miracle happens. The man in the shirt laughs.

He has a nice smile, and a nice laugh. We talk for a while and . . . well . . . it *is* 1982, after all – the age of sex without worry. The summer before the plague.

My first one-night stand. Not bad. The next weekend I am back in the Village – still nervous, but also filled with excitement. This time, I try a different bar, Uncle Charlie's, a few blocks from Christopher Street. It is less grimy. I like this bar. It shows something called music videos on large screens as attractive young men mill about. Annie Lennox of the Eurythmics is singing "Sweet Dreams (Are Made of This)" on the music system when I see a guy my age holding – of all things – a box of Entenmann's cookies. Talk about *sweet* dreams! Once again I dream up a clever opening line (I *am* growing confident – although the cookies make it easier). I stride up to him. This will be no one-night stand, but the start of my first romance.

Summer, 2012 and a call from the editor of this volume. Exactly three decades after my summer of love. The perfect opportunity to reflect upon my coming-out process and how it has shaped me. I am wary of idealizing coming out as a neat, one-time event, a transformative developmental milestone that, once achieved, is neatly completed and folded away – like an alligator shirt. After all, when did my coming out actually begin? On Christopher Street in 1983? On the night I broke up with Lynn? When I first told my counselor? In each pre-dissociative moment of my youth when awareness of my sexuality bubbled up in my mind, only to be quickly banished?

In a similar way, I am made uncomfortable reading analytic papers in which difficult enactments are magically solved and the treatment is forever trans-formed. I worry that it causes shame in other analysts who cannot live up to these lofty standards (Sherman, 2005). My experience as a gay man has made me particularly sensitive to issues around shame. Having spent so many years hiding, it is imperative for me to be as open as possible, especially in my writing. I purposely include struggles and failures that may not always cast me in the most positive light. Having grown up without any positive gay role models, I want to be a role model as a supervisor, writer, and analyst by sharing my blind spots, not closeting them.

For me, writing is a form of coming out, regardless of whether I am writing about my sexuality, though I suppose one could say I'm always writing about that since it is an intrinsic part of who I am. It makes me extraordinarily anxious to expose myself on paper. Once again, I yearn to be accepted, to fit in. But it's not only scary. I am filled with the same heady excitement and uncertainty that accompanied my walk down Christopher Street in 1982. Will I be criticized or ostracized by the cool kids, in this case well-respected analytic thinkers? Will I be found wanting? Alternatively, might I be praised? Will I feel too exposed, ashamed of my desire to connect and even show off? Perhaps each time we present our work – whether on paper, at conferences, or in supervision – we take a risk and contact a new part of ourselves. Even when we are cloaked in relative anonymity in the consulting room, we can think of practicing psychoanalysis

ERIC SHERMAN

as a form of coming out, infused with vulnerability, discovery, and personal expression.

Thus my concern with treating coming out in some picture-perfect way that could be shaming to those who still struggle, and which misrepresents the messiness I still sometimes experience. Maybe it's time to dust off and reconceptualize the process, to take it out of the closet so to speak. Rather than a discrete event, the complex process of owning one's sexuality may best be understood as a lifelong experience that forever shapes and reshapes the individual. As Drescher (1998) writes: "There is not *a* closet, or *the* closet but a whole panoply of closets" (p. 259) (see also Galatzer-Levy & Cohler, 2002). Each person's ongoing relationship to his or her coming out should be treated as a multifaceted construction, open to new interpretations based upon life events, changing relationships with self and others, and opportunities for revision and reflection. The process ought to be pondered from time to time, particularly by those of us who are psychoanalysts. Additionally, it might be helpful to expand the concept of coming out to include all the ways in which we get in touch with dissociated parts of our personality throughout life, regardless of our sexual orientation. In fact, one could see coming out as a metaphor decoupled from sexuality. Gay or straight, we all have experiences of shame and hiding. It can be challenging to venture into our metaphorical closets and poke around the mess. It can be daunting – and remarkably fulfilling.

Even after the summer of 1982, it would take years of therapy before I would become completely comfortable being gay. Wait – have I just ignored my own suggestion and idealized coming out? Is it really possible for anyone to be *completely* comfortable being gay in our society? Or straight, for that matter (Chodorow, 1992)? Perhaps some sliver of internalized homophobia never completely evaporates. It becomes better integrated, available for self-reflection, propelling us to question in the healthiest sense just who we are and how we view ourselves.

I believe that my experience growing up as a relatively isolated outsider primed me to be a relational analyst. I am drawn to its focus on the complexities of human connection and the power of the analytic relationship in healing. I am particularly interested in the concepts of dissociation and multiple self-states, as well as in self-disclosure (Sherman, 2007) and the analyst's unique subjectivity (Sherman, 2005). Having been both marginalized and categorized, I am leery of a tendency to put people into neat boxes, even as I am aware of my propensity to do just that. I try to help patients see new possibilities they never would have dreamed imaginable – just as, on the eve of breaking up with Lynn, I could never have imagined myself being a (reasonably) well-adjusted gay man. I want to bust out of black-and-white thinking. Leave it to a gay man to add a splash of color.

The relational concepts of multiplicity and paradox also fit neatly into both my personal and professional worldview, particularly given my experience in the closet. Depending upon the circumstances, I can feel out and proud or succumb to a pang of shame most wicked and dicey. I am a queer conformist. A cockeyed pessimist. I can work a room or hide in the corner. Like everyone, I am all the

116

colors of the rainbow flag. In this way, my experience dovetails with the idea of multiple self-states, each with their own complex history, affects, and relationship to other parts of the self. This is how I make sense of my adolescence, when a part of me could feel aroused, hopeful, and desirous even as another shut that down with breathtaking efficiency.

My own experience of shame and dissociation – of being both aware and not aware at the same time – is not uncommon. Growing up gay and different can pose a threat, intrapsychically and interpersonally. Most of us live for a period of time with a dangerous secret, making our early lives potentially traumatic in ways that differ from other minority groups. When you are gay, you can – sometimes *must* – hide, even (especially) from your own family. An inherent part of who we are risks condemnation by peers, authority figures, and the very parents to whom we would otherwise turn to make sense of overwhelming feelings (Blum & Pfetzing, 1997; Frommer, 1994; Sherman, 2005). What I longed for as much as anything from the boy in math class wasn't sex – it was acceptance.

I did begin to find some acceptance in college. The counselor who provided me with recognition when I came out to her did nothing short of stand in the spaces (Bromberg, 1996), helping hold together parts of myself filled with hope and dread (Mitchell, 1993), concepts which I find useful in my work today.[1] She did not rush in to take away my shame which probably would have only exacerbated it. Nor was she shocked or judgmental. Intuiting the importance of the moment, she allowed me to tell my sneaker, and she touched my soul. Here was the recognition I had always craved.

Because of my background, the concept of mutual recognition (Benjamin, 1990) has always spoken to me. However, I know I must be ever vigilant not to force my subjectivity on patients due to my own discomfort at feeling unacknowledged. I am aware of how easy it is to unburden myself and injure a patient in the name of authenticity or of providing a supposedly relational experience. Being an analyst requires us to tolerate sometimes not being known, to decide when to hold back, to endure our patient's fantasies even as they cause us discomfort. This can be particularly challenging for me at times, since it can feel too close to once again being in the closet. I can sometimes retaliate through dissociation, withdrawal, or sarcasm – all mechanisms honed in my youth. My white-man's Afro – alas, most of my hair – may be gone, but the acerbic wit can still sting.

At times like this, remembering my coming-out experience can be helpful. In doing so, I am able to give myself the recognition that my patient cannot or will not provide. In those moments, I can better understand why he or she may need to hold me at a distance, to keep me in the closet. Is it my closet, theirs, or both? I catch myself feeling like the awkward teenager, but I know that is not the sum of me. Here, too, a model of multiplicity is useful. When I am able to stand in my own spaces, I can try to use my contradictory feelings of curiosity and consternation to enliven me and to contact a part of the patient having a hard time finding direct expression. Has he or she withdrawn in response to something I have done, a threat to the patient's self integrity? How are we impacting one another? Is my patient, too, feeling alone?

None of this is easy. Certain patients in particular can stimulate a familiar sense of hiding, holding a dangerous secret, or the fear of being found out. I have written about how my experience of feeling humiliated by a hyper-masculine straight patient caused me to unconsciously adopt my own combative, macho stance (Sherman, 2005). This prevented me from getting in touch with the shame and longing for acceptance both of us were projecting into the other. Patients like this can represent the peers whose rejection and ridicule most stung – and whose acceptance I most longed for. Sitting with these patients can make me feel like I am back in high school gym class – awkward, different, emasculated. I have compared notes with several openly gay male colleagues who, like me, catch themselves thinking twice about which patients they will see before wearing a pink shirt. Will it out us? Going to gay resorts like Provincetown or Fire Island can cause anxiety when heterosexual patients ask where I will be spending my vacation (Sherman, 2005). Can I get away with simply saying "the Cape?" It can feel like I am back on Christopher Street in 1982, anxious about being found out.

In recent years, I have gotten better at not worrying so much. This allows me to notice and utilize my anxiety when it does come up. I am able to consider whether the patient might know or want to know what I may be trying to avoid. What does my shame communicate? What would be so terrible if he or she did not approve? Of course, many of my heterosexual patients have already figured out my sexual orientation. Some have intuited it, some know because of the referral source, some came across my book or information about me on the Internet. In the age of the Internet, as we are learning, no clinician, regardless of sexual orientation, can really hide.

The more comfortable I have become around patients' curiosity about my sexuality, the more they have begun to simply ask me. Some straight and gay male patients speak openly about how working with me has challenged their homophobic assumptions in positive ways, and has made them more comfortable with their masculinity.

Nonetheless, I can understand why lesbian, gay, bisexual, and transgender (LGBT) therapists might prefer working with LGBT patients. It can feel like a safe haven to do so. Yet here too I sometimes find challenges, particularly working with patients who have shame around – and sometimes wish to hide – their sexuality. My own experience with the pain of being closeted, and the ultimate freedom of coming out, has sometimes made it difficult to tolerate what I can easily label as a patient's "resistance" to coming out. Nonetheless, I sometimes struggle with how to respond to the men and women who insist that they haven't a scintilla of internalized homophobia, when their self-loathing is on evident display. They cling to that magical fantasy that coming out is a one-time event that erases any trace of unease like a psychic Etch-a-Sketch. I treat this much the same as when patients with traumatic pasts insist they had an idyllic childhood; I proceed with caution, trying to understand the need for this rigid idealization and denial. As an adolescent who mastered the art of not seeing what was right in front of him, I can certainly relate. Sometimes the identification makes it difficult to respond as empathically as I might like.

I am currently working with a gay man in his 40s who has never had sex and who entered therapy to get rid of his dangerous homoerotic urges. For the longest time, the treatment remained stuck as I labored to rid him of his shame and help him come out, rather than understand what the shame was about. Ultimately, I realized that he has to make his own decisions about his life. At first, his wish to remain in the closet too closely resembled my own struggles in adolescence for me to be comfortable enough to tolerate it, even though he needed me to. Similarly, I have written about how I unconsciously pulled away from, and inadvertently shamed, a flamboyant gay man who represented how I feared people would see me when I first came out – in fact, might still see me (Sherman, 2005). In both cases, my eventual ability to recognize my actions and their effect on the patient helped deepen the work. Still, I find it ironic: I wanted to yank the first patient out of the closet, and shove the second back in!

On the whole, my experience as an Other has made me sensitive to any outsider struggling to find his or her place – sensitive to all the Wicked Dicey Ones, regardless of their sexual orientation. Here, too, a model of multiplicity, coupled with thinking of the closet as metaphor, can be remarkably helpful. We are forever trying to expand how we see ourselves, how many internal voices we can bring into a dialogue.

Despite the challenges of overidentification, I have been able to help a number of patients navigate particularly challenging coming-out experiences. Some of their stories are heartbreaking, like the man whose family has not spoken to him for decades because of the shame they say he has caused them by being gay. There is the heterosexually married father who sobs that he can never feel the passion with his wife that he had felt for his one great love – another man he had known decades ago. He broke off the relationship when his pastor counseled him that homosexuality is a sin, and a therapist warned that gay people can never be happy. Recently, I worked with a man who, while in college – the same time I was coming out – nearly took his life rather than accept who he was. I feel fortunate – and sometimes deeply challenged – sitting with them and witnessing, in ways sharing, their struggles. I resonate with their stories of confusion and hope, excitement and dread. I have to be careful to catch myself when I project my own history, beliefs, and values onto them (see also Goldstein & Horowitz, 2003).

I recognize that each of these stories is more dramatic, more heart-rending than my own. Yet I know something of their suffering, I know what it's like to hate yourself simply because of who you are. Working with patients to accept and integrate their desire not only helps them, but also helps to heal the frightened young man who felt so much shame, but who, on a warm summer night in 1982, reached down and found strength. Reached down and found himself.

When I became a therapist, there was never a question that I would be open about my sexuality, including in my training. I was dumbfounded when a colleague at another Institute told me he was keeping his sexual orientation secret from his supervisor on the recommendation of his analyst. After so many years of hiding, I could not imagine doing it again. Closets are for alligator shirts, not people.

Much has changed since I was the only openly-gay candidate at the National Institute for the Psychotherapies in the early 1990s. I teach there now, and there are a number of out candidates, members, and faculty. In addition, I am one of several gay men and lesbians on the board or training committee at the Center for Psychotherapy and Psychoanalysis of New Jersey, where I am the Associate Director of Training. Societal attitudes toward homosexuality have changed drastically since I first came out – except for where they haven't. The back and forth around same-sex marriage, still only legal in a handful of states but embraced by a president, is a perfect example. Each step forward results in a temporary jolt back. It is a little like the coming-out process, filled with heady achievements and occasional disappointments. But progress is undeniable.

On a personal note, I have been with a wonderful man with unfeathered hair for the last 18 years. Dennis bakes me cookies; no need for Entenmann's. We happen to have met on a gay ski trip, not in a bar. He swept me off my tangled feet. He still does.

The McDonald's where I sat sipping Coke and gaining strength before my Christopher Street experience is still there. It looks exactly the same from the outside. To this day I smile when I walk by, and I even get a little choked up sometimes. Ironically, my office is down the block from the former bar where the Eurythmics sang of sweet dreams and I met my first love. It is now a very heterosexual Irish pub. Dennis and I recently had brunch there – a somewhat surreal experience. Although it looks nothing like Uncle Charlie's, I was able to point out where I stood when I met Mr. Entenmann's during the wonderful summer of 1982.

The Eurythmics – long since broken up – remains one of my favorite bands. Dennis likes them too. Sweet dreams, indeed.

Note

1 Interestingly, Steven Mitchell (1981) wrote an important early paper pointing out long-standing homophobia in psychoanalysis.

References

Benjamin, J. (1990). Recognition and destruction: An outline of intersubjectivity. *Psychoanalytic Psychology*, 7(Suppl.), 33–47.

Blechner, M. (2003). Psychoanalysis in and out of the closet. In B. Gerson (Ed.), *The therapist as a person* (pp. 223–239). Hillsdale, NJ: Analytic Press.

Blechner, M. (2005). That gay Harry Stack Sullivan: Interactions between his life, clinical work, and theory. *Contemporary Psychoanalysis*, *41*, 1–20.

Blum, A., & Pfetzing, V. (1997). Assaults to the self: The trauma of growing up gay. *Gender & Psychoanalysis, 2*, 427–442.

Bromberg, P. M. (1996). Standing in the spaces: The multiplicity of self on the psychoanalytic relationship. *Contemporary Psychoanalysis, 32*, 509–535.

Chodorow, N. (1992). Heterosexuality as a compromise formation: Reflections on the psychoanalytic theory of sexual development. *Psychoanalysis and Contemporary Thought, 15*, 267–304.

Drescher, J. (1998). *Psychoanalytic therapy and the gay man.* Hillsdale, NJ: Analytic Press.

Frommer, M. (1994). Homosexuality and psychoanalysis: Technical considerations revisited. *Psychoanalytic Dialogues, 4*, 215–233.

Galatzer-Levy, R., & Cohler, B. J. (2002). Making a gay identity: Coming out, social context, and psychodynamics. In J. Wiener, J. Anderson, B. Cohler, & R. Shelby (Eds.), *The annual of psychoanalysis: Rethinking psychoanalysis and homosexualities* (Vol. 12, pp. 255–286). Hillsdale, NJ: Analytic Press.

Goldstein, E., & Horowitz, L. (2003). *Lesbian identity and contemporary psychotherapy: A framework for clinical practice.* Hillsdale, NJ: Analytic Press.

Mitchell, S. (1981). The psychoanalytic treatment of homosexuality: Practical considerations. *International Review of Psychoanalysis, 8*, 63–80.

Mitchell, S. (1993). *Hope and dread in psychoanalysis.* New York: Basic Books.

Sherman, E. (2005). *Notes from the margins: The gay analyst's subjectivity in the treatment setting.* Hillsdale, NJ: Analytic Press.

Sherman, E. (2007). With this ring: Intersubjectivity, self-disclosure and sexual orientation in the analytic dyad. Presented at International Association for Relational Psychoanalysis and Psychotherapy Conference, Athens, Greece.

Part II

LATER LIFE EVENTS, CRISES, AND DEVELOPMENTAL PASSAGES

10

MOMENTS THAT COUNT

Michael Eigen

In my 20s, the following two statements helped orient me. The first by Thomas Merton: "The secret of my identity is hidden in the love and mercy of God." The second by Paul Tillich, and I believe I'm paraphrasing, "A man is only as big as the diabolic in himself that he can assimilate."

Such deep relief I felt reading the first. Such challenge, reading the second. The two together provided support and direction.

The secret of our identity is divine mercy. It's hard to describe the relief and uplift this brought. To think mercy, loving kindness of the Other, is the heart of my being – not my own strident efforts and struggles. At the heart of my struggle was divine love. I did not have to do everything or "know" who I was. Each time I tried to know myself, identity faded from view. Ego chasing its tail, like the tail of a disappearing dog. But God's mercy? A sense that God's love was deeper than self gave me support, buoyed me. The pain of being an individual, of having to know who I was dissolved in the enigma of being supported by infinite love. I felt myself more fully through this love than by frenetic efforts to be someone. A deep pain of my being met bottomless care: solution-less pain momentarily lessened, at times dissolved, when it touched divine mystery, love deeper than pain.

The second statement also provided relief, but its challenge grew. To assimilate the diabolic in myself. Tall order. What if I was a devil, or partly so? Assimilate myself? I knew the mythic theme of turning bad into good, the alchemical formula, base into rare. A radical theme of the story of Jesus, turn life into death, death into life. Or Freud's version of the great spiritual dare: id into ego.

Renunciation seemed part of spirituality. To transcend or transform lower into higher was part of spiritual paths, east and west. To transcend oneself, transform oneself. What can this mean? If I was diabolic, what do I give up, renounce, remove, transform? My I? Surely that is not all that is afflicted. All the psychic twists, deformations, wounds, horrors, and pleasures of self-centered lies?

Yet Tillich's words freed me. Even if the task was impossible, it was a relief to hear his words. They validated the demonic and gave a kind of permission to acknowledge one's makeup. The demonic is real, part of human being. People are devils; devils are people. I am not alone in needing to work with evil, my evil, a task confronting humankind. Take a look around you – the mean, cruel aspect of life. Gratuitous cruelty, greed, injury. Why? We might as well be devils. Or, rather, we conceive of devils to give expression to the depth and reality of hate in us. Images of demons express how we feel, how we taste and look to ourselves in some way. Not entirely, not essentially. But importantly. Devils are part of poetry, and poetry expresses and forms life. There is nothing more real than feelings to which poetry bears witness. Emotional imagination is real. Tillich sets an enormous task, a necessary vision. How will the human race work with its destructiveness?

Freud spoke of sublimation. Channeling, even transforming instinctual life creatively. Transformational processes have long been part of spirituality. Yet, often, a model of taming and control is center stage, controlling lower nature, taming it. Results have often been horrendous. Prisons, punishment, threats, rewards, wars, self-crippling, and the battery of mechanisms psychoanalysis charts, rerouting of what is "tamed," "controlled" in ways that overturn, break through, rebel. The wild within damages the controller.

Can we find a better model? Not control nor idealized sublimation. Can we partner our capacities, work *with*, not just against them? Learn who we are, what we can do, what we are up against? Assimilate, digest, not just fight, push away, break. Let life in – how?

In my 30s. Writing. I should say writing and writing and writing. I thought of people like Lawrence Durrell, who could write for weeks non-stop. Many writers could do that, write and write. For me, tension built, much too much tension. Red lines broke out on my neck and down my chest. It was impossible. The Vision – to give expression to – It, the Real Thing, Life – IT. The more I tried, the more I failed.

A few years later I came across Merleau-Ponty's writing on Cezanne. Cezanne wanted to capture the snowiness of a tablecloth Balzac described. Try as he would to paint the snowiness evoked by Balzac's words, he failed. Finally, he gave up and just tried to paint a tablecloth. And there it was, snowiness and all.

Sometimes you have to give up on the thing itself, the real-most X, and do what you *can* do.

Two moments stand out. The first a vision of mortality. Something like a voice told me that if I was to write, I had to accept mortality. The voice was my own being, a dream voice. It was *me*, perhaps a transcendent me, an inner guide. We have a guiding function that helps if we can tap it. This happened by itself, unsought, likely owing to the build-up of intensity of trying with all my might, trying too hard. It was a flash, a seeing, felt realization. My work would be imperfect. It would miss the thing itself, X, the Truly Real. It would be less than I wanted. To write, this had to be accepted, tolerated, admitted, like death. I would have to bear my work not being what I wanted it to be. I would have to live with it as it is, as it develops, warts and all. There was no way around this. To write, I had to be mortal. To pass through this tunnel, this veil. To simply be. To write I would have to be a failure. A pain a writer, at least this writer, must live with. A releasing pain.

The time was coming when I could stop throwing everything I wrote away. The time was coming when I could write because I failed.

The great surprise – like Cezanne and Balzac's snowiness – over the years, accepting or tolerating or living with necessary failure, gave birth to moments I despaired of finding, moments of X, the real thing itself, truth and life and beauty, what I hoped for but gave up on. It came by itself through the doing, acceptance of what I could and couldn't do, mining openings.

Mining mortality was one thing, but the tension continued. I accepted or was on the way to accepting my plight as a writer. But I did not have a clue how to go about working with the tensions writing plunged me into. The more I wrote, the more tension mounted, and I was semi-oblivious to the pressure I was living. Then one day, without quite knowing how, I found myself on a plane for Paris. Apparently I could not take the intensity and something blew or perhaps almost blew, and my system's way of handling it was to fly to Paris. There I roamed the streets a little like Woody Allen's protagonist in *Midnight in Paris*. But I was not so lucky to meet great authors and musicians of the 1920s. One thing about this trip, I wrote nothing and was lucky to make two French friends, male and female, who took me to their favorite places. I felt taken care of, nursed, nour- ished. The man kept saying *jouissance* left Paris, and so he was going to move to the country. Both said they could not believe I was American. They had a very different picture of "Americans."

The trip lasted longer than I expected. I went to Israel, Greece, Italy, then back to London, where I called R. D. Laing and D. W. Winnicott.

Laing didn't have time to see me. I heard only the voice of a secretary. Winnicott picked up the phone himself. His "hullo" was cheering, and we set a time. When I walked in the door, he shook my hand and greeted me saying, "Hullo, Dr. Eigen. I'm sorry I haven't read your books." Well, I was just a struggling graduate stu- dent. No books, no articles. No doctor. I was having a hard time in school, although I got much from parts of it. Other parts were torture, what I called the slave stage, learning a foreign language I'd never speak. It took 11 years to get my doctorate, going part-time, working in schools, treatment centers, and clinics. I was no one he could or should know. Yet to Winnicott I was special, Dr. Eigen, writer of books he hadn't read and I hadn't written. What a lovely feeling he engendered.

He served sherry, and as we spoke said, "Are you seeing Laing? So many want to see him now." He was curious why I was seeing him and not R. D. Laing. I couldn't say I called Laing first and he didn't see me. He bantered along thought- fully – thoughtful banter – saying, "We're worried about Laing. We're afraid fame will lead him to lose contact with clinical practice." By lose contact he meant something more than not doing it. He meant something like doing it without the nitty-gritty.

Years later I was consulted by a former Laing patient, although the word *patient* does not quite fit. Contact would be more like it – moments of significant contact.

He had important moments with Laing, especially on LSD, but afterwards, when the high faded, Laing lost interest. He was not interested in the "working through," just the intense points. The slow, hard drudge of daily practice did not appeal. The man who consulted me got a lot from these "psychic hits," but was raw and dangling from lack of work in the trenches, the work that assimilates. This reminds me of a remark by Chogyam Trungpa in the 1960s. When a student complained of a boring place Trungpa picked to meditate, the latter said something along the lines of, "Boredom, exactly what you need." He was thinking of "highs" and speed Americans were addicted to and thought boredom might help. Winnicott was prescient, not boring, but also had staying power.

I felt called upon to say something, and said how much I liked his paper on manic-depressive tendencies, which among other things he likened to death and resurrection, up and down movements. He shrugged my praise off saying, "Oh that. I wrote it to enter the Society." I really did like it but had to take in the political intent that was part of it. I felt a little embarrassed but touched by his open practicality.

As we got into the visit, Winnicott seemed unconscious of time. It's difficult to pin down this feeling. I felt it with Bion too. A loss of time consciousness. Just into the thing that was happening now, the present reality. It felt like we had all the time in the world; our time together would never end. Now I think it was because it was always beginning. Both Winnicott and Bion were always beginning.

Winnicott was a mixture of stillness and quirky movement. He could sit still in compressed concentration and without warning, change positions, go to another part of the room. For a long time he sat at the edge of his therapy couch, screwed himself up, a corkscrew. He put a lot of physical strength into his thought, a thin man with kindly, electric tension. His face seemed female. Yet an angular, masculine strength came through too. I thought of Jung's remark about older women becoming more masculine and older men more feminine. I don't know how true Jung's remark is, but Winnicott combined both.

He was trying to find the best way to tell me something, to convey something to me about the way he worked. Not simply how he worked but something about psychic reality. He wanted me to get a sense of something he felt was important, searching to find a way to evoke in me a reality that was real to him. He already made several attempts but was not satisfied that I got it. My sense was he was not dissatisfied with me but with how he went about it. He was trying to communicate a significant area of experience that I was not locating. It took me awhile to take in the realization that from his point of view, I was missing it or it was missing me, that there was something in the room that did not find me. I thought I was following him and had no sense I was missing it.

He seemed a little satisfied after telling me the following story. A woman he worked with was trying to center his image in a hand mirror, while he was seated behind her. He bent over and could see his face slightly off-center and moved to center it. He knew immediately he made an error. Next session she told him, had this happened six months earlier, she'd be back in hospital. He played the helpful mother who could not stand being off balance. Keeping his image off-center was precisely what his patient was doing, and he was unable to let it happen. He had to fix it, "right" it. His little story got through to me how important it is to tolerate off balance states. Life is filled with them. Trying to tidy them up to maintain imaginary homeostasis clouds reality.

I thought of the case in Winnicott's transitional object paper in which the child had to keep her mother in good repair, help her feel balanced (1953). The child functioned as a kind of transitional object, keeping her mother in life. Her mother could not let the child's aliveness wax and wane. The mother's aliveness depended on her child's aliveness, and loss of aliveness in the child meant loss of aliveness in the mother. It was quite a pressure, keeping oneself emotionally alive to stop mother's feeling from dying off.

Near the end of our meeting, Winnicott offered me books by Fairbairn, Guntrip, and himself. I had read Fairbairn and Guntrip, so he found another Guntrip I hadn't seen, published in London, *Healing the Sick Mind* (1964). We spoke about Guntrip and Fairbairn and what he valued in them. One of the books he gave me was a series of his BBC talks on mothers and babies, which I reread many times with melt-in-your-mouth pleasure (Winnicott, Shepard, & Davis, 1967).

He mentioned he was considering an invitation to speak in New York and wondered how he would be received. He was concerned and worried. I was taken aback that he would ask me, so little equipped to tell him. It was near the end of August, 1968. I said if they were like me, they would want to hear him, but I feared there was a wide mix of people in the field, many defensive and biased, and it depended who he spoke to. Later, I learned that he came to New York and spoke to an unreceptive, aggressive group, a meeting with a bad outcome. I wrote him once or twice afterwards and he wrote back, keeping things open, saying something like, "We'll see. We'll see."

I met Winnicott near the end of his life, his creativity in full bloom. I was left with a profound sense that if he could be him, I could be me. He was so himself, quirky, awkward, unapologetic about his intensity, that it freed me to be more myself. A deep kind of permission that if a sensibility like his could exist, then a sensibility like mine could too. This may sound presumptuous but it springs from his need to share his own sensibility, his sense of reality, a spontaneous striving.

After I came back to New York, I had a dream. I was painting large canvases. I'm not sure, but there was a sense of frustration. The image changed, and I was painting small pictures and was told I should paint on small, not large canvases. I awoke with a sense that I was trying to do too much and should pour myself into smaller frames. I was able to do a lot in smaller, more contained works, more able to distill intensity. With this as a guide, I was able to begin and finish papers, leading to my first psychoanalytic publications in 1973, five years after meeting Winnicott. Trying to do less, I found myself able to do more.

In 1978, at the age of 42, I met W. R. Bion. He gave a week of seminars in New York City under the auspices of the Institute for Psychoanalytic Training and

Research. I attended the seminars, the party, the public lecture, and had two therapy sessions. I felt I was learning something, although I was not sure what.

It is hard to unpack the moment I walked into his hotel room for a session. A tall man quickly adapting to my shorter height, making room. It's hard to define such moments of tact, they happen so quickly. I had a fleeting impression that he looked like a bug. Now years later, I wonder, did I see my own buggy self? I could have felt threatened but, if I did, I also felt reassured. I felt here was someone I could try to talk to and began testing the waters. Did I see hints of fear? If so, that added to kinship across distance. We were such different people, from different ages. He had a kind of formality and yet was gracious, accepting, inviting. I thought of the word "under-stand," to stand under, to provide an emotional floor simply by being present. What did we share? Perhaps love of the psyche, the respect, caution, and risk this love requires.

We spoke of many things, and at one point he said that ordinarily he wouldn't say so much but we had so little time. I wonder if he, too, felt something simpatico. I'll tell you some of what I remember in the order it comes to me now, rather than strain to re-create the order in the sessions, which I doubt I can do. A quality of the flow involved things that seemed to come to him out of the blue. In his seminar talks, the only writer who had worked in America that he mentioned was Theodore Reik, author of *Surprise and the Psychoanalyst* (1936). Surprise with deep psycho-logic.

A theme that emerged was the difficulty involved in finding, being, creating one's self, the "nasty business" (his words) of being real. I spoke to him about difficulties I was having with a former supervisor who had been so helpful. Now at meetings he became abusive. After my publications started coming out, his attitude towards me changed. Actually, my publications affected my status at the clinic where I worked in many ways. The head of the clinic suddenly paid attention to me. When we discussed an issue, he would turn to me and say, "Let's see what Mike says." I can see how this aggravated my former supervisor. Bion spoke of difficulties being an individual, perceiving differently. I got the feeling he was speaking from experience. He encouraged me to go my way and meet difficulties this brought.

When he heard about my intricate relationship with a former analyst and the latter's unresolved influence on me, he felt I must break away, struggle with the nasty business of finding myself. He spoke of Rickman saving him from Klein. John Rickman was Bion's earlier analyst and had a wider, undogmatic, independent perspective. Bion gained from Klein's more narrow, deep view, but felt a need to retain autonomy, which his previous analysis supported. He had a keen appreciation for the struggle to be a person, and I felt him trying to support my struggle.

At one point I remarked, "You remind me of Marion Milner." He said, "A lot of people tell me that." I was thinking of ways each was concerned with self. I met Milner three years earlier and was struck by a similarity. Perhaps no accident, too, that Winnicott, Milner, and Bion were, in their own ways, artists. In one of his last seminars, the Paris seminar, he spoke of the psychoanalyst as artist.

I told him a dream which involved a wild figure, something like King Kong, a gorilla in the jungle. It's vague now, but was alive then. He must have felt I played it down in some way because he sided with the wild one and said, "You know, it's real." Meaning the dream, the emotional reality of the dream is real. He spoke of it being part of myself, then paused and corrected himself. "You know, we speak of parts, parts of yourself, but they're not parts. They're *you*." I immediately felt the wholeness of the fragmented dream experience, a wholeness of being in my fragmented states. Me, not parts of me. The dream figure that scared me was me myself. I scared myself. I am afraid of myself. I thought of the common expression, "It's only a dream," often used to reassure a child who lacks capacity to take in and assimilate the terror of the night, so intimately related to the terror of the day. I felt both Bion and I shared this fear.

Out of the blue, Bion said, "Do you know the Kabbalah? The Zohar?" There was no warning or precedent for this remark that I knew of. Maybe his perception that I was Jewish. Several years later I came across remarks in a seminar in Brazil that showed Bion's consciousness of "race" in one case with a Jewish individual who disowned or was not aware of or rooted in the richness of his background, a denial that characterized much in his life, not just his Jewishness. Was he testing the depths, my moorings? Did he pick something up about the realness of spiritual life for me? Was he touching a convergence between us I did not take in? How did he know religion was such an important part of my sensibility? Was it like the dream, he taking as real something I was afraid to value as much as I did? This was an emergent theme than ran through our disjointed, seemingly unrelated communications – he valuing what in myself I feared to fully value and fully live.

"Yes, I mean, well not really, no, yes," I replied. I read aspects of Kabbalah for many years. "I mean, I read the Zohar, but don't really *know* it." I read intermittently, haphazardly, parts of Zohar and other writings over 20 years. He quickly replied, "Yes, likewise. I read it, but don't really *know* it." He paused, then added, "I use the Kabbalah as a framework for psychoanalysis." I was floored, motionless. It is a remark I am still mining.

By the time I met Bion, I heard Joseph Campbell use the *chakras* and Hindu mythos as a framework for Freud and Jung. But Bion came to me within psychoanalysis itself. His remark blew open a shell and brought me to a new level of freedom. I cannot do justice to all the themes of our contacts, but freedom was one of them, going along with the realness of oneself, one's life. This past year or two, a member of my Bion-Winnicott-Lacan seminar invited me to give seminars on Kabbalah and Psychoanalysis for the New York University Contemplative Studies Project. How he got to this, I don't know. It was not something I had in mind, but I can feel Bion's impact in the background.

The momentary awkward back and forth about "knowing" Kabbalah reminds me of Bion's end of sessions' behavior. He never told me the session was over. We kept talking and I began to wonder, was it up to me to end? As minutes ticked past the session time, I grew uncomfortable, and stood up. Neither of us hid a sort of semi-awkwardness, as if we were getting the feel of what to do moment to moment. He seemed in no rush, no rush at all. Likewise, payment. What would have happened if I hadn't asked? Would we still be sitting there today? Obviously not – but what is this mutual sensing, leaving it to me? Perhaps in an inner sense, we *are* still sitting there today, sensing, exploring, tasting.

In one of our meetings, I found myself talking about Rilke, who creates realities as he writes, creates new possibilities of sensibility as combinations of words are born. Someone told me that Rilke lacked humor. I found myself recycling this remark and blurted to Bion, "There's something joyless about you." It was as if I took in a foreign voice and spoke from it, funneling a narrow vision of my own, perhaps demon me, fearful me. What faith must it take to be Rilke, opening worlds at the edge of what it is possible to experience, hearts of experience. Bion writes of faith in face of unknown emotional reality. Yet I called him joyless. Was I saying what I saw, or defending against an experience our meetings were creating?

He responded, "Well, if joy is important to you, it must be in your body, your being, your skin." That is, if I was joyful, it can't just be in my head. It has to be cellular, in my pores, enfleshed in my life, lived joy, not theory. It was a remark I've thought about many years. It applies to much we say. We can talk about feeling, but living feelings, experiencing experience is another matter.

At the end of the IPTAR seminars (Bion, 1980) Bion looked at me (did I imagine it?) and said something like, "Odd, how going through something as grueling as this work can bring such joy."

Two of my girlfriends saw Bion for sessions, likely spurred by my seeing him. He had glimpses of me from other perspectives than mine. I spoke to him about difficulties with women. At one point, out of the blue, he said, "You should get married. Marriage is not what you think. It's someone you can speak truth to and help mitigate the severity to yourself."

Without expecting it, a whole, deeper field of experience opened. Someone to speak truth to and help mitigate the severity to yourself. The words, the sentiment cut through primitive fears, whatever they were – fear of engulfment, feeling trapped, being let down, abandoned, wounded beyond repair, unimaginable loss, fear of my own murderous rage, you name it.

I spoke about the women I was seeing and wondered whether I should seek someone new, seek a fresh start, my relationships were so blemished. He referred to a paper I gave him, published in the *International Journal of Psychoanalysis* (1977) "On working with 'unwanted' patients." It summarized 10 years of clinic work with intractable dependency, wounded dependency, and especially hostile dependency. He said, if not laconically, in a low-keyed way: "Do you need more hostile dependent relationships?"

At some point he said, "Stop analysis. You've had enough analysis." It was time to live my life, not keep analyzing it. The two are not incompatible, but he felt my tie to analytic work was keeping me from marriage, another kind of commitment. I picture jumping into oceans other than ones I knew. He touched a deep core and longing. I wanted to marry, to be a father and ever since I can remember assumed this would happen. I worked with children as a young man and expected to get married and become a father in my 20s. I entered analysis instead. Contact with the living psyche took on a kind of priority, a lifelong work. Twenty years passed.

Someone else could have said what Bion said. My father might have said it. But Bion's voice carried weight, touched psychic reality, resonated. A mere stranger, but I could believe him. He spoke from a place I believed. He was not a girlfriend, not my parent. Perhaps he simply said what was true for him, his own emotional truth, which touched mine.

When I wrote my "unwanted patient" paper (1977), I did not fully see I was addressing my own hostile dependency, wounded dependency, to be dependent and push or run away, intractably dependent and dependency phobic. But I was aware Bion was giving me a compassionate push towards further development, another stage of life, one I almost slid past.

Later I thought of Freud working from unconscious to unconscious and Bion from psychosis to psychosis. The fact that Bion so acutely touched faces of madness made his faith in living the more valuable to me. Facing the diabolic in oneself? Yes, but Bion went further (Bion, 1970; Eigen, 1998).

I wondered, the semi-oracular pronouncements Bion made – stop analysis, get married. Did he say the same thing to everyone? What did he tell my girlfriends? One I was in a very painful–pleasurable, in–out, hostile–dependent relationship, did he tell her to stop analysis and get married? He told her she had a father problem that would wreck a marriage. He told her not to get married but have more analysis. He had a more favorable response to the other woman. I wondered if he was blessing the latter relationship and advising against the former.

There was a third girlfriend he did not meet, and three years after seeing Bion we married and started a family. How that happened is another story, worth telling, but not now. I became a father at age 45, my wife 36. To say everything changed is an understatement. Challenges I never dared face became imperative. If I wanted my marriage to work and my family to survive me, I would have to undertake a rapid rate of growth that psychically resembled something like the rate of physical growth an embryo–fetus undergoes. Life was beginning in new ways which made the previous decade almost look like a standstill.

Similarly, my practice. I always tried my best with patients and all aspects of my work. But to begin to feel towards them a sense of care that paralleled aspects of what I felt towards my children, brought new affective resonance, new spirit. I was the same old me, limitations, warts and all, the failures patients have to put up with if they stay with me. Even so, other dimensions of care and possibilities opened, hard to define, but real. You can't give what you cannot access. Bion, I feel, supported me in accessing more.

I'd like to mention a few odds and ends relating to Bion's visit to New York in 1978. At the party, I was one of those who stood around him as he recited passages from Milton's *Paradise Lost*. My father used to recite Milton's "L'Allegro" and "Il Pensoroso" and tell me what they meant. Both Bion and my father appreciated poetry. Heine was my father's favorite poet.

You might find it odd to see a renowned 80-something psychoanalyst at a party reciting Milton's *Paradise Lost*. All kinds of thoughts raced through my head – does he have difficulty relating? Is he autistic? Schizoid? Yet the fuller message was: he was being himself, his idiosyncratic self. As with Winnicott, a message came through: if he could be Bion, I could be me. Seeing him recite Milton at a New York social gathering made me feel freer to be me.

In his public lecture, he spoke of being in a tank that shook like jelly. Metal turns to jelly. He spoke of fear in battle and fear in analytic sessions. He gave the impression that with no fear, you're out of contact with reality. Without fear, you're out of contact with the session. He felt they decorated him wrongly for bravery in action; he was a frightened soldier who got the idea that you can get killed running away from the enemy as easily as going towards him. Hearing him speak, being with him, I had no sense he was going to die the next year. His last year was filled with seminars, reaching others, sharing whatever he had, stimulating growth.

As he spoke, I thought of our two sessions. He was encouraging me to move towards life, my life. The metal that surrounded me like skin shook like jelly. To be afraid is part of living in reality. What one makes of it is something else.

References

Bion, W. R. (1970). *Attention and Interpretation*. London: Karnac Books, republished 1984.

Bion. W. R. (1980). *Bion in New York and Sao Paulo*. Perthshire: Clunie Press.

Eigen, M. (1977). On working with "unwanted" patients. *International Journal of Psychoanalysis, 58*, 109–121.

Eigen, M. (1998). *The psychoanalytic mystic*. London: Free Association Books.

Guntrip, H. (1964). *Healing the sick mind*. London: Allen & Unwin.

Merton, T. (1972). *New seeds of contemplation*. New York: New Directions.

Reik, T. (1936). *Surprise and the psycho-analyst: On the conjecture and comprehension of unconscious processes*. London: Kegan Paul.

Winnicott, D. W. (1953). Transitional objects and transitional phenomena. *International Journal of Psycho-Analysis, 34*, 89–97.

Winnicott, C., Shepard, R., & Davis, M. (Eds.) (1967). *Babies and their mothers*. New York: Addison-Wesley.

11

GUESS WHO'S GOING TO DINNER?

On the arrival of the uninvited third[1]

Steven Kuchuck

Hoping for the best

Five years ago, almost to the day of writing this, Michael walked into my office and took his usual place on the couch. Forty years old, handsome, personable, gay, and perpetually single, Michael first came to see me about six years before this to address longstanding feelings of depression and anxiety. At the time, he felt stuck financially and professionally, and found himself in constant conflict with his parents and many in his wide family and social circle. It soon came to light that drinking and substance use would also need to be addressed, and now, sober for about the last three years and more comfortable with himself and others, Michael felt ready, probably for the first time in his life, to meet and date men with the potential to become long-term partners rather than merely discardable sexual objects. Deeply longing for, but yet afraid and unsure of how to navigate intimacy, loneliness and its sometimes seemingly impossible antidotes now consumed our therapeutic hours. Narcissistic defenses were no longer as effective as they used to be; sadness, the pain of aloneness, often permeated. As is the paradox in these situations, we felt more good than not about having arrived at this difficult place. Still, we struggled.

Even before he spoke, I felt something different that day. Michael looked more relaxed, lighter even, as he layed down on the couch. A smile crept onto his face as he settled in and began to speak. "Well," he said, "I have some possible good news on the dating front, for a change." Only recently, after years of false starts and stops, his friends had once again begun trying to fix him up, and Michael felt cared for and appreciative of their efforts. "My friend Jonathan met someone at a party and got his number for me – the guy sounds so nice, and Jonathan thinks we might really hit it off. Actually, we spoke yesterday – for almost an hour, which I don't think either one of us expected. The conversation was great – he seems really smart and funny, and I know you give me shit for putting too much emphasis on looks, but I checked out his website, and I'll tell you, he's pretty hot." I smile to myself as I listen. Michael is happy and hopeful, and – at this point – I am too. But it's only a very few seconds before his description of this man becomes a bit more detailed and leads to a vague sense of

135

discomfort that I feel in my body, before conscious awareness sets in. A second more and my stomach feels as if it's sinking; my heart pounds. First flushed, then clammy and probably pale, my mind races; I'm grateful for the couch. Michael is describing my closest friend.

Hoping for the worst

As the reader might imagine, multiple, competing, overlapping thoughts and feelings rushed through my mind and body during the remainder of that session and day. First things first: I knew I couldn't – wouldn't – say anything to interrupt my patient's process – not yet, at least. I'm glad I knew at least this, because even after more than two decades of practice, in that moment I didn't feel like I knew very much about how to proceed beyond letting the process unfold – for a while, anyway. Assuming they liked each other, I knew the situation would not be tenable. All I could do, I remember thinking, is hope the first date goes poorly, and that will be the end of that. This thought was one of the earliest but by no means the only example of an experience of badness that began to permeate.

I felt anxious, queasy, and distracted for the rest of that day and many to follow. One of the dominant feelings that emerged almost immediately was betrayal. While I felt confident about my initial decision not to disclose that first day, it still didn't feel good to withhold this information from my patient and, as more time passed, from my friend. There was also a feeling of betraying myself as well as real and imagined internal and external professional objects. No matter what course I chose, some or all of us were bound to urge a different tack. Conflict between internalized objects and professional self-states seemed particularly acute; disappointment and hurt feelings were probably inevitable.

Searching for answers

Informal consultations with a few trusted colleagues began immediately, though as I was to discover, no one felt particularly confident in their counsel – this was new for all of us and fraught. I realized, of course, that this lack of an absolute rudder is one of the hallmarks of contemporary psychoanalysis. If there ever were a how-to manual, Hoffman (1994) had the right idea about "throwing away the book" (p. 187); each dyad does need to recreate psychoanalysis anew, as Ogden (2009) puts it. My peer group at the time urged containment and held and contained me while I weighed the options. I wanted Michael to have time and space to explore, and perhaps I needed that as well. One of my challenges was to try not to feel too bad, though that was tricky – it felt bad to consider disclosing and ruin the experience for him, and it felt bad to keep this from him and risk his feeling betrayed if he learns what I withheld. Nothing like a nice lose–lose. If there was comfort to be gained from any of this, though, it was through the realization that it was likely there would eventually be therapeutic value in the working-through to come; I did believe that this was a patient who could understand and appreciate the dilemma I'd been sitting with, the recognition of my separate subjectivity being a developmental achievement he had mostly mastered (Benjamin, 1990).

As the weekend of my patient's date arrives, I find myself reflecting on the clinical situation and what it stirs for me. This is of course while avoiding my friend, lest he tell me what I already know, and making a mental note to stay away from his favorite date spots in our sometimes too-small-for-comfort world.

Hearing voices

As I alluded to earlier, and as I suspect a lot of you do too, I hear voices, as Henry Smith (2001) puts it – my own and others, which of course are also now mine. I hear my early, Freudian analyst, perhaps ironic to put it this way since his silence and remove were legendary. His voice embodies an early identification and mode of practice that has been useful, but these days more often one that I struggle to distance myself from or at least own as one of many options. I hear his colleagues, my early teachers and supervisors at the first of two institutes I attended, urging their students to refrain from any expressions of subjectivity, lest they contaminate the treatment. "Don't tell Michael, don't show that you're flustered, analyze and contain the countertransference responses," I hear them say. These voices have been useful guides. They have at times also been stifling and depleting. I've written about the toll this hiding has taken on me and a generation of colleagues and patients (Kuchuck, 2008).

I hear other voices too, though. I hear self psychologists, object relations theorists, interpersonalists and humanists who years ago began to soften, if only so slightly, some of the sharp edges of those earliest professional voices. These voices reassure and remind me that my primary task is to track my patient's selfobject and other needs, though I hear them reminding me to keep an eye on my own as well. They tell me to recognize the multiplicity of internalizations, fragility, and resilience we are each subject to and capable of. Most of all, though, regardless of what theoretical labels they or I might attribute, I hear the voices of a generation of contemporary psychoanalysts. Among these are a more recent analyst, supervisors, mentors, students, colleagues, and friends, many of them relationalists and intersubjectivists but even some contemporary Freudians and Jungians, who speak and write about the challenges of asymmetry, the need for authenticity, recognition of intersubjectivity, and – particularly useful to me in this context – the importance of recognizing not only the patient's but also the analyst's subjective needs.[2] These more recent and increasingly more firmly embedded voices are the ones that seem closest to resonating with my own authentic voice, especially when held as a dialectic among the many others, each competing for attention and dominance, and, in the end, co-constructing a third voice out of this psychic, theoretical melting pot. It's this dialectic that inspires and informs – but it's also what can at times lead to the feelings of guilt, sense of disloyalty to early professional objects, and resistances to moving beyond primary professional identifications that many of us struggle with. While not always comfortable, I believe it's a useful struggle when one considers the likely alternatives of orthodoxy and stagnation. It's a road I've been down before in my work with Michael and other patients.

One of the ironies in a case replete with so many is the fact that this is a patient who, more than many or even most of my patients, wrestles with both a tremendous hunger to know and fear of knowing me. Many tears have been shed as a result of this longing and conflict, and we have had to work carefully together to decide what would be useful for him to know. The tears are multi-determined. They reflect a deep sadness about the limits of our relationship, sadness and embarrassment about the depths of his need and wish to know me differently and outside of the room, the many times articulated wish to meet and know my partner and others in my life, and the frustration over never running into me outside of the office or encountering others who know me. But the tears are also tears of envy, as he imagines an enchanted life of a perfect partner, fine living, splendid vacations and country homes that he believes he can never have, and, alternatively, tears of disappointment in himself for how cruel and devaluing he can be of himself, me, and others when we don't measure up to his impossible standards. I've shared with him the line I feel I must walk to protect both of us from the at times overwhelming envy and wish to render me (and him) helpless, empty, and incapacitated. This line, and my patient's voice, are part of what now guides my choices as I consider where we are and might soon need to go.

Collisions

There is an additional irony that finally tips this scale for me quite close to Jung's (1970) concept of synchronicity. Just several days before the session in question, my friend – who is not a therapist – and I were engaged in a lively conversation about how and whether or not it would be appropriate for an analyst to be on Facebook, as well as related burdens of privacy and discretion that the analyst carries. I shared with him a brief treatment I conducted at a clinic many years ago when I was just starting out: I suddenly realized during the first session that the patient had been a childhood neighbor of mine, delivering groceries to our house, and mutual friends with a classmate of mine. Here, by the way, is another voice, this time of a supervisor telling me not to say anything about this to the patient, though this voice is an easier one to question, if not dismiss, with the passage of time. I also relayed an even more awkward experience of a first session with a new referral also many years ago, but not so far back that it doesn't still cause me to squirm a bit: midway through the patient relaying his story, I had the uneasy feeling of having heard this before and the dawning realization that we had met at a party and then had a date many years before the consultation. This time, the voice was clearly mine and loud though quavering, as I shared with this patient what I remembered and why our work would likely not be able to proceed. All of this was discussed over lunch with my friend, less than a handful of days before I learned he was going on a date with my patient this weekend.

Monday arrives, and Michael comes in buoyed; my heart sinks. As I feared, this is apparently not going to go away so easily. The date was wonderful, he relays; this is a man he can imagine dating and, possibly, maybe even one day being in a relationship with. As he describes the date – an initial coffee that turned into an afternoon that turned into an evening – I hear a voice, my voice, that says now is the time to tell him what I know, a voice that says if I allow this to go any further, I will be acting unethically. But of course, as you know about me now and probably know from your own experiences as well, mine is/ours are heads filled with many voices. Another voice, just as clear and ultimately louder, suggests that I wait, that "it might not quite be the time . . . not just yet." A few beats later, Michael tells me his only hesitation is that he's not certain whether or not he's attracted enough to this man. Hope springs eternal, as does anger on behalf of my friend and disappointment in my patient for an inflated sense of his own attractiveness that in my estimation, gets in his way far too often. Still, I edge toward relief until he tells me, with pride, that he's been hearing my voice, and he knows he should and wants to give this more of a chance. A second date, this time for dinner and maybe a movie, has been scheduled for the coming weekend, and I brace myself.

Another weekend, another chance to reflect, to ruminate, to avoid my friend who I miss. More and more, I realize that the discomfort I've been feeling is not just about figuring out what to do and the careful timing of the intervention, though certainly that's foremost in my mind. But also coloring all of this is a feeling of resentment I have for needing to keep what I know from my patient and of course from my friend. While probably clinically wise for at least a short while longer, this makes me feel lonely and like I'm hiding again. It also becomes clearer to me that these feelings are disturbing enough to distract and disrupt my ability to be fully present in our sessions; this alone is helping me to know that I may need to tell my patient in the very near future, though I'm still hopeful that this might play itself out without my needing to intervene. Given my history of having to hide my sexual identity and other aspects of my subjectivity, especially in the context of early training and practice and according to the prevailing wisdom at the time, I understand why this is a source of some of the badness that I feel. This realization is helpful. Further complicating the picture for me is a heightened sensitivity to boundaries and potential violations, professional and otherwise. Ours was a house of emotional intrusions and violations, and to a lesser but still significant extent, physical violence. At a very early age, I began the aforementioned long-term classical analysis with a man whose wife referred me to him, she the individual, couples, and family therapist for every person in my family as well as close family friends, relatives, and intimates of these friends and relatives. I can never take lightly crossing, muddying, or confusing boundaries.

Invading thirds

Overstimulation, dysregulation, and a sense of unease were now constant companions. A professional voyeur, I found myself titillated by what I might and did hear and troubled by what felt like a boundary violation on my part, despite colleagues' assurances to the contrary. Perhaps you've already realized that this is a story of thirds: colleagues, internalized voices, Michael, my friend and I invading thirds for each other and still others not yet mentioned or too numerous to list again at this point in the telling but already referred to, crowding these pages, the treatment room, and all the rooms I inhabited during those days (Benjamin, 2004; Ogden, 2004). Certainly my friend was ever-present as both my patient's object and my own, present in the room and now I in his room, in their room. Pre-Oedipal and Oedipal feelings abound as, finally, it is not Michael who feels left out but rather I who feels banished from the bedroom, even as I listen in horror and delight just outside the door. Jealousy has entered the scene, sexual and emotional hunger is stirred, and I feel driven to possess each of these men without the other's interference.

At times, I feel like crying. I get a stomach ache which reminds me of the stomach aches I had as a young child during separations and Oedipal and other losses. I feel like I owe it to the three of us to say something now, before stronger attachments form between them. It's been clear to me from the start, of course, that they cannot continue to date while he remains my patient. But it's even more complicated than that. There are additional thirds that I haven't yet mentioned. Besides seeing me for individual treatment, Michael is also in a psychoanalytic group that I run, and I am well aware of the potential for disruption and loss in this most important of spaces for Michael and the others who have become such a significant part of each other's lives over the course of many years. I anticipate the impact of this disclosure on the others who also struggle with their own versions of wanting and not wanting to know more about or share me, and I am troubled by what I imagine to be the potential impact if he were to choose dating this man over remaining in treatment. But I'm getting ahead of myself, which, fortunately, I was at times able to keep in mind even then, despite what the following dream might indicate. I dream that Richard, a group member, invites me to join him and his best friend to pay to watch a couple have sex. I agree, and then try to reverse this when I realize it would be an inappropriate bond that Richard and I would share that others in group wouldn't be able to be a part of. Thirds – me included – continue to impinge.

As luck would have it, during the weekend before the beginning of the resolution – though I couldn't have known that then – I headed to Boston for a conference where I was presenting a paper in which a colleague and I explore various fantasies and forms of owning that emerge between parents and children, patients and analysts, spouses, and so on. In our work, we are particularly interested in owning as experienced in the context of losing something or someone that was once yours, and the wish to reclaim (Atlas-Koch & Kuchuck, 2012). I think about the feelings of possessiveness that have emerged during this period: anger at Michael for taking my friend, to a lesser extent at my friend for taking Michael, at both for taking an otherwise relatively peaceful period in my practice and my life. I think about Michael's fantasies of wanting to own or co-own my space outside of the office, by meeting and spending time with my partner and friends. In the paper, we ask who owns the treatment and its contents. And in our paper and over this weekend, I think about the concept of co-owning and co-constructing the ideas and interpretations that populate a treatment, and how much less control we have over the circumstances that occur in and out of the office than we like to think we do.

Hide and seek, lost and found

This is my cue for returning to earlier themes of hiding, irony, and yes, perhaps even synchronicity again. During a conference break, I was having coffee in the hotel with a friend and analytic colleague from my peer group in town for a couples therapy conference being held, by coincidence, on the same weekend and at the same hotel as the psychoanalytic conference. While filling her in on the events of the past weeks, I also mentioned that my cousins live in a suburb of Boston, but that I had decided not to call them this trip; it would be all I could do to find the time to attend the many presentations and catch up with friends and colleagues. As I was in the middle of telling her this, I noticed a man slowly approaching our table from the opposite side of the lobby, mouth wide open and shaking his head in amazement. Well, as they say, you can run, but you can't hide. My cousin is a social worker and family therapist and, as it turns out, was at the hotel for this other conference, called his wife to say that there was a man in the lobby coffee shop who looks just like me, and finally decided to try to get a closer look.

Once we began to get over the shock and whatever awkwardness surrounded this surprise encounter, my colleague and I filled him in on the circumstances of the case. My cousin is not analytically trained or particularly oriented that way in his thinking. Our relationship is such that we've rarely if ever discussed cases or other aspects of our work. Having said this, for all of the theoretical conversations I had that weekend and during the weeks that preceded – real and illusory – his was the voice that was about to ring loudest in my head. I'm not sure whether or not that would have been the case without the other voices and circumstances revealing themselves and unfolding in the ways that they did or the processing that had already been occurring. I suspect it was also the vulnerability I was feeling that helped me to hear his voice, as well as the reminder that theoretical – in this case psychoanalytic – knowledge, acuity, and clinical experience were not necessarily enough, even though (along with personal and psychological resources) they are often all that we have. It wouldn't surprise me if in that moment, in that weekend, following weeks of difficult stirrings, it was being with someone who I knew loved me and whom I loved and whose personal history and emotional landscape resonated with my own that allowed for an intermingling of personal and professional in a particularly profound and useful way.

I no longer have the exact words, but basically my cousin suggested something seemingly very simple. He proposed that I now put aside theory and instead just try to think of my patient and me as two human beings who are relating and in an unusual situation of having our lives cross outside the room. I know something that my patient doesn't, he reminded me, and carrying this secret is making it difficult for me to be with him in ways that he needs. I've given it the necessary time to unfold, he continues, and now it's time to let my patient in on what's been happening. It's true that by this point I was headed to or almost there myself – or at least I'd like to think so. But my cousin's words carried me the extra distance I needed to travel from where I had started – not just weeks but rather decades ago – to where I now lived with my patient, my friend, my various theoretical and personal self-states. In no uncertain terms, I now knew what needed to happen next.

Resolved

As I open the door to the waiting room, resolved to tell my patient what I know if he and my friend are considering a third date, Michael greets me with an expression not unlike that of my cousin's two days before. "Well," he says, smiling and excited, "It's finally happened. After more than five years, our paths have finally crossed!" While I knew this was a possibility, I didn't think it likely, and of course among other thoughts and feelings, I was relieved and intrigued to hear more. Apparently, the topic of therapy came up on their date, and while describing his experience, where my office is, and the like, my friend interrupted to say that he thinks he knows who Michael's therapist is, and that the two of us are friends. Michael tells me how excited he was by this news, and the questions he wanted to ask my friend about me. Interestingly, he is able to refrain, and before my friend has a chance to tell him any details about me or our friendship – which he probably wouldn't have done – Michael tells him that he has all these questions but won't ask because we don't talk a lot about my life. "You know I think he's a lovely man," Michael tells me. "He's the kind of friend I would imagine you to have, which raises you in my estimation . . . I don't think there's enough of an attraction or sexual chemistry though." We agree that in a way this is fortunate and makes things less complicated for us.

We talk about his sadness that this won't be moving forward, and his pride and hopefulness about getting this far and handling my friend's disclosure in a way that doesn't overwhelm him or cross a boundary he's reluctant to cross. He shares a fantasy that I would say to my friend, "run away as fast as you can, this guy is too sick," and bursts into tears. We sit quietly while he cries, the shame and sadness enveloping us. Later, I appreciate his capacity and kindness in recognizing my subjectivity when he gently asks if and when I knew and what this has been like for me. I share some of the dilemma and my wish to give him space to explore this, while not wanting him to feel tricked or betrayed if this were to be revealed at a later time. Michael is moved by this, and says it feels like what he needed, and that he can imagine how difficult this must have been for me. I confirm and we are able to laugh together: "What are the chances," we say, and "careful what you wish for – yes, you got to meet someone from my life outside." At this point, whatever anger, resentment, and envy he may also be feeling are held at bay, and I note to myself that the similar feelings I'd been carrying are overshadowed by tenderness and relief. Michael talks more about the brief but important experience of dating this man, and how during the last date he channeled my voice when giving some advice about a family issue my friend had shared. I again hear and remember all the voices that I'd been keeping company with and think about how they are a part of Michael, too. For the moment they are receding, but I know that for better or worse, they will never be too far away. In this time, in this place, I mostly hear the sounds of our breathing, Michael's crying, our laughing, his fingers tapping on the couch, my shifting in the chair, and the sounds of just our two voices filling the room.

Final thoughts

For some time, I wasn't sure whether or not to include this piece as a chapter in the current collection. In some respects, I see this as less a tale of the analyst's subjectivity affecting theory and practice than as a story in reverse; when the professional becomes personal, if you will – the impact on, rather than the clinical implications of, the psychoanalyst's life experience. Still, I think of Paul Wachtel's (2009) cyclical psychodynamic model and its elaboration of behavior as bidirectional, reciprocal, and mutually contextually embedded rather than linear, and Adrienne Harris's (2000) similar understanding of behavior as viewed through the lens of nonlinear dynamic systems theory and chaos theory. My entry into the current telling may initially emphasize Michael's impact on my personal life, but as I hope becomes apparent, this in turn soon leads to a struggle with emergent clinical concerns, theoretical dilemmas, choices, voices, professional ancestors, and ghosts (Harris, 2009; Loewald, 2000) as I bring my history to bear in work with Michael, the two of us devolving and evolving as each affects and is affected by the other. The personal and professional interpenetrate circularly, as they do in all treatments.

The story doesn't quite end here, of course. While it might seem that the narrative comes to rest in a place of smooth, neat resolution, questions remain, as perhaps they always do. Although it was my sense that Michael was already beginning to determine that his attraction to my friend wasn't strong enough to warrant continuation of the relationship, I have tried to explore – albeit with limited success – to what extent the end might also have been ushered in by Michael's wish to reinstate the old boundaries, preserve our relationship, and reduce any anxiety or guilt that he might have been feeling. It was indeed clear to me that Michael appreciated my disclosed attempts to give him space for things to unfold. I wonder, though, how much he might also have become aware of my personal interests and needs (when he discovered who he'd been dating), and our therefore intertwined but conflicted agenda. To what extent did Michael feel he must behave in accordance with those unarticulated but perceived wishes by prematurely aborting the relationship (Pickles, 2012; Slavin & Kriegman, 1998)? Assuming at least some amount of compliance, there would be anger and resentment to contend with at a later date.

This is a story not just of containment, of course, but also of multiple disclosures to multiple parties: Michael's, my friend's, and mine; to each other, to Michael's therapy group, to my colleagues and cousin and, more recently, to listeners and readers, with Michael's awareness of the latter. And these disclosures also represent what Jonathan Slavin (2013) calls moments of truth, opportunities to *speak* and *explore* the truth rather than merely *disclose* it, allowing my patient the opportunity to secure possession of his own mind by gaining access to mine, and his analyst to experience something similar, in ways that his (and my) parents were not always able to do for us.

Through the years, Michael and I have had numerous opportunities to revisit these issues and questions – to more fully explore these moments of truth, most recently when I sought his permission first to present and then publish our work. These reminiscences have opened up space to experience positive feelings of growth and appreciation for the intersection of our lives, both then and again when thinking about my telling of his story. We have also reexamined issues of anger, resentment, and envy as mentioned above, as well as shame – his resurrected and articulated in the treatment, and mine contained more than spoken during the initial events and while in the midst of these most recent explorations. And finally (though additional iterations and insights may of course transpire with the passage of more time and growth), we have encountered feelings of pride as well, especially since these most recent reflections occurred in the context of Michael's first long-term, live-in relationship, initiated less than a year after he said goodbye to his dating partner, my friend.

Notes

1 This chapter is a modified version of a previously published article entitled "When two become four: Patient, analyst, lover, friend," in *Psychoanalytic Perspectives, 10* (2), 2013.
2 For example, Aron (1996); Atwood and Stolorow (1993); Bach (2006); Fosshage (2007); Frank (2005); Knoblauch (2008); Loewald (2000); Mitchell (1993, 2000); Samuels (1989).

References

Atlas-Koch, G., & Kuchuck, S. (2012). To have and to hold: Psychoanalytic dialogues on the desire to own. *Psychoanalytic Dialogues, 22*, 93–105.

Atwood, G. E., & Stolorow, R. D. (1993). *Structures of subjectivity: Explorations in psychoanalytic phenomenology*. Hillsdale, NJ: Analytic Press.

Aron, L. (1996). *A meeting of minds: Mutuality in psychoanalysis*. Hillsdale, NJ: Analytic Press.

Bach, S. (2006). *Getting from here to there: Analytic love, analytic process*. Hillsdale, NJ: Analytic Press.

Benjamin, J. (1990). An outline of intersubjectivity: The development of recognition. *Psychoanalytic Psychology, 7* (Suppl.), 33–46.

Benjamin, J. (2004). Beyond doer and done-to: An intersubjective view of thirdness. *Psychoanalytic Quarterly*, *73*, 5–46.

Fosshage, J. L. (2007). The analyst's participation in co-creating the analytic relationship: Implicit and explicit dimensions of analytic change. *International Journal of Psychoanalytic Self Psychology*, *2*, 147–162.

Frank, K. A. (2005). Toward conceptualizing the personal relationship in therapeutic action: Beyond the real relationship. *Psychoanalytic Perspectives*, *3*(1), 15–56.

Harris, A. (2000). Gender as a soft assembly: Tomboys' stories. *Studies in Gender and Sexuality*, *1*, 223–250.

Harris, A. (2009). "You must remember this." *Psychoanalytic Dialogues*, *19*, 2–21.

Hoffman, I. Z. (1994). Dialectical thinking and therapeutic action in the psychoanalytic process. *Psychoanalytic Quarterly*, *63*, 187–218.

Jung, C. G. (1970). *The structure and dynamics of the psyche: Collected works of C. G. Jung* (Vol. 8). Princeton, NJ: Princeton University Press.

Knoblauch, S. H. (2008). Attention to the analyst's subjectivity: From Kohut to now . . . How are we doing? *International Journal of Psychoanalytic Self Psychology*, *3*, 237–239.

Kuchuck, S. (2008). In the shadow of the towers: The role of retraumatization and political action in the evolution of a psychoanalyst. *Psychoanalytic Review*, *95*, 417–436.

Loewald, H. W. (2000). On the therapeutic action of psychoanalysis. In *The essential Loewald: Collected papers and monographs* (pp. 221–256). Hagerstown, MD: University Publishing Group.

Mitchell, S. A. (1993). *Hope and dread in psychoanalysis*. New York: Basic Books.

Mitchell, S. A. (2000). *Relationality: From attachment to intersubjectivity*. Hillsdale, NJ: Analytic Press.

Ogden, T. H. (2004). The analytic third: Implications for psychoanalytic theory and technique. *Psychoanalytic Quarterly*, *73*, 167–195.

Ogden, T. H. (2009). *Rediscovering psychoanalysis: Thinking and dreaming, learning and forgetting*. London: Routledge.

Pickles, J. (2012, October). Discussion of Steven Kuchuck's "Guess who's going to dinner? On the arrival of the uninvited third." International Association for Psychoanalytic Self Psychology Annual Conference, Washington, DC.

Samuels, A. (1989). Analysis and pluralism: The politics of psyche. *Journal of Analytical Psychology*, *34*, 33–51.

Slavin, J. H. (2013). Moments of truth and perverse scenarios in psychoanalysis: Revisiting Davies' "Love in the afternoon." *Psychoanalytic Dialogues*, *23*, 139–149.

Slavin, M. O., & Kriegman, D. (1998). Why the analyst needs to change: Toward a theory of conflict, negotiation, and mutual influence in the therapeutic process. *Psychoanalytic Dialogues*, *8*, 247–284.

Smith, H. (2001). Hearing voices: The fate of the analyst's identifications. *Journal of the American Psychoanalytic Association*, *49*(3), 781–812.

Wachtel, P. L. (2009). Knowing oneself from the inside out, knowing oneself from the outside in: The "inner" and "outer" worlds and their link through action. *Psychoanalytic Psychology*, *26*, 158–170.

145

12

BECOMING AN ANALYST

At play in three acts

Philip Ringstrom

Shortly after the February 2010 IARPP conference in San Francisco, the editor of this volume approached me asking if I would be interested in contributing a chapter to the collection. What inspired his invitation was hearing me and my wife, Marcia Steinberg, being interviewed by Jeanne Wolff Bernstein on our experiences of infertility and miscarriages over two decades before. My comments in particular fell neatly into the narrative form that he was seeking for a book which would examine how very personal experiences in analysts' lives have a shaping effect, both in terms of their theoretical epistemology as well as their praxis. Taking license from this invitation, I began to associate to several life experiences. Each was profoundly informative of what I now recognize as organizing themes that have dramatically shaped my sense of psychoanalysis, both theoretically and clinically.

The first theme I will be discussing emerged from my experience with infertility and our first miscarriage. These proved to be seminal in shaping many thoughts about trauma. Among these are what I think of as unimpeachably trauma, but also my concern (a concern that I have subsequently heard is shared by many in our field) that our employment of trauma as an explanatory system is suffering from considerable overuse in manners that are potentially deleterious to our work.

Further pondering what I would write for this chapter led to another theme – the role of *expectancy systems* in psychoanalytic thinking as different from the current near fetish-ization of trauma. Clearly, although trauma represents a variety of an expectancy system, expectancy systems cover a vastly broader domain than trauma alone can capture. Though this may seem obvious, it was becoming clearer and clearer that virtually every case I was hearing about from clinicians was ensconced in trauma as the formulation of the root problem in the patient's life. This observation prompted me to review my own life, and in reflecting upon my two psychoanalyses I recalled several personally profound unconscious transference systems, all of which were seminal in my development, though not based in trauma per se. The analysis of these transferences led to illuminations that were quite liberating.

Free associating off this point reminded me of life experiences germane to what has often made me chafe at fixed systems of thought. While this applies broadly to my perspective on all things cultural, political, and so forth, it applies especially to my feelings about psychoanalysis. From this association emerged another recollection that powerfully influenced me growing up: being raised in a family in which both the concepts of ecumenicalism and dramaturgy were pretty much a daily lexical staple – whether spoken or not. It is clear that their combination was very important to my embracing pluralistic thinking.

This reverie further reminded me of my fascination with how our fictional world (i.e., the world of our imaginary) presses up against the experientially real world of our daily life. This collision is potentially enormously enlivening so long as we are capable of also distinguishing between what we subjectively codify as our fictional and our reality perspective on experience.[1] Nevertheless, I take to heart Stephen Mitchell's (2000) comment that, "Fantasy cut adrift from reality becomes irrelevant and threatening. Reality cut adrift from fantasy becomes vapid and empty. Meaning in human experience is generated in the mutual dialectically enriching tension between fantasy and reality; each requires the other to come alive" (p. 29). It was upon all of this reflection that I was finally able to more deeply understand my fascination with the role of improvisation in psychoanalysis.

The remainder of this chapter focuses on three principle themes: distinguishing trauma from expectancy systems; the revisitation of the connection of expectancy systems with transference, independent of trauma; and how the pluralistic values of ecumenicalism, coupled with the world of drama, became an experiential segue into the fascinating and often challenging world of operating psychoanalytically from an improvisational perspective.

"Trauma, trauma, everywhere and not a thought to think"[2]

In January, 1984, my wife and I married after two years of courtship. Each of us had pursued personal and professional goals independent of one another, and we married fully expecting that our union would lead to a shared goal of creating a family. In 1984, Marcia was finishing the second year of her MSW program, and between that and her desire to graduate and begin her practice, we delayed trying to have a child.

In the meantime, we knew that we were both in excellent shape and enjoying excellent health. The weekend we first began attempting to conceive in earnest, we also hiked to the bottom of the Grand Canyon and back up to the top in a day. In this context, we imagined that we would have no difficulties having children as soon as we were ready, a course upon which we commenced in August of 1987. For me at least, an implicit *expectancy system* – a point I will be elaborating upon considerably shortly – was in place that filled me with an unwavering confidence that our success in conceiving and thereafter having a child would only be a matter of a few months away.

After close to six months of trying, we awakened on Valentine's Day morning, 1988, to the realization that Marcia might be pregnant. We took the home pregnancy test and, giddy with delight, discovered that indeed she was. In a state of what retrospectively might be thought of as a kind of manic defensiveness – a sense of omnipotent fantasy – we were, at least in my mind, suddenly enveloped in the completely irrational sense of having created life, as if for the first time, literally, as if we were the first couple on earth to have a child. Even though at the time I sensed that this seemed a tad delusional, it felt too wonderful to dismiss. I completely and readily embraced my omnipotent fantasy, with no protective reflection to spare me. I did so consciously primarily because, in an uncanny way, this conviction felt like "it" embraced me!

Over the next two weeks, my omnipotent fantasy made me feel as though we were viscerally floating through the world. In my mind, we were surrounded quite literally by a protective "bubble" insulating us from any harm, impervious to the unthinkable things that beset ill-fated and unfortunate others. We were now three, with my even personifying our union further by naming our future unknown off-spring, "Embry-O." It was in this context that the miscarriage that occurred two weeks later completely shocked me in a manner that left me not simply devastated, but traumatized. (This miscarriage was the first of three, prior to a fourth pregnancy in 1991 that led to the birth of our daughter, Lena, now age 21. We were never able to conceive again.)

The nature of my omnipotent fantasy, and my incapacity to imagine anything otherwise, completely made me vulnerable to the "assault of the unimaginable." Equally important, however, is that Marcia was not traumatized. She was devastated for sure, and in some respects as emotionally distraught as I, but there was also something profoundly different about our experiences of what was ostensibly the same event: our miscarriage. For Marcia, at least, as horrible as the thought was of potentially having a miscarriage, the possibility of it fit within the larger domain of her expectancy systems.

Nevertheless, my experience was instrumental in compelling me to ask many questions, such as: What is trauma? What do we mean by trauma? What happens when we employ trauma as an etiological explanation, when perhaps an alternative explanation might be better suited to a patient's presentation? In taking up these questions, I want to take up what is for me an unequivocal version of trauma: the "assault of the unimaginable." Trauma, Van der Kolk (2007), Grotstein (1997, 2000), and Ringstrom (1999, 2010d) all argue, arises precisely when we are assaulted by the "unimaginable" – in effect, we have not been able to "create" in our mind, prior to its occurrence, the event or situation that becomes traumatic to us. Grotstein (2000) writes: "Trauma is the premature encounter with the impact of objects that we lacked the capacity to 'create'" (p. 211). Human beings are intrinsically makers of meaning, and as such create versions of reality as much as reality discloses itself to us. We are constituted by innumerable expectancy systems, and their violation has an enormous range of implications to our psychological health. In fact, I believe that one primary thing that may differentiate the same shocking event from becoming traumatic to one while not so to another is that the former had no chance (or perhaps the capacity, no emotional belief system) to imagine (and therefore to create in the imaginary) the event in advance. Hence, the same traumatic event or situation that literally "shocks" one (Bromberg, 1998, 2006) ends up not shocking the other, despite how bad its consequences also are for the latter. Furthermore, and most importantly, we are all the more devastated in circumstances when we are assaulted by the very thing our unconsciously omnipotent fantasies lead us to feel we are impervious to. This was certainly the case for me, and I would submit also for Robert Stolorow's loss of his wife Dede in 1991. He writes: "Her death tore from me the illusion of our infinitude" (2007, p. 41).

Trauma, in the case of expectancy systems, arises when one is overwhelmed so as to shatter heretofore illusions about reality and therefore to render one helpless in the face of unbearable feelings until these can be taken up with others, a key task of psychotherapy. The salient point is about the *violation of expectancy*, but this topic is enormously complex insofar as violations of expectations are also very normal aspects of human relating in ways that are just as much positive as negative. For example, our delight in any joke involves the punch line's violation of our expectation borne of the joke's set-up. Furthermore, in many respects, it is the violation of the expectancies of a patient's negative transference that involves one of the most salient mutative impacts on the outcome of any treatment.

The troubling aspect of the overuse of trauma is that it "universalizes" it to the point of poignantly diluting its meaning. For example, Philipson (2010) notes that Stolorow's definition of "developmental trauma"[3] involves "the absence of adequate attunement and responsiveness to the child's painful emotional reactions that renders them unendurable and thus a source of traumatic states and psychopathology" (Stolorow, 2007, p. 10). She argues that given this model of trauma, it is hard to imagine anyone who has not been traumatized during some part of their development.[4] This definition of trauma, she further notes, expands it to include potentially anything that might violate a child's expectancies or disrupt his or her organization of experience. Philipson writes that this definition, ". . . militates against what Mitchell (1988) has called 'the inevitable emotional conditions of early life . . .'" (p. 22) She notes that Mitchell argued that babies are born with a wide range of potentialities, but that these necessarily become reduced by the degree to which they are either recognized and responded to or not. Meanwhile, it is inevitable that caregivers offer up other possibilities for the child, some of which may not correspond to his or her as the temperamental potentials. In short, Mitchell is suggesting how that which Stolorow encompasses as potentially traumatizing malattunement is mostly about inherent, inescapable reductions of the child's originating potentialities in any given caregiving surround.

She goes on to say:

> If malattunement to painful emotional states gives rise to trauma, it follows then that trauma becomes not exceptional but common, not unimaginable but painfully expectable, not the property of the few but the experience of the many. It is withdrawn from the category of being

outside of normal human experience, to being virtually definitional of that experience. Thus it would make sense that it would assume salience in child development and clinical presentation.

(p. 22)

Thus, it appears that what is getting lost in the overuse of trauma is the role of expectation (the psychoanalytic domain of which is largely unconscious) – in other words, the role of expectancy systems. Even more to the point, it further sets the stage for how violations of expectancy play a common disturbance in life, but are equally important in cultivating highly mutative potentials, especially in psychotherapy.[5]

Beebe and Lachmann (2002) relate expectancy systems to Stern's (1985) idea about "representations of interaction generalized" (RIGs). Both of these ideas are constituted by cognitive, affective, and communicative processes involving implicit (procedural, emotional, and non-conscious process) and *explicit* (conscious, verbalizable, symbolic narrative) elements, as these processes generalize to expectancies about interaction. It is a tiny leap to seeing how all of this is formative of what reveals itself as the patient's transference organization,[6] which takes me into the illumination of highly constraining, though not traumatically created transferences.

Three transferences

I must confess that I chafe a bit whenever my patients invoke the term *normal*. I loathe the self-objectification of the construct as much as I also appreciate that this is – dare I say – about as normal as any human tendency. Still, this reductionism flies in the face of the liberating forces of the psychoanalytic perspective I revere. I think that whatever is normal for us is borne of our fundamental emotional convictions that we were raised with, those that inform what is both imaginable and, just as often, what is not. Of course, one's sense of normal may be grounded in trauma, but I am more inclined to think of the world of "normal" in terms of transference constructions. This conviction was certainly borne out in terms of three profound relational systems in my development that formed the basis of several distinct expectancy systems. I would have never been able to embrace this but for what became analyzed in over 16.5 years in two separate analyses. I came to refer to these as my "father," "mother," and "brother(s)" modes of transference.

What was of great importance in the illumination of these three transference systems was that while they all evidenced episodes of malattunement, invalidation, and misrecognition, none of this culminated in my thinking of them as belonging to the world of developmental trauma. This is not to say that I escaped trauma in my life; I have had my share of it as I believe most people do. I am not sure I have met anyone that hasn't had some experience constitutive of trauma as I have defined it in terms of the "assault of the unimaginable." In each case, it is apparent that the imprint of these traumatic experiences is profound, though I

150

am less certain that they are as character-defining as much of the current trauma literature seems to insist.

Meanwhile, the illumination of my three transference modes was most helpful in aiding me to see that I was not a victim so much as a participant, albeit unconsciously, in a system of convictions soft-assembled in the context of what I came to expect. Loosely, the first transference to be tackled in my analysis was to my father. Growing up, he loomed large. I idealized him tremendously, and in his largeness he represented a considerable source of castration anxiety for me. By castration, I mean the abdication of one's own sense of meaning relative to the presumed all-knowing authority, especially when having a mind of one's own was felt, at least in certain circumstances (whether in fact or fantasy), to be too threatening to one's affective tie. In this manner, I take castration anxiety (for both men and women) to be a universal potentiality, but one that should not be confused with developmental trauma.

A very early recollection of the power of my idealization to my father occurred perhaps at age three or four during a fight I had with my middle brother (I am the youngest of three sons) about whether our father could (if he chose to) become the President of the United States. I was horrified at my brother arguing that our father couldn't, and argued vehemently, bordering on hysteria, that he most certainly could! Preserving my idealization of my father was emblematic of something essential to me, though during my years of analysis I would come to realize being idealized by me was not necessarily so important to my father. In later conversations about this, my father found my childhood fantasy puzzling, especially in the context of his never feeling this toward his father.

My father was a very loving man and cared (along with my mother) more about his three sons than anything else. Nevertheless, he could be firm and strict, and if crossed, he would become loud and frightening (though never physical). Still, as I was always a creative and imaginative boy and was eager to explore the world in ways that would not necessarily have been acceptable to him, I was careful to always stay below his radar, to take careful notes of how my brothers seemed to fuck up, and to ultimately learn how to manage to stay off my father's disciplinary map. None of this was very clear to me beyond a procedural way of operating until my analyses.

During my years on the couch, I also learned that much of his bravado masked his own fears of the world. His father, a Swedish immigrant, had very little interest in his family, and my father had to take care of his ever-worried Swedish immigrant mother and his younger (by seven years) brother, who was wholly unwanted and resented by his father and worried to death about by his mother. My father was conscripted into an unfair role. But he was also a fair and compassionate man, and in effect, a relatively clear transference object with which to work out the authoritarian aspects of my transference neurosis, especially regarding the castration anxiety element. One of the most powerful lessons to come out of the analysis of my transference to my father was to not let fear stop me from important things in my life, in the manner that it seemed to have sometimes paralyzed my father.

My "mother transference," on the other hand, was far, far murkier. In a moment I will say more about her background in theater and in drama and the lifelong impact that has had upon me. But perhaps the easiest way to describe her impact is the story she told me more than once wherein her mother said to her: "Wilma, if you cannot realize your ideals, then idealize your real." In one swipe, my grandmother had encouraged my mother to never let reality get her down, but instead to make things up wherever necessary. My mother became the personification of the message, "If life gives you lemons, make lemonade."

Meanwhile, her relationship with her mother was complicated. Her mother was very dictatorial regarding whatever talents she detected in my mother, which were several. My mother was talented in drama, in diving, in a host of performative activities for which her mother became the proverbial "stage Mom," who was convinced that with enough trophies, her daughter could marry rich by becoming some man's "trophy wife." Her mother's intrusions were mighty, which led to my mother's conviction that she would never attempt to coerce her children as she had been coerced by her mother.

When she told this to me as an adult, in the midst of my first analysis, I realized that she had inadvertently "confessed" a huge blind spot in her conscious awareness. Consciously, she believed that she could escape being an influence in the direction of our lives by never being a direct influence, though unconsciously she was attempting to persuade all of us how to be (for our own betterment) concealed in a kind of plausible deniability of what she was actually doing, a deniability that she could fully believe was the case because of her erstwhile commitment to not be a pressuring influence in our lives. Meanwhile, the effect of her omnipresent influence could never really be protested by any of us. Ironically, I have often thought that had my mother ever been in analysis, her transference to her mother would have been far more easily discerned and reconciled than mine to her.

My point is, however, that while never for a moment questioning my mother's love, I eventually began to question how real what she said was, even to her. This left a long trail of confusion that I did not experience with my father. He was less complex in this sense, but infinitely clearer. My expectancy system for him was much more easily negotiated, whereas that with my mother wasn't. My transference with my mother led not to fear of castration, but to the repetition of feeling aroused and dropped, aroused and dropped, and frequently confused without knowing why.

It seemed the course of my analyses had to follow first getting clear about dad, then, in a much longer process, getting clear about my mother's lack of clarity. Eventually, as these two modes of transference expectancy systems became clearer, a third one emerged relative to my transference to my older brothers: my middle brother older by five years, and my oldest, older by ten. My story of being the youngest sibling is a pretty common one. I idolized my brothers, and they never, ever seemed to grasp or embrace this fact.

My oldest brother was off to college by the time I entered third grade. Up to that point, our worlds were so far apart that they had little or nothing to do with one another. He built things for me, assisted in teaching me how to walk and later to ride a bike. He also gave me our first family dog and completely overhauled an ancient tuba so that I could play it in my elementary school band. But his interest in who I was, was seldom in evidence. Meanwhile, my middle brother was sandwiched in between the two of us and was full of envy, jealousy, and anger, which was not hard to understand. My oldest brother was presumed our father's favorite, and I, the youngest, was the presumed the favorite of my mother. To compound matters, our female cousin came to live with us for one year precisely when both she and my middle brother were age five. Neither my parents, nor my oldest brother, nor even I could suppress our delight in having a little girl (surrogate "daughter/sister"), and my cousin was an expert at milking the attention while dismissing my middle brother. As an outcome, he became moody and prone to being petulant and sometimes even abusive when in a dark mood. I never questioned his love, but I did learn to track his moods closely and work around them. And, I think bitter in my own way about his non-recognition of my adulation, not to mention his intermittent abuse, I found ways to poke at his vulnerabilities and torture him a bit psychologically.

These three stories of transference barely touch the magnitude of our lives together. Still, they hopefully capture how much my character was shaped by these systems and what I cobbled together about what to *expect* from growing up in them. From my father, I eventually learned to expect that when he was frightened, he would become angry and prone to displacing blame on others for things he feared reflected some inadequacy of his own. Of course, he was not conscious of this. From my mother, I learned to expect that she would compulsively put a positive spin on everything, making her quite poor at empathy in moments of her family's pain or loss, though she was not entirely without sympathy. From my brothers, I learned that no amount of idolizing them would induce the same powerfully positive affect from them towards me, though in adulthood, on occasion, some admiration sometimes has sneaked through.

But mostly what I have learned from these transferences is that each of us builds a myriad of expectancy systems that arise in various relational contexts for the remainder of our lives. These systems organize how in different circumstances we come to expect something about ourselves vis-à-vis something about the fantasized other. But that doesn't mean that this should be codified as traumatic.

In writing this chapter, I realized several critically important questions about my practice. I begin with a murky, messy, and perhaps indeterminable one: Does developmental malattunement necessarily create trauma? Or, instead, is it clearer to think of malattunement as simply implicated (in a sense, "normal") in creating expectancy systems, many of which may well be piss-poor and really, really crappy, but not by definition traumatic? These expectancies may be ones from which we suffer (sometimes tremendously), but are they ones from which we could be misled by codifying them as trauma? Certainly, there is little question that attunement and validation and recognition were all central in shaping my expectancy systems, including affect regulation and sense of agency. Likewise, malattunement, invalidation, and misrecognition must play key roles in creating my less desirable expectancy systems, but also roles in which I was not simply a victim, but rather, played parts born of my larger family drama.

All of this got me thinking: Why should we care about designating the etiology of some forms of psychopathology as traumatic versus expectancy systems definitive of a closed system of predictable lousy "sequences of reciprocal exchanges"? In the latter, a person's perspective on life and relationships exhibits a highly constrained manner in which he imagines how he will be responded to. But what is so important about distinguishing the latter from trauma?

The answer: quite a lot, actually. However, to capture the complexity of this issue, I first need to situate my argument in the topic of the fundamental problem human beings have of devolving into binaries, the gravitational pull that tugs us into either/or, black-and-white ways of thinking and feeling versus both/and, shades-of-gray ways. Jessica Benjamin (2004) and Lew Aron (2003, 2006) have studied this dyadic phenomenon better than anyone else I can think of. They see this natural gravitational pull in terms of the dyadic systems' vulnerability to collapsing into patterns of dominance and submission whenever there are *essential* beliefs in conflict. This happens in dyads of all shapes and sizes: evidence on the nation-state level is the tension between the Israelis and the Palestinians and the Protestants and Catholics in Northern Ireland; on the intrapsychic level, it is found between dissociated self-states; on the intersubjective level of the dyadic structure of two people relating, it is easy for them to slip into the binary wherein one experiences being the "done-to" by another who is then deemed "the doer." (More importantly, a common experience of the person who feels "done-to" is that he sees the "doer" in a domineering position relative to his state of submission.) Of course, as frequently happens, both parties are convinced that they are the "done-to," the victim as it were, not recognizing that in complementary (character) form, each needs the other to define their own position. There can be no "doer" without a "done-to," no sadist without a masochist, and in either of these cases there is an imminent reversibility of roles. The point is, these conditions of dominance and submission are the death knell of play in general and of improvisation in particular. They can only be reckoned with through the introduction of a "third" unbound (non-binary) point of view that recognizes that a much broader sense of the selfhood of each participant often involves *both* the positions of the "doer" and the "done-to" and even, sometimes, the sadist and the masochist. Absent this recognition, one is doomed to split off one half of the binary, project it, and induce the other to act in accordance with the projected half. It is the mutuality of this process that makes for the concept of "mutual inductive identification" (Ringstrom, 2007a, 2008b, 2011, in press). So, in answer to what is important about distinguishing expectancy systems from trauma, it is the attempt to not readily fall prey to the victim/abuser binary which can so easily happen once the trauma construct has been invoked.

My intuitive sense of the problematic of binary thinking compelled me to recall my parents' strong belief in ecumenicalism. I am fairly certain that without design, but perhaps more out of serendipity, my parents found in each other partners who were deeply ensconced in ecumenical thinking long before they had ever considered the meaning of the word.

From ecumenicalism to improvisation

My parents' religious upbringings were wildly disparate from one another's. My mother's family were devout members of the Mayfair Methodist Church in Chicago; my father's parents were Swedish immigrants who were essentially atheists, and my father's father even associated with various communist organizations. Nevertheless, perhaps in youthful defiance, my father developed something of an interest in religion, and was very taken with my mother's commitment to her church. When they married, they did so as Methodists.

One decade later, we moved from Chicago to Kansas City where, finding the Methodist church not so much to their liking, they joined a Presbyterian church. It seemed that having some religious faith of the Christian variety was important to them, but what form it took was less important. Curiously, they both shared deeply rooted suspicions about organized religion, disliking its politics and its commercialism. The more pomp and circumstance and rules of observance any religion had, the more they raised their eyebrows. They were especially critical of religious rules and "do's and don'ts" that were based on superstitions formed eons ago and that no longer made sense in modern times, and of religious organizations "robbing the faithful" for their own institutional needs.

What did remain important to them was the goodness of any religious faith. They felt all people should find a faith that appealed to them, and that one's faith should be respected. Included in this was even respect for not having faith, as was tested by my announcement to my mother at age 13 that I thought I was an atheist. She asked me to speak with a youth minister, and I did, which merely fortified my conviction. She said she hoped I might someday have a restored sense of belief in God, but she also respected my thoughtfulness and never once criticized me for my stance. Hence ecumenicalism – a word typically not in the lexicon of a small boy – was embedded very early in my speech and in my worldview. This broad-mindedness of my parents also carried over in other areas, including progressive views about civil rights, race relations, women rights, the protection of freedom of thought and its expression, as well as the protection of the environment.

This picture of my parents might make them sound like progenitors of the cultural revolution of their son's "baby boomer" years, a road trip from the beatniks to the hippies. That, however, was hardly the case. They were as Midwestern and "white bread" as any in our mostly Republican, largely protestant community. Humorously, it was never clear in any presidential election which one would vote Democrat and which Republican. Nor did it appear they ever told each other, though they often joked that this could be another year in which their votes might cancel out.

There really wasn't much overt evidence of their convictions, and yet, when occasions arose to speak about organizations of any type, especially religious ones, they always spoke in a manner underscoring the importance of an ecumenical attitude. They had their Presbyterian faith, but never for a moment did they believe it superior over any other religion. For my parents, the first order of business was for all religions to accept one another's existence. They had zero patience for any religion that was bent upon the eradication of other rival religions.

Something of the deep structure of their convictions powerfully informed my developmental sensibility. In adulthood, my love affair with psychoanalysis has been ensconced in a kind of theoretical ecumenicalism. I have often joked – though I mean it – that I am the Will Rogers of psychoanalysis, in that I have never met a theory I didn't like. Like Roger's admonition that he could find something good in anybody he met, so too have I been able to find something good in every psychoanalytic theory with which I have become acquainted. And like my parents' view of religious rivalries, I have little patience for psychoanalytic theories that are bent on the eradication of competing points of view. Still, the question that hounds psychoanalysis is: How does one utilize aspects of divergent theories, some of which, it has been argued, have incompatible premises? Here is where I wind my way to improvisation.

My fascination with improvisation bore roots in a family background ensconced in theater. I don't remember a day growing up in which drama was not an important consideration. As a girl in Chicago, my mother fell in love with the theater. She acted well into early adulthood, when she got a contract with an agency to pursue a career in acting and modeling in New York City. At the time, she was a dead ringer for the actress Jean Harlow, and that was the heyday of Jean Harlow's Hollywood stardom. Within a week in New York my mother was introduced to the proverbial "director's couch," and in terror fled home back to Chicago, met my father, and got married six months later. Shortly thereafter, she gave birth to my oldest brother, and that put a quick stop to her life in professional theater and modeling. After my family moved to Kansas City close to a decade later, she became very involved in directing, writing, and acting at the Village Presbyterian Church in Prairie Village, Kansas (the second largest Presbyterian church in the United States at the time). From this, she drew the attention of various theologians interested in returning drama as an art form to the church. With them, she became the co-founder of what eventually was named the Ecumenical Council on Dramatic Arts (ECDA). Surrounded by doctors of theology, this was quite an accomplishment for a woman who never went to college.

In 1965, we moved to St. Louis, where she continued her dramatic work with the Webster Groves Presbyterian Church as she had done in Kansas City. From that day forward, the ECDA was a huge part of her world, and therefore also ours. For all 31 years that my parents lived in St. Louis, they had season tickets to Webster University's prized Repertory Company. Until 1996, when she and my father moved to Virginia, she was active in writing, teaching, directing, acting, and conducting drama workshops all over the United States. The workshops were about bringing the arts back into religion, back to where it all began. Up until she began slipping into Alzheimer's in her early 80s, there was hardly a conversation that we ever had that did not at some point find its way back to the dramatic arts.

As noted earlier, though my background exposure to ecumenicalism would seemingly have been sufficient to have made me the pluralistic thinker that I am, clearly the world of drama enlivened those ecumenical spirits. I believe that it was this unique, synergistic influence that led to the cultivation of an improvisational attitude in psychoanalysis that has been a topic of fascination since the early 1980s, when I joined an improvisational theater group organized by Drs. Norman and Evelyn Tabachnick. The group was composed mostly of psychoanalysts and a few other professionals, and was led over the years by a succession of professional actors who would provide us with the exercises that led to improvisational scene work.

Improvisation differs from convention in powerfully significant ways. It can create possibilities between people that are less likely through conventional means of interaction. For starters, while people frequently have at least some implicit sense of what they are doing together in an improvisation, there is little the two participants know in advance about the present moment experience that they are about to co-create. Neither knows where they are going, but if they adhere to the primary dictates of improvisation (i.e., to listen, to never reject what the other poses, but to in fact play-off-of-and-with the other's suggested reality), they will inevitably build a story. Furthermore, all of the elements of it will be co-authored, and therefore will arise not simply from each one's unconscious, but also culminate in the instantiation of moments of relational unconsciousness and the emergence of thirdness that is the property of both and not one or the other. Improvisation, in short, is a powerful antidote to binaries.

In over a dozen articles and chapters (Ringstrom, 2001a, 2001b, 2003, 2005, 2007a, 2007b, 2008a, 2008b, 2009, 2010a, 2010b, 2010c, in press), I have explored how improvisation is a fitting metaphor for many aspects of contemporary psychoanalysis. In the context of accepted systems concepts that the analytic relationship is inextricably mutually influential, the three ideal pillars of classical analysis no longer stand so steadily. With the understanding of so much implicit (nonverbal, affective, sub-symbolic) communication going on, the ideas of "abstinence, neutrality, and anonymity" seem pretty illusory and, in fact, potentially harmful in relationship to what we now understand about attachment systems and the profound interaffectivity of the analytic pairing. Indeed, to the degree analysts continue to try to uphold the "three pillars," they become caricatures of some past scripted world.

Thus, improvisation (like ecumenicalism) opens up how to think about vistas of possibility in contrast with the expectable narrowing of what constitutes each patient's character (i.e., his recursive self-defining personality traits), and this applies as well to the analyst's character. Improvisation does not suggest that the vicissitudes of each participant's character or script can be evaded – they can't. But it offers the possibility that character, organizing principles, transference, and countertransference can be more than simply illuminated and analyzed; *they can be played with*, and in the play lies the new possibility. This latter point is of critical importance to the topic of the violation of expectancy systems, and in particular, those that represent entrenched, closed systems of transference and sometimes even countertransference when the analyst is more wedded to adhering to the dictates of her theory than being with her patient. Such expectancy systems (whether the patient's or the analyst's) convey certain perspectives regarding the world, often perspectives that elide what is actually going on, and instead substitute one's own rigid set of rules that constrict engagement in reality rather than playing with the possibility of something different, something new. Indeed, one of the areas in which I find improvisation most moving is in actually playing with negative transference. This is a delicate phenomenon and needs to be carefully explored on a case-by-case basis, since in some cases such play can feel to the patient like mocking, while in others it communicates a profound understanding of the patient along with a means for both thinking and acting outside his negative transference box.

In this context of understanding, awareness of our human penchant for binaries suggests what can be problematic in the over-attribution of trauma, especially when applied as a universal construct such as developmental trauma. Unfortunately, the moment we invoke the word *trauma*, we inadvertently invite the construction of a binary. After all, once one is said to have suffered trauma, one has become a victim of something or someone. This latter formulation can rapidly devolve into the role of the other being the perpetrator of the trauma. *Voilà* – we are instantly into a binary and the space quickly closes down the creativity of thirdness, of another potentially liberating way of seeing and experiencing one's life circumstance.

This perspective, wedded to an improvisational point of view, has resulted in my saying on numerous occasions, "I do not work with trauma victims. I work with patients who among many things have likely also suffered some trauma in their lives." Calling a patient a "trauma victim" ironically invokes a great deal of reductionistic thinking as well as objectification. Speaking of my patient (or myself) as an open-ended subject, constituted by a myriad of experiences both terrible and good, makes me feel much less hogtied by the fear I recurrently hear analysts bemoan these days of either retraumatizing or shaming/blaming their patient. These latter fears completely undermine the analyst's capacity to play, and paraphrasing Winnicott (1971), if the patient can't play he must be taught, and if the analyst can't play, no psychotherapy can occur.

Conclusion

Having had the good fortune to be invited to contribute to this volume gave me an opportunity to capture the developmental origins of several powerful organizing principles that influence how I embrace theory and how I practice psychoanalytically. Psychoanalysis, for me, is a vehicle for personal liberation, but that feat must occur in the context of an analytic relationship. Requisite to that happening is the degree to which the field of that relationship is open to possibility. Trauma clearly is an impediment to that, but so too is its overuse, especially when an alternative, historical analysis of transference keeps things open in a manner that binary thinking about trauma can foreclose. As discussed, my background in a family that valued ecumenicalism as well as theater served to shape these ideas, as did my later experiences with my wife's miscarriages. Writing this chapter has presented me with an interesting review of my development, which leads me to encourage all analysts to investigate the developmental roots of their thinking as an invaluable part of the work.

Notes

1 Strenger (1998) indicates: "The more the individual's image of a life worth living is formed by images created in fantasy, the more the distance between actual life and a life informed by authorship is increased. The fantasy image transcendentalizes the idea of a 'real' life to the point where nothing in actual life could correspond to it anymore. In therapeutic work this manifests itself by the patient's contemptuous rejection of real-life options which could provide a step toward authorship, because he or she cannot see any connection between these steps and the image of real life they have gotten used to in fantasy" (p. 180).

2 This title is a play on words from Samuel Coleridge's famous poem *The Rime of the Ancient Mariner*.

3 Stolorow (2011) writes: "Developmental trauma originates within a formative intersubjective context whose central feature is malattunement to painful affect – a breakdown of the child-caregiver interaffective system – leading to the child's loss of affect integrating capacity and thereby to an unbearable, overwhelmed, disorganized state. Painful or frightening affect becomes traumatic when the attunement that the child needs to assist in its tolerance, containment, and integration is profoundly absent" (p. 27).

4 We know from Fonagy's (2003) research that the most optimal parenting imaginable wouldn't be able to be attuned more than 50% of the time and an average caregiver score of optimal attunement of 33% would be extraordinary, something like two decades of having a consistent batting average in the 300s in baseball. Nor, for that matter, would pure attunement be a good thing in development. Overattunement often heightens the child's sense that his mind is being perpetually invaded. This experience of intrusion includes a sense that assumptions are being made, some of which may prove to be true of him, but nevertheless assault him because he didn't have a chance to formulate them on his own. Is it any wonder that (Winnicott, 1971) posits a dialectic between the powerful desire to be recognized and also to maintain exquisite privacy? In the latter, we formulate that which isn't necessarily ready for "primetime."

5 The discourse on expectancy systems reunites us with earlier and perhaps currently arcane psychoanalytic discourse on self-"deficits," as distinguished from intrapsychic conflict. Beebe and Lachmann (2002) updated the language of structural defects to that of "patterns of experience," always in process and therefore potentially transformative. These patterns represent *"expectancies of sequences of reciprocal exchanges"* and are associated with "self-regulatory styles." They write: "The concept of expectancies shifts the focus to the *process* in which patterns of interaction became organized in the patient's history and are becoming organized in the treatment relationship" (p. 13).

6 And, of course, also the analyst's countertransference during the course of psychoanalytic treatment.

References

Aron, L. (2003). The paradoxical place of enactment in psychoanalysis: Introduction. *Psychoanalytic Dialogues*, *13*(5), 623–632.

Aron, L. (2006). Analytic impasse and the third: Clinical implications of intersubjectivity theory. *International Journal of Psychoanalysis*, *87*, 349–368.

Beebe, B., & Lachmann, F. (2002). *Infant research and adult treatment: Co-constructing interactions*. Hillsdale, NJ: Analytic Press.

Benjamin, J. (2004). Beyond doer and done to: An intersubjective view of thirdness. *Psychoanalytic Quarterly*, *73*, 5–46.

Bromberg, P. M. (1998). *Standing in spaces: Essays on dissociation, trauma, and clinical process*. Hillsdale, NJ: Analytic Press.

Bromberg, P. M. (2006). *Awakening the dreamer: Clinical journeys*. Mahwah, NJ: Analytic Press.

Fonagy, P. (2003). Some complexities in the relationship of psychoanalytic theory to technique. *Psychoanalytic Quarterly*, *72*(1), 13–48.

Grotstein, J. (1997). Autochthony and alterity: Psychic reality in counterpoint. *Psychoanalytic Quarterly*, *66*, 403–430.

Grotstein, J. (2000). *Who is the dreamer, who dreams the dream?* Hillsdale, NJ: Analytic Press.

Mitchell, S. (1988). *Relational concepts in psychoanalysis*. Cambridge, MA: Harvard University Press.

Mitchell, S. (2000). *Relationality: From attachment to intersubjectivity*. Hillsdale, NJ: The Analytic Press.

Philipson, I. (2010). Pathologizing twinship: An exploration of Robert Stolorow's trauma-tocentrism. *International Journal of Psychoanalytic Self Psychology*, *5*(1), 19–33.

Ringstrom, P. (1999). Discussion of Robert Stolorow's paper "The phenomenology of trauma." Paper given at the 22nd Annual Conference on the Psychology of the Self, Toronto, ON.

Ringstrom, P. (2001a). Cultivating the improvisational in psychoanalytic treatment. *Psychoanalytic Dialogues*, *11*(5), 727–754.

Ringstrom, P. (2001b). "Yes, and . . ." – How improvisation is the essence of good psychoanalytic dialogue: Reply to commentaries. *Psychoanalytic Dialogues*, *11*(5), 797–806.

Ringstrom, P. (2003). Crunches, (k)nots, and double binds: When what isn't happening is the most important thing: Commentary on paper by Barbara Pizer. *Psychoanalytic Dialogues*, *11*(5), 193–205.

Ringstrom, P. (2005). Essential enactments: Commentary on paper by Taras Babiak. *Studies in Gender and Sexuality*, *6*(2), 155–163.

Ringstrom, P. (2007a). Scenes that write themselves: Improvisational moments in relational psychoanalysis. *Psychoanalytic Dialogues*, *17*(1), 69–100.

Ringstrom, P. (2007b). Reply to commentary by Daniel N. Stern. *Psychoanalytic Dialogues*, *17*(1), 105–113.

Ringstrom, P. (2008a). Improvisational moments in self-psychological relational psychoanalysis. In P. Buirski & A. Kottler (Eds.), *New developments in self psychology practice* (pp. 223–237). Lanham, MD: Jason Aronson.

Ringstrom, P. (2008b). Improvisation and mutual inductive identification in couples therapy: A discussion of Susan Shimmerlick's article "Moments in relational psychoanalysis." *Psychoanalytic Dialogues*, *18*(3), 390–402.

Ringstrom, P. (2009). Selfobject as dramatis personae: Cultivating the improvisational in self-psychological psychoanalysis. In N. Van der Heide & W. Coburn (Eds.), *Self and systems: Explorations in contemporary self psychology* (pp. 174–203). New York: The Annals of New York Academy of Sciences.

Ringstrom, P. (2010a). Reply to commentaries. *Psychoanalytic Dialogues*, *20*(2), 236–250.

Ringstrom, P. (2010b). "Yes Alan!" and a few more thoughts about improvisation: A discussion of Alan Kindler's chapter "Spontaneity and improvisation in psychoanalysis." *Psychoanalytic Inquiry*, *30*(3), 235–242.

Ringstrom, P. (2010c). Commentary on Donna Orange's "Recognition as intersubjective vulnerability in the psychoanalytic dialogue." *International Journal of Psychoanalytic Self Psychology*, *5*(3), 257–273.

Ringstrom, P. (2010d). A review of Robert Stolorow's book: *Trauma and human existence: Autobiographical, psychological, and philosophical reflections*. *Psychoanalytic Psychology*, *27*(2), 241–249.

Ringstrom, P. (2011). Principles of improvisation: A model of therapeutic play in relational psychoanalysis. In L. Aron & A. Harris (Eds.), *Relational psychoanalysis, vol. V: Evolution of process* (pp. 447–478). New York: Routledge.

Ringstrom, P. (in press). "Inductive identification" and improvisation in psychoanalytic practice: Some comments on Joye Weisel-Barth's article on complexity theory. *International Journal of Psychoanalytic Self Psychology*.

Stern, D. N. (1985). *The interpersonal world of the infant: A view from psychoanalysis and developmental psychology*. New York: W. W. Norton.

Stolorow, R. (2007). *Trauma and human existence: Autobiographical, psychoanalytic and philosophical reflections*. New York: Analytic Press.

Stolorow, R. (2011). *World, affectivity, trauma: Heidegger and post-Cartesian psychoanalysis*. New York: Routledge.

Strenger, C. (1998). *Individuality, the impossible project: Psychoanalysis and self-creation*. Madison, CT: International Universities Press, Inc.

Van der Kolk, B. (2007, October). Annual Conference of the Los Angeles County Psychological Association.

Winnicott, D. W. (1971). *Playing and reality*. London: Tavistock.

13

PERSPECTIVES ON GAY FATHERHOOD

Emotional legacies and clinical reverberations

Noah Glassman and Steven Botticelli

Noah: girlyboy losses and family romance fantasy

It didn't take long for us to notice we were raising a "boy" boy. As two gay men, we were naturally alert to the signs, though perhaps no more so than anyone in our gender-attuned times. This realization would occur repeatedly, almost anew each time, taking me by surprise. On one occasion, it was not until we reached the baseball field that I realized how anxious I was, holding our five-year-old son's hand with sweaty palms. We had arrived for his first little league practice, and when I saw the field I was gripped by the old dread so powerfully associated with team sports: the nauseating mix of fear, shame, and anger so typical of some proto-gay boys. My own brief foray into group athletics – approximately five minutes of little league at the same age – consisted mostly of shock and fear in relation to the coaches, who seemed loud, rough, frightening, existing only to belittle. I felt completely "other," out of place among boys who seemed to take the shouting directives of the father–coaches in stride, even thrilled by the intensity of the practice, the rough-and-tumble play. I, of course, didn't yet have the words – nor had I heard their analogs hurled at me yet – for the unformulated experience of being a "girly" boy among seeming "boy" boys (Corbett, 1996; see also Drescher, 1998).[1] Even when I managed to get aspects of the stereotypical "boy" boy gender performance right, I was not part of the team: a few years later in a middle school phys ed baseball game, I caught the ball – through the miraculous intervention of some magical fairy godmother – and tagged out one of the more popular jocks. He promptly called me "faggot" for the indignity of losing a run on my "nellie" account. My teammates seemed to agree.

In forming a family through adoption, as soon as we knew our son's birth mother was pregnant with a boy, we imagined what it might be like to raise a male child who would probably, statistically speaking, grow up straight, and also a "boy" boy. Although I knew sports would likely be part of the picture, I somehow failed to anticipate fully what it would be like to navigate this masculine terrain with my child. So I walked onto the baseball field with him, this time as a 45-year-old man, taken aback by how awash I was in vulnerability. And yet, I was even more stunned to watch my son take in the scene with grinning excitement. He ran from me to a group of boys he didn't know (shy he is not), as I took in his difference; it now felt like difference, somehow, rather than the alienating "otherness" of my own little league experience. I watched as he threw himself enthusiastically into competitive camaraderie, following the guidance of a coach who seemed so much kinder than those of my boyhood (are fathers so much gentler now?). Over time, something new, perhaps long dormant and unclaimed, emerged in my experience as I found myself looking forward to games – baseball, soccer, basketball – and even following televised team sports. Suddenly, the World Series had meaning (see Harris, 2010, for a moving and eloquent "rereading" of baseball for its femininity and androgyny). I had expected to feel merely inept about sports with my child; I had not expected to feel something like terror, followed by his pleasure and my healing at the former site of trauma, accompanied by a sadness over my shame and loss: among other things, loss of a communal boyhood experience, a feeling of gender adequacy, and an acceptance of my own particular gender experience/performance. Parenthood had deepened a need for mourning that, while always in the background, had not previously taken me over in the way I was now experiencing. I wondered what else I had lost, never had, never knew I had fantasized about, and had not adequately mourned. In delineating the impact of the analyst's own unmourned losses as contributing to clinical impasse, Harris (2009) highlights the risks of "melancholic foreclosure" as ". . . the omnipotent stance, always beckons, because the move into deep loss and then into terror, is very frightening – for analyst or analysand" (p. 14).

I sat listening to my patient Taylor, a heavily muscled single gay man in his mid 20s with a traumatic childhood history of abuse, betrayals, and abandonments by parents and other family members. Despite his hulking linebacker-like exterior, I knew he had experienced himself as unlike other boys, in gendered and other ways, but so often the traumas in his family life had occupied most of my thoughts. He, like many if not most of the gay men I've worked with, made fleeting references to having been taunted as a boy. Reflexively, without thinking, I felt I "knew what he meant" when he had mentioned it; my own "bright spot" (a variant of blind spot, Goldberger, 1993). After all, I had many of my own memories to draw from and had heard many others. Although "many gay men have femme ghosts in their closets, many do not . . . [T]here are multiple homosexual boyhoods" (Corbett, 1996, p. 435). Similarly, there are multiple versions of the femme ghost in the closet. In becoming a father and revisiting my own girlyboyishness, I suddenly realized how little I knew about Taylor's experience, how little I had pressed him to say more. I asked for details about the taunting, what kind, what was it like, who knew, unprepared for Taylor's description of being spit on, kicked, pelted with stones – in addition to the "usual" outbursts of "faggot" and "fem-boy," I was even more unprepared for Taylor's trembling lip, his tearing eyes, his cracking voice – so different from the invulnerable, flat, shut-down seeming man–boy I usually faced. This, then, would become our entry point to his fragmented feeling states, and a point of connection between us. The shame and losses suffered by his girlyboy self became part of the language used for talking about other, earlier losses, as well.

Family narratives, family romance, and parental relationship to loss

Before becoming a father, when I contemplated adoption, my initial focus had been on our child-yet-to-be, his potential losses in not being raised by heterosexual birth parents – especially a birth mother, in a culture that so often constructs narratives of a mother's fundamental, innate capacity to soothe, to nurture a baby and young child. My own internal relationship to loss was not yet part of my conscious thinking. Instead, I wondered about our son's birth family, their loss of him, and how this would be woven into his and our relationship with them over time. Choosing an open adoption, in which we would have an ongoing connection with some members of our son's birth family, made me mindful of the evolving family reveries we might develop with our child (i.e., stories about how our son came to be and how we came to be a family), with room for wondering about and imagining those who were part of the story yet absent from our lives (Corbett, 2001a). After our son's birth, though, as he's grown and become more gendered, I've become more aware of my own losses related, in part, to gender and sexual orientation. These have been woven into my daily experiences with my son, extending beyond baseball.

Once his interest in superheroes and other male fantasy figures began, I thought here would be one area of "boy" boy overlap between us, one in which I would not feel incompetent. Sport was not something I could excel in, but my knowledge of superheroes is encyclopedic, left over from a boyhood steeped in comic books. I welcomed his delight in Iron Man and Spider-Man, I relished reading the Harry Potter books, I forgave him his one lapse in taste with the Power Rangers. But I began to notice another difference between us. His interests seemed, to me, flexible, relatively lightly held, readily yielding to his preference for playing with his friends. By contrast, my own childhood involvement with superheroes, I now realized, was early, deep, prolonged, and fixed. I remembered how, as a boy, I fantasized often about the eventual discovery of my own super powers and the revelation of my "true" origin. Aquaman and the Sub-Mariner, in particular, occupied my daydreams. Both able to breathe water and air, straddling the worlds of land and sea, possessed of great strength. I loved to swim and wished I could be like them. I imagined that one day while swimming I would suddenly find that I could breathe underwater, and I'd be discovered by my long lost brethren from Atlantis, my "true" family, taken to live with them in their more advanced underwater civilization. These fantasies were exciting, private, and wistful. In them expanded my desire to be seen, wanting to be "big" (Corbett, 2001b), and, I imagine now, a longing to recapture a sense of special place and belonging that I may have lost from earlier in my childhood. I think of these as my own family romance fantasies (Freud, 1909; Widzer, 1977).

Family reverie is a group/family experience of openly shared fantasies about birth "others" who are part of the conception story (Ehrensaft, 2008), whereas *family romance fantasy* (Freud, 1909; Kaplan, 1974; Lehrman, 1927) is usually a "solo" activity, in which there is the wish to be the child of other parents, a fantasy of not belonging to one's family (Corbett, 2001a, however, argues for the likely interdependence and interpenetration of these activities). The notion that family romance is a *universal* fantasy used throughout life to help regulate feelings about the self (Kaplan, 1974) resonated with my sense of unmourned girlyboy losses. Some analysts believe the fantasy originates early in life, gaining articulation and traction throughout later childhood and adolescence (Horner & Rosenberg, 1991; Kaplan, 1974; Wieder, 1977). Its themes are reflected in some fairy tales (Horner & Rosenberg, 1991) as well as adventure stories or comic books (Widzer, 1977). Superman, for example, was raised by earthly foster parents but hailed from otherworldly beings, his alien heritage granting him amazing abilities.

The fantasy often involves being the biological child of parents of "higher standing," such as celebrities or royalty (did I mention that Aquaman is a king and the Sub-Mariner a prince?), and of having been adopted into the current family. Inevitable disillusionment with one's current parents can stir the fantasy. The disillusionment can have many causes, such as the feeling that the child's love for the parents is not fully reciprocated (perhaps because of the parents' exclusive bond with each other), sibling rivalry, or any strong sense of parental love being withdrawn. In an effort to self-regulate, manage the injury, and actively master the situation, the child imagines that the "true" (other) parents are perfect beings – the same perfect beings experienced, perhaps, during infancy. As Greenacre (1958) put it: "The germ of the family romance is ubiquitous in the hankering of growing children for a return to the real or fancied conditions . . . when adults were Olympians and the child shared their special privileges and unconditional love without special efforts being demanded" (p. 10, as cited in Kaplan, 1974).

"[R]escue . . . is an inherent feature of the family romance in its latent content. The child wishes to be rescued by his [or her] parents in order to restore a situation in disrepair and to bring him [or her] back to where he [or she] belongs . . ." (Kaplan, 1974, p. 175). In its broad clinical relevance, the family romance fantasy may contribute to a patient's willingness to enter into a therapeutic relationship, to search for the lost love object in the person of the analyst, perhaps even become the analyst's "favorite" and be rescued by – or rescue – the analyst (e.g., Frosch, 1959).

I knew that the psychoanalytic literature speculated that the family romance fantasies and intrapsychic development of the adopted child are influenced by his or her awareness of there being *actual* other parents out in the world (e.g., Blum, 1983; Wieder, 1977) – although much of this theorizing assumed closed adoptions, in which the child had no direct experience of birth parents (e.g., Hodges et al., 1984). This literature predated the world of open adoption and assisted reproduction (e.g., with sperm/egg donors and gestational carriers), where nontraditional family narratives are increasingly common, expanding notions of extended family and adding complexity to conception stories told to children.

Moreover, much of this literature focused "almost exclusively on the emotional world and fantasy life of the adopted *child*, often disregarding the adoptive *parents'* fantasies" (Bonovitz, 2004, p. 2). Adoptive parents may have rescue fantasies, fantasies about a "perfect baby," or fantasies about a genetically related baby – fantasies that likely reflect parental losses, such as losses from earlier attempts at pregnancy, especially for some heterosexual couples. The adoptive parents' relationship to loss is likely to interact with the developing internal world of the child (just as the analyst's losses contribute to the intersubjective field with the patient). Family romance fantasies – of adoptive parents, their children, and everyone – may also reflect losses because these fantasies are, in part, a response to disillusionment with one's own parents as a result of the loss of an earlier version of more loving, benevolent, and omnipotent-seeming caregivers (e.g., Horner & Rosenberg, 1991; Kaplan, 1974). In becoming a parent, in which so much is gained, I found myself (re)connecting with losses from the past, losses which now took on feelings and associations not fully experienced in my own analysis, losses intertwined with being a variety of girlyboy.

Family romance fantasy and the girlyboy

For proto-gay boys and the girlyboys among them, feeling "other" relative to same-sex peers can be paralleled or preceded by rejection, overt and covert, from parents – perhaps, historically, fathers especially. The bases for this rejection may be multiple, such as the parents' discomfort and shame in having an other-gendered boy unlike their gender-stereotyped fantasies, or the father's unease with the kinds of longings such a boy may have toward him (e.g., Drescher, 1998; Isay, 1989; Lewes, 1988). Shame may develop for some proto-gay boys at this point: a daughter saying, "Daddy, I want to marry you," may seem adorable to parents, but reactions might be quite different if a son expressed the same wish (Goldsmith, 1995). In contrasting the Oedipal development of heterosexual and homosexual boys, Phillips (2003) proposes that the crucial distinction resides in the basis of the paternal rejection. For heterosexual boys, the father "declares" the mother, a *specific* woman, taboo, while encouraging the boy's desire for *women* in general. In homosexual Oedipal development, the boy's *desire itself* is often condemned: desire not just for *this particular* man (the father), but for *any* man. These are powerful bases for the proto-gay boy and girlyboy to feel rejected by parents, cast out (if not literally, as sometimes happens, then emotionally), adding, perhaps, to the self-regulating burden of the family romance fantasy.

My own superhero wishes, I imagine, contained not only the homoeroticism I was forbidden from more directly experiencing and expressing, but also a yearning to recapture my father's lost affection and involvement from earlier in my childhood. Although my father was loving and rarely overtly rejecting, I believe something shifted between us as my girlyboyishness became more apparent; a hesitance, a distance, a self-consciousness developed. Perhaps in becoming a superhero, I thought I would possess the masculinity I believed my father, and others, would embrace. Perhaps in fantasizing that my "true" super-origin was with another family, a super one, more like me, I yearned for the father I could be like and who could love me because of the likeness. I notice only now that the setting for my family romance fantasy – the ocean – was an early mutually shared love for my father and me, an area of overlapping pleasure that later on became more elusive for us. And if we are all engaged in some effort to find our lost love objects, I think of my partner, Steve, who could not possibly be more drawn to water (anyone who knows him knows he is, quite literally, Aquaman), and we have a son who is never happier than when he's at the beach. Maybe I now have my family from Atlantis.

In later sessions, Taylor has moved in and out of thinking/feeling about being raised by a shifting cast of extended family members after his biological parents demonstrated their inability to raise him without abuse and neglect. In disturbing dream material, he had gotten closer to his early experience of his father's sometimes violent disgust with Taylor's boyhood effeminacy, a revulsion that could border on murderous. Taylor is now moving away from this, describing his concern that people in his current life will "see" him for what he is, will uncover his shame and his shameful family. In his young adult persona, he has imagined himself as different from everyone in his family, more intellectual, more interested in the world, better, superior. At times he was, indeed, Superman, in body and mind, and, I imagined, I was also a superhero, trying to rescue him. I find myself remembering my leave of absence from my practice, a few years earlier, to be my son's primary caregiver after his birth. Patients had various reactions to my absence, some wanting to know what was going on in my life, others not. Taylor did not. He knew that I was gay, but he did not want to know anything else about me. At the time, I felt I was just emerging from my maternal/paternal preoccupation with my son, re-engaging with patients, and having the unbidden, pleasant, and emotional experience of feeling that I could easily "see" what each patient had looked like as a baby. I could see Taylor's infant face and felt I had abandoned him during my leave, as he seemed more remote, closed off, upon my return. It would be several months before I'd see a trace of emotion and vulnerability again. Taylor brings me back to the current session when, suddenly, he looks at me – infrequent for him – and says, "You have a child, don't you . . .," more a statement than a question, in a small voice. I feel caught and disoriented at first, again flush with the sense I had abandoned him. I don't want to evade this uncharacteristic direct engagement with me. I tell him yes. He lets out a long breath, and when I ask what's happening for him, he speaks haltingly with long silences. It's important to him, he tells me, to imagine that I "didn't do the surrogate thing," but rather, adopted, making it more possible, he feels, for my child to be like him – perhaps a reflection of his having been shuttled among several caregivers while growing up. He begins to imagine what it would have been like to have had a "gay father" who, in this fantasy, would not make him "feel small," whom he could feel "like," who would not have to hate him for being effeminate, who might even know something

167

about Stevie Nicks "twirling in shawls." He's looking down, smiling. Perhaps my girlyboy fatherhood could provide access to some of his distant longing and might offer less risk in having them.

Kinship and belonging

As proto-gay children, we emerge into families unlike us, often without a sense that anyone *is* like us – either out in the world, or within our own biological family structures. We often do not get to know of the gay uncle, the lesbian aunt. These relatives have often been closeted, or if not, then disowned, their very existence sometimes eliminated from family trees or narratives. And, in past generations, even when there has been a gay parent, often the closeted and painful nature of living a "dual life" complicates, if not obscures, possibilities for identification, feelings of "likeness," or belonging. In the desire to find a sense of place even in one's experience of otherness, family romance fantasies may be a means of attachment and separation (Corbett, 2001a). These fantasies may sometimes arise just as a child is beginning to grasp complicated interpersonal relationships in the world, including notions of kinship (Horner & Rosenberg, 1991). In terms of kinship and processes of identification, perhaps gay people of certain generations have been largely denied a type of "kinship" knowledge and experience (e.g., Levi-Strauss, 1969). Maybe we have something in common with those adopted children who may feel some lack of a sense of genetic continuity, who may feel different from their adoptive parents, either in temperament, or in more obvious physical ways.

Back to the baseball field: in my new sense of entry and inclusion through my son's joy in team sports, there is part of me wary of being someone for my son to rescue, wary of my desire to be a rescuer – both of which (ghosts from my past, femme and otherwise) would burden my son (and patients) with functions that are not his (theirs) to fill. And yet, patients, and children, do sometimes heal us, in part, even though it is not their responsibility. I think of Harris (2010) quoting former Commissioner of Baseball, Bart Giamatti: baseball is "the only game where you start from home and try as hard as possible to return." I could not have imagined finding a home in baseball. I could not have imagined finding a home with our son's large birth family (his grandparents were early pioneers of the "modern family," with biological and adopted children of different races and sexual orientations). I could not have imagined that there would also be a space in my new family life for girlyboy sensibilities, as our son asks Steve and me to read to him at bedtime an occasional favorite book, *The Boy Who Cried Fabulous* (Newman & Ferguson, 2004) – the story of an irrepressibly enthusiastic boy who's mantra might best be captured by a queer-infused exclamation, "More life!" (Corbett, 2001c).

Steve: redemptive fantasies and fallacies

It didn't take long for us to notice we were raising a "boy" boy. As two gay men, we were naturally alert to the signs, though perhaps no more so than anyone in our gender-attuned times. I felt relieved: he'll never have to go through what I did, as a not-quite girlyboy who nevertheless came in for a good deal of mistreatment on this score during one period of my adolescence. And then felt shame at the relief, which felt like disowning the boy I was and all that he would go on to be. And then, further, chagrin at the shame: wasn't this part of what fatherhood (I now realized) was supposed to allow me finally to escape, the shame that attaches to being gay?

In *Feeling Backward: Loss and the Politics of Queer History*, Heather Love (2007) cautions us against turning our backs on our "backward" feelings – shame, sadness, loneliness, regret, despair (and this is just part of her list) – all the emotional "stuff" of our personal and collective gay pasts. With epigrams like "Still Hurting" and "The Art of Losing," she means to bring into focus those aspects of our histories (and current lives) that we may wish to put behind us as we try to look ahead to a bright gay future. Nevertheless, in a turn of thought that is familiar to us as psychoanalysts, she argues that the effort to maintain an "affirmative political vision" (p. 105) will be haunted by the specter of our unhappy gay past to the extent that this past cannot be openly acknowledged, and even felt. "[I]t is the damaging aspects of the past that tend to stay with us" (p. 1). We are inevitably and specifically shaped by the ways we've been injured; as she astutely notes, the major tropes of gay liberation, pride and visibility, are precisely the mirror images of the shame and secrecy that were the experience of the closet. Such seeming transformations are inevitably fragile: "Shame lives on in pride, and pride can easily turn back into shame" (p. 28). She questions the "culture of redemption" (Bersani, 1990) by which the history of antigay violence and stigmatization gets pressed into service to justify an insistence on progress and visions of an ever-improving gay future. Such insistence, she argues, "makes it harder to see the persistence of the past in the present" (p. 19).

For a same-sex couple, having a child can never happen by accident. The couple has to want a child, a lot. At the same time, the motivations for having a child can never be uncomplicated, for anyone. The very idea that we could adopt a child developed from seeing other same-sex couples having children, an option made possible by shifts in the culture and the easing up of laws that might have restricted us in the not too distant past. Certainly we couldn't have imagined this for ourselves when we got together in the late 1980s. Some of our motives were no doubt similar to those of any prospective parents. As our own parents grew older and became ill, we wanted something to look forward to. Having a child is a powerful way to orient to the future. Raising a child may also have seemed like a more dignified way of entering gay middle age than some of the apparent alternatives. Dan Savage has a funny, if somewhat homophobic, riff on these in his memoir of his and his partner's adoption of their son. He summarizes the three scenarios for gay men entering middle age as follows: "Stay in the game" ("Keep going to bars, and parties, and clubs, keep getting laid, keep drinking, keep taking drugs"), "Go places, see shit," and "Mr. and Mrs. Martha Stewart" (1999, pp. 34–35). One feels in Savage's satirizing of middle-aged gay men his effort to ward off shame – an effort that all of us, gay, straight, and otherwise, are involved in more of the time than we realize, as recent developments in psychoanalysis (e.g., Bromberg, 2006; Dimen, 2003) are helping us to appreciate.

Perhaps less consciously, we may have been moved to have a child by a wish to counter perceptions of us as gay men (which persist, despite many manifest changes) as immature, selfish, unwilling to contribute to society (say, by having children), "a drag on the process of civilization itself," (p. 7), as Love puts it. We were certainly aware we would be participating in a whole sociological phenomenon, a gay baby boom, part of a larger process of "gay normalization" and "the mainstreaming of gay life" (Love, 2007, pp. 154, 153) that has been underway for a few decades now. However dimly remembered, childhood and young adult experiences of having been stigmatized and marginalized shape powerful wishes to feel and to be seen as normal. As Love says, for gay people, "the desire to be recognized as part of the modern social order is strong" (p. 7). The relentlessly positive tone and aggressive wholesomeness of gay fathering narratives (e.g., Green, 1999; Strah & Margolis, 2003 – no tiger fathers here) attest to the strength of this wish, as if to say, look, straight people, we can do this even better than you can, we're more "normal" than you are. Maybe by having a child we could separate ourselves from "the long history of queer abjection" (Love, 2007, p. 158) once and for all.

How understandable (if this was part of our motivation), the wish to put pain and shame behind us. As Love puts it, "Given the scene of destruction at our backs, queers feel compelled to keep moving on toward a brighter future" (p. 162). For many of our generation, this scene included the mortifications of a gay adolescence and many losses to AIDS. Not all of us survived those adolescences; none of us, among all the gay men I've known over the years, survived without injury. How many more of us didn't survive AIDS, and more still suffered such painful losses to that disease, as I did.

Adrienne Harris has written of the way the very fact of having survived terrible things can engender a sense of "imaginary freedom, the feeling that survival itself has separated you from suffering" (2009, p. 3). My interest here is a corollary of Harris' idea. I believe that existing alongside and perhaps sustaining this sense of having escaped the worst there often lives a redemptive fantasy, a wishful belief that someone or something will make good the losses one has experienced, rescue one from one's painful sense of difference and exclusion, make up to one one's injuries and disappointments, and banish the shame that accompanied all of these. Parenthood provides a perfect vehicle for such redemptive wishes, as it may foster the fantasy of getting to be the perfect, omnipotent parent ("this time I get to decide how it's going to go"; Benjamin, personal communication, March, 2012) who, in tending one's child, attempts to repair the damage done to one's childhood self through the deficiencies of one's own parents, and perhaps as well the other injuries and injustices inflicted as one has made one's way through life.

If our own wish for a child was fueled in part by such a fantasy, it was only a matter of time before we would be disabused, made to face "the stark significance of the idea of irrecoverable loss" (Harris, 2009, p. 3), as well as "the surprising persistence of pre-Stonewall feelings" (Love, p. 19) in ourselves.

I met my first boyfriend during a trip to visit a friend in San Francisco over winter break in my senior year of college. Mike and I took up quickly with each other when I moved there the following year. We were kids together, creating a childhood world of silly names and games, perhaps making up for the childhoods neither of us had quite gotten to have. I had never felt close to another person like this before.

We took care of each other, looked out for each other. Crossing our dark street together one night I became aware of someone walking very close behind us. Mike (much taller than I) abruptly, reflexively it seemed, turned around to confront this person, who immediately backed off. Years later as Mike started to get sick it was hard to feel helpless to do anything to shield him from the ravages of his disease, in the way he had so often protected me.

We grew up together. One part of our growing up was coming into political consciousness. Our experiences as we entered the world of work were disappointing, at times degrading (this, especially for Mike, who worked as a "cater/waiter" while trying to pursue an acting career). The indignities involved in trying to make a living as twenty-somethings appalled us. When we moved to New York, we started attending the meetings of a socialist organization, whose ideas seemed to us to make only the plainest common sense. We started going to ACT UP demonstrations soon after the group formed in the spring of 1987, thrilled by the angry energy. Not the good little gay boys we'd been (had had to be) anymore! And so much at stake for us in those protests, more than we knew; Mike wouldn't be diagnosed for another two years yet.

"I want to be around to kick the shit out of the system," Mike said to me in one of the last lucid conversations we were to have. How much he had changed over the years I'd known him; no longer the cheerful, even Pollyannaish (the basis for my nickname for him) man I'd met years before, and how could it be otherwise after all he'd been through. "I'm so sad I could get violent," his sister told me he said to her two days before he died. The years before and after losing him were the deepest experience of suffering I'd known in my life.

Our son was born 11 years later, in the same month as Mike's birthday, which was also the month in which he died. Mike was not consciously much on my mind as Noah and I were deciding to adopt a child, but perhaps my memory of Mike's protective presence formed part of the basis for my desire to become a father. I wonder whether part of me was hoping to refind Mike in the child Noah and I would have together.

"Some people don't like gay people, black people, people who have just come to our country. When someone hurts any one of us, it's important for us to stick up for each other." I was trying to explain to our son why I wanted us to go to a protest/vigil that afternoon for a black man who had been shot and killed by a cop in the Bronx earlier that week. It has surprised me, and not just on this occasion, how hard it is to explain political protest to a six year old. In the effort to do so, I fumble for words and sometimes start to question the meaning and efficacy of my own participation in protest, disturbing myself in the process. My son tells me he hates going to protests and has in his opinion already been to too many. We don't go to the protest that afternoon.

"I look forward to Monday and getting to have some adult conversation," another therapist in my building, a mother of two kids, says as she greets me in the elevator one morning. At the time I am not yet a parent, haven't yet learned that the quality of adult conversation in parenthood can itself leave something to be desired.

Something about being a father seems to have made it hard to find the interesting parts of other people. I notice this especially when talking to other gay fathers. Men whose idiosyncrasies might have revealed themselves in conversations about movies, politics, or gossip remain stubbornly opaque throughout discussions of babysitting arrangements, choices over schools, and planning for playdates. Determined to confront this problem, Noah and I, before our next outing with a couple of other dads and their son, make a mental list of promising conversation topics, topics that might draw out the unusual opinion, personality quirk, or unexpected piece of history that must be there, that everyone possesses (right?), but it's no use – any telling, peculiar features of character seem to become undetectable under the smooth surface gloss of the new gay dad. And though we might not see it, we're probably no different; fatherhood seems to have had this homogenizing, pastoralizing effect on us all.

What is this clichéd, unimaginative version of parenthood (and personhood) we seem to be performing for each other? What's happened to our younger selves (and now I think), our flirtatious selves, our randy selves? For now I realize it's sexuality that seems to be missing. We behave as if in unconscious agreement with the cultural assumption that gay people are unfit to be parents. Our sexuality made us gay, so if we are to be parents sexuality will have to go back into the closet. Are we ashamed of these gay selves, of our sexual pasts (and maybe presents)?

But then, why should this come as a surprise? How could we not have absorbed the message (however much we might have resisted it) that gay men and children are not supposed to mix, the homophobic and persistent association we have with pedophilia? I've noticed, when setting up a playdate with the parent of a friend of our son's, having the unwanted question come to mind: Is this person worried that I'll molest their child? Perfectly lovely, liberal people, and the playdates always go forward – so why does the question arise in my mind again when the next playdate comes around? Fatherhood, it turns out, provides no rescue or respite from such introjections, indeed just calls my attention to the presence of something I didn't know was there. So here it is, to Heather Love's point: the shame and exclusion (in the sense of disconnection from other gay dads) of our adolescence, come back to roost in the present. And just when we thought that, maybe, finally, we had said goodbye to all that.

Recognizing the power of my redemptive wishes and their perhaps inevitable disappointment has helped me better understand something important about my patient Gary: his fierce attachment to the most unhappy parts of his childhood, his refusal to (from my perspective) make the most of his present, and his inability to imagine a future that could be different from either of these. From the beginning of our work together, it was clear that Gary lived in the grip of a redemptive fantasy. The signs of this were not subtle. "I want to be rescued," he told me. Gary's childhood had been unhappy: he'd grown up with an alcoholic father; witnessed his father screaming at and threatening his mother; had been homophobically taunted by neighborhood kids and some years (not all) by kids at school; and had, crucially, gone unmentalized by each of his parents. An unhappy childhood, but not manifestly much worse than that of many other gay men I've known or worked with in therapy who have managed to make emotionally sustaining and satisfying lives for themselves. By contrast with such men, Gary lived his life in accordance with a benighted vision of gay life that most contemporary gay men have made every effort to escape. Painfully lonely but finding so much to distrust and dislike about other people, especially other gay men, Gary spent most of his time by himself in his apartment. Attractive enough that he was sometimes approached by other men on the rare occasions he put himself in their company, Gary nevertheless restricted his sex life to assignations with hustlers. He lived his life in a mode of regret for missed opportunities and choices not made, never seeming to notice (despite my repeatedly calling it to his attention) how this preoccupation kept him from becoming aware of the possibilities of the present.

For Gary, his current life had been fully determined by the injuries and insults of his childhood, which he revisited with me in all its sad, shame-ridden detail. How different it might be if he had been raised by different parents in a different world and time, he mused. One day he saw my son and Noah (known to him by sight as my suitemate, not – consciously at least – as my partner) walking together outside the office. Noticing how carefully Noah seemed to be listening to our son as he spoke, he reflected bitterly on the lack of such attention he had received as a boy from his own parents.

How ashamed he felt about being gay. How often in telling me about a sexual image or fantasy would he next tell me about the disgusted reaction he imagined a heterosexual person would have to that image or fantasy. Often he was able to recognize the disgust as his own. "The idea of two old men as lovers – it's just gross," he told me one day. He was so immersed in living his shame, we never got to explore it. I knew what his shame felt like. I could empathize with him in these moments – to a point. I had had my own shame-filled childhood and adolescence, but lived now in a different relation to it than he. I remembered what it felt like to think and feel the way he did about men being physically and sexually intimate with each other, and listening to Gary I'd feel relieved I didn't think and feel that way anymore. In my own life, I had worked hard to get past the feelings he described. As I came to recognize my distancing and relief as a countertransference block, I tried to notice the moments in my listening when I would shift away from his perspective to a place of some remove, wondering whether it would make a difference if I could stay closer to him through his shame-ridden reveries. Sometimes I felt angry at having to make the effort. It was 2005 (2006, 2007 . . .) for Christ's sake, things were different now; why couldn't he get with the program, go with the flow, make the best of the new possibilities that had opened up for us – as I had? Why couldn't he be more like me?

I had not always received Gary's feelings with exasperation. In the first years of our work I felt quite a bit for and with him in the pain of his childhood and had not questioned his wish for me to rescue him, working implicitly in accord with Anna Ornstein's (1995) precept that patients' "curative fantasies – no matter how infantile – [need to be] accepted as a legitimate insistence on experiences that they consider to be essential for the completion of their self-development" (p. 115). Over time, however, perhaps influenced by the birth of my son and my new acquaintance with my own redemptive wishes, I became impatient. I could watch my son growing and changing every day; Gary, on the other hand, seemed to stay the same. Furthermore, no one, nothing, was going to make it up to us, I was learning; one had to mourn one's losses and get on with life.

Especially concerning to me was the way in which Gary's very agency was countermanded by his curative fantasy, its fulfillment contingent precisely on his not acting on his own behalf. It seemed that if he could be passive enough, make himself abject enough in my eyes, not step out into the world in any of the ways he frequently imagined but never acted on, then I would be moved to step in and rescue him. For several years, Gary's fantasy took the form of the romantic, sexual relationship we would have, to be initiated by me at some point in the future, for which this time in therapy was serving as a prelude, a kind of extended courtship. When I realized that what I had taken as an arena for play – our mutual creation of our life together as lovers – was for him a matter of deadly seriousness, I had gradually to disabuse him of its real-life possibility. My introduction of reality led to rupture and his feeling betrayed, from which it took us some time to recover. We continued in a sobered, lower key, his life now appearing all the more poor and involuted without the spark our flirtation had lent it, the desolation of his life and his passive relation to it all the more stark. He continued to seek little human contact outside our relationship, as if by such seeking he would reveal to me his agency and thereby forfeit the prize he was holding out for – the savior who would finally recognize his helpless, abject state and step in to make everything all right, make up to him all he had suffered.

This understanding helped me tolerate the lack of movement in the therapy, even as it suggested Gary and I were locked in a permanent impasse. I wasn't sure how any of this was going to change, and neither were the supervisors I consulted to help me think about my work with Gary. In the meantime, perhaps engaging in the kind of self-deception to which Slavin and Kriegman (1998) remind us we therapists are susceptible, I consoled myself with the thought that Gary's life would surely be worse without me. I never seriously considered referring him elsewhere; what would be different with the next person? In this, I may have been influenced

174

by Gary's odd acceptance of his lonely, abject state, his complaints resembling the plaints of the melancholic: I'll bear this unhappiness, as long as I can loudly berate you for it. I like Heather Love's take on this circumstance, expressed in her own, non-psychoanalytic language: "Backwardness can be deeply gratifying to the backward" (2007, p. 146).

Still, it was hard not to feel like a failure in my work with Gary, a feeling made worse by the fact that I wasn't the only one who could see it. I felt ashamed as I imagined what a bad therapist I must seem in the eyes of Gary's psychiatrist, who could observe how spectacularly unhelpful I had been to Gary after years of working with him. I cringed in listening to Gary tell me of his bitterly complaining to this person of my inefficacy, that I didn't encourage him enough. For his part, the psychiatrist (with whom I conferred occasionally by phone to discuss Gary's treatment) had long since started recommending to Gary CBT groups and other forms of therapy he might pursue.

It seemed that (in a manner of speaking) if I couldn't get Gary to join me as an apparently happy, well-adjusted 21st century gay man, he'd make me share in his own sense of shame, loss, and failure. In part, this was my punishment for having spurned his love, for refusing to rescue him. His wish for redemption – which he both insisted on, on his own terms, and refused, under any of the terms in which it might have in some senses been possible – consigned us both to disappointment and frustration. But in making his life a memorial to seemingly irreparable damage, Gary succeeded in forcing me to feel again the shame and failure of my own childhood and young adult life, made me confront my idea of having "moved on" as a turning away from something I could never fully separate myself from. Gary, to me: "You MUST remember this" (Harris, 2009, p. 17). Assuming the mirror image of the structure of homophobia itself, my repudiation of Gary's homophobia showed me just how much my and others' apparent acceptance of my own homosexuality was necessarily a partial and fragile achievement, built as it was on a foundation of exclusion, difference, and shame that can be disguised or displaced, but not done away with. Beneath the trappings of my normalcy – my career, marriage, and child – Gary and I had more in common than I wanted to think.

Heather Love (2007) writes movingly that sometimes we need to live with injury, without fixing it. To a therapist's ear, her quiet acceptance of this circumstance jangles, grating against our therapeutic ambitions, our will to repair, our wishes for our patients' (and our own) progress. Yet with some people it may be all we can do, all we're allowed to do, to be a witness to injury. As I discovered, the process of witnessing (however limited, however failed) may engage us with a patient in deep and unwanted ways that implicate our own histories, even if it does not always move toward what would conventionally be regarded as a therapeutically satisfying outcome. I present my work with Gary as a testament to the complex and deeply personal purposes to which our patients may put us, purposes undreamt of in the mind of the "evidence-based" treatment researcher. Testament, too, to the way in which our own unhealed wounds may curtail our empathic responsiveness to our patients.

Reflecting back from Gary to my son, I think of how being a parent, like being a therapist, has involved me in revisiting (and resisting revisiting) painful feelings from my childhood and young adulthood. Psychotherapeutic work with a deeply avoidant patient like Gary reminds one how badly the effort to steer clear of life's difficulties and discomforts backfires. I recall my relief at the thought my son would, in his life, be spared the pain around gender that I suffered, naïve for the moment to my knowledge of the inevitability of pain in any human life. Naïve as well to what I have learned, that there can be growth through pain, as I (like so many of us) can trace the origin of my calling to the vocation of psychoanalysis to the need to make sense of the ways I have been hurt. As Ken Corbett has reflected, "[F]or those who have been wounded by the shrapnel of shame, who have felt the shame of being hated, or have suffered the deeper wounds of trauma, understanding psychic pain may provide a way out" (1996, p. 458). Perhaps a better wish for my son would be that whatever the pain he experiences in his life, he's able to make the most of it.

Note

1 By "girly" boy I am referring here to a particular, and not necessarily universal, proto-gay boy experience of growing up with some sense of gendered atypicality – without the wish to actually be a girl (Corbett, 1996). Moreover, in using the term *girlyboy*, I am not foreclosing male homosexuality as a "differently structured masculinity" (Corbett, 1993; see also Blechner, 1998), nor am I assuming a central position of gender in the lives of gay men – as Corbett (1996), citing Sedgwick (1995), reminds us, "Some people are just plain more gender-y than others" (p. 435). In addition, proto-gay boys do not have the market cornered on feelings of masculine inadequacy, as several straight male patients have described to me their own sense of gendered otherness during childhood.

References

Bersani, L. (1990). *The culture of redemption.* Cambridge, MA: Harvard University Press.

Blechner, M. J. (1998). Maleness and masculinity. *Contemporary Psychoanalysis, 34,* 597–613.

Blum, H. P. (1983). Adoptive parents: Generative conflict and generational continuity. *Psychoanalytic Study of the Child, 38,* 141–163.

Bonovitz, C. (2004). Unconscious communication and the transmission of loss. *Journal of Infant, Child & Adolescent Psychotherapy, 3,* 1–27.

Bromberg, P. M. (2006). *Awakening the dreamer: Clinical journeys.* Mahwah, NJ: Analytic Press.

Corbett, K. (1993). The mystery of homosexuality. *Psychoanalytic Psychology, 10,* 345–357.

Corbett, K. (1996). Homosexual boyhood: Notes on girlyboys. *Gender and Psychoanalysis, 1,* 429–461.

Corbett, K. (2001a). Nontraditional family romance. *Psychoanalytic Quarterly, 70,* 599–624.

Corbett, K. (2001b). Faggot = loser. *Studies in Gender and Sexuality, 2,* 3–28.

Corbett, K. (2001c). More life: Centrality and marginality in human development. *Psychoanalytic Dialogues, 11*, 313–335.

Dimen, M. (2003). *Sexuality, intimacy, power*. Hillsdale, NJ: Analytic Press.

Drescher, J. (1998). *Psychoanalytic therapy and the gay man*. Hillsdale, NJ: Analytic Press.

Ehrensaft, D. (2008). When baby makes three or four or more: Attachment, individuation, and identity in assisted-conception families. *Psychoanalytic Study of the Child, 63*, 3–23.

Freud, S. (1909). Family romances. In J. Strachey (Ed. & Trans.), *The standard edition of the complete psychological works of Sigmund Freud* (Vol. 9, pp. 235–244). London: Hogarth Press, 1953.

Frosch, J. (1959). Transference derivatives of the family romance. *Journal of the American Psychoanalytic Association, 7*, 503–522.

Goldberger, M. (1993). "Bright spot": A variant of "blind spot." *Psychoanalytic Quarterly, 62*, 270–273.

Goldsmith, S. J. (1995). Oedipus or Orestes? Aspects of gender identity development in homosexual men. *Psychoanalytic Inquiry, 15*, 112–124.

Green, J. (1999). *The velveteen father: An unexpected journey to parenthood*. New York: Ballantine Books.

Greenacre, P. (1958). The family romance of the artist. *Psychoanalytic Study of the Child, 13*, 9–36.

Harris, A. (2009). "You must remember this." *Psychoanalytic Dialogues, 19*, 2–21.

Harris, A. (2010). Baseball's bisexuality. *Contemporary Psychoanalysis, 46*, 480–503.

Hodges, J., Berger, M., Melzak, S., Oldeschultes, R., Rabb, S., & Salo, F. (1984). Two crucial questions: Adopted children in psychoanalytic treatment. *Journal of Child Psychotherapy, 10*, 47–56.

Horner, T. M., & Rosenberg, E. B. (1991). The family romance: A developmental-historical perspective. *Psychoanalytic Psychology, 8*, 131–148.

Isay, R. A. (1989). *Being homosexual*. New York: Farrar, Straus & Giraux.

Kaplan, L. J. (1974). The concept of the family romance. *Psychoanalytic Review, 61*, 169–202.

Lehrman, P. R. (1927). The fantasy of not belonging to one's family. *Archives of Neurology and Psychiatry, 18*, 1015–1023.

Levi-Strauss, C. (1969). *The elementary structures of kinship* (2nd ed.). Boston, MA: Beacon Press.

Lewes, K. (1988). *The psychoanalytic theory of male homosexuality*. New York: Simon and Schuster.

Love, H. (2007). *Feeling backward: Loss and the politics of queer history*. Cambridge, MA: Harvard University Press.

Newman, L., & Ferguson, P. (2004). *The boy who cried fabulous*. Berkeley, CA: Tricycle Press.

Ornstein, A. (1995). The fate of the curative fantasy in the psychoanalytic treatment process. *Contemporary Psychoanalysis, 31*, 113–123.

Phillips, S. H. (2003). Homosexuality: Coming out of the confusion. *International Journal of Psychoanalysis, 84*, 1431–1450.

Savage, D. (1999). *The kid: What happened when my boyfriend and I decided to get pregnant: An adoption story*. New York: Plume.

Sedgwick, E. (1995). Gosh, Boy George, you must be awfully secure in your masculinity! In M. Berger, B. Wallis, & S. Watson (Eds.), *Constructing masculinities* (pp. 11–20). New York: Routledge.

Slavin, M., & Kriegman, D. (1998). Why the analyst needs to change: Toward a theory of conflict, negotiation, and mutual influence in the therapeutic process. *Psychoanalytic Dialogues, 8*(2), 247–284.

Strah, D., & Margolis, S. (2003). *Gay dads: A celebration of fatherhood.* New York: Jeremy T. Tarcher/Penguin.

Widzer, M. E. (1977). The comic-book superhero: A study of the family romance fantasy. *Psychoanalytic Study of the Child, 32*, 565–603.

Wieder, H. (1977). The family romance fantasies of adopted children. *Psychoanalytic Quarterly, 46*, 185–200.

14

THE IMPORTANCE OF FATHERS

Hillary Grill

My news

I was in the office when I got the call from one of my brothers telling me about the brain tumor. That information made no sense to me. My father was so healthy, so sprightly, so able to take care of himself. Suddenly a wave, fast and furious, crashed all around and destabilized me – in that instant, I realized he was going to die. I hadn't truly considered that possibility until just then. Of course, we all know our parents will die, as we know we will – but I hadn't fully considered either of those facts to be facts that I needed to fully feel until right then. There must have been a tacit assumption deep in me that let me believe he would always be there, an omnipotent figure, even if I didn't like to ascribe that much power to him. And I must have also somehow believed that we could fix our relationship someday. But my time was up for indulging my responses and thoughts – I had a patient waiting. I had to try and suck in my experience, turn it inside out. No visible tears, no sharing statement like, "I just found out my father has a BRAIN TUMOR." Just the barest hint of a smile, and a move to focus on the story unfolding from the person before me. A BRAIN TUMOR kept flashing through my mind. I tried to banish those words and the thoughts and feelings that were stirred by them, although at times as my patient talked, I'm sure I wasn't taking very much in, as if he were suddenly speaking a foreign language.

Her news

Lara told me that her father, a man who stubbornly resisted medical treatment, was taken to the hospital for symptoms that looked like a heart attack or stroke. I know those stubborn men well. My father was just like that. He *never* went to a doctor. In fact, when he found some sort of small growth on his arm, he cut it out by himself, bandaged it up and thought nothing much more about it. I recalled that my father's symptoms, similar to Lara's father's, were what finally brought him to seek medical attention; his doctors, too, initially assumed he had a stroke. Trying to focus on Lara as she relayed her story, I found myself drifting in and out of my own story, my father's story – and many layers of feelings.

179

My father died eight years before Lara told me about her father's medical incident. I remember a fleeting moment from when I was very little and felt that my father and I had a special relationship. At times back then, he would take me out somewhere – to a movie, to lunch – or he would let me watch him build something. In those singular moments of just the two of us, I felt important and loved. But that aspect of us is so far from what we became. The thread of the connection we had was insubstantial and easily frayed. Our relationship could not withstand the various developmental shifts and separations. He didn't know how to relate to me as a separate individual, a willful individual, a sexual individual – and ultimately the autonomous woman I became. He pulled away; I grimaced with resentment. That grimace stayed put until he got sick.

Lara's father, we eventually found out, also had a brain tumor. The initial shock I felt was not entirely unlike the shock I felt upon hearing the news of my father's tumor – my reactions to her and her situation were blindingly informed and steeped in my own experience. I wasn't conscious of this in the moment, but later, the fallacy and impossibility of separating her experience from mine came into sharp focus. Objectivity and neutrality, concepts that always seemed like impossible (albeit dubiously useful) ideals, faded into fanciful notions, as our experiences mixed together into a pot of intersubjective soup. Whose brain tumor are we talking about? Your father's, my father's? Who is the daughter of the man with the brain tumor? You, me, we?

Our fathers: whose experience/father is it?

This confluence of events – our father's similarities in illnesses and personalities – was disorienting at first. There were moments when I felt fuzzy, and our experiences seemed fused. It was difficult to determine where my experience stopped and hers began. It was more than the situational facts that caused me to feel this way – those facts not only obscured but also laid a foundation for a deeper connection. The facts we shared seemed uncanny in their uniqueness. The sense of mystery inherent in the random confluence allowed for unconscious receptivity to be enhanced in me and I believe, in turn, her. Early on, Freud (1919), and more recently Bass (2001) and Suchet (2004), among others, discussed the ubiquitous and uncanny nature of unconscious communication. They reported that they and their patients dream in ways that reveal an inexplicable knowledge of each other. Each participant is tuned into the other on such an exquisite level that they know the other in ways that are not yet consciously recognized (see also Bollas, 1987, and Stern, 1983). As I listen to Lara, I know exactly what she is talking about. Or do I? I know the horror, the terror, the impotence – but whose? I want to tell her I understand fully – that I'd been there, that my bones were rattling in recognition of her experience. I want to be able to tell her that she isn't alone – because if she's not, then neither am I.

Lara had a complicated, emotionally fraught relationship with her father. He was hard to reach, dismissive, prone to angry outbursts, stubborn, iconoclastic, liked to build things . . . the similarities suddenly struck me in a way they hadn't before. In sessions, I struggled and bit my tongue. I tried to understand what the impulse to share was about (Cole, 2001; Gerson, 1996; Kuchuck, 2009; Mendelsohn, 1996; Morrison, 1996; Pizer, 1997; Silverman, 2006). Was it a narcissistic need to show I understood, that I could be perfectly empathic, that I knew her uniquely in a way no one else could? I wanted recognition for recognizing her, in much the same way that I longed for this from my father. It can be lonely inside our own subjectivities.

The hellish time of my father's illness, dying, and death was complicated on a multitude of levels – our relationship was complicated enough without him being sick and dying. When he became gravely ill, I lost my equilibrium. I had grown accustomed to our distance, to the push–pull of wanting more of a relationship and accepting the meager frame of what we had. When he became ill, I found myself more in the relationship than I had in many years, or perhaps ever – until he died.

My father was one of those loner-types – a distant man, in personality and miles. He was not easy, and so he was alone, living in the middle of nowhere, many miles from me. It wasn't just the miles though; we weren't particularly close even when we lived in the same house. He wasn't much of a phone person, so we didn't speak often. And neither of us made any substantial effort to see each other – so we didn't. Maybe twice a year. I didn't really miss him – perhaps defensively so, since I was angry and resentful that he didn't try harder. He prided himself on his self-sufficiency; relationships were hard for him. He coped by making sure he didn't have to rely on anybody, and by insulating himself from intimate relationships. His energy was abundant, and he used it to take care of himself. He was never sick and never seemed like an old man, even as he aged.

For years, I refused to visit him in his house. His place was a mess. He never made the effort to clean up, to make his place safe for my two little kids – his grandchildren. Now I see we were both stubborn – I am my father's daughter. At the time, I was convinced it was just him – he was the problem. That was all I could see. The only thing I could feel was that he did not care enough. That was it, that was the script, the complementarity (Benjamin, 2012) that permeated. We cheated each other of a fuller relationship, and we cheated my kids. Their memories of him are sparse.

A very long time ago and in a very *Mad Men*[1] sort of way, my father left my mother for his much younger secretary. I was 16, and we were riding the subway together. In a distorted reprise of the earlier, brief, daddy's-little-girl phase of our relationship, he leaned over conspiratorially and proudly told me he was in love with a woman (not my mother), and she was pregnant. It was our secret, and I was not to tell anyone – certainly not my mother, and not even my younger brother. Thanks Dad.

That information, heavy and contaminated, was not easy to hold. I felt guilty about conspiring with my father, and also felt a hint of specialness that I could not let myself revel in. Mainly, I was confused and torn knowing my mother would be doubly hurt by the information itself, and the fact that I was holding it. It became all the more sordid when I met the woman. She was only a few years older than I! We were almost peers, so we bonded – kind of. I liked to go to the apartment they shared on Avenue C in Manhattan to hang out – an apartment that my mother did not know existed. There was a coolness factor about it that attracted me; after all, it was the East Village. Smoking cigarettes in front of them and being their confidante made me feel very grown up. This bred a form of pseudo-closeness between my father and me. But it was a tainted closeness, as it would also be when he was dying. In each of these cases, there was a connection developing, but it was more about him, and the circumstances made it impossible to feel the satisfaction one might hope for in less encumbered, less emotionally loaded situations.

My father eventually married, and then divorced the woman he told me about that day on the train. Later, there were other women, but by the time he got sick, he was alone. There were virtually no people in his life. He never made lasting friendships, and was estranged from his own parents before they died. Since he was estranged from them, I was too, and had no contact. After many years of separation, I was surprised to get a call from a cousin telling me that my grandmother committed suicide in a nursing home. I hadn't seen her in many years, and didn't even know she was in a nursing home. She left no note, no explanation – just what I imagined was unbearable despair. My father always had a hard time with his mother. She was cold and harsh, and like my father, had difficulty showing interest in others. Again, in some mash-up of roles, it was up to me to tell him what had happened to his mother. His response was like hollowed steel, and he refused to go to her funeral. In a veil of emotional confusion and ragged allegiances, I attended.

Revelation of rage

Lara's father underwent brain surgery 10 years after my father did. As she speaks, I find myself back in the pre-surgical holding area with my father, anxious, as I was then. Nurses, anesthesiologists, and surgeons poked, prodded, and shaved. With charts in hand, they interviewed and questioned us – some even provided platitudes of reassurance. Although my father's tumor was strangling the speech centers in his brain so he could barely form words, he strained to communicate his optimism to us. He went off into the surgical suite smiling. My mind left my father at the door to the operating room and returned to Lara. I expected her to tell me about the anxiety and the optimism, but the emotional landscape of her pre-surgical scene was entirely different from mine. There was no smiling and there was no optimism. The moment her father was taken to be operated on, Lara turned to her family and said very matter-of-factly that they would be better off if he never returned from surgery. I was stunned. She was stunned. She felt guilty and ashamed. This confession also seemed to be a release – powerful feelings finally exhaled. It was raw and real – and I admired that.

My relationship with my father was fraught too, and I wondered if Lara was verbalizing something I felt but wasn't able to say – something as yet unformulated (Stern, 1983), unthought (Bollas, 1987). Or was it simpler than that – was this anger and wish to destroy something all of us experience at times but don't always recognize? Maybe that feeling wasn't as prominent for me – I had certainly felt anger toward my father in the past, but not such vivid annihilation fantasies. The questions were churning, even if I was unclear about exactly what I felt. What I was clear about, was that what I was feeling was both familiar and new. There were many parallels in our histories, which gave the illusion of sameness and overshadowed the differences. I somehow wanted the sameness; there was comfort in knowing her and she knowing me. I was experiencing a sibling-like feeling, as Silverman (2006) described in her deeply moving paper about similar life experiences she shared with her patient. Spending time with Lara, I felt less alone. I was not the only daughter with a complex relationship with a difficult father who had a brain tumor.

I believed I knew Lara's experience, and I did – but as I came to realize, I only knew something about it. Perhaps knowing is always a matter of degree. Until the moment of her revelation, I thought I knew anger and hate – feelings that arose in reaction to being minimized, overlooked, and rejected, what it's like to absorb the other's anger. I thought I knew this dynamic, the feelings that can occur between a father and a daughter. But I only knew a piece of those feelings – my version. My patient's anger and hate were so piercing it pained me, scared me, and ultimately taught me. In a deeper and more visceral way than I had known before, with Lara I began to understand the value of using my experience, knowledge, and empathy without making fixed assumptions about the other. No matter how much I believed I knew about Lara's situation or psyche, my experience with her underscored the value of a Sullivanian (1954) "detailed inquiry" of thoughts and experience for the closest approximation to true understanding. Beyond that, I realized from our interactions that I had my own knotted-up complexities to tease out about my relationship with my father and my response to his death before I could more fully understand my patient.

During the time leading up to my father's illness, he was too emotionally and physically removed to cause any current-day problems for me. I didn't need to wish him dead, didn't need to get rid of him. There was no such urgency for me; he was already gone in so many ways. Perhaps his existence didn't matter enough for me to have that degree of emotion, and this thought filled me with profound sadness – a new nuance to my mourning, realized in the dynamic between my patient and me. Did I wish he mattered that much? Lara's father had a cruel, sadistic self-state that terrorized her family while she was growing up – and still. Lara, married with children of her own, was presently enmeshed with her parents in ways that kept them close but also caused her continuous pain. I was beginning to realize that I not only wanted to help her untangle herself from them, but that I had also longed for some kind of closeness with my father, and wished for that aspect of her relationship with her family for myself.

After my father's diagnosis, a new piece of me emerged, a part of me born in his dying. I was able to risk more closeness with him as I dove into educating myself about his tumor, and engaged in providing care for him. While I had already been acutely aware of my penchant for caretaking, that part of me hadn't been expressed so directly in relation to my father before. What was most new was being needed and valued by him. I had only felt the barest whisper of that when I was a very young girl, and then later when I was his adolescent accomplice. Now, a new kind of intimacy was developing between us. There was no escaping his accelerated aging and illness. His speech was slow and almost incomprehensible. It was an act of will for him to try to speak and for me to try to listen and make sense of it. It was unnerving and discombobulating to observe his shuffling gait. He was moving like a sick old man, and that was hard to reconcile with the man I always knew – the energetic maverick. The awareness that he would never recover – or at least never be the same – shattered the innocence I still maintained about his invincibility – and mine. He had never been vulnerable in front of me before and now he was. I was moved that he let me know that part of him, and by the invitation to be in something piercingly real with him.

My father's illness, which lasted for two and a half years, felt like an opportunity for me to right our relationship. When he got sick, the tensions, the conflicts, the distance began to melt away. He was in need, completely alone, and I was there. This was my call to action, and I became an intimate witness to his pain, a participant in his care. At the time, in the face of his physical devastation, it was too dangerous and destabilizing for me to allow for much anger or disappointment. I was too busy trying to fix things – his body, our relationship. I made the hours-long trip to his house every couple of weeks, loaded his freezer with healthy, cancer-fighting foods I cooked for him, and with my siblings, researched and found the best neurosurgeon in his area. That all felt right to me at the time. He needed to be taken care of, and I needed to take care of him. While there was plenty of emotion – sadness, pain, even pleasure in our reconnection – the resentment and anger I held for so long seemed to evaporate, and consciously, I barely noticed it was gone.

Reliving my crisis – witnessing hers

The ordeal of her father's illness opened up a deep well of resentment and pain in Lara. She became more acutely aware of the ways in which her father caused difficulties in her family. Up until then, she was somewhat inured to his derisive, manipulative, anger-driven behavior. She coped by being the "good girl" in order to win his approval. Before he got sick, her anger simmered, almost imperceptibly. She protected him and protected herself from a fuller scorch, and at times I was frustrated by this. I could feel the anger emanating, almost see the steam. His treatment of her seemed so maddeningly unfair – I wanted her to fight back. But Lara rarely did. She maintained the pattern of coping, managing, and pleasing until he got sick. Her fantasies of what life would be like if he were gone were unleashed only when the possibility of that became more real. She could sense what being relieved of the burden of him and the constant high-alert to his behavior would feel like, and little by little, material emerged that she didn't have access to before. She found new meanings and made connections from her experiences. What had been long simmering began to boil over.

The intensity of her anger touched a place in me that I had previously cordoned off. Lara's anger toward her father had been dissociated until he got sick. His tumor opened up wounds deep within her that she had been carefully tending for years. I had the inverse reaction to my father's tumor – it served to seal my wounds with almost surgical precision. During his illness, I dissociated the angry feelings I had lived with for most of my life. Allowing those feelings prominence would have made it more difficult for me to be there with him throughout his illness. As similar as our experiences and fathers were, I came to see that aspects of our reactions stood in stark contrast. I became less angry and Lara only more so.

My mind was firing in response to my patient. I was feeling, thinking about, understanding aspects of myself and my reaction to my father's death in ways I hadn't had access to before. I realize now that in many ways, I had protective blinders on throughout his illness. Without those, not only would I have felt more anger, I also would have felt my heart breaking. The sadness of his decline from empowered father, to old man, to helpless, wordless child was too much for me to fully bear at the time. I wasn't able to own my sadness then – a sadness that included the impossibility of ongoingness with a dad who had only just arrived. And, with the layers of history, experience, and emotion stirring as I sat with Lara, I was beginning to grasp the complexity of who my father and I were to each other – and the maddening ambivalence I am left with.

A second chance to mourn: my patient helps me grieve

Residing on the border between unconscious and preconscious was the sense that I had unfinished grieving and work to do on understanding my relationship with my father. And there it stayed until Lara's got sick. The unabashed honesty of Lara's revelation of her murderous fantasy was an invitation to be more honest with myself about my experience with my father. Unconsciously, it seems to me now, I feared that acknowledging the long-held resentment and anger – and the loss forever of the fantasied kind of relationship I had always wanted – would negate the actual positive experiences I was able to have with him during his illness. Instead, as I have told patients countless times (but lost sight of for myself), the eventual acknowledgment made it all feel more real, more true to the entirety of our relationship – and it felt oddly relieving. I now held a more genuine representation of my father and me, which enabled me to have a fuller experience of him and us. I am grateful to Lara for bringing this part of herself to our relationship. With fathers in mind, I am reminded of a forward-thinking psychoanalytic forefather – as a Ferenzcian feel was developing in the treatment. While our experience was no mutual analysis (Ferenczi, 1995), we were on a reciprocal see-saw of mutual influence (Aron, 1996; Frank, 2012) that had moments of tipping toward the patient providing for me. For a long period of time, I wasn't even aware of this aspect of our relationship. It was an evolution and an unfolding between us, much of it happening just outside of awareness. Our mutual engagement was transformative and enabled me to identify my need to unpack the grief I had stowed away. Tracing back the trajectory, the moment Lara revealed her wish that her father would die in surgery, was the moment that shocked me out of my reverie about what it means to have a father with a brain tumor, and what it means to mourn while loving and hating. Ultimately, facing and feeling my father's death more profoundly led me to know more viscerally, almost tangibly, about pain and the complexity of relationships, an awareness that resonates every day with patients. The resultant richness of the work Lara and I have been able to engage in since belies the necessity for her to know explicitly about her role in the way that Ferenczi's patients did.

Possibilities for personal disclosure

Many things changed for me after I learned about my father's tumor. It was so shocking, so invasive – it was not only spreading in his head, it was spreading in my life. Although not fully aware of this at the time, parts of me were functioning on autopilot. The desire to do something – to fix it, to stop it, to make it go away somehow – was powerful. Like many aspects of my life, I didn't bring this directly into the treatment room. It felt like a trick to keep this thing engulfing my life out of my work, in itself a consuming and significant part of my life. The confused, scared, daughter self-state stayed outside of the room – or so it seemed. Do we ever bring all of ourselves into the treatment room? Yes, but . . . or is it a question of foreground and background?

When more personal, vulnerable self-states threatened to take and stay center stage, my analytic self-state (Morrison, 1996) moved forward and relegated the personal to a behind-the-scenes spot. For years, my father was expected to die many times – and each time he rallied. My siblings and I often questioned his quality of life, but he seemed to want to live no matter what. He couldn't walk, couldn't talk except to yell out curses on occasion, but he could sing, laugh, and eat. As sad and scary as it was to witness his decline, and as difficult as it was to care for him and make decisions for and about him, it was also easier to have a relationship with this kind of dad. Life was different for him, stripped down to the basics. He listened without interrupting and could no longer say hurtful things to me. Somehow, his blue eyes were amazingly alive and twinkly as he sang, laughed, and enjoyed meals – even if we had to cut his food into almost baby-food consistency.

With all of that going on during the years of my father's illness, although pulled toward telling patients, it didn't seem necessary. I didn't have to miss much work, especially not unexpectedly – and when emergencies did occur, I simply explained that there was a family illness. It felt self-serving to discuss it further with them, even if at times I wanted to. I wonder now if the longstanding distance in my relationship with my father was part of why it seemed relatively effortless to keep my experience of his illness, and then death, out of the treatment room. Even as I

186

was rattled and consumed, I felt able to shut it off and shut it out. Certainly I was dissociated – in part adaptively so. It was a necessary relief to not think about him or feel for periods of time. And I wonder if I was enacting the long history of emotional distance I experienced with my father, with my patients.

Just as I felt conflicted about revealing my circumstances to patients while my father was so ill, I struggled with similar feelings and questions when he succumbed. Since I had just begun my summer vacation, there was only a crack of an opening in the window for disclosure. On top of that, shortly after he died, New York City experienced a blackout. That event lifted me out of the hollowness of loss and filled me with purpose. Stranded for days on an upper floor of an apartment building without electricity or water, I was forced to focus on taking care of my daughters. When I finally returned to the office, the feelings surrounding my father's death seemed less pressing. Certainly it was on my mind, and I was undoubtedly distracted at times. There was a part of me that wanted to tell each and every one of my patients, but there didn't seem to be a convincing reason for me to do so. It wasn't very different from the way I felt in the presence of just about everyone in my life. I wanted to talk about it in order to process what had happened, and what was happening to me. I wanted their comfort, and at times I wanted to be the focus. In some ways, not talking about it made it a non-event, which I only partly wanted and needed it to be. I didn't quite want to sit Shiva[2] with my patients, but the complete silence seemed like an over-correction or over-reaction on my part. Doing so perpetuated the aloneness that enveloped me.

Missing the opportunity to process my loss with those I was intimately involved with affected me in ways I wasn't aware of at the time, and I now believe this contributed to the foreclosure of my mourning process. Still, as mentioned, my need to grieve did not seem enough of a reason for me to have disclosed to my patients (Elise, 2007; Greenberg, 1995; Mendelsohn, 1996; Mitchell, 1997, 1998; Pizer, 1997; Singer, 1971). That would have turned the analytic relationship on its head in ways that make me and many in the field uncomfortable. Searles (1981) has another take on this though, arguing that for many patients, it becomes part of the therapeutic action to be therapist to the therapist, and may even be an essential part of the treatment, somewhat akin to Ferenczi's mutual analysis. Perhaps this was not only a missed opportunity for me in my grieving process, but also a missed opportunity for at least some patients to have felt effective and useful.

As Searles (1981) described it, this aspect of the therapeutic endeavor need not be spelled out to be effective. Accordingly, he said,

> I rarely if ever acknowledge, in any explicit way, and surely not in any formal way, that I am receiving such help from the patient. The more I can comfortably accept these strivings as inherent to the treatment process, the more, I feel certain, does my whole demeanor convey an implicit acknowledgement that the therapeutic process involves both of us.
>
> (p. 121)

Although Searles wrote this almost 40 years ago, and many of us today might be likely to definitively acknowledge our experience with the patient more often, his observations remain useful as we – and particularly I, in this case – struggle with questions about what to reveal, in what way, and to whose benefit.

Like many current thinkers in our field (e.g., Aron, 1996; Bromberg, 2006; Frank, 2005; Kuchuck, 2009; Mitchell, 1997; Renik, 1999), I continue to grapple with how much self-disclosure is useful. Part of this equation involves assessing what they and I need. Aside from my desire to talk about and share my experience with others, there was a nagging feeling that I "should" disclose, that it was inauthentic of me not to – that I was not being relational enough. This begs the question: How much do we need to disclose to approach authenticity and honesty in any relationship, especially the analytic one? While there has been a focus of late on the "real" relationship, it has also been argued that direct disclosure of thoughts, feelings, personal history, or events is not necessary to conduct a relational analysis or to achieve authenticity (Aron, 1996; Mitchell, 1993, 1997). In fact, articulation may serve to detract from the felt experience and dilute it or cause self-consciousness (Mitchell, 1997). Without explicit processing with patients, though, I worry that they have no way to contextualize what they may experience as my sadness, distraction, or distance. Even though I know conscious and unconscious choices about what to reveal about ourselves in themselves are not the arbiter of authenticity, I was uneasy feeling that I was presenting a false-self, and in that sense, it seems as if authenticity was thrown out the window. Perhaps the struggle we engage in about what is best for patients communicates an aspect of authenticity that is meaningful without being overt. What carries the most weight is affective authenticity (Frank, 2005), and I hope that is what was felt between my patients and me, and Lara and me in particular.

Alone and together in our subjectivities

There were many occasions when I wanted to reveal to Lara my experience with my father. I was not theoretically opposed to doing so, as discussed above, but I was torn. Thoughts and emotions were bubbling just below the surface, pressing for release. Especially during the period of time while her father underwent tests and then surgery, I struggled and held back because I needed to be clear with myself that any personal revelation would be for her, or both of us, and not only for me. As it turned out, not only was her reaction to her father's diagnosis different and unique from mine, her father's tumor was also different – it was not malignant. His surgery cleanly removed the tumor, and he eventually recovered. The news that Lara's father would live made my loss seem all the more mournful. She had time, something I no longer had, and with that came possibilities. I envied her options. Maybe Lara and her father could find a way to work out their relationship. I had begun that process with my father only as he was dying.

We were, and are still, each struggling with our feelings about our fathers. In lockstep, what was happening to Lara in real time triggered a re-experiencing of

188

my past. We were in it together, even while ensconced in our own subjectivities. As she was living through her trauma and I was reliving mine, we each yearned for the other's emotional touch and holding, consciously and unconsciously. Like an endless hall of mirrors, we reflected one another (Hoffman, 1994), and the impact was felt between us. I did not call attention to my subjectivity; instead, I was an organically involved participant with her, as she was with me. For moments it felt as though we were dancing the same dance in a syncopated rhythm, until the music changed and we moved away a bit to regroup. We came back together in a slightly different configuration, creating a space where we were able explore our love, hate, and sadness – separately and together.

Recognizing fathers, recognizing loss

Experiencing my relationship with my father and the loss of him anew altered my understanding of him, fathers in general, and myself. Viscerally understanding the importance of fathers is something that developed more fully out of my experience with Lara. It is now a part of me that I bring to every clinical encounter. As psychoanalysis has historically used a soft-focus lens on fathers, so had I, personally, theoretically, and clinically. I underplayed the significance and centrality of my father – and all fathers.

Acknowledging this means feeling the full brunt of the loss. I discovered that my grieving was truncated only by witnessing Lara's experience with her father, and living through her turmoil. Only now has it become deeply clear to me that mourning never ends. It's ongoing, and we cannot predict what event or experience will add another layer to the process. While this is knowledge that was previously held in some part of my mind, to unlock it and make it accessible, I needed another. Lara risked exposing her dark fantasies about her father to herself and to me. Her fearlessness led the way for me to risk knowing myself in relation to my father and to experience more deeply the complex pain of losing him. Without our relationship, Lara may never have known that shadowy corner of her internal world, and I may not have known the story of my father and me.

Notes

1 *Mad Men* is a dramatic TV series, produced in 2007 and continuing into the present, depicting American social and office culture in the 1960s.
2 Shiva, a Jewish ritual, commonly known as "sitting Shiva," is the seven-day mourning period following a funeral in which first-degree family members gather together to receive visitors.

References

Aron, L. (1996). *A meeting of minds: Mutuality in psychoanalysis*. Hillsdale, NJ: Analytic Press.
Bass, A. (2001). It takes one to know one; or, whose unconscious is it anyway? *Psychoanalytic Dialogues, 11*, 683–702.

Benjamin, J. (2012). Beyond doer and done to: An intersubjective view of thirdness. In L. Aron & A. Harris (Eds.), *Relational psychoanalysis, volume 4: Expansion of theory* (pp. 91–129). New York: Routledge.

Bollas, C. (1987). *The shadow of the object: Psychoanalysis of the unthought known.* London: Free Association Books.

Bromberg, P. M. (2006). *Awakening the dreamer: Clinical journeys.* Mahwah, NJ: Analytic Press.

Cole, G. W. (2001). The HIV-positive analyst. *Contemporary Psychoanalysis, 37,* 113–132.

Elise, D. (2007). The black man and the mermaid. *Psychoanalytic Dialogues, 17,* 791–809.

Ferenczi, S. (1995). *The clinical diary of Sándor Ferenczi* (J. Dupont, Ed., M. Balint & N. Jackson, Trans.). Cambridge, MA: Harvard University Press.

Frank, K. A. (2005). Toward conceptualizing the personal relationship in therapeutic action: Beyond the "real" relationship. *Psychoanalytic Perspectives, 3,* 15–56.

Frank, K. A. (2012). Strangers to ourselves: Exploring the limits and potentials of the analyst's self-awareness in self- and mutual analysis. *Psychoanalytic Dialogues, 22,* 311–327.

Freud, S. (1919). The "Uncanny." In J. Strachey (Ed. & Trans.), *The standard edition of the complete psychological works of Sigmund Freud* (Vol. 17, pp. 217–256). London: Hogarth Press.

Gerson, B. (1996). An analyst's pregnancy loss and its effects on treatment: Disruption and growth. In B. Gerson (Ed.), *The therapist as a person* (pp. 55–69). Hillsdale, NJ: Analytic Press.

Greenberg, J. (1995). Self-disclosure: Is it psychoanalytic? *Contemporary Psychoanalysis, 31,* 193–205.

Hoffman, I. Z. (1994). Dialectical thinking and therapeutic action in the psychoanalytic process. *Psychoanalytic Quarterly, 63,* 187–218.

Kuchuck, S. (2009). Do ask, do tell? Narcissistic need as a determinant of analyst self-disclosure. *Psychoanalytic Review, 96,* 1007–1024.

Mendelsohn, E. (1996). More human than otherwise. In B. Gerson (Ed.), *The therapist as a person* (pp. 21–40). Hillsdale, NJ: Analytic Press.

Mitchell, S. A. (1993). *Hope and dread in psychoanalysis.* New York: Basic Books.

Mitchell, S. A. (1997). *Influence and autonomy in psychoanalysis.* Hillsdale, NJ: Analytic Press.

Mitchell, S. A. (1998). The emergence of features of the analyst's life. *Psychoanalytic Dialogues, 8,* 187–194.

Morrison, A. P. (1996). Trauma and disruption in the life of an analyst: Enforced disclosure and disequilibrium in the "analytic instrument." In B. Gerson (Ed.), *The therapist as a person* (pp. 41–54). Hillsdale, NJ: Analytic Press.

Pizer, B. (1997). When the analyst is ill: Dimensions of self-disclosure. *Psychoanalytic Quarterly, 66,* 450–469.

Renik, O. (1999). Playing one's cards face up in analysis. *Psychoanalytic Quarterly, 68,* 521–539.

Searles, H. (1981). The patient as therapist to his analyst. In R. Langs (Ed), *Classics in psychoanalytic technique* (pp. 103–135). New York: Jason Aronson.

Silverman, S. (2006). Where we both have lived. *Psychoanalytic Dialogues, 16,* 527–542.

Singer, E. (1971). The patient aids the analyst. In B. Landis & E. Tauber (Eds.), *In the name of life* (pp. 56–68). New York: Holt, Rinehart and Winston.

Stern, D. B. (1983). Unformulated experience: From familiar chaos to creative disorder. *Contemporary Psychoanalysis, 19*, 71–99.

Suchet, M. (2004). Whose mind is it anyway? *Studies in Gender and Sexuality, 5*, 259–287.

Sullivan, H. S. (1954). *The psychiatric interview*. New York: Norton.

15

WORKING THROUGH SEPARATION
Personal and clinical reflections

Eric Mendelsohn

Life changes

In the summer of 2011, my wife and I separated after 29 years of marriage. Our decision had countless points of origin and evolved imperceptibly and precipitously, emerging from a process that was both deeply considered and selectively inattended, one that was both shared and unilateral. It was a choice defined by sorrow and hope. The separation has been an experience my wife and I have gone through together and apart, in ways that reflect the dynamics of our marriage, while also engaging aspects of ourselves that have been unanticipated and that feel stunningly new. Our separation will culminate in divorce.

The separation is *ours* and *mine*. It is a jointly held and individually endured experience that is, on the one hand, of us and between us (*our* separation), while also being precipitated by one of us (*my* separation). In both of these constructions, it has also been an object of reflection, something to be thought about and considered (*the* separation). It is inescapably and painfully public, while being irreducibly and equally painfully private. It can and should be talked about, although its details and emotional heart remain personal, and its essence eludes what can be communicated clearly and perhaps what should be shared openly. While the wish to be known and the need for privacy inform all that we say and do, I am especially aware, in writing this chapter, of both my desire and my reluctance to speak, and of the need to be tactful and circumspect. This tension is more keenly felt than has been the case in writing any previous paper. Beyond the limits of my self-knowing and expressive ability, I am concerned about the privacy and sensitivities of my wife and children, and for my own as well. Despite this, I am opting for public dialogue and for some measure of sharing. I have tended to write in a personal voice about personal matters while always holding to considerable formality and reserve, and these dissonances inform this writing.

The ending of our marriage can be regarded in many ways, but, inescapably, our separation feels like a failure. The failure is ours; the failure is mine. We failed because we could not sustain a sufficient basis for mutual pleasure and sharing, because we could not hold a joyful center for family connectedness, and because cumulative losses inclined us toward withdrawal and shadowed our intimacy with the specter of grief. I failed because disappointment evolved into alienation, and because genuine risk-taking too often gave over to effortful coping. The feeling of failure has become a presence and companion. Sometimes I take it to heart, embracing it with disheartening literalness. But at other times I regard it skeptically, seeing it as the expression of an all too familiar and reflexive guilt. I can then know it to be overstated and misguided, even as being distractingly off-point. At times, I am burdened and self-critical, yet I also feel an affirming freedom to be.

Our separation has had a shared emotional foundation, but I feel the burden of responsibility for much of its impact and effect. To feel this way is both fitting and self-aggrandizing. What is hopeful and promising is often accessible and seems evident, and this is deeply encouraging – but, at times, this part of things is obscured, enfolded within blanketing layers of anxiety and guilt. I work to hold these divergent perspectives, and concern myself with the well-being of my three daughters.

When a marriage ends, personal disappointment and discord enter more fully into the arena of the public and observable. While much remains unsaid, more is visible and openly acknowledged. This form of presence has had an impact in different sectors of our lives. Our children know what they have always known, but now they know more, and what they know is known in new ways. Impressions that were tentative and provisionally held now have sharper edges, and memories and interpretations of the past will now be shaped by the experience of what has more recently unfolded. Our friends and extended families have been deeply affected; they feel with us and for us, project onto us, and are distressed for us and by us. Some envy us, some judge us, and many share resonant experiences. Colleagues lend support, reassure, raise necessary questions, watch, and identify, projectively and concordantly.

The ending of a marriage transforms, irrevocably and shockingly, the possibilities and limitations of our marital connection and the nature of our collaboration. A life partner – with whom no matter how deep or intractable the schisms, there was always an unquestioned reliance – is now a newly minted stranger and potential adversary. Commonly held goals are now trumped by competing interests, and areas of mutual commitment become more difficult to access and hold. The move toward common ground is sometimes blocked by the press of security needs and the allure of self-justification.

While I cannot escape the sense of failure, I also experience our separation as a bold, improbable, and hopeful act. It is an achievement that is both a culmination of and an inception of processes that hold promise. It expresses a willingness to undergo destabilization, and it carries a hoped for renewal and revitalization of personal possibilities and family bonds. There is, in the separation, the wish to transform yet maintain cherished connections, and to preserve what is nourishing and loving for our three daughters. It also moves us toward reworking our relationships in ways that will more fully reflect and express our strengths and the passion of our caring. My hope is that our participation as parents will now more fully and freely carry our loving and creative presence.

I can also regard my separation as an act of courage. It risks a loss of security, raises the specter of loneliness, and disrupts the experience of ongoingness and familiarity in every way imaginable. I tell myself that preserving a marriage can, under certain circumstances, reflect a failure of imagination, a flight from risk, or a depressive resignation. Remaining married may express a need for self-validation, it may reflect an effort to maintain the moral high ground, or it may inflict hurt while seeming to express commitment. At the same time, I recognize that all of what I have just written can be said, at least in part, to serve defensive aims.

My separation is still relatively new, yet its prehistory had been sufficiently extended and the attendant emotions so sufficiently integrated that, once actualized, it almost immediately came to feel familiar and right. At the same time, it has also felt stunningly novel and disorienting. Its course and effects are experiences in process, and I realize that my perspective will be different, perhaps radically so, in a year, in five, in ten. I also know that these perspectives will be shaped not only by my subjective states, but by how my family fares, and by the evolving course of our relationships. Rightly and wrongly, fittingly and narcissistically, I anticipate feeling responsible.

My wife and I separated soon after I turned 60. The implacable presence of limited time was a precipitating factor, and the feeling, "If not now, when?" a haunting companion. There was a sense of purpose that led to a narrowing of my attention. There was much to question, even while I convinced myself I was sure of my course. Managing a separation requires a narrowed and sustained focus, and a willingness to endure unprecedented levels of logistical and interpersonal disruption. Separation necessitates attentiveness to a myriad of tasks, processes, details. I feel simultaneously at home in a new context, in the sense of living in ways that more closely reflect what is felt and wanted, and also dislocated, wrenched from what is familiar and catapulted into spaces that feel new and not yet known. Along with the companionship of regret, guilt, hope, and excitement, I discover an affirming sense of having arrived, a sense of rightness, and an unnerving embrace of disarray. For the first time, I am forgetful, and can recognize that there is simply too much to keep in mind.

While assigning a point of origin for any decision is invariably confounding, I believe that bearing responsibility for decisions and effects is meaningful and right. As guilt has been an intimate companion from early on, I am concerned about my tendency to deny myself opportunities to embrace and enjoy what determination and happenstance have provided. At the same time, I draw strength from the encouragement, understanding, acceptance, love, and even from the anger that is directed my way. I see and recognize changes that are of us and from us, of me and from me.

Working through a time of preoccupation

There is the task of working, with this, and within this separation.

In this section, I will revisit issues raised in an earlier chapter (Mendelsohn, 1996), now in a different context. In that previous piece, I considered the experience of working as an analyst during the time of my daughter's illness and after the time of her death. This was a time of preoccupation and mourning, a time when life changed irrevocably. Anna had illnesses that cut her life short, and decisively changed the lives of my wife, my oldest daughter, and me, while casting a shadow over the lives of our twins, born three years after Anna died. During that time, my wife and I struggled to think through agonizing medical decisions, assimilate unbearable information, and maintain connectedness with family, friends, clients, and patients. We feared for Anna, for our older daughter's well-being, and for our marriage, and I worried about my ability to work and be present with my patients.

In my practice, I wrestled with the clinical and ethical dilemmas of what felt like massive disturbances of the analytic space. The struggle was to transform my preoccupation and, later, my mourning into personal presence. I worked to integrate what was happening into experience that felt sufficiently part of me so that I could be with my patients as a preoccupied, grieving, but connected therapist whose sense of pain and loss was accessible enough to be held, seen, known, and accepted, or knowingly ignored, by both participants. My earlier chapter described the experiential foundation, the conceptualization of therapy process, the technical decisions, and the clinical unfolding of this effort.

For reasons that will surely take further shape over time, this current time of personal preoccupation has a different emotional valence. While I feel deeply connected to my passage through a time of disruption and hope, I am suffused with feelings that are more difficult to tolerate and hold within the clinical space. In some ways, what I experience feels more private and personal, more complicated to share, and more informed by defense than was the case when I was living and working as a heartsick and then grieving parent. To live through a separation and divorce is to simultaneously inhabit a tumultuous emotional position and to generate, and become a magnet for, an array of deeply personal and intensely emotional projections, projections which are inevitably taken in and lived by patient and analyst alike. To my way of thinking, this may be the case whether or not the facts of the therapist's life circumstances are explicitly shared with patients. The presence of these feelings and projections within the context of my own experience introduces them into the intersubjective space, where they become objects that are more or less obtrusive, and more or less accessible as subjects for shared experience and analysis. In these ways, my internal experience – particularly insofar as it is suffused by shame and guilt – works its way into the experiential field, informing, distracting, and shaping the flow of shared attention and receptivity. What is present and pressing for attention in the mind of one, is felt and absorbed within the mutually constituted field of experience. My preoccupation and grief in regard to Anna felt unbearably painful but was assimilable and sharable, whether in explicit terms or simply via affective presence. The turmoil, disruption, and excitement of divorce seek and find a more uncertain place.

Loneliness

In a recent chapter that considered loneliness as it is experienced in the context of working analytically with candidates in training (Mendelsohn, in press), I noted that while loneliness may be sponsored by interpersonal aloneness and loss, it involves, at heart, a form of self-alienation. To be lonely is to be blocked from access to sustaining internal objects, and to aspects of self-experience that require integration and communicative expression. When analysts are not free to think or feel, it is often because experience is, rightly or wrongly, thought to be unspeakable (Levenson, 1983; Wilner, 1998). The best way to manage the desire to speak of something disturbing is to not think it in the first place.

In the context of an intimate, clinical field of experience, the disturbance engendered by my separation and divorce has heightened my need for connection and recognition while sponsoring recourse to privacy, insularity, and defense. There has been a yearning to unburden, to feel known, to invoke the assurance of intimate sharing, and to engage opportunities for free and deeply connecting exchange. At the same time, I have been aware of, and feel strongly, the inhibiting impact of raw, turbulent feelings, heightened anxiety, the companionship and blanketing presence of fatigue, and the preoccupying self-involvement sponsored by shame and guilt. These feelings and states have engendered loneliness and induce me to "coast in the countertransference" (Hirsch, 2008). Since the separation, on more occasions than I care to admit, I nod and intone "uh-huh," in some semblance of attentiveness. Despite this, in better moments, feelings of loneliness are mitigated and counterbalanced by a sense of vitality and hopefulness. Along with shame-filled constriction, I experience a freedom to feel and be.

In my previous chapter about working during that earlier time of preoccupation and loss, I wrote about the affirming, nourishing aspects of clinical relationships. In the context of my separation, that kind of experience has been harder to find; while not altogether absent, it is sometimes limited by the loneliness that follows when experiences of intimacy that might occur are not actualized.

Boundaries

Boundary issues abound. First, with regard to the experience of writing this chapter: when we share autobiographical content, we tend to feel safer and more firmly grounded presenting stories that have a coherent narrative arc and a relatively positive resolution. We try to put our best foot forward. I recall attending a conference some years ago entitled, "The Good, The Bad, and The Ugly." Panels were assembled to discuss facilitative, obstructive, and chaotic clinical experience. It was striking to me how even the "bad" and "ugly" clinical stories we publicly share tend to be inspiring and uplifting, usually evoking admiration and even envy among the audience. It is much harder, for understandable reasons, to openly speak about clinical experiences that do not go well, stories that do not feature ourselves at our best, or narratives of experience that are fluid, open to critical interpretation,

196

or disturbing and ambiguous as to outcome. In these latter contexts, we tend to be more anxious and circumspect, and to withhold as much as we share. In writing this chapter, I am aware that I am succumbing to the temptation and need for circumspection while sharing experience that is painful, hopeful, and ambiguous with respect to outcome.

There are also multiple, complex boundary issues that arise in the work with patients. Some of these are in the realm of internal experience, involving the issues discussed in the context of loneliness. In that realm, what is at issue is the struggle to integrate and hold painful experiences that threaten to become preoccupying and distracting presences in the work. These processes of internal self-regulation and working through are also informed by, and interpenetrate with, boundary issues that are negotiated interpersonally. As will be discussed later, these issues often organize themselves around questions regarding the explicit sharing of personal information.

Much of the clinical work I do takes place over periods of years, often at a schedule of multiple times a week. My relationships with patients tend to be quite close, and there are opportunities – taken, avoided, analyzed, and simply lived – for deep mutual knowing (Mendelsohn, 2007). Often, information about aspects of my life circumstances is accessible. This aspect of knowing and being known is facilitated by the fact that many of the people I work with are in the field, often members of the professional communities within which I teach and enjoy lasting and close friendships. Often there are few "degrees of separation" between us, and a number of patients and supervisees are likely to hear about major developments in my life even when these are not explicitly taken up in therapy or supervision.

Two issues have followed from this. When my wife and I separated, I began telling friends and colleagues in the professional communities within which I affiliate. Though at first I wanted to tell people personally, and asked those I told to keep the information private, inevitably the sharing took on a life of its own and became available through the grapevine. While thoughts, desires, and disinclinations to share this news with patients and supervisees had already begun to take shape, I soon realized that – whether nor not I wanted to discuss this with patients and supervisees, and whether or not I thought this kind of sharing was a good idea – it was likely that many with whom I work would soon hear about my personal life from third parties. It was not hard to imagine circumstances in which some patients might hear news about me from colleagues who were unaware of my patients' relationships with me. Balanced against this were many considerations, including my awareness of the ways in which I *wanted* to share news of the changes in my life. In many instances, there was an aspect of this that had to do with wishing to be recognized, to be seen and known by patients with whom I feel close and with whom I enjoy a considerable sense of affirmation and support. In addition, I felt uncomfortable promoting (through silence) erroneous depictions of my life circumstances.

Particularly in therapies that had taken place over many years, ones in which my being married was known as fact, patients' and supervisees' continued references to my married state now had a different status than they did previously, and my allowing this to stand would now take on a range of meanings that were complex and troublesome, including the sense that I was being misleading. Finally, there were questions regarding the decision to share information about my changed circumstances from the vantage point of my sharing it at my initiative. It is one thing to recognize that patients might feel exposed and taken aback upon hearing personal information about me from third parties, and for them then to realize that I *could have* told them myself, and quite another to *choose* to preempt even a distressing experience by telling patients, to take an active role in assuming this kind of controlling and protective (including self-protective) position. Of course, what becomes apparent is that no technical position avoids the risks of therapeutic activism and avoidance, no position more clearly respects the patient's initiative and resilience, and none bypasses countertransferential anxiety and self-protectiveness. Moreover, the very act of trying to think this through can be said to express a counterresistant position (Wilner, 2000). At the time of this writing, these issues and dilemmas play themselves out in various stages of resolution and irresolution.

One of the backdrops for this aspect of clinical thinking through involves the place of personal information in the construction of transference (Jacobs, 1991). The asymmetrical tilt of the analytic relationship (Aron, 1996; Hoffman, 1998), and the historical depiction of the analyst's role as involving at least a certain form of anonymity, invite us to conflate the withholding of personal information with the importance of allowing and facilitating the play of transference. While we recognize that anonymity in any absolute or literal sense is impossible (Singer, 1977), we remain careful and measured about sharing biographical and personal information, adhering to the notion that patients should retain considerable choice about exposing themselves to details about who we are outside of the consulting room, and that too freely or extensively sharing certain kinds of information takes us too far in the direction of fostering orchestrated or controlled versions of transference, and limiting the patient's freedom to construct needed forms of experience. There then remains a tendency to mistake the sharing of personal information with the restriction and manipulation of transference experience.

A contrasting view is that transference and countertransference are meaningfully shaped by the dynamics and processes enacted around the sharing or withholding of content, more so than they are by the nature of the information itself. As Schafer (1958) pointed out, form and content interpenetrate in the telling of a story and, by extrapolation, in the construction of transference stories. To illustrate: many years ago I worked with a young woman, Diane, who struggled with fertility issues. She longed for a pregnancy and was bereft at the prospect of relinquishing her dream of having biological children. At the time, I was in my late 30s, and my wife and I had endured a sequence of pregnancy loss, illness, struggles to conceive, failed fertility treatments, and derailed attempts at adoption. During this time, Diane constructed and elaborated, in unsparing detail, a picture of the idyllic suburban life I shared with my wife and two children. We were, in fact, childless and lived on 110th Street in a then fairly unglamorous part of Manhattan. I found her insistently drawn version of my life to be subtly alienating, but persistently gratifying, as it comforted me and offered an idyllic space I could inhabit as I struggled to endure feelings of loss and disappointment.

One night, I encountered Diane at a meeting of Resolve, an organization devoted to assisting those contending with infertility and seeking alternative routes to parenthood. Neither my patient nor I expected the other to be there. At the meeting, we briefly greeted each other and exchanged hellos. I found myself apprehensive, but I also looked forward to the next day's session with considerable relief at having been "outed." In ways that I had not fully registered, the aspect of the transference story that involved my life as a fulfilled parent had felt oppressive and confining. There was something about it, beyond the poignant content, which felt caricatured and idealized in a defensive, restrictive way. When I asked Diane about her experience of seeing me at the meeting, she said she wasn't a bit surprised. She had always had the impression that I knew a great deal about adoption and infertility, and it was obvious that my attendance at the meeting was part of my extensive research in this area.

I was floored. For the next two months, I struggled with my frustration. I now felt a heightened need to loosen her attachment – and mine – to what increasingly felt like a powerfully held position of denial, one aided and abetted by my collusion. I thought about my feelings of gratification and comfort, and my attachment to the role of the admired and envied older brother, one that had deep resonance in my personal history. I thought further about Diane's somewhat subservient, subtly self-denigrating posture in relation to her older brother and to a series of male supervisors and mentors. In the end, I revisited our Resolve encounter and told her I had been there as a prospective adoptive parent. We were then able to explore together the ways in which we had constructed a transference–countertransference intersection that played out meaningful issues from both of our histories. We could see how attachment to those scenarios had served to restrict us from experiencing the dimension of our relationship that was expressive of mutual identification and shared experience. In this instance, the transference had less to do with the content of transference projections (e.g., I was the father of two, or I was childless), and more to do with how these stories were played out in the *form* of our transactions. We were, together, constructing and perpetuating an experience of me as privileged and enviable, and of her as wanting, admiring, and secretly resentful, while avoiding the complementary experience of mutual identification and shared feelings and struggles.

This vignette from an earlier time in my clinical work has bearing on the negotiation of boundary issues in the context of my separation. While I feel both a pull to share and to maintain privacy with respect to my personal life, I have tried to privilege the emotional situation that shapes and expresses itself in the patient–therapist relationship. In a lyrical, comprehensive, and movingly honest paper about her experience of divorce, Basescu (2009) recounts several clinical stories that involved some degree of sharing with patients about her personal circumstances and struggles. In her examples, while information was exchanged, the process lived between Basescu and her patients was of primary concern, and the disclosures that did occur often took the form of responding to something the patient had discerned and generatively, rather than defensively, projected (Singer, 1965), or they built upon and elaborated a platform of mutual identification. It is worth noting – in Basescu's work, and I believe in my own as well – that the recognition and exploration of mutual identification does not diminish, and may in fact facilitate the kind of benign idealization that is often a component of the therapeutic process in analytic therapy (Hoffman, 1998).

Idealization, safety, and holding

Jenny, a long-term patient, has, with considerable struggle, opened herself to an intimate, collaborative working relationship with me, one that is founded upon considerable mutual candor. She has, in some ways for the first time in her life, experienced what feels to her like a safe-enough reliance upon another. This sense of partnership has become a platform for the relinquishing of suicidality, substance abuse, an entrenched pattern of masochistic relatedness, and forms of self-neglect. The working through of these emotional and behavioral issues has taken place over many years in the context of an intense but safe-enough erotic transference. For Jenny, my marriage contributed to her experience of a necessary boundary, a way of holding deeply felt experience. She could undergo and share intense longings in the context of an experience of me as attached, fulfilled, unavailable romantically and sexually, and committed to a way of living and a value system that relegated to the background, just sufficiently, the presence of my sexual, romantic, and narcissistic selves. While Jenny always recognized intellectually that it was my role as her therapist, rather than my married state, that defined the crucial boundary, my being married helped. A lot.

After my separation, I struggled with the issue of how to carry and share the changes in my life circumstances in the work with Jenny. Over a period of months, Jenny's continued reference to my being married, her recognition of my fatigue and occasional preoccupation and distractedness, and associative material that suggested her "prehension" (Sullivan, 1938) of changes in my life circumstances, contributed to feelings of discomfort about continuing to endorse Jenny's identification of me as married. Balanced against this was concern about disrupting what sometimes felt like a "needed" (Stern, 1994) aspect of transference, and worry over the inevitable foregrounding of erotic and romantic countertransference that had long been held, within an intricate, mutually engendered construction of recognition and illusion. My decision to share with Jenny that my wife and I had separated, facilitated by a growing sense of collusive falseness, moved us into an extended period of turbulence and intensity, in the course of which the conditions of safety, the configuration of boundaries, and the nature of facilitative forms of idealization have had to be renegotiated (Pizer, 1998). One of Jenny's reflections on this process has been to elaborate on her heightened recognition of the ways in which she experiences us as more closely allied through the medium of shared and common experience, including a more vivid appreciation of the ways in which my life experience, like hers, must also be characterized by some degree of disruption, risk-taking and destabilization, features in relation to which she had felt herself, heretofore, to have had more exclusive dominion.

In another therapy, Josh, the husband of a married couple I have worked with, said, "So here's what we heard about you." Through a friend of theirs in the community who is also a friend of my wife, Josh and Natalie learned that my wife and I had separated nearly a year before. They also heard, in some detail, reports and commentary about how the separation had occurred, their friend's impressions of my wife's personality and mine, and many other welcome details. Josh and Natalie discussed this with me with a mix of muted excitement and apprehension, and with considerable concern regarding the impact of this disclosure on me and our work. They had briefly considered not sharing this with me, but felt that, for them, the experiential cat was out of the bag, and non-disclosure would have been untenable.

While I felt exposed, embarrassed, and anxious about the rendition of a less than complimentary narrative about my marriage and separation by a couple I was seeing to work with on their marital issues, my sense of exposure and annoyance, as well as my embarrassment and anxiety, were held and mitigated by the sense that Josh and Natalie were more concerned about my response to what they were saying than they were about what they had heard. We discussed what they were interested in knowing, defined what they felt to be the meaningful issues, and considered how these revelations shaped their experience of me as someone able to discern and address their marital problems. What was especially meaningful to them was their sense that, while the separation had taken place nearly a year earlier, they (in contrast to Jenny) had not discerned a meaningful difference in the quality of my work with them. I had not appeared less attentive or attuned. Whatever assumptions there had been about my experience of being married (they knew me to be married and met with me in the suburban home office I continue to use), and whatever ways that these had been woven into facilitative idealizations, were reconfigured into revised versions of transference and observation (Greenberg, 1991) now built around my non-defensiveness, connectedness to what I was doing, and willingness to be open.

Idealization, of course, is a two-way street. It is hard for one person to idealize another who fails to seek and accept the idealization (Hoffman, 1994). The experience of separating has made more apparent to me specific ways in which, over the years, patients have tended to represent my married state, and has helped me more fully recognize how those transferential narratives have served to nourish certain of my own split-off, idealized, and consoling self-representations. The changes in my life circumstances, and the resultant shifts in constructions of transference, have helped me appreciate the degree to which my patients' idealizations of my married state – especially versions of the story that emphasized the presumed harmony and richness of my family life – supported my tendency to seek refuge and derive comfort from these part-truths and consoling illusions. Indeed, I have come to consider how these ways of experiencing myself through the eyes of my patients, and my readiness to identify and bask in the glow of these representations of my experience (while simultaneously feeling considerable sadness with respect to their contrast with my lived experience), may have helped to sustain me during my many years of marriage. To the degree that my participation in my marriage required, over the course of time, the management of sadness and longing, these elements of countertransference feeling became sources of comfort. I now wonder if and how my work with patients contributed to the construction of a complexly constituted holding environment that, for better and worse, made living with some considerable measure of sadness manageable, and kept the possibility of separating, when it was neither thinkable nor feasible, unformulated and at a safe distance.

Dynamic shifts

In the time preceding and following the separation, there have been shifts in the thematic and tonal quality of many therapies. Interestingly, the kinds of changes that have been most apparent to me have occurred both in those therapies in which there has been open discussion of my changed circumstances, and those in which there has not – therapies in which, presumably, patients do not know I am no longer married. This commonality is consistent with the impression that analytic therapy is carried more by the analyst's attentiveness and openness to affective and relational experience enacted within the field of therapy, and less by content qua content.

Two trends have stood out. In many long-term therapies, the past two to three years (which include the considerable pre-separation conscious and unconscious preparation period) has been a time of significant disequilibrium and foundational change. In many therapies, there have been breakdowns of entrenched patterns of impasse and restriction, significant (but usually well-considered) emotional risk-taking, and the reconfiguration of important commitments and attachments. While in only one case have these kinds of changes taken the form of actual divorce, in many instances there have been symbolic separations and divorces. Examples include:

- making career changes that move the person from dependence upon a secure but restrictive corporate position to the freedom and risk associated with self-employment,
- the relinquishing of a position within a marriage of resigned, claustrophobic servitude and, through facing the *possibility* of separation without the typical attendant panic and guilt, being able, for the first time, to feel freely engaged within the marriage,
- separating from enthrallment to an addictive and largely self-endangering long-term affair, and

- feeling sufficiently separate from a compulsively enacted counteridentification with a mother's malignant and dramatized helplessness to permit the acceptance of dependencies associated with chronic illness.

While these and many other signal changes can be seen as the ordinary outcomes of intensive analytic work, their frequency and scope have been impressive. In each instance, these changes have been ushered in by a sense of disruption and disequilibrium, and my patients have linked these changes with changes they can discern in me and in the quality of our relationship.

Those patients who know about my life changes have said things like the following: "Seeing and knowing what you have done has been with me as a kind of presence, serving as an example, and even as a kind of sanction for making these changes"; or, "It seems to me that, over time, you have become more sensitive to and comfortable addressing the ways in which I feel stuck and avoidant, you seem freer"; or, "The atmosphere in the therapy feels more open. More can be questioned and accepted, and the consequences feel less dreadful." While, of course, attitudes and observations like these are always multi-determined, and derive from and are expressed within the unique context of each intersubjective field, the frequency and vividness of these sorts of shifts are consonant with changes in my internal states as well as my openness to experiences of destabilization and change. More specifically, I suspect that the loosening of internal states of stagnation and self-alienation has had a facilitative effect on many therapies.

An important dimension of the shifts occurring within a number of treatments has been a growing emphasis on what Hoffman (1994) has termed the pole of "common humanity" in the analytic relationship. In Hoffman's view, many of the important dimensions of therapeutic relatedness – including transference and countertransference, ritualized and spontaneously expressive participation, and interpretation and action – organize themselves in dialectical terms. That is, these major constituents of analytic role relatedness, while appearing to be in distinct and even complementary relationship to each other, are, at heart, mutually constituted, interpenetrating, and mutually defining. The poles of idealization and common humanity take this dialectical form. Our idealizations of each other gather much of their meaning and power against a background appreciation of all that we share and struggle with together, and our identifications via our shared vulnerabilities and consolations take shape in the context of the recognition of how we differ and what we admire and draw strength from in each other.

Merton Gill (1983) observed that, if one could study the record of multiple therapies conducted by a single analyst, one could discern the imprint of that analyst's personhood. That is, the analyses would be unmistakably *his* as well as being reflective of the unique dyad. My sense is, that during this time of flux in my life, there has been a heightened influence and presence of the "pole of common humanity" in many, if not most therapies. Patients now frequently comment on how I seem accessible and available in ways not previously felt, how I seem more able to identify with and appreciate their struggles, how they experience me as less critical, of myself as well as them, as offering participation that recognizes and embraces their efforts at considered risk-taking, and as sensing that this presence flows from personal sources within me. What is striking to me and, I admit, encouraging, is that these clinical experiences occur in the context of my often feeling defensive, preoccupied, wrestling with shame and guilt, private, self-protective, and so forth. While I cannot say I fully understand this, it may reflect at least some degree of recognition and acceptance on my part of my anxiety and defensiveness and at least some degree of willingness to make *those* aspects of my participation accessible for mutual inquiry. It may well be that the freedom to actualize a desired change in my life circumstances has facilitated an enhanced openness and responsiveness to internal experience.

One final clinical note: all that I am describing in a global sense must be offered with the caveat that selective inattention undoubtedly remains present in the work. As I described recently (Mendelsohn, in press), the time immediately preceding and following our separation was characterized by glaring evidence of shared selective inattention. During the year before my wife and I separated, none of my patients commented, or seemed aware, that I had stopped wearing my wedding ring, a ring that had been, in many instances, the subject of considerable attention and affectively saturated interest. Even in the work with patients with whom I shared information about the separation, none commented on the absence of a ring, and when I raised *that* as an issue, not a single patient said he or she had noticed. To me, this clearly signaled the communication of my preference that the changes that were occurring in my life should be off limits for mutual observation and inquiry. I assume that, as time goes by, I will become aware of additional manifestations of shared avoidance and inattention.

Separating

I am writing about experiences that are in process, and that are emotionally fraught, in many ways painful, irreducibly private and public, and whose outcome is unknown. At the same time, there is a quality of the ordinary in this that must be underscored. As I noted many years ago (Mendelsohn, 1996), psychoanalysis is the work we do over the course of a professional lifetime. It is of us, and reflects our deepest passions and commitments. We engage in what we do with the entirety of our beings during times of relative equanimity, and times of disturbance and destabilization. Who we are gets carried in our work. Inevitably, in ways we see and appreciate, and in ways we miss and perhaps come to see belatedly, our responsive and embattled selves enter and shape our clinical work. We notice, learn, and work things through with the help of our patients.

References

Aron, L. (1996). *A meeting of minds*. Hillsdale, NJ: The Analytic Press.

Basescu, C. (2009). Shifting ground: The therapist's divorce and its impact on her life and work. *Contemporary Psychoanalysis*, *45*, 44–64.

Gill, M. M. (1983). The interpersonal paradigm and the degree of the therapist's involvement. *Contemporary Psychoanalysis*, *19*, 200–237.

Greenberg, J. R. (1991). Countertransference and reality. *Psychoanalytic Dialogues*, *1*, 52–73.

Hirsch, I. (2008). *Coasting in the countertransference: Conflicts of self interest between analyst and patient*. New York: The Analytic Press.

Hoffman, I. Z. (1994). Dialectical thinking and therapeutic action. *Psychoanalytic Quarterly*, *63*, 187–218.

Hoffman, I. Z. (1998). *Ritual and spontaneity in the psychoanalytic process: A dialectical-constructivist view*. Hillsdale, NJ: The Analytic Press.

Jacobs, T. J. (1991). *The use of the self*. Madison, CT: International Universities Press.

Levenson, E. A. (1983). *The ambiguity of change*. Northvale, NJ: Jason Aronson.

Mendelsohn, E. (1996). More human than otherwise: Working through a time of preoccupation and mourning. In B. Gerson, (Ed.), *The therapist as a person: Life choices, life experiences, and their effects on treatment* (pp. 21–40). Hillsdale, NJ: The Analytic Press.

Mendelsohn, E. (2007). Analytic love: Possibilities and limitations. *Psychoanalytic Inquiry*, *27*, 219–245.

Mendelsohn, E. (in press). The loneliness of the training analyst. In A. A. Lynch, A. K. Richards, and L. Spira, (Eds.), *Encounters with loneliness: Only the lonely*. New York: IP Books.

Pizer, S. (1998). *Building bridges: The negotiation of paradox in psychoanalysis*. Hillsdale, NJ: The Analytic Press.

Schafer, R. (1958). How was this story told? *Journal of Projective Techniques*, *22*, 181–210.

Singer, E. (1965). *Key concepts in psychotherapy*. NY: Basic Books.

Singer, E. (1977). The fiction of analytic anonymity. In K. Frank, (Ed.), *The human dimension in psychoanalytic practice* (pp. 181–192). New York: Grune and Stratton.

Stern, S. (1994). Needed relationships and repeated relationships: An integrated relational perspective. *Psychoanalytic Dialogues*, *4*, 317–346.

Sullivan, H. S. (1938). The data of psychiatry. In *The fusion of psychiatry and the social sciences* (pp. 32–55). New York: W. W. Norton & Co., published 1964.

Wilner, W. (1998). Experience, metaphor, and the crucial nature of the analyst's expressive participation. *Contemporary Psychoanalysis*, *34*, 413–443.

Wilner, W. (2000). A legacy of self: The unique psychoanalytic perspective of Benjamin Wolstein. *Contemporary Psychoanalysis*, *36*, 267–280.

16

A BIRD THAT THUNDERS
My analysis with Emmanuel Ghent

Bonnie Zindel

I began treatment with Emmanuel Ghent, M.D. twice a week in the fall of 1994. These were momentous years for me. He was helping me contemplate a divorce after 25 years of marriage, and I had just completed my graduate studies at Columbia University at age 52 – where I was euphemistically referred to as a "mature student." Following that, I began a four-year analytic training at the National Institute for the Psychotherapies in New York. My work with Mannie Ghent continued for nine years until his death in 2003, when it came to an abrupt and sudden end. In the pages that follow I have relied on contemporaneous notes to capture some of the work we did together.

One of the most defining moments of my life was my mother dying when I was 16 years old. Or had I just turned 17? Dates always elude me, blur between one number and the next. Was my wedding anniversary to Paul, when we married in London, October 26th or 27th? Did my mother die on her birthday, November 11th, or early the next morning on the 12th, 10 hours into her 46th year? Or was it her 47th? I always felt I would not live to see my 47th birthday. Breast cancer wiped out all the women in the family. Maybe this time confusion had to do with my false birthday. My parents wanted me to begin first grade that autumn and falsified my birth certificate by whiting out the month of May and adding the month of March. So in first grade, as I was turning five, I had to make believe that the false day, March 3rd, was my birthday. My mother brought cupcakes to school, and Mrs. DeVito, the teacher, led the class in singing happy birthday on a day that meant nothing to me. Then, on my real birthday, May 3, turning five, I had to contain my enthusiasm and act as if that was just another day. I hated it. I had to keep this secret. It felt dishonest. What was the big rush? My mother went to great effort to push me.
   "Do you know what today is?" Mannie asked me. "No, what?" I wanted to know. "March 3rd." I didn't know. This is my phony, make-believe birthday. Yes, he added, your un-birthday. She wanted you to be famous at five. She sent you a message that you were not good enough.

Who am I more like, my mother or my father? Some of the following narrative summarizes work with Mannie over the course of a few months – collaboration

206

between two minds. My therapy was a re-authoring of my life story from fragmented and chaotic experiences. My father was intellectual, funny, and very real. Nothing phony about him. He'd read stories to me at night. Never let me go to sleep without a kiss goodnight. We had a ritual. He'd light up a cigar, take the paper ring off, and then give it to me. And I would wear it for hours before adding it to my collection in a white canister. When the bad ones opened and fell of my finger, I was heartbroken. Mannie jotted a few notes down.

My father was a CPA, and I grew to hate numbers, because numbers took him away from me. He was in medical school and had to give it up to support his family and six younger siblings when his own father got ill. Look at me. In a way I am a doctor too. My mother was the most important person in my life, and I never made any decision without thinking first what she would like, what she would want me to do. She trained me for that, and I never learned to express my needs. I grow silent. Mannie heard a yearning to be known, my essence to be recognized (Ghent, 1990). My mother made me feel like I was disloyal to her by liking my father. Needs are created (Ghent, 2001). Where did you just go? Mannie asked. I am in my walk-in closet. It is the only place I could feel. "In the dark your feelings come out," Mannie offered. "Tell me what you need, and I'll be your mother," he said. "I want you to see me, really see me," I answered without a pause.

When my mother died, I went to my room and cried and cried and cried. I remember sitting at the edge of my bed weeping, or wailing for hours all alone until depleted. Then days. Then months. No one was there. My father returned home after work at 6 p.m., and I made dinner for him. Then he would stare into space listening to the radio at the kitchen table in mourning for his wife of 25 years. I would return upstairs to my bedroom, close the white shutters for the evening, and re-enter alone my devastating state of sorrow, of despair and dissociation. Eventually I did come out of that room when aunts and cousins urged that I see a psychiatrist for a short time and begin college like other kids my age.

Then came work and marriage. I met Paul at the Cleveland Play House where I was PR Director. I had my own radio show and interviewed Paul when we were doing his play, *The Effect of Gamma Rays on Man-in-the-Moon Marigolds*. We married a few years later in London, having first set up a 60-day residency at the Dorchester Hotel. We arrived for our 9 o'clock appointment a bit late. He surprised me by ordering a yellow Rolls Royce convertible driven by a hippie with a pony tail, and drove though the streets of London, onto Oxford Street then to Caxton Hall, a British registry, with my pink voile hat blowing in the wind. We made two stops. First we picked up our two friends, and when they saw us, only then did they know they were the designated maid of honor and best man and were going to a wedding. As people went on with their daily morning rush hour rituals, we got married. It was on the 26th of October – or was it October 27th? Recently I found the box with my wedding dress, and on it I had written October 29th. We sailed back on one of the last crossings of the SS *France* as man and wife to begin our newly married life together as a writing couple in New York.

And over the course of those years we had two children, a Great Dane, Darwin, and Alfie the sheep dog, some rabbits, and a boa constrictor. For Paul's career as a writer, we moved three times back and forth from New York to California, putting our children in The Dalton School in New York or John Thomas Dye School in Bel Air in LA. Somewhere in all these moves we grew apart. I went back to Columbia University School of Social Work to become a therapist. Then I applied for four-year analytic training. He left the city for a peaceful writing life in the country, and I stayed on the Upper West Side to begin training as a psychoanalyst.

In my search for a training analyst, I got Mannie Ghent's name from a supervisor who had read his paper "Paradox and Process" (1992) and thought his interest in creativity would be a good fit. I remember reading that neediness is often confounded with genuine need, and designed to keep the real need from being known by the analyst, let alone by the patient. And that neediness, garbed in protective coloration, is the impersonator. I also knew that he had been in analysis with Clara Thompson, who had been in her own analysis with Sandor Ferenczi. I called and set up an appointment. On the first week of October at 11 a.m. I headed for his office in Soho, excited to start my analysis.

That Tuesday, I took the D train to Broadway Lafayette and got up out of the subway in Soho on a street I had never been on before. It was a clear sunny morning, and I was filled with hope. Weaving along cobblestone paths lined with warehouses turned into lofts and unusual shops, I felt I was walking in a dream. I liked the newness, the excitement and intensity, and then turned right onto Prince Street. I was standing in front of a green entryway, and then opened the door to a small anteroom. I was a few minutes early. I took a deep breath, calming nerves, and pushed the button: Emmanuel Ghent. 5th floor. He had told me the signal: one long buzz followed by one short, like the beginning of a symphony. I did as he told me, and then waited. He buzzed me in. The elevator opened, and a dog looked startled. I went up to the only apartment on the 5th floor. A bench resembling a church pew seemed like the place to sit while expectantly staring at a painting of a Rembrandt-like face and another impressionist painting that I imagined a patient had created. In a few minutes I heard shuffles from inside, voices grew louder as Mannie held the tapestry curtain aside, letting a man with a briefcase out of his session, focusing only on their goodbye. The patient and I did not exchange glances. Then Mannie turned his complete attention to me, smiled, and held the curtain open as if in a choreographed dance while I passed a black sculptured silhouette of a lithe dancer at the doorway and entered another world. "Come in," he said with a smile, closing the wooden door behind, and inviting me into his sanctuary. On the inside of the door was a black and white poster of a sun-dappled forest. I imagined the blurred trunks of tall trees gave Mannie a sense of inner peace and expansiveness, his surrendering to a quiet meditation. Thoreau's words came to me, "A light from within." So began my twice a week analysis.

His greeting always included studying my state, and meeting me wherever I was in that moment of transition between my outside world and what was to become my birthing room with Mannie.

Where should I sit? "The chair, the couch or you can sit on the floor if you want," he said playfully, giving me permission to be whoever I am, do whatever I wanted. I'll sit in the chair. There was an unspoken freedom. The room was small and cozy, and I sat in a brown leather chair, a bit worn from all the lives that passed in here. Across the room was a leather couch covered with a woolen blanket. In a black turtleneck, he sat in a large comfortable worn red leather chair, with his relevant papers where he kept his master schedule on one sheet of paper. And right next to him, on a small side table, lay his lovely black fountain pen. It reminded me of my father filling his green Parker fountain pen, shaking excess off, then drying it meticulously with a tissue. Blue ink. I wondered how many stories Mannie heard in this chair. How many lives he entered. I told him that the best work I had done was raising my kids. "So far," he said.

He had kind eyes that twinkled, knowing wise eyes that could see beyond the visual, and a white beard that he sometimes stroked as he listened. His slender build could hold a universe. Keys rattled in his pocket like he could open many doors. Sometimes he slipped his shoes off and, curling his feet under him, sent an invitation for me to relax too. Other times he stretched his legs out in front of him, closed his eyes, and listened in the deepest way, to places inside that he wanted only me to find while right there with me. So close. And when he looked at me with his very blue blue eyes, it was as if he could see right into the deepest part of my emerging self. He was beaming into internal states. He could sense if I was sad or pensive or light and joyful. He never intruded. He listened very quietly. Like a Buddhist mediation. I talked first. Always. When I spoke jibbersh he slowed me down. He encouraged surrendering to the emotional moment. He helped me live with uncertainty, urging me to go deeper inside myself. After three years, I eventually got on the couch. I knew immediately that different things were valued in this room than in other rooms.

I was thrilled when he took out a 5x7 yellow index card and wrote down my first dream in treatment about a young earthy woman expected to die in a few hours. She is giving into it, but she doesn't very much like it. Occasionally, a sound is uttered. The mother wraps her in a gauze-like shroud, preparing her for burial, when a slight movement is seen. We can't put her in the dark lonely ground and cover her with earth; she still may have some feelings. The next thing I know, I cut the gauze off, and the woman raises her hands up in the air with a sense of freedom. And with an effervescent radiant smile, the young woman says, "I am going to live each day the way I want." I jump out of bed a bit nauseous, throw water on my face, and get dressed. This is the first day of my analysis with Mannie.

I began writing notes after each session. Following each visit, I would sit in Dean & Deluca on Prince Street over a café latte and write reflections on the session. Mannie seemed to set the buried part of me screaming to exhume (Ghent, 1990). The ritual, always writing. What does that mean? Does writing hold my feelings? Does it prevent me from forgetting, or is it a way for dissociating or avoiding dissociation? Does writing hold me in some unexplainable way? Does it help me remember or help me forget? Does it contain my anxiety? Is it an expression of my creativity? Is it a blessing or a curse? Do I use writing to hold onto me? To hold onto Mannie? To hold onto my being? Am I using words for a deeper resonance or to slip away? Or is it that I need to write to be human? Or to hold me together and bind me? Does writing digest emotions, or freeze them? I am a writer, and it seems like I have no choice but to write.

A slight nervousness tinged with excitement filled me each time I rang Mannie's buzzer. The times he didn't answer right away, I became filled with an overwhelming sense of fear that I would never see him again. But he always responded. The first part of treatment we talked about my mother and her living through me. I always felt she stole me. What was she like? Mannie wanted to know. Powerful, smart, dynamic, a director of people's lives and unhappy in her own. I was designated to make her happy and fulfill her unfilled life. "Soul rape," he said. I yelled at her and cried with her and got mad at her, but it was hard fighting her in the grave. I wish she had lived longer and that I could speak to her, stand up to her, be a woman with her. Mostly, though, I found it hard to forgive her for not seeing me, not teaching me the basic rudiments of being a person, appreciating who I was. And, most of all, I could not forgive her for dying and leaving me so young and unprepared for life. Tell me what you need, and I'll be your mother, he said.

And Mannie became my mother; he mothered me and nurtured me, and he twinkled for me. Also, he taught me to not know. That seemed to be his credo (Ghent, 1989) – the fundamental need of people for the expansion and liberation of the self and the dismantling of the false self. In our sessions together, Mannie listened to the rumblings of the nascent parts of me that began bubbling up from the deep. He helped me get rid of my red lipstick (my nickname in high school was ruby lips) and red nail polish, to which I had an addiction. My body became nervous when I had naked nails. Men liked a natural woman, he told me.

I would see different people come and go. Unconscious sisters and brothers. The same man left before me for many years. I wondered who he was. He always left an impression on the little pillow on the couch. I breathed his air. A woman entered after me. She breathed mine. For much of the time I wanted Mannie for myself, but when he died, I was happy to have unconscious siblings.

When Dean & Deluca closed, Mannie suggested Untitled Space around the corner on Mercer Street. After each session, I would write on 3x5 ruled Filofax refills. I never missed writing notes after a session, even if it was on the D train heading back uptown to see a patient. Eventually, I filled up three brown leather volumes. The last book was very thin.

Book One of my Filofax contained analytic work on my mother having me take six dance classes a week even though I was not very good, how I pushed feelings down, never learned to make decisions on my own, and never asked for what I wanted or developed a sense of agency. Mannie called me an emotional virgin. Then, in early adolescence, when most pierced earlobes or stayed out late, I did not have the opportunity to rebel when she became seriously ill. I had tap shoes and toe shoes but never learned to walk. I could not rebel against a dying mother. He takes his pen, fills it up with ink, touches the tip, and jots a few notes down. Then, one year right before the August break, I was frightened that Mannie would not come back from his vacation. When you lose a mother at 16 – or had I just turned 17? – abandonment takes over, and goodbye is forever.

Somewhere in the second year of treatment, when a jackhammer under the window invaded our space, Mannie moved us mid-session to his other office across the hall, a space where his music lived; his oboe and other instruments. Digital music equipment filled the room, and in here, his two passions lived – music and psychoanalysis. A section was set aside for analysis – a couch and two chairs. Here was the musical Mannie, reflected in his love of music and his love of psychoanalysis, both suffused with rhythms, tones, and emotional moments. I knew he had won a Guggenheim Fellowship to pursue pioneering work as a composer of electronic music, creating new sounds as he did in psychoanalysis. Among his best-known compositions is "Phosphones," a work for dance. It was the first time he used his computer system to synchronize lighting cues with an electronic score. The inventor Mannie. When performed, light bounced around the stage, on cue, among the performers, and the audience begins to perceive the light as another dancer. Mannie was also an amateur oboist, and it's therefore not surprising that in our work together, at times, we listened to the sounds and not the words.

In the middle of a session, as I was talking about an early experience with my mother, he moved the ottoman closer to me. Surprised, I began to cry. I do not know where the tears came from. The tears surprised him too. I found it hard to accept his kindness. His caring took my breath away. "Is the time up?" "Another minute," he said. I didn't know if my heart could take it; I rested my feet back on the ottoman. "I am letting your kindness in. It feels so unfamiliar to be given to." "I give to you because I want to," he said quietly.

Soon he tapped lightly on the side of his chair. "Time to go." He walked me to the door, and off I went. I felt overwhelmed. Exposed. This was a new country. He offered me an experience of being seen, and it felt scary. Giving to me without my asking seemed impossible to take in. Years later, I read about Mannie covering the lap of a woman patient with a Scottish throw. Her first words were "I didn't even know I was feeling cold" (Ghent, 1995). And then she wept profusely. He satisfied her unthought need. I had not read the paper when the ottoman moment happened. I didn't know I wanted the ottoman until he pushed it over towards me, and only then did I realize that he had given me something I needed. He touched a place in me that he saw.

Mannie offered this paradoxical statement: a need is something you don't know you have until someone happens to gratify it, validate it – and then this mundane act becomes vividly transformational. Adam Phillips (2001) said the need to be looked after could never be a new need. Mannie believes that even if the need had been dissociated, it now becomes connected in this creative moment. All of this was unspoken in our experience. He encouraged my surrender, a longing for the wish to be found, recognized, and penetrated to the core so as to become real.

After the summer break we spoke a lot about my father, who played second fiddle to my mother. She needed to be the chosen one in our family dyad. She met my dad when they were in Brighton Beach, Brooklyn, and in the middle of a baseball game with friends; he accidentally hit her on the head with a fly ball and knocked her out. When she came to, he took her home to the Bronx (even though he lived in Brooklyn), and before you know it she wanted to get out of her own house. He proposed, and they got married. So goes the family lore. She was 19. So young.

My father wanted to be a doctor. But his father got ill, and he had to leave medical school to support the family. He was not bitter or resentful, but he would have been a wonderful doctor. Mannie shook his head knowingly. My mother never wanted me to be close to him, and it was through my work with Mannie that I got to really know my father, who was still alive when I entered treatment. My mother didn't like my father very much. He could never please her. Only once in all the years growing up did I see them hold hands on the couch. When he died at 94 (twice the age of my mother), the kids and I were with him in the hospital, and we sang every song that he would have sung the coming year when he would no longer be here, even the one from his fraternity days when he met my mother. We sat on the bed singing "If you knew Suzie," "Over the river and through the woods," "Oh horsey, keep your tail up, keep your tail up, keep your tail up, oh horsey keep your tail up, keep the sun out of your eyes." My father sang that silly song from his college years, a fraternity song that meant nothing, that meant everything.

A guard stood sentry at the first floor elevator. I want to see my father. He called up and then said, "You can't go up." I started trying to push my way past this 250-pound security guard. "You'll have to shoot me to keep me from seeing my father," I said defiantly.

For me, surrender embodied the release of a precious dissociated state that had been inaccessible before (Ghent, 2001). When we speak of need, Mannie speaks of transcendent experience. In the language of complexity theory, Mannie would refer to this state as a system poised on the edge of chaos; one that's optimal for change (Ghent, 2001).

In my next session, I told Mannie that on the last two visits with my father, we each took back what was rightfully ours. I gave my father his freedom – having thought about me much of his adult life, now he should do what he needed to do. I would be all right. And in the end, he gave me back my strength. And my aggression. I told Mannie my father gave me life twice – once when I was born, and again when he died. I cried with Mannie. I cried for my father. I cried for myself.

The session after my father died, I brought a copy of my first published novel that I had dedicated to and given to my father (Zindel & Zindel, 1980). I was now giving this book to my analytic father. He kept it on the table next to him. One time he held the book, pointing to the cover artwork: a girl with her mother, strings attached to the girl like a puppet. Before I had seen the girl. Now I saw the strings. I had never seen them before. You weren't ready to see them, he told me. He wrote that one has a longing for the birth, or rebirth of the true self (Ghent, 1990). Mannie said: "You feel you have to perform for me. You only have to do what you want to do." We were in a space of total commitment to change and uncertainty. He did write about the fundamental need of a person for the expansion and liberation of the self (Ghent, 1990).

Winnicott (1992) says that regression offers hope for a new opportunity to unfreeze. Mannie understood this to mean an opportunity for the birth or rebirth of the true self. Every time I came into session, I would check that the book was still there. It always was. I felt safe and protected and loved. When the new millennium came, and I arrived at his office for the first session in the year 2000, the book was gone. "Where is the book?" I asked, surprised. He was taken back. "I didn't know you cared." "Of course I cared. I looked for it each time I entered the room." "I didn't know," he said, "you never told me." "I liked that you kept it there without me asking, and that you did it because you wanted to." It felt very Winncottian to me. How then did he, a man who taught Winnicott, forget about transitional experience (Winnicott, 1953) and the unspoken agreement that it was never to be talked about? "Here it is" – he got up and went to the closet and brought out the copy. "I will keep it in here," Mannie said. It made me sad that time moves on. "I guess every thousand years it is good to do a cleaning," I responded. And so started a new millennium.

Steve Mitchell and Lew Aron (1999) refer to Mannie's paper (Ghent, 1999), and say that Mannie's psychoanalytic goal is not insight but transformation, as patients come in contact with frozen parts of themselves that are yearning to be known and recognized. Mannie always said that Steve was his best friend.

Around that time, Mannie lent me his copy of *The Work and Play of Winnicott* (Grolnick, 1990). He was teaching a course at the NYU Postdoctoral Program in Psychotherapy and Psychoanalysis (Postdoc), where he was among the founders of the Relational Track. I loved reading his underlines and notes in the margins. When I returned his copy, I bought my own.

Notebook #2

Here are some of the highlights with Mannie that I wrote in my book. Summer breaks, vacations, me bringing back a poster of the Cro-Magnon man from the Dordogne, his going out to California to visit his daughter, his writing his papers, me going to hear his presentations. Upon graduation from my four-year analytic training at NIP, feeling both losses and exhilaration, I wondered: "What now?" He responded: "The King is Dead. Long Live the King." "What do you mean?" "Life perpetuates itself. The king is dead and he has his children and then their children. Dreams give birth to other dreams. Life perpetuates itself."

Mannie loved silence. When I get lonely and feel the four walls and how it hurts, he said, "*A faire une omlette il faut casser une oeuf* – To make an omelet you have to break an egg. You have to crack one thing to make another, and this is trans-formation." We talked about echoes, all the decades of unfilled wants. "I'll tell you about echoes," he said. "Close your eyes and listen to them and feel who you have always been but never recognized – pure, free, unshackled." I welcomed my creative unconscious into the room as he invited my unconscious stories. "Do you want to close your eyes and go into your unconscious?" Here the words of Ranier Marie Rilke (2000) play in my head. I have faith in all that is not yet said.

I write some of these thoughts in my notebook at Dean & DeLuca. Mannie taught me to go inside and not cut myself off or run away from the experience of being. I had never sat with anyone like this before. I don't know what is so scary about being seen. "You need to take it back, own the part you gave away." "Listen to the echoes and turn it inside and allow yourself to feel and see what will hap-pen instead of turning it outward." In these silences I felt held and seen. I could sit with the silence without doing anything. I just had to be. I open my eyes and tears that had been trapped pour down my face. I took an emotional photograph. "We are a camera with our own subjectivities, not a mirror," he says. I sit there feeling such love towards Mannie, towards myself, towards others. "You have to be ready when chance comes along." Some of these offerings are informed by Buddhism.

We shared reading and writing in sessions. Mannie would often read passages to me. I loved it when he did. I felt like I was a young girl, and he was reading me a bedtime story like *Alice in Wonderland*, and he was the white rabbit beckoning me on. I felt held and cared for and safe. What we shared always came from a place of deep resonance, something we talked about. He used literature and metaphor to speak to me from a deeper place and in another voice. My final paper in my fourth year of institute training was called "The Metaphor Goddess in Three-Quarter Time." This time, after talking about my father, he returned from his bookshelf in another room and brought back the poetic classic *Metamorphoses* by Ovid, verses translated from the Roman. He read "The Muir Tree." Time seemed to stand still when he read to me in the language of metaphor and the imagination. Another time, when we talked about a word, he got his humongous old *Oxford Unabridged Dictionary*, grabbed a large magnifying glass, squinted his eyes (he was losing his vision), and read the minuscule print. "Intimacy," he read – "intimacy is a way to be real, to let someone in, to be vulnerable."

One time, we talked about the theme of subjugating myself to second position in close relationships. Mannie got up from his chair and returned with an old book, yellow from age, pages falling out from wear. "Do you speak French?" he asked. "A little." Mannie grew up and attended medical school in Montreal, speaking French fluently, before moving to New York. He read from the poem, *Paroles*, a symbolic poem by the French poet and writer, Jacques Prevert (1972). Hearing Mannie speak French sounded like a compelling love song, his voice soft and melodic. Then, he translated the poem into English, enjoying being a poet for a moment.

Pour Toi Mon Amour
I went to the birdmarket and bought a bird for you, my dear.
I went to the flower market and bought flowers for you, my dear.
I went to the ironmonger and bought chains for you, my love.
Then I went to the slave market and looked for you, my love.
But you were not there.

"See," Mannie, said, resting the book on his lap. "The speaker in the poem went to find her in the market but was glad she was not there." I grab a tissue and wipe my eyes. I am free. "I want to hold onto this feeling," I say. "You can, it is right inside of you." The session is over, and I take the elevator down. "Falling in love with one's analyst is a form of surrender, even when infused with the elements of transference" (Ghent, 2001, p. 31). In describing nonlinear complexity theory, he says that when we fall in love we attribute the extraordinary experience we are having to the traits of the person we love.

Paul and I separate, and he spends more time writing at the lake house than in the city. I visit him on a weekend in February, gazing at the frozen lake through binoculars as we sit on the terrace watching ice fishing and waiting for rare winter birds. We rediscover each other through talking about Christopher Bollas, who I heard speak the week before on the nature of human character. Bollas (1993) explained that character means bringing along with one's articulating idioms those inner presences – or spirit – that we all contain. We compared character from a literary and then a psychoanalytic point of view.

Mannie talked about a number of psychoanalysts. The most dear to him was Steve Mitchell, who said that we have to have one foot in fantasy and the other in illusion. Some people build sandcastles even though they will be washed away. Others never build them. Mannie said the hardest part of living one's life is the loss of illusion, because illusion defies reality. He talks about being grounded and flying. Mannie, a master of illusion and paradox said, "If you fly too low you can be stuck in the waves. It is good to soar and fly but occasionally look down to earth and see where you are and not get chained to the rocks."

He paraphrased a thought of Marion Milner: "It is good to be on this earth and in reality, but it is also necessary to heed the beacon of hope." He sent me out to buy *On Not Being Able to Paint* by Marion Milner (1950), who had influenced his thinking about surrender. Milner, in her discussion of the nature of creativity, drew attention to the blanking out of ordinary consciousness – when one is able to break free from the familiar and allow a new unexpected entity to appear. This

215

is essential if something new is to be created, an essential part of the creative process. Mannie encouraged my creativity, and we often played in that space.

I remember some fragments of his thoughts:

Following a disagreement, he said, "I see I am back in your good graces." I smiled and paused. "Or maybe you are back in my good graces. Probably they are related," he mused.

"Just because it is your birthday doesn't mean it is the day you were born."

"All you need is a man whose arms are big enough to go around you."
"Your life is yours. Turn on the master switch."
"The thing about mystery is that you never know when it will appear and where it will take you."
"What is it you offer me?" I ask. "Freedom," he says.
"Don't be afraid of rejection, it is not important at age 55."
"Why not let your tears lead the way and see where they can lead?"
"If a kite is in the sky you can pull it down, but words once spoken can never be retrieved."
"Here are bamboozle glasses, wear when needed."
"In the land of concrete, speak concrete."
"Imagine if you allow yourself to feel that hate instead of being nice. Imagine what other feelings could come out."
"Is the unconscious willing to pick up the invitation at will?"
"The couch or the chair, which one do you think will help you today?"
"People go to school but never learn to take risks. It is always scary and daunting, but without taking risk you will not grow."
"You don't have to work so hard for someone's love."

The summer after our August break, he told me that he wanted me to hear this from him and not someone else: he had been diagnosed with lymphoma, a slow-growing, indolent leukemia that robbed him of his energy but that he could live with the rest of his days. He was then 76.

Around that time I brought in a dream. I go out at night and look up at the sky and see the most incredible colors illuminated on the glass window. The moon is bright and full and moving along its axis. Coming into full view, there is an unfamiliar planet. I recognize that this is a once in a lifetime thing, and it feels wonderful. I call out for someone to hear me, but I have difficulty finding words to describe it, and then clouds obscure the view. Suddenly I realize that the planet is me. That I am full.

For Mannie's 75th birthday, there was a two-day celebratory conference in May, "For Mannie Who Will Be Turning 75 in the Year 2000." Just an hour before,

Adam Phillips had arrived from London to open the celebration. He said Mannie worked against the latent and luring Procrustean in psychoanalysis, with a distinction of blending need and neediness, surrender and submission, and paradoxical process. Mark Epstein (2005) spoke of their shared interest in Buddhism, and its influence on therapeutic action in psychoanalysis. Interested in Eastern religion, Mannie had spent time in Poona, India. Michael Eigen (2005) mentioned how Mannie's writing resonated for him in profound ways, especially with Eigen's description of faith undertaken with one's whole being, with all one's heart and with all one's soul. Bass et al. (2005) found in Mannie strength and wisdom and a source of generativity.

Jessica Benjamin (2005) paid tribute to Mannie, and the many things she learned from him in the 1970s and 1980s, when Mannie was her analyst. In paying homage to Mannie, she said, "We need to find a way to affirm what is unique and growing in each of us." Carolyn Clement (2005) celebrated Mannie as a founder of the Relational Track at Postdoc, and as a founding member of the board of *Psychoanalytic Dialogues*. She spoke of Mannie's infinite exploration of what it means to be and feel human. There was a characteristic respect, love, and appetite for the new, and openness to the unknown as evidenced in a creative, playful, deeply appreciative responsiveness that was experienced by all who knew him as supervisee, analysand, and colleague. Eventually, she assembled the tribute issue in *Psychoanalytic Dialogues* (2005).

During our first session back, in the sprit of his 75th birthday, I read Mannie a chapter of a novel I had been working on that drew on work we were doing together. It began:

Her mother's name was Claire, "light" in French, but she wasn't happy with her own light so she took the light of her daughter, the light of a different moon, and the mother harnessed it as her own. The daughter, then, was left without light and died inside. No light. No life.

"Mannie," I asked, "when actually is your birth date?" "The same day as your husband."

Year seven. Untitled Space is closed. The Mercer Hotel on Prince Street, a half block away, with its small lobby restaurant and lovely shrimp salad seemed like a good place to continue writing session notes. Mannie began taking two months off in the summer, July and August.

One Friday morning, the phone rang as I returned home after a day of patients. A woman's voice. "Dr. Ghent has to cancel his appointments, and he will call you when he is ready to resume." In two weeks, he called and I went in. "A mild heart attack," he said. "But I am fine now, don't worry, I'll be here for some time." He said that with such reassurance, as if it were possible to know that. I wanted to believe him.

217

One time, we talked about termination. I said, "I can't see leaving treatment. You will have to be the one to leave."

I wrote a poem for you, I said, at the next session. Can I read it to you? He reclined and got into a listening position. We play in the area of psychoanalysis and creativity.

> *Birdtime*
> A bird flies off in the drowsy sky
> Then calmly dawdles back
> A robin in birdtime
> In its fragility and merciless beauty
> For a short time only, it rests and soaks the view
> And sings too-weet-woo-too-weet-woo-too
> Then the bird of wonder flies away
> A soaring duet of flying wings
> No shoulds. No coulds. No what ifs
> She thinks the bird will be there forever
> But it will not
> The wanderer of infinite grace
> Comes together and separates
> Dropping in for a visit and dropping away
> Where is the bird going? Will it come back?
> She wants it to return. What is this creature?
> People mull around and confer. What is this?
> Don't you know it is a bird.
> A bird that thunders.
>
> (Zindel, 2003)

In response to Adam Phillips' remarks on Mannie's 75th birthday, Mannie wrote this commentary: "What would psychoanalysis be like if it had emerged not from medicine or psychiatry, but from developmental studies, from spiritual studies, or from poetry?" (Ghent, 2001, p. 39). Maybe that is why he reads poetry and narrative and myth in our sessions.

Notebook #3

He taught me about risk: "What people don't teach you and what you need to grow is called risk. If it wasn't scary and terrifying, it would not be called risk. We have to experience it, for that is the only way we change." Years ago, I had taken a photograph on safari in Africa at the Serengeti Plains – a leopard is jumping from tree to tree – and it felt like what Mannie had been taking about, caught in the middle of a jump without a safety net. I called the photograph "Risk." And when my patients are experiencing a place in their life when they need to take a leap of faith, I point to the photograph on my office wall. The leopard's jumping from

218

one branch of a tree to another tree, and I call what happens in the middle risk. Many patients carry that photo in them; Mannie talks to them. One day, years later, the photo spontaneously dropped to the floor and shattered. The glass replaced, "Risk" stayed in my office.

In winter of 2002, with the children in California, and Paul and I divorced for five years, Paul was diagnosed with terminal lung cancer. Paul was petrified of death. This was expressed explicitly in everything he wrote. Characters' monologues in his plays and novels, personal interviews, and other dialogue reflected this terror couched in humor. During every session, Mannie and I talked about loss, and mortality, and I asked Mannie if he was afraid of dying. I asked because death had always frightened me, too, especially having lost my mother so young at 17, or was it 16? Seriously considering the question, he paused for a minute and then said, "No. I am not."

While sitting with patients, I began having fantasies about them, wondering which I would want to be with if I were to become sick or die. I realize that I would want to be with someone whose humanity I have often felt in sessions, and in those final moments could be with me in loving kindness. In the end, I would not want to be with someone who cannot recognize me as a separate person. Dying is a uniquely individual act; it is at the same time a relational experience.

I read Mannie a fragment of the short story I had just written called "The Day of Michelangelo" (Zindel, 2005), which takes place in the church of Santa Croce in Florence. I sat straight in my chair, papers in hand. The part he most responded to was this section:

> Near the end [of Michelangelo's life] he said to a friend, "I have reached the twenty-fourth hour of my day." He was not afraid of death. He figured if God had created such a good life for him on earth, the same must be waiting for him in heaven.
>
> (p.102)

Mannie audibly concured and shook his head in total agreement. I continue:

> It was said that with his left hand he sculpted the brilliance of sunshine and its softer tones of yellow and with his right hand, he sculpt the feelings of night, darker colors, browns and grays. Dark absorbs time. After his David, the Pietas and the Slaves and the Sistine Chapel, the Last Supper, architectural domes, the politics of art, the fighting and the loving and the struggles of family and creations and inner hopes and anguish, it all comes down to this. This dreamless place of nature that summons us, that inevitable moment, big or small, little or giant, it calls us, even Michelangelo. Here a man, like any man, he lies.
>
> (p. 102)

Mannie grew quiet. I could see that he and I were in some shared place of mortality. Of immortality. Of timelessness.

It was also during these days that I was preparing to present a paper on creativity for a workshop at my analytic institute. One morning when Paul was ill at home, I sat down next to him on the edge of the bed. I asked what he knew about creativity that might apply to psychoanalysis. He said, "epiphenomenology," an idea used by Shakespeare which means that while you work on one creative thought, other ideas emerge that fling off of the original idea. Epiphenomenalism is like shooting stars. "For example," Paul said, "the sun is spinning in the sky and the sun has these little flares that fly off the surface and these sparks go off while the main event is going on." I love that word and whenever I find occasion, I drop it into conversation and immediately, Paul is there.

While Paul was in New York in this final stage of his illness, a revival of his play, *The Effect of Gamma Rays on Man-in-the-Moon Marigolds,* was in rehearsal at the Jean Cocteau Repertory Theatre downtown. The production, which had been scheduled nearly a year before, as timing would have it, was now actually opening in a few weeks, on March 6th.

The story of the play is autobiographical. Paul once told me that it poured out of him in a few days. One morning, awakened from sleep, next to his typewriter, lay this play which went on to win many awards including the Obie, Drama Desk, The Drama Critics Circle Award, and the Pulitzer Prize. He was determined to attend the opening night performance. That was important to him. The kids and I took him to the theater. Before the house lights dimmed, the director came on stage and said the playwright was present that evening, and Paul stood up, acknowledging the audience as they applauded. He seemed so happy. They did not know he was dying. And that was his last professional engagement. The play begins: Tillie, the character who most represented Paul, embodies hope against great odds, and delivers the first lines of the play as a voice-over. The stage is in shadow except for a spotlight focusing on the young girl. "He told me to look at my hand, for a part of it came from a star that exploded too long ago to imagine" (Zindel, 1973).

That was the last play he ever saw. His own. We met when *Marigolds* was being presented at the Cleveland Play House in 1971, 31 years ago, or was it 1970, when we were both young and starting our lives? The play had been a motif. Because of the play, we met; we married, and had a family. It all seemed to have come full circle.

On my last visit with Mannie before Paul died, we talked about perfection and accepting my imperfections. At the end of the session, when I got up to leave, Mannie came over and gave me a hug. I didn't know why. He would do it on occasions when I had a hard session and he felt I needed something. But this time was not that way. All the way down the elevator and back on the subway uptown,

I searched myself as to what was different. Was there a different quality of our interaction? The feeling was unsettling.

Six weeks after returning to New York, Paul passed away on March 27th.

After making funeral arrangements, I left a message on Mannie's machine: "Paul died today and the funeral will be Sunday at noon at Riverside Chapel on Amsterdam Avenue."

When we greeted people at Paul's funeral, I looked up and there was Mannie. I ran over to him and he hugged me or I hugged him, grateful he was there. Once in the chapel, Mannie was sitting in the middle of the center row. Occasionally, his eyes closed. Was he listening or had he fallen asleep? Or was he remembering Steve Mitchell's funeral in this same place two years ago? Following the service, I did not see him.

The next afternoon after the burial in Staten Island, I went back to the city. In the car I checked my machine. A colleague, a senior analyst, had called and left a message. "I am in Mannie's office. Please call me back." What was she doing in Mannie's office? It felt like an intrusion on her part. Quickly, I called the number and I got Mannie's wife. "Mannie died late last night. Around midnight. A heart attack lying in bed." "Where is he?" I wanted to know. I was confused. She paused and stuttered, "Well, I don't know," she said. Then she said, "He is in the funeral home." I had seen Mannie at noon the previous day, and he died at midnight 12 hours later. Stunned. Speechless. I couldn't cry. I could only breath. I couldn't be anything except frozen. The thought of losing him was unimaginable. When I got to my office, I had a phone conversation planned with a colleague. "I can't talk today. I just got a call that Mannie died. I can't talk. I can't think." "No," he said, "this is what you need to do. Talk to me." And so we talked of hope about mortality. He said that it was a gift when Paul talked to me about epiphenomenology and was in touch with his brilliant mind.

A week later, I went back to Riverside Chapel where Paul's funeral had been, and now, in the same waiting room, Mannie's family was accepting condolences. One speaker explained that Mannie died on the cusp of March 31 and April 1, April Fool's Day. Midnight. Which day was it then? Did he die on a Sunday or a Monday?

These huge men in my life gone, two men who shared a birthday – May 15th – now closely shared their death day: Paul March 27, and Mannie March 31.

Tuesday arrived. After nine years, the fierce impulse to head down to Soho for my session overwhelmed me. Instead, though, I found myself walking towards Central Park. Exactly at 11 a.m., I sat down on a bench. I had wanted to talk with Mannie about losing Paul. Now I had to talk with Mannie about losing Mannie. Something about talking with Mannie in my mind helped me. Suddenly I became aware of sitting on the bench. I gazed at my watch and saw that 45 minutes had elapsed.

Somehow, between sessions, these two huge people were gone and my world had changed. Time was up according to my Mannie clock. I can talk to him outside of sessions. Walking down the street. I can summon his voice and when I need him, he appears. For him, in the real world, time is up, but in my being, our time is endless. If one can invent a clock, I can invent time.

I got up from the bench and headed out of the park – a patient without an analyst. How do I say goodbye when I never got a chance to say goodbye. Like Michelangelo, just a man at the end like any other.

References

Bass, A., Black, M., & Dimen, M. (2005). Reflections on flat mountain. *Psychoanalytic Dialogues*, *15*, 159–168.

Benjamin, J. (2005). Introduction. *Psychoanalytic Dialogues*, *15*, 185–201.

Bollas, C. (1993). *Being a character: Psychoanalysis and self experience*. London: Routledge.

Clement, C. (2005). Introduction. *Psychoanalytic Dialogues*, *15*, 119–124.

Eigen, M. (2005). Healing longing in the midst of damage. *Psychoanalytic Dialogues*, *15*, 169–183.

Epstein, M. (2005). A strange beauty: Emmanuel Ghent and the psychologies of east and west. *Psychoanalytic Dialogues*, *15*, 125–138.

Ghent, E. (1989). Credo: The dialectics of one-person and two-person psychologies. *Contemporary Psychoanalysis*, *25*, 169–211.

Ghent, E. (1990). Masochism, submission, surrender. *Contemporary Psychoanalysis*, *26*, 108–136.

Ghent, E. (1992). Paradox and process. *Psychoanalytic Dialogues*, *2*, 135–159.

Ghent, E. (1995). Interaction in the psychoanalytic situation. *Psychoanalytic Dialogues*, *5*, 479–491.

Ghent, E. (1999). Afterword to "Masochism, submission, surrender." In S. A. Mitchell & L. Aron (Eds.), *Relational psychoanalysis: The emergence of a tradition* (pp. 239–242) Hillsdale, NJ: The Analytic Press.

Ghent, E. (2001). Need, paradox, and surrender: Commentary on paper by Adam Phillips. *Psychoanalytic Dialogues*, *11*, 23–41.

Grolnick, S. (1990). *The work and play of Winnicott*. Northvale, NJ: Aaronson.

Milner, M. (1950). *On not being able to paint*. New York: Taylor & Frances.

Mitchell, S. A., & Aron, L. (1999). Editors' introduction to Ghent, E. (1999), "Masochism, submission, surrender." In S. A. Mitchell & L. Aron (Eds.), *Relational psychoanalysis: The emergence of a tradition* (pp. 211–242) Hillsdale, NJ: The Analytic Press.

Phillips, A. (2001). On what we need: A celebration of the work of Emmanuel Ghent. *Psychoanalytic Dialogues*, *11*, 1–21.

Prevert, J. (1972). *Paroles*. Paris: Gallimard.

Rilke, R. M. (2000). *Essential Rilke*. New York: Harper Collins.

Winnicott, D. W. (1953). Transitional objects and transitional phenomena – A study of the first not-me possession. *International Journal of Psycho-Analysis*, *34*, 89–97.

Winnicott, D. W. (1992). Metapsychological and clinical aspects of regression within the psycho-analytical set-up. In *Through Paediatrics to Psycho-Analysis: Collected Papers*. New York: Brunner Mazel.

Zindel, B. (2003). Birdtime. *Psychoanalytic Perspectives*, *1*(1), 91.

Zindel, B. (2005). The day of Michelangelo. *Psychoanalytic Perspectives*, *2*(2), 95–103.

Zindel, P. (1973). *The effect of gamma rays on man-in-the-moon marigolds*. New York: Harper Collins.

Zindel, P., & Zindel, B. (1980). *A star for the latecomer*. New York: Harper Collins.

17

STROKE AND THE FRACTURING OF THE SELF

Rebuilding a life and a practice

Deborah Pines

It was the end of March 2008. I was on vacation in Antigua, and I could hardly imagine feeling more fully alive. I was about to take over as sole editor of the journal *Psychoanalytic Perspectives* in June, after six months as its co-editor. My practice was busy, and I was fit and healthy. The weather was beautiful, the sky crystalline, and I began the day with a scuba dive. In the afternoon, I took a yoga class, after which I had a tennis lesson. Then I planned to go to dinner with my husband and another couple we'd just met.

Toward the end of yoga that afternoon, I was doing a shoulder stand and felt a sudden twinge in my neck. I didn't think anything of it, and after the class was over, I went to tennis. During the lesson, I had some heartburn, but again, I didn't think it was anything to worry about. With very little time before dinner, I ran back to my room to get dressed. I was taking a shower when I suddenly had a strange feeling in my eye.

"I feel like I'm having a migraine aura," I called to my husband, Tony, in the bedroom.

"Don't worry," he called back. "You've never had a migraine. I'm sure it's nothing."

We met up with our new friends, and after drinks at the bar, the four of us made our way into the dining room and sat down. Within moments, I noticed my silverware appeared to be moving around on the table. It was disconcerting, and I felt a moment of panic. But before I had a chance to say anything, I lost consciousness and fell to the floor. It was as if I'd been hit by a truck. One minute I was able to place my feet on the ground, and the next moment, the ground had disappeared from beneath me.

My life was torn asunder. It has taken me more than four years to try to put it back together.

This is a story about trauma, abandonment, loss, hope, love, and the painfully slow process of reconnection. It is about being abandoned by a brain that had served me very well for nearly 60 years – a brain that I completely took for granted. It's also about feeling abandoned by my family, friends, and colleagues when I needed them most, and the sense that my family and my patients had of being abandoned by me. It's about the gulf that grew between me and everyone I care about – the trauma I experienced, and the vicarious trauma they experienced. Finally, it's about my path to healing, and theirs, which continues in small but incremental steps to this day.

Back home

As it turned out, I hadn't lost any significant physical capacity, nor was my speech slurred, but this only served to mask the extent of the losses I had suffered. The world was swiftly spinning around me. Only rarely did I touch down long enough to sense what was happening.

It took Tony quite a while to get us a flight home, but the next day, we flew back to New York. At 8:00 the next morning, we were in the neurologist's office. She asked me a series of questions, which I answered in monosyllables, and at one point she told me to write down where I was. I wrote something like, "I'm lost." Tony was horrified, but I didn't even recognize that there was a reason to be upset. After a few more questions, the neurologist told me I'd suffered a stroke and admitted me to the hospital.

I spent a week there as they adjusted the dosage of the blood-thinner, Heparin, to assure that blood was reaching my brain so I wouldn't be at risk of a second stroke. I remember my younger daughter Emily taking me for walks up and down the hall and working with me on my language. "Okay, tell me all the nouns you know that start with B," she would say. After wracking my brain, I would finally find a word or two, but often they were adjectives or verbs. At one point, she recalls, I said, "Belligerent!" but I don't remember that or much of anything from that period. As confused as I was, I was aware enough to be stunned and to recognize that much of my memory had simply vanished. I assumed Emily was equally dismayed. Only later did I learn that while it was difficult for her, she was so convinced I would improve quickly that she didn't even feel worried, much less horrified.

What none of us said – but all of us were feeling on some deep level – is that I could have died. As I write this today, I am filled with sadness about what happened to me. It's as if an intruder broke into my house and bludgeoned me, and I was helpless against the assault. The shock of the stroke hid the first feelings of loss. But eventually, anger and depression would rise up in me. Today, the grief about all I lost sometimes feels overwhelming.

When I returned home from the hospital, one of the first things I did – at my neurologist's suggestion – was to call several speech therapists. They all assumed I was calling on behalf of the woman who'd had the stroke; I had to explain that I was the patient. My speech sounded normal, even though I was struggling to find words and form sentences.

I also called all of my patients to tell them I'd had a stroke and to explain that I would be back in a week or two. I thought I was telling the truth, but I was in such an altered state that I don't really know what my thought process was at the

time. That said, "whenever the analyst feels compelled or chooses . . . to reveal
something about herself to a patient, she remains responsible for that revelation as
she considers every subsequent interaction in the life of that particular treatment"
(Pizer, 1997, p. 457). I was not capable of thinking about the impact of my disclosure on each of my patients. That ability came only much later.

Each week, I called my patients back. "Next week," I told them. But as time
passed, it became more and more apparent that I was far from ready to return to
work. One afternoon, a friend – also a neurologist – said to me, "Just tell them
you're out for the count. You'll call when you're ready to come back." Those were
the hardest calls I've ever made, but he was right. I was in no state to resume my
work. I asked each of my patients if they wanted me to refer them to someone else,
but all of them said they would prefer to wait. As soon as I divulged this news to
them, I felt much better. Now I could focus on my own healing.

I spent the next two months walking three miles a day, visiting the speech therapist twice a week, seeing my own therapist three times a week, and even lifting
weights again. I started slowly, but returning to working out was a sign to me that
I was getting healthy again, at least physically. Each day, I took a two-hour nap
after lunch, which proved to be a crucial element of my healing. It was a time for
filing away things I'd relearned during the day, but also a time of complete peace
and a much needed respite from the challenges of the day (Taylor, 2008). I also
slept about 11 hours at night.

My mood during this time was relatively good, although Tony and my daughters said that I was almost completely flat in my expression. I simply wasn't
experiencing many emotions during this period. I was aware of feeling anger occasionally, as I did toward the speech therapist who wouldn't come to my house or
an acupuncture practitioner who said she could help me but didn't. Otherwise,
nearly all of my energy was focused on physical healing. I had very little left over
for either my own feelings, or the feelings of others.

Back to work

In the middle of June, two and a half months after the stroke, I decided to start seeing my patients again. I was frightened by the prospect, and I didn't have much to
offer, but I thought they needed to see me. I also felt I needed to see them to remind
myself that I was still a psychoanalyst. I needed to remember that I had a calling,
and that my life hadn't simply come to a full and permanent stop. I also needed to
see them because each patient was important to me, and I wanted to show them
I was okay and still available. I called each one and explained that I was coming
back to work and would see them once a week for the next six weeks. Then I'd
take my annual vacation in August, and be ready to resume my practice full-time
when I returned in September.

One of my patients, who had emailed me several times during the preceding
three months, had been struggling with some minor physical problems. When we
met, she asked me how I was, and when I said I was feeling pretty good, she went

on to discuss her own ailments. I felt relieved to have someone else's problems to think about, but I wasn't aware that because I looked and sounded okay, it was difficult for her to see that I was still deeply impaired. Still, I was able to be empathic around her struggles with work and her physical condition. This was a patient whom I'd been seeing for five years, and I remember feeling that she was particularly warm and loving to me that first day back. Being able to connect with her helped me to feel that I was going to heal eventually.

When I asked another patient how he was feeling about my absence, he said he had been worried about me and that he cared a lot about my health. At my prodding, he then added that he might be a little angry with me. I asked him to say more, but he declined to delve deeper. I was gratified that he was able to say even this much, but as I look back, I realize that like many of my patients, he probably felt deeply abandoned by me. I wish I had been able to recognize this at the time, but I was still so limited in my ability to perceive and articulate my observations. Paul Russell (2006) says that the patient needs us to know what we do not know: "Some experiences are so scorching, some feelings so frightening or painful, that, at whatever cost, the patient will know far more about it than we do. The most important source of resistance in the treatment process is the therapist's resistance to what the patient feels" (p. 635).

A third patient emailed me several times while I was recovering. In the last note I received from her, she wrote the following:

As for the apparent "resistance" to therapy, there are two things that cross my mind, though I don't know their significance. One was that I THOUGHT you said you would be in touch with me by the end of May to set up an appointment. When I didn't hear from you by June, and saw the checks were not paid, I started to wonder if you were dead, or dying, and if not, wondered why no call and no cashed checks.

The other thought is that I have tons of questions about your illness, as I feel like it relates to me. We are both post-menopausal women, and with my weight and diabetes, I have stroke-related risks that might be greater than yours. I am not sure what I want to ask, or what would be crossing the boundaries of our relationship. This makes me uncomfortable.

Today, I can see that this woman was deeply in pain. Prior to my stroke, she would never have even asked how I was feeling, much less written these words. Now she was forced by circumstances to imagine I was dead or dying. However shocking she found my actual illness to be, she realized, probably with tremendous fear, that her own risk of a stroke was even greater than mine had been. Today, I'm able to recognize her terror and confusion about why I – and not she – had the stroke, and I feel deeply empathic about her fears of the future. At the time, however, I didn't have the resources to understand what she was experiencing. In response to her note, I wrote that I was sorry for the delay in getting back to her, and I invited her to ask me any questions she'd like. She was 30 minutes late for our first session, and she spent the final 15 minutes avoiding my inquiry about why the lateness might have happened.

After one more uneventful, pre-vacation session, my patient wrote me a long email in which she talked again about her fear of having a stroke like mine and, even more frightening to her, of dying alone. I wrote a brief response that neglected to acknowledge the raw emotions she revealed. Six months after my summer vacation, she stopped coming to therapy altogether. After nine years, she simply left, with no opportunity for a termination process. She said it was because she could no longer afford to pay for sessions. I assume her fear about her own health risks and my inability to connect with her feelings about the loneliness of illness were among the real reasons it felt impossible for her to continue with me. Had I been further along in my own healing, I would have asked what it was about becoming ill that was so terrifying, and what made it seem so probable and so hopeless. I also might have shared some of my journey with her, in an effort to soothe her and to serve as a source of identification. But I simply wasn't yet capable of that.

All of my patients seemed reticent to express what they were feeling about my long absence. Upon my return, they each asked how I was, but when I said I was doing pretty well, they didn't ask for more. In large part, I suspect this was because they were there to focus on their own concerns and my absence had already interrupted that process for three months. Probably, I unconsciously encouraged that inclination. I looked fine to them, they wanted me to be fine, and when I brushed off their worry, they seemed happy to accept my answer. The problem is that my own denial about the extent of my illness did not allow for exploration. Our collusion in mutual dissociation did not serve any of us well. I was going about my life as if nothing was different or wrong, but in truth, I was struggling every day to come up with the words to express even the simplest things, and trying to understand what was happening to me. Only in retrospect have I realized that I was unable to think deeply about what was going on with my patients, or what was happening between us.

I went back to work because I felt that it was important to me and to my patients to begin again. At the time, I didn't realize that I wasn't yet able to really do the work. My husband, my analyst, and my supervisor all said that I should go ahead and try. Once again, I suspect there was mutual collusion and dissociation. None of us was comfortable seeing me as wounded and limited. We all wanted the old Deborah back, and in our different ways, we pretended that she was. Today, now that I am able to see so much more of what I was missing with each of my patients – when I realize how much they were experiencing that I simply could not comprehend or address – I feel shame and sadness. At the same time, I suspect and of course hope that, on balance, I made the right choice in continuing to see them. They needed as much of me as could be present, and for all my limitations, I still provided them with continuity and kindness, and some measure of empathy. I wasn't bringing any of them what they deserved from a therapist, but I don't believe I was hurting them either. The only patient who clearly wasn't getting what she needed chose to leave.

The beach

Tony and I took our summer vacation that year at the beach. We rented a house, sight unseen, that turned out to be lovely. Our daughters came out for the first week, which I thought would be great. However, Emily, then 23, was going through significant struggles of her own. One day, she spent an hour sitting with us in the kitchen, explaining that she didn't want to work but instead wanted to have a baby right away. Emily is very persuasive, and I certainly didn't have the resources to argue with her. Tony tried, but she was in such an extreme state of mind that even he didn't have much success.

After the conversation was over, I went to the beach and met up with my older daughter Kate, then 27, who was visiting with a friend. I started to explain the situation to them, and Kate became furious. I couldn't defend myself because I didn't understand her anger, nor could I summon the words to express my confusion. She was upset at what was happening with her sister, and at the fact that Tony and I hadn't been more forceful in responding to Emily. All I remember feeling was that she should be directing her anger at her sister, not at me. Kate and her friend left the beach immediately, but I stayed behind. I felt wounded and bewildered, and I tried to make sense of what had just happened. Kate clearly had no idea of the extent of the larger struggles I was confronting, and I was unable to share this with her. What I needed most were kindness, empathy, and encouraging words. I wasn't prepared to deal with anything else.

Only years later did I understand that the cause of this disconnect between my family and me was rooted in a failure of communication. My husband and especially my two children assumed I had recovered by this point because that was the message I conveyed with the limited vocabulary I had access to. When they asked me how I was doing, I always said fine. My capacity for self-awareness remained limited. More recently, when I spoke with Kate about that beach confrontation, she told me she had no idea that I was speaking through the lens of my stroke. She heard my description of the conversation with Emily as passive and enabling of something that might not be in Emily's best interest. It sounded to her as if I wasn't challenging her sister's unrealistic plans. It never occurred to her that I simply didn't have the resources to stand up to Emily. Today, I recognize that the disparity between what I said about how I was feeling and how I actually behaved was not only confusing, but also added strain to my relationship with each of my family members. We were like distressed ships passing in the night.

In thinking about all of this, I've been drawn back in time. As a child, whenever I would cry, my mother would send me upstairs to my room and tell me to not come back down until I had a smile on my face. This screen memory is vivid, and the ramifications still feel stunning and devastating. That little girl with the required smile on her face was the one who appeared before my family – and everyone else in my life – in the weeks and months after my stroke. I was at least partly reliving the trauma of my childhood. In the family of my adulthood, I had always been the rock – the person who comforted others. My reluctance – my inability even – to share my real feelings, was borne of a very early fear that to show up with anything other than a smile on my face would only insure my rejection and abandonment. It was too dangerous to be vulnerable, even at my time of greatest need.

During the second week at the beach, Tony and I had the house to ourselves. I welcomed this quiet time together, but almost immediately, I became very anxious. I was anticipating the coming September, which seemed overwhelming. I was intending to see my patients again on a regular basis, while also starting a Supervisory Training Program (STP) at my institute. As mentioned, I was also taking over as sole editor of the Journal, and planning to hold a retreat at my home for the entire Journal staff in September. I wasn't ready to take all of this on so early in my recovery, but the train was about to leave the station, full steam ahead, and I saw no way of stopping it.

My return

As September loomed, my anxiety was at a fever pitch. Labor Day came and went, and I began to see my patients again. As it was I was barely getting by, but then I started STP and had my first Journal meeting. Both were very difficult. STP was hard because my memory had been decimated – I remembered virtually nothing I had read during my psychoanalytic training and retained very little from what I was currently reading. I was also assigned two supervisees right away, and I had very little to say about the cases they were presenting to me.

Then there was my first Journal meeting. Two members of the editorial board, among the most senior members of my institute, asked me to send long and detailed emails out to the staff, twice a week. I was barely able to type a single sentence at that point. The notion of writing two comprehensive emails a week was completely unimaginable – even impossible. I told the board members that if this were required of the editor, they'd have to find someone else to do the job. We all knew that there was no one else available at the time, so I carried on.

Today, I realize the issue was not the exact number of weekly emails that needed to be sent. These colleagues thought it important to keep the editorial staff abreast of what was happening, and I understand now that this was the job of the editor. If I'd been in possession of all my senses, I might initially have felt defensive, but I would have eventually realized their request was valid.

Late in November, I began to feel that my supervision program was simply too difficult for me, and I wondered if I should quit. I was not learning much in class, and I was contributing very little to the group. I also believed I was not giving enough to my two supervisees – one of whom I found particularly difficult to supervise. I couldn't talk to these students about theory, and I didn't have the wherewithal to talk to them much about their patients. To make matters even worse, I felt depressed, which was probably partly attributable to the demands I was facing, and partly to the organic nature of the stroke itself. I discussed the idea of dropping out of the program with my analyst. He seemed to agree, saying that I could leave the program and take it up again the next time it was given, which was in another two years. I called the head of the STP program, who was also my teacher that semester, and told him how I was feeling. He was distressed that I was thinking of quitting, and suggested that I come in at least one more time to tell the group what I was thinking.

The following Wednesday, I met with the group, and we had a long dialogue. They were kind enough to say they wanted me to stay, but that was small solace. I was anticipating, among other things, having to write detailed evaluations about each of my supervisees, and then present those evaluations at a meeting with of a number of faculty members and supervisors. The two tasks seemed overwhelming, but I finally had an idea that seemed plausible. We would all be assigned individual senior supervisors in February to assist us with our supervisees. I suggested I might be able to begin with my supervisor as early as December, and perhaps she could help me with the evaluations. The group thought this was a great idea.

As it turned out, I stayed in the STP. It was very difficult for me, but it became more manageable as the year progressed and my anxiety subsided.

Family matters

As a family, we continued to have a difficult time. Kate, who was in graduate school when I had my stroke, had come home as soon as she heard the news and arrived at the hospital shortly after I was admitted. She visited me every day of that week. When she went back to school, she called me each day to see how I was doing. It was wonderful to have someone to talk to – someone I really loved. But Kate assumed I would get better quickly, and that I'd return to being the nurturing mother I had always been. That didn't happen, and after several months, I realized she had become very angry. This was a time of great struggle in her own life. Not only was she in her first year of a three-year MFA program at graduate school and directing her first play, but she had also recently broken up with her boyfriend of six years, after realizing he wasn't the person she wanted to marry. Even so, he had been a great caretaker, and that was very much the role I'd always played in our family – a reliable listener, the person who helped everyone else sort out their feelings, the good mom. Kate had lost her boyfriend and me at the same time, and she was lonely. She was furious that the stroke had happened, and that I wasn't getting better faster, and she felt abandoned and unseen by me. I wished I could have been there for her, but it wasn't possible. All I wanted at the time was for her to be empathic to me. Perhaps we could have been more successful at giving those things to each other had I been able to share my struggle with her, but that would have required more fully recognizing it in myself and then feeling safe enough to acknowledge it.

Christmas arrived, and we had invited a dozen people for the holiday dinner – another venture I took on as I always had before, but which I soon learned I wasn't equipped to manage. Kate and Emily were a wonderful help to me as we spent the day preparing the meal. Shortly before everyone was expected to arrive, I realized I was utterly exhausted. I went upstairs to shower, but before I did, I lay down on my bed to take a brief rest and fell fast asleep. I missed numerous calls over the intercom from Kate, as she grew anxious about finishing the cooking and greeting the early guests. Suddenly, she burst into my room, woke me up, and yelled at me for leaving her to complete the meal herself. It was another moment of disconnect. I couldn't meet her needs, and she didn't recognize mine.

The next morning, she apologized. We had a long talk in which I explained how exhausted I had felt the night before and generally, and how important and unavoidable the lengthy recovery time was turning out to be. It was good to hear her apology, but the incident and of course overall experience of my illness and slow recovery was so painful for both of us. Looking back on that evening and the following morning, I recognize that I wasn't the only one in denial. The fact that I fell asleep was unprecedented on an occasion like this. What did Kate think had happened to me? Why didn't she come up sooner? We were unconscious co-conspirators in denying the painful reality of my situation.

"The distance and turmoil the issues [of stroke] bring in their wake can divide a family, just when support is needed most. Without help, your emotional state can unravel. The family can disintegrate further, with each member feeling more and more alone" (Senelick, 2010, p. 215). Indeed, my husband and children had lost the person who in many ways held us all together. Simultaneously, I was feeling profoundly alone – and this was only the beginning. The mutual misunderstanding would last for nearly four years.

During this early period, several of my patients became very angry with me as well. One young man actually walked out of the office about ten minutes early because he was enraged and upset. In the following session, he denied that it had anything to do with my stroke or my subsequent absence. When he told me that he was feeling abandoned by his friends and his mother, I failed to recognize that he was also saying he felt abandoned by me. Today, I would be able to ask him about these feelings – how I had left him for several months, and perhaps even that when I came back I wasn't the same therapist he had known. But we were both disconnected from what was happening between us. Dissociation that occurs within the psychoanalytic session does more than keep one from feeling threatening feelings. It also destroys the actual self that experienced the trauma (Bromberg, 1993). I couldn't help my patient with this reenactment of his original trauma, because I was suffering from trauma of my own.

As a result of my stroke, I have suffered tremendous shame with my patients, my colleagues, and my family. I still have the sense that I am less than they are, less than I was, and I'm constantly afraid I will always be less than I hope to be. I am determined to share this shame with my patients when I am aware of it, and when I can do so without burdening them. Often, however, I don't know that it is there, and even when I do, I am frequently unable to articulate it. I'm working with my supervisor and my therapist to recognize when these feelings arise at work, and to find ways to manage or address it in the treatment. Although contemporary psychoanalysis has looked for ways to minimize shame, there is no way to avoid it all together (Orange, 2008). "There are times when we . . . make judgments about ourselves out of a sense of total isolation . . . At such times, we may feel frighteningly alone, yet simultaneously observed under a spotlight by a harsh audience" (Morrison, 2008, p. 75). My imaginary audience is made up of all the psychoanalysts who, I believe, are judging me critically, whether or not they actually are. Shame is difficult to process, both for my patients and for me.

The following August, I decided to go away for a long weekend with my two daughters. I was vaguely aware that the effects of the stroke were going to make our time together more difficult, but I thought we could weather it. As it turned out, the girls were irritated with me – Kate had already made that clear. Emily had begun the trip believing I was doing very well. By the end she was more aware of my limitations, and couldn't understand why I seemed to be denying them.

When we arrived home, the girls and Tony confronted me about the growing chasm between their perception of me, and their understanding of my perception of myself. They wanted a straight story: How was I really? They were angry because they believed I was purposely hiding my ongoing deficits.

Tony and the girls told me I was less attentive and less empathic than before my stroke. They felt that I often didn't fully attend to, process, or consider information that was presented to me. They described my memory for details of conversations as having decreased significantly, and noted that I was often silent. I felt attacked, and I didn't really know how to respond, but I knew their perceptions were accurate.

My husband and two children are very different from one another, but they are all highly intelligent, exceptionally verbal, and extraordinarily sensitive to their own needs. Before my stroke, they experienced me as insightful, caring, empathic, and very tuned in. Our overt dynamic was that I attended to their needs more than they did to mine, and they had come to rely on my availability and on the container that I provided for each of them (Bion, 1963). In hindsight, I recognize that we were all not just traumatized by my stroke, but also retraumatized regularly by our inability to communicate. Consciously, I felt I was simply trying to get better. My level of self-awareness, verbal capacity, and even empathy were dramatically diminished and that was in part because I was using all of my available resources in the service of healing. I didn't have much left over to give, cognitively or emotionally.

As a result of my ongoing struggles, I just wasn't the mom and wife my family had known. They felt undernourished, and I felt surprised and hurt that they didn't seem to recognize the significant progress I was making. We were at a painful impasse. At the end of the confrontation, I told them I had learned of a neuropsychologist who might be able to help me, and promised to make an appointment to see him.

Several weeks later, I spent the whole day at the neuropsychologist's office, taking a huge battery of tests. Two weeks after that, I went back for the results. My IQ was 112, more than 10 points below what it had been before the stroke. I had predicted I would do poorly on many of the tests, but it was very depressing, none-theless, to hear these numbers. The only thing the neuropsychologist offered was medication aimed at improving my focus. He gave me a list of four medicines to try, and one by one I did. But each one kept me awake at night, so I couldn't use them. He did say one thing I found reassuring. In his experience, it took at least three years for someone to overcome the effects of a stroke like mine. This was a great source of solace to me, and to my family. It gave us all hope that I would eventually fully recover.

During this time, however, my relationship with Tony continued to be a chal-lenge. Aware now that my recovery was going to take longer than we initially anticipated, it had become even harder for him to deal with my language prob-lems, my lack of intellectual curiosity, and my relative emotional flatness. Tony suggested we visit my analyst together. What I didn't realize was how angry he was at this man. When we got there, he immediately launched into a tirade. He had expressed concern in the past that I hadn't acknowledged my deficits, and he was convinced that my therapist wasn't seeing me accurately, or recognizing the extent of my limitations. My therapist didn't react to my husband's anger and went on with the session. He did help us both see, perhaps for the first time, how traumatized Tony and our daughters were feeling as a result of my stroke, and how much they were suffering, as I was in a different way. Tony became more aware of how much pain his anger was causing me, and how much empathy and under-standing I needed. The session lasted more than an hour and a half, and when we left, Tony seemed quite moved. But very quickly it became clear that he still felt my therapist wasn't recognizing the extent of my limitations, or truly challenging me to take them on.

Back to the beach

We went back to the beach in August, more than three years since my stroke. During the vacation I spent a good deal of time working with the *Psychoana-lytic Perspectives* lawyer on a contract with Psychoanalytic Electronic Publishing (P-E-P), and writing a paper for a conference the following March. I felt as if I was "back."

One afternoon, about a week before we were scheduled to return to our home in New York, Tony asked me to take a walk to the beach. It seemed like a wonderful idea. As we strolled away from the house, he began to tell me that he and the girls thought I had made great strides over the past several years. But he was concerned that there had been little additional change in recent months. He felt I had become too accepting of the way I was, with no motivation to improve. He had begun to worry that if nothing changed, our marriage would not survive. I felt blindsided and shocked. For a long time, he had been urging me to think more reflectively and to challenge myself to understand what I was feeling, but these comments seemed harsh. It wasn't fair that he was painting such a grim portrait, when – in my mind –

234

I had improved so much. Still, I tried to keep an open mind and not let my defenses take over. Tony made many suggestions that proved to be helpful. For one thing, he encouraged me to keep a journal and to think deeply about what I was writing. He also thought that we should go into family therapy, to which I readily agreed. Additionally, we decided to reinstate the Saturday morning conversations we'd engaged in faithfully for the 15 years before my stroke. In these conversations, we discussed everything on our minds, which had been hugely important in our marriage, because it meant that we always had a specific time to talk about the things that were bothering each of us.

We have resumed our talks, and the four of us spent a number of sessions in family therapy. The talks and sessions allowed us to speak honestly and openly about the pain each had suffered. During that time, I decided to leave my therapist after it became clear that he was coming between my family and me, painting them as enemies, and himself as my only ally. It proved to be a difficult but healthy decision. Tony worked closely with me on this chapter, as did both my daughters. We all feel that with each passing day, I am finding my way back to the attentive, engaged, caring, insightful person I was before the stroke. They have also learned to be more patient, aware that I still sometimes have trouble finding my words and articulating my needs. We're much better able to understand one another, and our connection and closeness feels restored.

I know now what it's like to struggle for words and to lose access not only to knowledge and understanding I've spent a lifetime accumulating, but also to my deepest emotions. I know what it's like to feel I've let my patients and my family down, and how painful it is not just for me but for them as well. I know what it's like to feel terribly alone, and to want only to be comforted. I wish my stroke had never happened. It has been a harrowing, humbling and, at times, humiliating experience.

At the same time, I have learned a great deal, not just from living the experience of my stroke over the last four years, but also from writing this chapter. I've learned that the trauma I experienced in my childhood is much greater than I ever knew, and that the smile on my face is a mask for a great deal of pain I find threatening to share. I've also learned that keeping these experiences to myself has been hurtful to many of the people I care about in my life – not only my family, but also my patients and colleagues.

I've discovered that my default defense is to dissociate and compartmentalize my emotions. But I've also learned that I have a wonderful ability to see and appreciate the world around me in new ways, perhaps because I've had to rely more on my right hemisphere since my stroke. I take immense pleasure watching the birds in my yard alight in the trees and around my bird feeders, much as I do observing the brilliant full moon shining brightly in the sky.

Most important, I've learned that all the pain I have felt and the shame I've experienced from my stroke are not my destiny. Step by step, with much work, patience, and resolve, I'm reclaiming my life. The journey back to health continues.

References

Bion, W. R. (1963). *Elements of psychoanalysis*. London: Heinemann.

Bromberg, P. M. (1993). Shadow and substance: A relational perspective on clinical process. *Psychoanalytic Psychology, 10*, 147–168.

Morrison, A. P. (2008). The analyst's shame. *Contemporary Psychoanalysis, 44*, 65–82.

Orange, D. M. (2008). Whose shame is it anyway: Lifeworlds of humiliation and systems of restoration (or "The analyst's shame"). *Contemporary Psychoanalysis, 44*, 83–100.

Pizer, B. (1997). When the analyst is ill: Dimensions of self-disclosure. *Psychoanalytic Quarterly, 66*, 450–469.

Russell, P. L. (2006). The negotiation of affect. *Contemporary Psychoanalysis, 42*, 621–636.

Senelick, R. C. (2010). *Living with stroke*. Birmingham, AL: Healthsouth Press.

Taylor, J. B. (2008). *My stroke of insight*. New York: Viking.

18

PSYCHOANALYSIS IN OLD AGE

The patient and the analyst

Martin S. Bergmann

My admission

Before I begin, I have to tell you that this chapter has a special significance for me. It is an admission paper to a very exclusive club called "Gerontocracy," those who have remained creative in old age. So far, its members are Sophocles, Goethe, Verdi, Bertrand Russell, and George Bernard Shaw. Since I am nearly 100 at the time of this writing, I am entitled to membership, but only if this chapter is good enough.

The current economic meltdown has made it clear that we live in a society that cannot plan. The marriage between capitalism and democracy is in trouble. The current problem of old age has a sociological aspect. Progress in medicine has prolonged life beyond expectation, but our social capacity to make these last years productive – or at least tolerable – has lagged significantly behind the capacity of medicine to keep old people alive.

Old age is often associated with illness, loneliness, and bereavement. As a result, many middle-aged men and even more women spend a great deal of their life's energy taking care of those aging parents. "Honor thy father and thy mother" has become a burdensome commandment. After decades of separation, parent and child are now once more in very close contact. Wounds of infancy that have not completely healed are reopened; with them, Oedipal conflicts are reawakened. A large literature within psychoanalysis and in popular culture has emerged describing the horror of old age. I do not wish to contribute to this literature. The aged and aging population offers a professional challenge to psychoanalytic therapy, and I want to examine this challenge. This vast caretaking population often requires what we are accustomed to call supportive psychotherapy to help alleviate their burden, but this therapy will not be the subject of this chapter.

The older patient population falls into two groups: those so burdened by what old age brought that they need support, and those who need and can bring about new insight and some change. Fortunately, there are therapists willing to give patients in the first group support, but we do not ask these patients to be capable of intrapsychic change. It is important that we do not confuse the two populations and the two tasks.

The older patient in analysis

Freud, it is well-known, did not believe that older people should be analyzed. In "Sexuality in the Aetiology of the Neuroses," published in 1898 (before *The Interpretation of Dreams*), he says:

> Psycho-analytic therapy is not at present applicable to all cases. It has, to my knowledge, the following limitations. It demands a certain degree of maturity and understanding in the patient and is therefore not suited for the young or for adults who are feeble-minded or uneducated. It also fails with people who are very advanced in years, because, owing to the accumulation of material in them, it would take up so much time that by the end of the treatment they would have reached a period of life in which value is no longer attached to nervous health.
>
> (p. 282)

Freud feared that their analysis would only lead to the recognition of mistaken and lost opportunities, without the capacity to use this new knowledge gained by psychoanalysis for new and more productive ends. He feared that under such conditions, the analysis would not "pay for itself." I find this attitude of Freud's too commercial, as if psychoanalysis has to be financially profitable to be worth the effort and expense. Instead, I have adopted the slogan of the shipping industry when they were competing with transatlantic airlines: "Getting there is half the fun." Psychoanalysis should return benefits from the first hour when the patient meets the analyst who knows how to listen, not condemn, and who knows that he or she must know a great deal about a patient before venturing an opinion or an interpretation. Or, to put it in the language of the structural phase, we know now that insights obtained in the course of an analysis can be appropriated by the superego to punish the patient for opportunities lost; they can also be grabbed by the id and lead to acting out, or be used by the ego to master past traumatic events. Which one of the three possibilities takes place will not depend on age but on the analyst's skill. As therapists, we are responsible for delivering our understanding in such a way that the patient's ego can make use of them and not for the superego to attack the patient or for the id to endanger the patient by acting upon the revelations. We must make sure our interpretations are of use to the ego and not subject to the commands of the id or the superego.

Having said all that against Freud, he is not so easily dismissed. As we get older, we become more dependent on the very environment we have created. A couple may be unhappy together, but they have a house they are attached to, they have children and pets in common, and a circle of friends they fear losing. They fear the empty house, the loss of the caretaker in illness, and that they do not have enough libido for a new relationship. So let us assume that after due deliberation the analysand decides that no change is possible. Does that mean the whole endeavor had been for naught? The American ethos would be inclined to say yes. I would argue that there is a difference between having examined the situation constructively, and having reached a decision that no change is possible and having been afraid to attempt this examination. The issue is whether the examined life is richer than living in fear of such an examination. Psychoanalysis has its roots in the conviction that the examined life, regardless of whether it was fulfilling or not, is richer than a life in which such an examination was not undertaken out of the fear that such an endeavor would result in depression.

One of the main characteristics of old age is the disappearance of the future as a dimension. We are not always aware of it, but our lives consist of remembering or reanimating the past, a sense of the present, and hopes for the future. In old age, the future as a dimension disappears, and there is nothing to hope for. The loss of the future tends to accentuate the past, popularly known as "memory lane." This compulsory re-examination, this looking back, can often become needlessly painful. There is much to be said in favor of not undertaking this re-examination alone, but rather with a benign and objective therapist. The therapist's main function in the examination of the life lived is to not allow it to fall under the domination of the superego and result in a depression.

Presenting problems of the elderly patient

I have noticed that as I have gotten older, my patients have also gotten older. What are the problems of the patients who seek our help in their upper 60s and beyond? If my practice is any guide, and if we exclude those who have been hit by cruel old age and largely need supportive therapy (that is, ordinary aging men and women), the most prevalent problem is the relationship to their adult children. Often, their children are clinging and unable to move away from home into a world that appears too strange, too hostile, or too rejecting. In other words, neither they nor their parents have mastered the final step of separation. Many of these children have become accusatory or hostile, without the capacity to move away. One benefit of analyzing older patients is that their relationship to their adult children will undergo a change for the better.

The next problem of this population is in the sphere of love. In a long marriage, the formerly romantic partner can become either parent or child, but is no longer the sexual partner: for the woman, the husband has increasingly become a father figure; for the man, the wife becomes a mother figure. In these cases, the incest taboo has caught up with the couple. Freud visualized the Oedipus complex as the kernel of the infantile neurosis: if it is not overcome in childhood, it threatens adult sexuality by transferring the Oedipal taboo to the adult relationship. The Oedipal taboo will manifest itself in impotence, premature ejaculation, or frigidity. In long relationships, therefore, the partners are in danger of being transformed from sexual lovers to each other's parents. Thus, after many years, the Oedipal taboo that may have been successfully overcome now returns. Husbands slip and call their wives by their mother's name, and women refer to their husbands by their children's name. Psychoanalytic help may be necessary to prevent such a return of the Oedipus complex and the incest taboo. When this help is not available or fully successful, a new love relationship may be sought, which often creates new guilt. I remember one of these patients realizing, "My trouble is I have a woman I love and the other woman I cannot live without." Psychoanalytic work revealed that the wife became the early mother, without whom the patient could not exist, while the other woman could be loved because she represented the mother after separation. Both were mother figures who stood in for the mother at different periods of the man's life. Once this dichotomy was understood, the choice could be made. It is characteristic of the primary processes that the two wishes can be activated at the same time.

Existential patients

I come now to another category of older patients, whom, for lack of a better term, I will designate as "existential patients." Their basic complaint is that they have not lived their lives fully, and do not want to die without having fully lived. Here we often see a degree of depersonalization, as if somebody else is living their lives. Often, sexual inhibitions are involved, or there is an excessive need to please others. Psychoanalytically speaking, we can see in these patients an excessive use of ego defense mechanisms, which have become too expensive and strong and have exacted so much energy from the person that the feeling of aliveness was jeopardized. Our society, with its emphasis on success, may have contributed to this problem. As life comes to its end and there is nothing left to conquer, this feeling that life was partly or largely wasted can become overwhelming. Such patients need our help to mourn, for they do not allow themselves to do so. In summary, the older patient often needs our help, and we can make the difference between a deepening intrapsychic conflict in old age and one that can be mastered.

The prospect of retirement is often the reason why elderly people need therapy. Work offers all of us certain gratifications. A workplace is often an outlet for needs to love or be loved, and for many people it is also an outlet for aggression. To be suddenly deprived of this outlet will disturb the inner equilibrium and require therapeutic help. I am familiar with a case in which a woman looked forward to retirement as a chance to explore foreign countries, but upon retirement discovered that her husband was afraid of flying. In another instance, a manufacturer was very successful financially, having worked very hard since he was in his teens; his work was synonymous with his life. Now it is time for retirement. Should he sell his factory or give it to his workers as a cooperative? Or should he give it to some relatives for whom he never cared? And what will he do if he does not get up every morning to go to work? To the wife, being together with an ever-anxious, repetitive husband is boring, and being together 24 hours a day is unbearable.

In a third example, a man who held an important political position 10 years ago but has since experienced painful political defeats is now reaching 80. He fears a depression is coming, based on a reliving of his defeats in reality and in his dreams. A few years ago when newly discovered drugs were hailed as the solution to depression, many thousands of people were put on a combination of drugs. But the limitation of this solution has now been experienced, and the need for therapy in old age is more acceptable.

My personal philosophy

As to my own philosophy of life and death, I no longer remember when I first realized that the two belong together. Only what is alive can and must die; the inanimate alone knows no death. Some butterflies live only a few hours while the redwoods in California live hundreds of years, but everything that lives is subject to death. We are the only species that knows death is inevitable. And yet history shows that we have done so very much to deny this knowledge, beginning with the Egyptian pyramids and continuing through the belief in an afterlife and heaven and hell. All are denials of the simple fact that life is final. Why is it, then, that we encounter patients who are afraid of death, or that we ourselves are afraid? Think of Hamlet's famous soliloquy, "To be, or not to be":

> To sleep: perchance to dream: ay, there's the rub;
> For in that sleep of death what dreams may come
> When we have shuffled off this mortal coil,
> Must give us pause.
>   (Shakespeare, 2008a, III.i.65–68)

What happened to Hamlet, happens to many of our patients and perhaps to some of us: the denial of death has backfired and become transformed into a fear of the afterlife.

Why is it that some people can accept death as inevitable and life as final, while others cannot? Why is it that some people do not mind donating their corpse to a hospital for residents to learn how to operate, while others cannot? If my clinical experience is any guide, it is our capacity to have good internal objects that enables us to accept death, and here it is helpful if as children we were wanted by our parents, particularly the mother.

It is very much to the credit of psychoanalysis that it had something new to say on this subject. We sleep well and are rested in the morning when we sleep with our good objects, which love us and wish us well. We are restless, have nightmares, and are tired in the morning when we have slept with our bad objects. Hamlet's fear of death turns out to be the fear of the power of bad objects. By contrast to Hamlet, I cite one of the poems I cherish by Emily Dickinson (1890); here are the first eight lines:

> Because I could not stop for Death,
> He kindly stopped for me;
> The carriage held but just ourselves
> And Immortality.

241

We slowly drove, he knew no haste,
And I had put away
My labor, and my leisure too,
For his civility.

We thank the poet for her capacity to transform her fear of death into these wonderful lines. What Emily Dickinson did in this poem has a psychoanalytic term: she libidinized death. Note the line, "The carriage held but just ourselves." To the poet, death has become a monogamous lover. This is not an outright denial of death, but by transforming death into a romantic companion, it is a form of denial. Freud did something similar in his 1913 paper, "The Theme of the Three Caskets":

We might argue that what is represented here are the three inevitable relations that a man has with a woman – the woman who bears him, the woman who is his mate and the woman who destroys him; or that they are the three forms taken by the figure of the mother in the course of a man's life – the mother herself, the beloved one who is chosen after her pattern, and lastly the Mother Earth who receives him once more. But it is in vain that an old man yearns for the love of woman as he had it first from his mother; the third of the Fates alone, the silent Goddess of Death, will take him into her arms.

(p. 301)

Freud personified death as a mother figure, but in Western art death is usually represented as a jealous man who separates the happy lovers. In the Bible, when a man dies, he is "assembled unto his fathers," not his mothers.

There is no goddess of death who takes us into her arms. I admit that it is not likely that I will ever persuade my unconscious to accept what I just told you, that life and death are intertwined and cannot be separated. My dreams tell me that in my unconscious, I have not even accepted the death of my parents.

In an often-quoted passage in "Beyond the Pleasure Principle" (1920), Freud felt "compelled" to say, "The aim of life is death and looking backward, that inanimate things existed before living ones" (p. 38). The hidden difficulty here is in understanding what Freud means by the word *aim,* which might be closer to what we would call *direction.* I aimed (intended) to get this paper published, but it is not in the same sense that the aim (direction) of my life is death. I do not believe that the organic living world has a wish to return to the inorganic, as Freud thought. The Darwinian view of the survival of the fittest speaks against it, but we older folks alone, who know death and know that death exists, can also develop a desire for it, perhaps because it is as an aim of life. However, psychoanalysis considers those who wish to die as depressed and suicidal and regards these wishes as pathological. If the aim of life is death, then depression should be a normal, expectable state. It is surprising that after the concept of the death instinct was formulated,

242

the question of depression was not re-examined. Once more Shakespeare extends his hand to me:

Falstaff: I would it were bed-time, Hal, and all well.
Prince: Why, thou owest God a death.
Falstaff: 'T is not due yet: I would be loath to pay him before his day. What need I be so forward with him that calls not on me?
(Shakespeare, 2008b, V.i.125–128)

In this matter, I side with Falstaff rather than Freud. We need not be forward with death; death is not the aim of our lives. But regardless of what our primary processes whisper to us, our secondary processes tell us that life and death are intertwined; neither one exists without the other. Freud (1900), citing this quote, made the famous slip, "Du bist der Natur einen Tod schulding," ("you owe nature a death") (p. 205). Two pages later, "since life is short and death inevitable" (p. 207) leads Freud to the Latin "carpe diem" ("seize the day"): one should always grab what one can, even if it involves doing a small wrong.

Practicing as an elderly analyst

We owe to Ferenczi's article "The Unwelcome Child and his Death Instinct" (1929) the insight that human babies do not enter life with a strong instinct to survive. We have to be persuaded by the mother's love that life is worthwhile, and for the rest of our life we remain dependent on love to successfully combat the death instinct in us, hence the permanent fear of succumbing to depression. In old age, death is always near, something like a neighbor. It falls to the ego both to resist the fear of death and the attraction of it. In a symposium not so very long ago, I thanked the profession of psychoanalysis for protecting me from "the swimming pools of Florida" when my co-speaker told the audience, "I just bought an apartment in Florida." Only half jokingly, I said, "We analysts can never retire; it takes us so very long to become any good." If I am any example, psychoanalysis can be practiced longer than many other professions. To my own surprise, it can even be practiced when a loss of memory is beginning to appear. As we get older we forget more, but not what is essential for our patients. Miraculously and thankfully, the *Gestalt* we need of our patients in order to make interpretations survives intact, even if we have forgotten many of the details.

In what way is practicing analysis in old age different than my work when I was younger? Before I answer, I ought to differentiate between changes that took place in psychoanalytic practice itself regardless of age, and changes in my own analytic work. In the past, I used to see my patients four or five times a week; now, three sessions a week is considered very frequent and most patients come twice a week. The other change is that the anonymity of the analyst has changed. New patients look me up on the Internet, and some even look for who my father was. The waiting room is no longer just a waiting room but now a cell phone zone. In

243

the past, my patients came because they wanted to be analyzed; now, it is more common for them to come to me for a more personal relationship rather than to be "merely" analyzed.

With these preliminaries out of the way, I believe I can point to two major differences that are due to old age. Eroticized transference, which caused so much trouble for Freud (1915), does not appear except in the latent content of dreams. However, the most important difference is the frequency with which the fear of my death appears. Sometimes, this is the main theme, hour after hour. It is difficult for patients to bring this topic up, but the demand to free associate – to say everything that occurs to them – leaves them no choice. Many times, I find this preoccupation helpful in making my death more objective, but at times it can be difficult to hear, particularly when the theme repeats itself in many sessions on the same day.

It is important to help patients recognize that in our unconscious, death is not a biological necessity but a desertion, to say, "If I die I am not leaving you, I just cease to exist. Death is not a desertion." Both my patients and I myself need to hear this.

Burden, artistry, and retirement

I once more call upon Shakespeare; King Lear expresses his wish to retire from responsibilities thus:

> To shake all cares and business from our age,
> Conferring them on younger strengths while we
> Unburdened crawl toward death.
>
> (Shakespeare, 2008c, I.i.37–39)

Lear, like many old men, experiences life as a burden, and the phrase "crawl toward death" implies that he equates future retirement with a return to infancy. Shakespeare (2008c) does not give this abdication wish a happy ending, and for a very interesting reason. As the fool tells him, "thou madest thy daughters / thy mothers" (I.iv.156–157). Lear's abdication wish has activated his Oedipal wishes and therefore the tragic end. In my experience, this wish to regress is stronger in men than in women. Some men see retirement as equivalent to carefree childhood and the days when there was yet no obligation to work, and as a result, no superego. Women seem to know that such a happy regression may be open to their husbands but not to them.

The idea of retirement seems to be a combination of two very different trends of thought. The first is that old age makes effective work more difficult. We retire because we cannot perform as well as we used to. Tasks that were easy when we were young become more difficult in old age. This is undisputable. However, there is also another idea: that work itself is a burden. We get paid for work because it is opposed to the pleasure principle. Here we encounter some important differences. Artists are supposed to love their work; that is why it is so hard to unionize musicians: they love to play even if they are not being paid. In psychoanalytic terms, when work itself yields pleasure, we can call it sublimation. Our language also acknowledges a third group, workaholics, people who work not because they enjoy it, but because not working evokes in them anxiety or depression. Where do we, therapists, stand? With artists or with those who consider work a burden? The only contribution I can make to this discussion is that our work becomes more pleasurable as we get older. The work of therapy is difficult if we do not know what to do; our work becomes more enjoyable as we increasingly master our trade. We also develop our personal style only over time, and this brings us closer to being artists.

Hands of time

What happened to me in old age – and I cannot be the only one who has experienced it – is a different attitude towards time. Time has become more precious. There are so many wonderful books to read, so much music to hear, so many paintings to study and remember, and so many meaningful and precious personal encounters, but so little time. With this realization comes a sense of gratitude for the richness that psychoanalysis gave to my life and with it a thankfulness that I survived the many dangers I lived through. With it comes a sense of gratitude I did not, perhaps could not, experience earlier.

References

Dickinson, E. (1890). Because I could not stop for death. In T. H. Johnson (Ed.), *The complete poems of Emily Dickinson*. New York: Back Bay Books, republished 1960.

Ferenczi, S. (1929). The unwelcome child and his death instinct. In *Final contributions to the problems and methods of psycho-analysis* (pp. 102–107). London: Karnac Books, republished 1994.

Freud, S. (1898). Sexuality in the aetiology of the neuroses. In J. Strachey (Ed. & Trans.), *The standard edition of the complete psychological works of Sigmund Freud* (Vol. 3, pp. 261–285). London: Hogarth Press.

Freud, S. (1900). *The interpretation of dreams*. In J. Strachey (Ed. & Trans.), *The standard edition of the complete psychological works of Sigmund Freud* (Vols. 4–5, pp. 1–627). London: Hogarth Press.

Freud, S. (1913). The theme of the three caskets. In J. Strachey (Ed. & Trans.), *The standard edition of the complete psychological works of Sigmund Freud* (Vol. 12, pp. 289–302). London: Hogarth Press.

Freud, S. (1915). Observations of transference love. In J. Strachey (Ed. & Trans.), *The standard edition of the complete psychological works of Sigmund Freud* (Vol. 12, pp. 157–171). London: Hogarth Press.

Freud, S. (1920). Beyond the pleasure principle. In J. Strachey (Ed. & Trans.), *The standard edition of the complete psychological works of Sigmund Freud* (Vol. 18, pp. 7–64). London: Hogarth Press.

Shakespeare, W. (2008a). The Tragedy of Hamlet, Prince of Denmark. In S. Greenblatt, W. Cohen, J. E. Howard, & K. E. Maus (Eds.), *The Norton Shakespeare: Based on the Oxford Edition*, 2nd Edition. New York: W. W. Norton & Company, Inc.

Shakespeare, W. (2008b). Henry IV, Part 1. In S. Greenblatt, W. Cohen, J. E. Howard, & K. E. Maus (Eds.), *The Norton Shakespeare: Based on the Oxford Edition*, 2nd Edition. New York: W. W. Norton & Company, Inc.

Shakespeare, W. (2008c). King Lear. In S. Greenblatt, W. Cohen, J. E. Howard, & K. E. Maus (Eds.), *The Norton Shakespeare: Based on the Oxford Edition*, 2nd Edition. New York: W. W. Norton & Company, Inc.

INDEX

247